CONSTITUTIONAL COURTS, GAY RIGHTS AND SEXUAL ORIENTATION EQUALITY

Over the last 15 years, constitutional issues regarding the rights of gays, lesbians and same-sex couples have emerged on a global scale. The pace of recognition of their fundamental rights, both at judicial and legislative level, has increased dramatically across different jurisdictions, reflecting a growing consensus toward sexual orientation equality.

This book considers a wide-range of decisions by constitutional and international courts, from the decriminalisation of sexual acts to the recognition of same-sex marriage and parental rights for same-sex couples. It discusses analogies and differences in judicial arguments and rationales in such cases, focusing in particular on human dignity, privacy, liberty, equality and non-discrimination.

It argues that courts operate as major exporters of models and principles and that judicial cross-fertilisation also helps courts in increasing the acceptability of gay and lesbian rights in public opinions and politics. Courts discuss changes in the social perception of marriage and family at national and international levels and at the same time confirm and reinforce them, forging the legal debate over sexual orientation equality. Furthermore, by promoting the political reception of the achievements of foreign gay movements in their own jurisdictions, courts play an essential role in breaking the political stalemate.

Volume 14 in the series Hart Studies in Comparative Public Law

Hart Studies in Comparative Public Law
Recent titles in this series:

Constitutionalising Secession
David Haljan

Parliaments and Human Rights
Redressing the Democratic Deficit
Edited by Murray Hunt, Hayley Hooper and Paul Yowell

The Right to Freedom of Assembly
A Comparative Study
Orsolya Salát

An Inquiry into the Existence of Global Values
Through the Lens of Comparative Constitutional Law
Edited by Dennis Davis, Alan Richter and Cheryl Saunders

The Scope and Intensity of Substantive Review
Traversing Taggart's Rainbow
Edited by Hanna Wilberg and Mark Elliott

Entick v Carrington
250 Years of the Rule of Law
Edited by Adam Tomkins and Paul Scott

Administrative Law and Judicial Deference
Matthew Lewans

Soft Law and Public Authorities
Remedies and Reform
Greg Weeks

Legitimate Expectations in the Common Law World
Edited by Matthew Groves and Greg Weeks

The Dynamics of Exclusionary Constitutionalism
Mazen Masri

Constitutional Courts, Gay Rights and Sexual Orientation Equality

Angioletta Sperti

•HART•
OXFORD • LONDON • NEW YORK • NEW DELHI • SYDNEY

HART PUBLISHING
Bloomsbury Publishing Plc
Kemp House, Chawley Park, Cumnor Hill, Oxford, OX2 9PH, UK

HART PUBLISHING, the Hart/Stag logo, BLOOMSBURY and the Diana logo are trademarks of Bloomsbury Publishing Plc
First published in Great Britain 2017

First published in hardback, 2017
Paperback edition, 2019

A catalogue record for this book is available from the British Library.

Library of Congress Cataloging-in-Publication Data

Names: Sperti, Angioletta author.

Title: Constitutional courts, gay rights and sexual orientation equality / Angioletta Sperti.

Description: Oxford ; Portland, Oregon : Hart Publishing, an imprint of Bloomsbury Publishing Plc, 2017. | Series: Hart studies in comparative public law ; volume 14 | Includes bibliographical references and index.

Identifiers: LCCN 2016054443 (print) | LCCN 2016055158 (ebook) | ISBN 9781782256427 (hardback) | ISBN 9781782256434 (Epub)

Subjects: LCSH: Gays—Legal status, laws, etc. | Constitutional courts.

Classification: LCC K3242.3 .S68 2017 (print) | LCC K3242.3 (ebook) | DDC 342.08/7—dc23

LC record available at https://lccn.loc.gov/2016054443

ISBN: HB: 978-1-78225-642-7
PB: 978-1-50993-211-5
ePDF: 978-1-78225-644-1
ePub: 978-1-78225-643-4

Typeset by Compuscript Ltd, Shannon

To find out more about our authors and books visit www.hartpublishing.co.uk. Here you will find extracts, author information, details of forthcoming events and the option to sign up for our newsletters.

To the memory of Alessandro Pizzorusso

Acknowledgements

In the reflection and work preparatory to this book I received the support and help of many people and institutions.

I would like to express my sincere gratitude to my friends and colleagues on the editorial board of GenIUS and Articolo29.it. I benefited greatly from the conversations I had with all of them in the last few years. My thanks go especially to Marco Gattuso for his insightful ideas and for welcoming me to the editorial board, to Luca Morassutto for answering my questions, and to Elena Falletti who kindly introduced me to some of the literature on comparative family law.

I am very grateful to the colleagues who forwarded me their writings or helped me in researching materials I needed for this book, in particular to Carmelo Danisi, Anna Gragnani, Elina Magnan, Anne Sanders and Caterina Severino. I am also indebted to Reva Siegel for sharing with me some stimulating ideas.

The University of Pisa provided funding for my research, and the Institute for Advanced Legal Studies in London and the British Library offered me the opportunity to finalise my bibliographical research.

My thanks go also to Bill Asquith and to the staff of Hart Publishing.

Even so, I would never have written this book without the continuous support and help of my family. My gratitude goes to Laura and Silvia for their great patience, to Michele for always encouraging me, to my parents for their help in bringing this book to its end, to my Aunt Pat and to my Uncle Enzo for promptly answering my questions.

This book is dedicated to the memory of Alessandro Pizzorusso who recently passed away. His passing was a great loss for me. His culture, his integrity and his uncompromising commitment to research will always serve as an example to me.

Contents

Dedication ... v
Acknowledgements ... vii
Table of Cases ... xiii
Table of Legislation ... xxi

1. Introduction ... 1
   I. Setting the Landscape ... 1
   II. The Aims of this Book ... 4
   III. The Comparative Method ... 6
   IV. Some Remarks on Courts' Use of Foreign Precedents ... 8
   V. Outline of the Book ... 15

2. The Private Dimension of Homosexuality: Courts and Decriminalisation of Sexual Acts ... 19
   I. *Dudgeon v UK* as a Global Landmark Case ... 19
   II. *Dudgeon* and the Recognition of Homosexuality as 'An Essentially Private Manifestation of Human Personality' ... 21
   III. The Notion of Privacy in *Dudgeon* and the Perpetuation of the 'Sexual Closet' ... 26
   IV. *Lawrence v Texas* and the Liberty of all Individuals in their Personal Relationships ... 30
   V. The 'Multi-Faceted' Notion of Privacy in *Lawrence* ... 33
   VI. The Legacy of *Dudgeon* in *Lawrence* ... 36
   VII. The Supreme Court of South Africa's Case in *National Coalition* and the Influence of *Dudgeon* ... 41
   VIII. The Right to Privacy in *National Coalition*: A Common Thread ... 43
   IX. The 'Boomerang Pattern Influence' of *Dudgeon* at International Level ... 45

3. Out of the Closet: Courts and the Same-Sex Couple as 'Family' ... 49
   I. Different Models of Regulation of Family, the Public–Private Dichotomy and the Purpose of this Chapter ... 49
   II. The Supreme Court of Canada and the Inadequacy of 'Unexamined Consensus' in the Definition of 'Family' ... 56
   III. 'Private Life' v 'Family Life' in the European Court of Human Rights' Early Cases ... 61
   IV. *Schalk and Kopf v Austria* and Recognition of the Same-Sex Couple as 'Family' ... 65

V. From the 'Perception of the Ordinary Man' to a Functional Definition of 'Family': The *Fitzpatrick* Case ... 67
VI. Same-Sex Couples as 'Spouses' in *Ghaidan v Godin-Mendoza* ... 71
VII. Some Final Remarks and a First Conclusion ... 74
VIII. A Digression on a Narrow Interpretation of 'Family' ... 76

4. Same-Sex Marriage: Judicial Revolution or Constitutional Inevitability? ... 80
I. Courts and Constitutional Change ... 80
A. From Civil Partnerships to Same-Sex Marriage: Courts, Constitutional Change and Judicial Backlash ... 80
B. The Path Towards Equal Marriage: On the Dialogue Between Courts and Legislators in Some European Countries ... 86
i. Spain (2005) ... 86
ii. Portugal (2010) ... 89
iii. France (2013) ... 92
iv. Germany (2001) ... 97
C. The Different Roles of Constitutional and Ordinary Courts in Promoting Equal Marriage in Europe ... 102
II. Arguments in Same-Sex Marriage Cases: Tradition v Constitutional Change ... 109
A. The Argument of Tradition in Constitutional Cases. Introductory Remarks ... 109
B. What is 'Tradition'? ... 115
i. Legal Tradition and the Difficult Identification of an 'Essential Core' of Marriage ... 115
ii. Cultural and Religious Tradition, its Indeterminacy and the Vicious Cycle that Perpetuates Discrimination ... 119
C. The Debate on Unenumerated Rights in the United States and its Teachings on the Normative Value of Tradition ... 122
D. The Normative Value of Tradition and the Risk of a 'Circular Reasoning' ... 132
E. Progressive Interpretations of Constitutional Clauses on 'Marriage' and Separation of Powers Concerns ... 134
F. 'A New Image of Marriage' and Judicial Cross-Fertilisation ... 137
III. Arguments in Same-Sex Marriage Cases: Equality, Liberty and Human Dignity ... 140
A. Equality and Diversity in the Present Debate over Civil Rights ... 140

B. Equality and its Implications in Same-Sex Marriage Cases ... 141
i. Equality and the 'Expressive' Value of Marriage ... 142
ii. Equality of Rights and Responsibilities Flowing from Marriage ... 146
C. Dignity as Synthesis of Liberty and Equality ... 149
D. The Different Meanings of Dignity in Same-Sex Marriage Cases ... 154
i. Dignity as a 'Claim of Recognition' and Equality ... 156
ii. From Exclusion to Inclusion: Dignity as Equal Value ... 158
iii. Dignity as Liberty and Self-Determination ... 161
E. The Different Purposes of Dignity in Same-Sex Marriage Cases ... 164

5. Addressing the Reality of Family Life: Parental Rights ... 171
I. The Debate over Parental Rights and the Principle of the Best Interests of the Child ... 171
II. The Constitutional Courts and the 'Procreative Nature' of Marriage ... 176
III. The Optimal Parenting Argument and the Child's Right to a 'Normal' Family Life ... 182
A. The Early Cases on Child Custody and Single-Parent Adoption ... 182
B. Second-parent Adoption ... 187
C. Joint Adoption ... 192

6. Concluding Remarks ... 196

Bibliography ... 197
Index ... 209

Table of Cases

International

United Nations Human Rights Committee

Edward Young v Australia, Communication No. 941/2000, U.N. Doc. CCPR/C/78/D/941/2000 (2003) 65

Joslin v New Zealand Communication no 902/1999, UN Doc A/57/40 at 214 (2002) 112–113

Toonen v Australia Communication No 488/1992, UN Doc CCPR/C/50/D/488/1992 (1994) 20, 47–48, 65

European Court of Human Rights

ADT v United Kindgom App no 35765/97, 31 July 2000, ECHR 2000-IX, [2000] ECHR 402 .... 27, 62

Chapin and Charpentier v France App no 40183/07, 9 June 2016, (2016) ECHR 504 .... 94, 189

D and Others v Belgium App no 29176/13, 8 July 2014 173

Dudgeon v UK App no 7525/76, 22 October 1981, Series A no 45, [1981] EHRR 5 .... 9, 11, 15–16, 19–34, 37–39, 41–43, 45–49, 62

EB v France App no 43546/02, 22 January 2008, IHRL 3284 (ECHR 2008) 61, 185–86

Fretté v France App No 36515/97, ECHR 2002-I, (2004) 38 EHRR 21 .... 184–186, 191

Gas and Dubois v France App no 25951/07, 15 March 2012, ECHR 2012-II 188–190

Goodwin v United Kindgom App no 17488/90, 27 March 1996, ECHR 1996-II, [1996] ECHR 16 110

Hämäläinen v. Finland [GC], App no 37359/09, 16 July 2014 189

Karner v Austria App no 40016/98, 24 July 2003, (2004), § 37 ECHR 2003-IX, 38 EHRR 24 .... 63, 169, 190

Kozak v Poland App no 13102/02, 2 March 2010, [2010] ECHR 280 .... 63, 169, 190

Manenc v France, App no 66686/09, 21 September 2010 61

Marckx v Belgium App No 6833/74, 13 June 1979, (1979) 2 EHRR 330, (1979) ECHR 2 .... 50, 66–67

Mata Estevez v Spain (dec) App no 56501/00, 10 May 2001, ECHR 2001-VI 61, 63

Mennesson v France and *Labassee v France*, App nos 65192/11 and 65941/11, 26 June 2014, ECHR 2014-III 173

Modinos v Cyprus App no 15070/89, 22 April 1993, Series A no. 259, (1993) 16 EHRR 485 .... 19, 46

Niemietz v Germany App no 13710/88, 16 December 1992, Series A no 251-B, (1992) ECHR 80 62

Norris v Ireland App no 10581/83, 26 October 1988, Series A no 142, (1991) 13 EHRR 186 .... 19, 27, 42, 46

Oliari v Italy, App nos 18766/11 and 36030/11, 21 July 2015, [2015] ECHR 752 ..... 77, 106, 174, 189
Paradiso and Campanelli v Italy App no 25358/12, 27 January 2015, [2015] ECHR 76 173
PB and JS v Austria, App no 18984/02, 22 July 2010 ..... 65, 67
Salgueiro da Silva Mouta v Portugal, App no 33290/96, 21 December 1999, ECHR 1999-IX 72, 169, 183–84
Schalk and Kopf v Austria App no 30141/04, 24 June 2010, ECHR 2010-I, (2010) ECHR 1996 ..... 29, 65–67, 94, 135, 189–90
Simpson v United Kingdom App no 11716/85, ECommHR (1986) 68
Vallianatos and others v Greece [GC], App nos 29381/09, 32684/09, 07 November 2013, [2013] ECHR 1110 189
van den Heijden v Netherlands App no 42857/05, 4 April 2012 67
WB v Republic of Germany App n 104/55, Commission Decision, 17 December 1955 22
X and Others v Austria [GC] App no 19010/07, 19 February 2013, [2013] ECHR 425 ..... 173, 189–92
X v United Kingdom App no 7215/75, 5 November 1981, Series A no 46, (1981) ECHR 6 62

Court of Justice of the European Union

Omega Spielhalle- und Automatenaufstellungs-GmbH v. Oberbürgermeisterin der Bundeststadt Bonn, C-36/02, 2004 E.C.R. I-09609 154

Domestic

Argentina

Freire Alejandro v. GCBA (expte. no 34.292/09) Juzgado en lo Contencioso Administrativo y Tributario No 15 de la Ciudad Autónoma de Buenos Aires, 10 November 2009 139
LSF y ACP, Family Tribunal of the 4th Court District of the City of Cordoba, Argentina RU 2003-5, 5, DJ 2003-3, 236, 6 August 2003 184

Austria

Verfassungsgerichthof, decision of 11 October 1974 2

Belgium

Cour d'Arbitrage, case no159/2004 of 20 October 2004 132

Brasil

Supremo Tribunal Federal of Brasil, Ação direta de inconstitucionalidade 4.277, 5 May 2011 139

Canada

Barbeau v British Columbia 2003 BCCA 251 (Court of Appeal for BC, May 1, 2003) 136
Canada v Mossop (1993) SCJ No 20 ..... 56–61, 67, 69, 80, 179
Canada v Mossop, Federal Court of Appeal (1991) 1 FC 18 57

EGALE Canada, Inc. v Canada (2003) 13 BCLR 4th 1 (Can. B.C. C.A.) 81, 112, 180
Egan v Canada (1995) 2 SCR 513 .... 45, 80, 160, 169, 180
Haig v Canada (1992), 16 CHRR D/226 (Ont. C.A.) 169
Halpern v Canada (2003) OJ No 2268, 65 OR (3d) 161 (Can. Ont. C.A.) 81, 111, 133, 136, 143–44, 149, 157
Halpern v Canada (Attorney General) 95 CRR (2d) 1 (Ontario Superior Court, July 12, 2002) 136, 178
Hendricks v Quebec (2002) RJQ.2506 (Quebec Superior Court, September 6, 2002) 112, 136, 144
Hendricks v Quebec (2004) 238 DLR 4th 577 (Can. Que. CA) 81
Lavigne v Ontario Public Service Employees Union, [1991] 2 S.C.R. 211 14
Law v Canada (1999) 1 SCR 497 156
Layland v Ontario (Minister of Consumer and Commercial Relations) (1993) 14 OR (3d) 658 (Ont. Div. Ct.) 111
M v H (1999) 2 SCR 3 80–81
Mossop v Canada, Canadian Human Rights Tribunal (1989), 10 CHRR D/6064 56
Reference Re Same-Sex Marriage (2004) 3 SCR 698, 2004 SCC 79 .... 114, 118, 132, 134–36, 139
Rosenberg v Canada (1998) 158 DLR (4th) 664 80

Colombia

Constitutional Court, *Sentencia* C-481/98, 9 September 1998 20
Constitutional Court, *Sentencia* C-577/11, 26 July 2011 .... 9, 139

Ecuador

Constitutional Tribunal, case no111-97 TC, 22 November 1997 20–21

Fiji

McCoskar and Nadan v State (2005) FJHC 500 .... 20–21, 45

France

Conseil constitutionnel, Décision no 71-44 DC, 16 July 1971 93
Conseil constitutionnel, Décision no 74-54 DC of 15 January 1975 2
Conseil constitutionnel, Décision no 99-419 DC. 9 November 1999 .... 93–94, 106, 108
Conseil constitutionnel, Décision no 2010-39 QPC, 6 October 2010 188
Conseil constitutionnel Décision no 2010-92 QPC, 28 January 2011 .... 95–96, 106
Conseil constitutionnel. Décision no 2013-669 DC, 17 May 2013 .... 96, 170, 193–194
Conseil d'Etat, 1/2 SSR, no 230533, 5 June 2002 185
Cour de Cassation, Arrêt no 511, 13 March 2007 94
Cour de Cassation, Arrêt nos 221 and 224, 20 February 2007 188
Cour de Cassation, Secher v Air France, 11 July 1989 92
Cour de Cassation, Vileda v Weil, 17 December 1997 92
Court of Appeal of Paris, 10 April, 1959 172

Germany

AG Frankfurt/Main (1993) NJW 940 99
BVerfGE 6, 55 (1957)—Joint Income Tax Case 98
BVerfGE 10, 59 (1959) 98, 119

BVerfGE 1, 27 (1962)—Microcensus case ... 151
BVerfGE 30, 173 (1971)—Mephisto case ... 44
BVerfGE 31 58 (1971)—The Spanish Marriage case ... 98
BVerfGE 39, 1 (1975)—Abortion Case I ... 2, 51
BVerfGE, 45, 187 (1977)—Life Imprisonment case ... 151
BVerfGE 88, 87 (1978)—Transsexuals case I ... 110
BVerfGE 53, 224 (1980)—Civil Divorce case ... 98
BVerfGE 75, 369 (380) (1987)—Political satire case ... 154
BVerfGE 88, 203 (1993)-Abortion II Case ... 51
BVerfGE 105, 313 (2002)—Civil Partnership Act case ... 99–101, 119, 139, 180–81
BVerfGE 115, 1 (2005)—Transsexuals case III ... 101
BVerfGE 121, 175 (2008)—Transsexuals case V ... 110
BVerfGE 124, 199 (2009) ... 101
BVerfGE 126, 400 (2010) ... 102
BVerfGE 128, 109 (2011) ... 110
BVerfGE 133, 59 (2013) ... 102, 191
BvL 1, 1/11, BvR 1, 3247/09 (2013) ... 174–76
BvL 2, 2/13 (2014) ... 102
BvR 1, 640/93 (1993) ... 99, 102, 107–108
BvR 2, 855/06 (2007) ... 102
BvR 1, 1164/07 (2009) ... 169
LG Frankfurt/Main (1993) NJW 1998 ... 99

Hong Kong

Court of Appeal, *Leung v Secretary of Justice* (2006) 4 HKLRD 211 (CA) ... 20, 48

Hungary

Case no 8/1990 of 23 April 1990 (IV. 23) AB ... 167
Case no 48/1998 of 18 November 1998 (IX.23) AB ... 153

India

Naz Foundation v Government of NCT of Delhi (2009) 160 Delhi Law Times 277 ... 12, 20

Ireland

McGee v Attorney General [1974] IR 284 ... 178
Murray v Ireland [1985] IR 532 ... 178
Quinn's Supermarkets Ltd. v Attorney General, [1972] IR 1 ... 153
T v T [2003] ILRM 321 ... 116
Zappone and Gilligan v Revenue Commissioners [2006] IEHC 404 (14 December 2006) ... 10, 13, 16–17, 129, 133, 139–140, 165, 177–178

Israel

Ben-Ari v The Director of the Population Administration in the Ministry of the Interior, HCJ 3045/05 ... 139
El-Al Israel Airlines v. Danielowitz, HCJ 721/94 ... 14, 75
Yaros-Hakak v Attorney General, CA 10280/01, 10 January 2005 ... 191

Italy

Constitutional Court, case no 27 of 22 January 1975 2
Constitutional Court, case no 161 of 23 May 1985 152
Constitutional Court, case no 561 of 10 December 1987 152
Constitutional Court, case no 356 of 14 October 1996 104
Constitutional Court, case no 352 of 2000, 25 July 2000 78
Constitutional Court, case no 138, 15 April 2010 .... 78, 105–08, 114–17, 129, 134, 164–165, 169, 173–174, 178
Constitutional Court, case no 170 of 11 June 2014 ('compulsory divorce case') 78, 105, 107, 110
Court of Appeal of Milan, Labour Section, Judgment no. 7176/12 of 29 March 2012 105
Court of Appeal of Milan, case of 16 October 2015 106
Court of Appeal of Naples, case of 30 March 2016 106
Court of Appeal of Turin, case of 29 October 2014 105
Court of Cassation, case no 1808 of 20 May 1976 115
Court of Cassation, case no 1304 of 22 February 1990 115
Court of Cassation, case no 3572 of 14 February 2011 174
Court of Cassation, case no 7877, sez. I Civ., of 9 June 2000 115
Court of Cassation, case no 4184 of 15 March 2012 .... 106, 111
Court of Cassation, sez I civ, case no 601 of 11 January 2013 191
Court of Cassation, case no 2400 of 9 February 2015 106
Court di Cassation, case no 15138 of 20 July 2015 110
Court of Cassation, n 12962 of 26 May 2016 174
Tribunale dei Minorenni di Bologna (Bologna Juvenile Court), decree no 1948 of 17 April 2013 174
Tribunale dei Minorenni di Roma (Rome Juvenile Court), case of 30 July 2014 105
Tribunale dei Minorenni di Roma (Rome Juvenile Court), case of 22 October 2015 105–06
Tribunale dei Minorenni di Roma (Rome Juvenile Court), case of 23 December 2015 106
Tribunal of Grosseto, case of 3 April 2014 105
Tribunal of Grosseto, case of 17 February 2015 105
Tribunal of Milan, case no 9965/11 of 13 June 2011 105
Tribunal of Palermo, decree of 13 April 2015 105
Tribunal of Reggio Emilia, ordinance of 13 February 2012 105

Mexico

Acción de Inconstitucionalidad 2/2010, 10 August 2010 .... 9, 139

Portugal

Acórdão no 359/2009 (9 July 2009) 90, 105–108 117, 119, 129, 134, 136, 164
Acórdão no 121/2010 (8 April 2010) 9, 91–92, 136, 138, 149, 180
Lisbon Court of Appeal (Tribunal da Relação), 9 January 1996 183–84

South Africa

Certification of the Constitution of the Republic of South Africa, 1996, In Re: Ex parte Chairperson of the Constitutional Assembly 1996, Case CCT 37/96, 1996 (4) SA 744 (CC); 1996 (10) BCLR 1253 (CC) 121

Coetzee v Government of the Republic of South Africa, Matiso v Commanding Officer Port Elizabeth Prison, CCT19/94, CCT22/94, [1995] ZACC 7, 22 September 1995 167
Du Toit v Minister for Welfare and Population Development Case CCT 40/01, [2002] ZACC 20; 2002 (10) BCLR 1006 194–95
Minister of Home Affairs and Another v Fourie, Case CCT 60/04, [2005] ZACC 19 .... 10, 14, 22, 139, 146, 149, 157, 160–61, 179
National Coalition for Gay and Lesbian Equality v Minister of Justice, Case CCT 11/98, (1998) ZACC 15, 9 October 1998 .... 8, 20–21, 41–45, 48
National Coalition for Gay and Lesbian Equality v Minister for Home Affairs, CCT10/99, [1999] ZACC 17; 2000 (2) SA 1 .... 74–76, 179
Mashia Ebrahim v Mahomed Essop 1905 TS 59 112

Spain

Case no 11/1981, 8 April 1981, SCT 153
Case no 53/1985, 11 April 1985, SCT 152
Case no 120/1990, 27 June 1990, SCT 152
Case no 101/1991, 13 May 1991, SCT 153
Auto no 222/1994, 11 July 1994, SCT 86, 89, 107–108
Case no 292/1994, 20 July 1994, SCT 153
Case no 41/2006, 13 February 2006, SCT 169
Case no198/2012, 6 November 2012, SCT 8, 13, 15, 88, 118–119, 132, 134–135, 137–138, 149, 163, 165–166, 180–181, 191, 194

United Kingdom

Bellinger v Bellinger [2003] UKHL 21 110
C v C (A Minor) (Custody: Appeal) [1991] 1 FLR 223 183
Corbett v Corbett (otherwise Ashley) [1970] 2 W.L.R. 1306 .... 110, 113, 120
Fitzpatrick v Sterling Housing Association Ltd [2001] 1 AC 27 .... 53, 68–72, 76
Gammans v Ekins [1950] 2 KB 328 71
Ghaidan v Godin-Mendoza [2004] 2 AC 557 .... 72–74, 161
Harrogate Borough Council v Simpson [1985] 17 HLR 205 67–68
Hyde v Hyde and Woodmansee [1886] L Rev 1 P &D 130 111
In Re D (An Infant) (Adoption: Parent's Consent) [1977] AC 602 183
Re W (Adoption: Homosexual Adopter) [1997] 2 FLR 406 183
Wilkinson v Kitzinger [2006] EWHC 2022 (Fam) 179–180

United States of America

Adoption of IM 48 Kan App 2d 343 (2012) 187
Adoption of Tammy 416 Mass 205, 619 NE2d 315 (1993) 83
Baehr v Lewin 74 Haw 530, 852 P2d 44 (1993) 1, 82–85, 113, 139, 141, 143, 176
Baker v Nelson 291 Minn 310, 191 NW2d 185 (1971) 120
Baker v Nelson 409 US 810 (1972) 112
Baker v State 744 A2d 864 (Vt. 1999) 83
Bostic v Rainey 970 F Supp 2d 456, 22 (E.D. Va. 2014) 2, 163
Bostic v Schaefer, 760 F.3d 352 (4th Cir. 2014) 2
Bowers v Hardwick 478 US 186 (1986) 9, 20, 34, 36–37, 40, 124–27
Braschi v Stahl Associates 74 NY2d 201 (1989) 60

Brown v Board of Education of Topeka 347 US 483 (1954) ... 82, 84, 196
Campaign for Southern Equality v Mississippi Department of Human Services 2016 U.S. Dist. LEXIS 43897 (2016) ... 187
Cohen v California 403 US 15 (1971) ... 162
Constant V v Paul CA 344 Pa Sup Ct 49, 496 A.2d 1 (1985) ... 183
Doe v Doe 16 Mass. App. Ct. 499, 452 N.E.2d 293 (1983) ... 184
E.N.O. v L.M.M. 429 Mass 824, cert denied 528 US 1005 (1999) ... 83
Eisenstadt v Baird 405 US 438 (1972) ... 33, 64
Goodridge v Department of Public Health 440 Mass 309 (2003) ... 83–84, 133, 144, 159, 163, 176
Gottlieb v Gottlieb 108 A.D.2d 120, 488 N.Y.S.2d 180 (1st Dep't 1985) ... 184
Griswold v Connecticut 381 US 479 (1965) ... 64, 123
Hernandez v Robles 7 NY3d 338 (2006) ... 133
In re Adoption of BLVB 160 Vt 368, 628 A 2d 1271 (1993) ... 187
In re Adoption of Luke 640 NW 2d 374 (Neb. 2002) ... 188
In re marriage cases 43 Cal 4th 757 (2008) ... 144, 159–60, 178
In the Matter of the Adoption of John Doe & John Doe I 156 Idaho 532; 328 P.3d 512 (2014) ... 188
Kitchen v Herbert 961 FSupp2d 1181 (D. Utah 2013) ... 163
Lawrence v Texas 539 US 558 (2003) ... 9, 11–12, 15, 19–21, 30–41, 43–44, 48, 114, 123–27, 150, 162, 168, 182
Lewis v Harris 188 NJ 415 (2006) ... 109, 112, 144, 147
Lewis v Harris 378 NJ Super 168 (2005) ... 121, 133
Loving v Virginia 388 US 1 (1967) ... 2, 120, 128, 144, 176
Matter of Adoption of Evan 583 NYS 2d 997 (Sur Ct 1992) ... 187
Maynard v Hill 125 US 190, 211 (1885) ... 176
Michael H v Gerald D 491 US 110, 141 (1989) ... 123, 128
MT v JT 140 NJ Super 77 (1976) ... 112
Obergefell v Hodges 576 US, 135 S Ct 2584 (2015) ... 4, 65, 127, 130–131, 134–35, 142, 145–46, 148–50, 157, 159, 162, 165, 168–169, 176–77, 181–182, 187–88
Perry v Brown 671 F3d 1052 (9th Cir 2012) ... 144, 178–179
Petition of L.S. for Adoption of Minor (T.), 1991 WL 219598 (D.C. Super. Ct. 1991) ... 187
Planned Parenthood of Southeastern Pennsylvania v Casey 505 US 833 (1992) ... 33, 35, 37, 162
Plessy v Ferguson 163 US 537 (1896) ... 18
Poe v Ullman 367 US 497 (1961) ... 123–24, 127, 129
Printz v United States, 521 US 898 (1997) ... 13
Reynolds v United States 98 US 145 (1878) ... 112
Roe v Roe 324 S.E.2d 691 (1985) ... 182–83
Roe v Wade 410 US 113 (1973) ... 2, 33, 82, 84–85, 196
Romer v Evans, 517 US 620 (1996) ... 38
Rosenblatt v Baer 383 US 75 (1966) ... 162
Singer v Hara 11 Wn App 247, 522 P 2d 1187 (1974) ... 112
SJLS v TLS 265 SW 3d 804 (Ct. App. Ky. 2008) ... 187
Skinner v Oklahoma ex rel Williamson 316 US 535 (1942) ... 176
Snyder v Massachusetts 291 US 97, 105 (1933) ... 123
Thompson v Oklahoma, 487 US 815 (1988) ... 13
Truax v Raich 239 US 33 (1915) ... 133
Turner v Safley 482 US 78 (1987) ... 128

United States v Carolene Products Co 304 US 144 (1938) ... 32
United States v Then, 56 F 3d 464, 469 (1995) ... 11
United States v Windsor 133 S Ct 2675, 570 US (2013) ... 2, 38, 144–45, 147–48, 157, 159, 165, 168
Varnum v Brien 63 NW2d 862 (2009) ... 133, 144
VL v EL 136 S. Ct. 1017 (2016) ... 187
Washington v Glucksberg 521 US 702 (1997) ... 123–24, 128, 168
West Virginia State Board of Education v Barnette 319 US 624 (1943) ... 162
Zablocki v Redhail 434 US 374 (1978) ... 128, 176–177

Zimbabwe

Banana v State [2000] 4 LRC 621 ... 20, 48

Table of Legislation

International

Convention on the Rights of the Child, 1989
art 3 ... 172
art 21 ... 172
European Convention on Human Rights, 1950 ... 24, 27–28, 55, 72, 78, 94
art 8 ... 19, 21–23, 26, 29, 38, 49–50, 61–62, 64–65, 66–68, 72, 92, 94, 106, 110, 173, 179, 184, 186, 189–90
art 8(1) ... 26, 41, 49, 62
art 8(2) ... 26, 50
art 12 ... 50, 66, 94, 106, 110–11, 135, 180, 189
art 14 ... 21–22, 63, 65, 68, 72, 94, 140–41, 169, 173, 179, 184, 186, 189
European Convention on the Adoption of Children, 2008 ... 186
International Covenant on Civil and Political Rights, 1966 ... 47–48, 65, 112
art 2(1) ... 48
art 17(1) ... 47, 65
art 23(2) ... 110, 113
art 26 ... 47–48, 65
UN Declaration of the Rights of the Child, 1959
principle 2 ... 172
principle 7 ... 172
UN Universal Declaration of Human Rights, 1948
art 16(3) ... 49, 110

European Union

Charter of Fundamental Rights of the EU, 2000
art 7 ... 50
art 9 ... 50
art 21 ... 141
art 24(1) ... 172
art 24(2) ... 172
Directive 2004/38/EC ... 55
art 3 para 2(a) ... 55
art 3 para 2(b) ... 55

Domestic

Austria

Civil Code (*Allgemeines Bürgerliches Gesetzbuch*)
art 182, §2 ... 173, 189
Registered Partnership Act (*Eingetragene Partnerschaft-Gesetz*) ... 65–66

Australia

Tasmanian Criminal Code 20
  s 122(a) 47
  s 122 (c) 47
  s 123 47

Belgium

Constitution, 1831
  art 22(1) 50
Act of 13 February 2003 132

Brasil

Constitution of 1988
  art 226(3) 110

Canada

Canadian Charter of Rights and Freedoms 1982 .... 14, 80–81, 136
  s 1 136
  s 2 (a) 136
  s 15 81
  s 15 (1) 135–136
Canadian Human Rights Act 1985
  s 2 56–57
  s 3 57–58
Civil Marriage Act 2005
  c. 33 81
Constitution Act 1867
  s 91(26) 112, 135
Family Law Act 1990
  c. F.3, s 29 81
Old Age Security Act, R.S.C. 1970
  s 2 80
Modernization of Benefits and Obligations Act 2000
  s 1(1) 112

Colombia

Civil code
  art 113 139

France

Code Civil, 1804 52
  art 4 103
  art 6–1 .... 95, 193
  art 75 95
  art 144 .... 95, 111

art 343 (1) ... 184
art 365 ... 188
art 514(4) ... 93
art 515(1) ... 93
Constitution of French Republic, 1946 Préambule (preamble) ... 96
Constitution of French Republic, 1958 ... 110
art 1 ... 96
art 61 ... 3, 95
Declaration of the Rights of Man and the Citizen 1789
art 2 ... 193
Loi constitutionnelle no 2008-724 of 23 July 2008 (de modernisation des institutions de la Ve République) ... 188
art 29 ... 188
Loi no 99-944 of 15 November 1999 (relative au pacte civil de solidarité) ... 92, 94, 96, 147, 188
art 1 ... 93
Loi no 2013-404 of 17 May 2013 (ouvrant le mariage aux couples de personnes de même sexe) ... 94–96, 89, 193
art 13 ... 95, 193

Germany

Basic Law (Grundgesetz), 1949 ... 153
art 1(1) ... 101, 151, 155
art 1(2) ... 151
art 2(1) ... 97, 99, 101, 102, 151, 153, 155
art 2(2) ... 155
art 3(1) ... 100, 151, 169
art 3(3) ... 100
art 6 ... 98–101
art 6 (1) ... 51, 97–98, 100–01, 110, 119, 175, 181
art 6(2) ... 175
Civil Code (BGB) ... 97
s 1416 ... 111
s 1742 ... 175
Civil Partnership Act 2001 (*Lebenspartnerschaftsgesetz*) ... 99, 101–102, 119, 147, 181
s 9(1) ... 174
s 9(2) ... 174
s 9(7) ... 175
Gender Transsexual Act 1980 (*Transsexuellengesetz*) ... 110
Law for the Execution of the Judgement of the Constitutional Tribunal on Successive Adoption for Civil Partners, 2014 ... 102
Law on marriage (Ehegesetz, EheG) 1946 ... 97
Reich Constitution of 1919 (Weimar Constitution)
art 119 ... 98
Registered Life Partnership Law (Revision) Act, 2004 ... 101

Termination of the Discrimination of Same-Sex Couples:
Civil Partnerships Act, 2001 .... 99, 174
Weimar Constitution of 1919
art 119 ff 98

Greece

Constitution,
art 9(1) 50
art 21(1) 50, 110
art 21(3) 50, 110

Hungary

Constitution of Hungary of 1949, as amended in 1989
art 54 153
Constitution of Hungary of 2011
art 2 153

Ireland

Civil Registration Act 2004 (no 3) 116, 140
s 2(2) (e) 140
Irish Constitution of 1937 (Bunreacht na hÉireann)
art 40 153
art 41 117
art 41(1) 116
art 41(2) 116
art 41(3) 116
Criminal Law (Sexual Offences) Act 1993 46

Italy

Civil Code of 1942 116
art 12 (preleggi) 103
art 107 111
art 108 111
art 134 79
Constitution, 1948 .... 51, 77
art 2 .... 44, 77–79, 152, 164
art 3 .... 152, 164
art 3(1) 152, 169
art 3(2) 151
art 29 .... 77–78, 105, 116, 173
art 29(1) 50, 77, 51, 110, 115–116
art 29(2) 51, 77, 116
Law no 87 of 11 March 1953
art 28 103
Law no 164 of 14 April 1982 .... 78, 110
Law no 184 of 4 May 1983
art 44 174

Law no 40 of 19 February 2004 179
Law no. 76 of 20 May 2016 (Civil Unions) 16, 77, 79, 97, 105, 108–109, 143, 147, 164, 174, 179
  art 1 (1) 79
  art 1 (7) a 79
  art 1 (10) 79
  art 1 (11) 79
  art 1 (12) 79

Mexico

Constitution of Mexico of 1917 (as amended in 2015)
  art 1 169

New Zealand

New Zealand Human Rights Act 1993
  art 27(2) 169
  art 45 169
  art 59 169

Portugal

Constitution, 1976 91
  art 13 (2) 89–90, 169
  art 26(1) 50
  art 36 .... 91, 136
  art 36(1) 50, 89, 110, 117
  art 67 91
  art 67(1) 50
  art 67(2) 50
  art 278 (1) 91
  art 280(1) b 90
Civil code of 1966
  art 1577 90
Decreto no 9/XI 90
Lei no 7/2001
  art 1(1) 90
Lei no 9/2010 90

Spain

Constitution, 1978 110
  art 10(1) 149,152, 163, 169
  art 14 169
  art 18(1) 50
  art 32 .... 88, 110, 118, 169
  art 32(1) 86
  art 39 88
  art 39(1) 50, 194
  art 39(2) 194

art 149 ... 87
art 149 para 8 § 1 ... 86–87
Codigo Civil (Civil Code), 1889 ... 111, 119
art 44(2) ... 86, 88
art 175 ... 88
art 175(4) ... 194
Ley de Matrimonio Civil 1870 ... 111
Ley de Matrimonio Civil 1932 ... 111
Ley Orgánica 6/1985 (Ley Organica del Poder Judicial)
art 5, s 3 ... 104
Ley 10/1998 (Catalonia) ... 87
Ley 6/1999 (Aragón) ... 87
Ley Foral 6/2000 (Navarre) ... 87
Ley 18/2001 (Balearic Islands) ... 87
Ley 1/2001 (Valencia) ... 87
Ley 2/2003 (Basque Country) ... 87
Ley 13/2005 ... 86, 88–89, 135, 138, 149, 180, 194
art 1 ... 86, 88
art 7 ... 88
Ley 2/2006 (Galicia) ... 87

South Africa

Child Care Act
s 17(1) ... 194
s 17 (2) ... 194
Aliens Control Act, Act 96 of 1991 ... 74
25(2) ... 74
Constitution, 1996 ... 14, 121, 135
art 1 ... 153
art 7(1) ... 153
art 9 (1) ... 41, 74, 158
art 9 (3) ... 20, 41, 158, 169, 195
art 10 ... 20, 74, 153
art 10(1) ... 153
art 14 ... 20
art 28(1)(b) ... 195
art 36(1) ... 9, 153
art 39(1) ... 153
Child Care Act
sect 17(1) ... 194
sect 17 (2) ... 194
Marriage Act (no 25 of 1961) ... 122
s 30(1) ... 112
Sexual Offences Act 1957
s 20(a) ... 41

Switzerland

Civil code, 1907
art 2(1) 103

Sweden

Constitution of Sweden of 1974, as amended in 2012
art 1(2) 169

United Kingdom

Adoption Act 1976 183
Adoption and Children Act 2002
s 144(4) 192
Civil Partnership Act 2004 .... 73, 179
Criminal Law Amendment Act 1985
s 11 21
Criminal Law (Sexual Offences) Act 1993 46
Gender Recognition Act 2004 110
Human Rights Act 1998 .... 72, 184
s 2 56
s 3 72
Homosexual Offences (Northern Ireland) Order 1982, 1982 No. 1536 (N.I. 19) 28, 45
Housing Act 1980 67
s 50(3) 67–68
Housing Act 1988 71
s 39(2) 69
sch 1, para 2(2) 68
sch 4, para 2 68
sch 4, para 3 68
Increase of Rent and Mortgage Interest (Restrictions) Act 1920
s 12(1)(g) 70
Matrimonial Causes Act 1973
s 11 (c) 110–11
Marriage (Same Sex Couples) Act 2013 .... 111, 179, 192
Northern Ireland Act 1998
s 75(1) 169
Offences Against the Person Act 1861 46
s 61 21
s 62 21
Rent Act 1977 68–72
Sch 1, Para 2 (2) 68–69, 72, 74
Sch 1, Para 3(1) 68–69, 72
Scotland Act 1998
schedule 5, part II, subheading 2, head L, L2 169
Sexual Offences Act 1967 .... 25, 27
s 1(2) 27

United States of America

California Family Code
s 308.5 ... 178
Constitution of the United States of America, 1787 ... 13
V Amendment ... 148, 150
IX Amendment ... 129
XIV Amendment ... 17, 30–31, 34–35, 38, 123, 127–130, 150, 159, 162–63, 169
Civil Rights Act of 1964 ... 84
Defence of Marriage Act of 1996 (DOMA) ... 82, 85, 112, 159
s 2 ... 148
s 3 ... 148
New Jersey Domestic Partnership Act, L. 2003 ... 147

Zimbabwe

Constitution, 1981
art 23 ... 48

1

Introduction

I. SETTING THE LANDSCAPE

WHEN IN 1993 the Supreme Court of Hawaii released its groundbreaking judgment in *Baehr v Lewin*,[1] holding, for the first time in the world, that denial of marriage licences to same-sex couples amounted to a violation of equal protection under the State Constitution, only a few commentators would have defined equal marriage as an 'inevitable' constitutional development.[2] Although the case—'possibly the biggest lesbian and gay rights legal victory ever'[3]—was the result of a long-term legal, political and cultural battle for sexual orientation equality starting in the United States as early as the 1950s,[4] the mere prospect of a widespread recognition of the right to marriage for same-sex couples unleashed a political and social firestorm at both state and national level.[5]

Needless to say that in many parts of the world, gays and lesbians still suffer overt discrimination, and full sexual equality is a long-term goal to be achieved through a daily and painful struggle. But since *Baehr*, the pace of recognition of gays' and lesbians' rights at both judicial and legislative level has increased dramatically across different jurisdictions, reflecting a rapidly growing consensus toward equal rights for gay men and lesbians. Many pivotal cases have been released at domestic and international level, and in many countries equal marriage is probably the most significant—and symbolic—achievement in a long series of piecemeal victories of LGBT movements in the last 15 years, ranging from decriminalisation of sexual acts, to family and parental rights, to the right to have relationships legalised, to social and workplace benefits.

Although in many countries, especially in Europe, these victories were mostly the result of legislative reforms, courts—especially supreme and constitutional courts and the European Court of Human Rights (ECtHR)—have played a key role in forging the legal debate over sexual equality and stimulating a 'virtuous cycle' in

[1] *Baehr v Lewin* 74 Haw 530, 852 P2d 44 (1993).

[2] See LH Tribe, 'The Constitutional Inevitability' of Same-Sex Marriage (2012) 71 *Maryland Law Review* 471.

[3] E Wolfson, 'Crossing the Threshold: Equal Marriage Rights for Lesbians and Gay Men and the Intra-Community Critique' (1994) 21 *New York University Review of Law and Social Change* 567, 572.

[4] See J Pierceson, *Same-Sex Marriage in the United States. The Road to the Supreme Court* (Lanham, Rowman & Littlefield Publishers, 2013).

[5] WN Eskridge, 'Backlash Politics: How Constitutional Litigation Has Advanced Marriage Equality in the United States' (2003) 93 *Boston University Law Review* 275, 283 ff.

which every single achievement has led to a further advancement towards sexual orientation equality.

In the past, other social movements mobilised themselves, ensuring historic victories before constitutional courts across different jurisdictions. Similarly to the debate over gay rights, those achievements became conceivable because of the enormous changes in the surrounding social and political contexts.[6]

For instance, in 1973, the United States Supreme Court landmark case in *Roe v Wade*[7] gave rise to a worldwide debate over abortion and women's reproductive rights. It was followed by remarkable constitutional court judgments in Europe,[8] which in turn inspired legislative reforms.

More recently, when the United States Supreme Court released its judgment in *United States v Windsor*[9]—holding it unconstitutional to restrict the federal definition of 'marriage' and 'spouse' to opposite-sex couples—President Obama compared that victory to *Loving v Virginia*,[10] the 1967 case on interracial marriage.[11] The analogy has been also emphasised by scholars[12] and lower courts.[13]

Nonetheless, some peculiarities differentiate the present debate over gay rights.

Since the 1950s, with successive waves of democratisation, the European model of constitutionalism[14]—based on an entrenched and written constitution and its combination with judicial review of legislation—has spread across the world. The establishment of new constitutional courts and the introduction of judicial review of legislation has 'become the norm of democratic constitution-writing',[15] frequently marking the transition to democracy and a new economic system.[16]

[6] MJ Klarman, '*Windsor* and *Brown:* Marriage Equality and Racial Equality' (2013) 127 *Harvard Law Review* 127, 129 ff.

[7] *Roe v Wade* 410 US 113 (1973).

[8] See, Italian Constitutional Court, case no 27 of 22 January 1975; German Constitutional Tribunal, 39 BVerfGE 1 (1975) (Abortion I case); French Conseil constitutionnel, Decision 74–54 DC of 15 January 1975; Austrian Verfassungsgerichthof, decision of 11 October 1974, [1974] *Erklaerungen des Verfassungsgerichtshofs* 221.

[9] *United States v Windsor* 133 S Ct 2675 (2013).

[10] *Loving v Virginia* 388 US 1 (1967).

[11] See also President Obama's Inaugural address, 2013 *Daily Comp. Pres. Doc.* 32, 21 January 2013.

[12] On the *Loving* analogy, see WN Eskridge, *The Case for Same-Sex Marriage. From Sexual Liberty to Civilized Commitment* (New York, The Free Press, 1996) 127 ff. See against Y Merlin, *Equality for Same-Sex Couples. The Legal Recognition of Gay Partnerships in Europe and the United States* (Chicago, University of Chicago Press, 2002) 288 ff.

[13] See eg the Virginia District Court's ruling in *Bostic v Rainey* 970 F Supp 2d 456, 22 (ED Va 2014) and the Court of Appeal for the Fourth Circuit's ruling in *Bostic v Schaefer* 760 F3d 352, 390 (2014). See also 'Virginia gay marriage fight echoes past battles over interracial marriage' in *Huffington Post*, 4 June 2014 (available at www.huffingtonpost.com/2014/04/06/virginia-gay-marriage-ban_n_5100602.html).

[14] M Shapiro, A Stone Sweet, 'The New Constitutional Politics of Europe' (1994) 26 *Comparative Political Studies* 397, describing Western Europe as the epicentre of a 'new constitutionalism', a model of democracy that rejects dogmas of legislative sovereignty and prioritises the protection of fundamental rights through constitutional review of legislation.

[15] T Ginsburg, 'The Global Spread of Constitutional Review' in GA Caldeira, DR Keleman and KE Whittington (eds), *Oxford Handbook of Law and Politics*, Oxford Handbooks on Political Science (Oxford, Oxford University Press, 2008) 81.

[16] R Hirschl, *Towards Juristocracy* (Cambridge MA, Harvard University Press, 2004) at 8 arguing that in post-communist countries the new constitutions and the introduction of the judicial review of legislation are part of a transition to both a Western model of democracy and a market economy.

'Centralised' constitutional courts have been introduced, for instance, in Southern Europe after the collapse of the authoritarian regimes at the end of the 1970s, and in Central and Eastern Europe after the fall of communist regimes in the 1990s. In those countries the constitutional courts became 'the main institutional vehicles for countering the forces of the ancient regime, or of authoritarianism, of rights-threatening nationalism'.[17] In South Africa, a Constitutional Court was established in 1995, after the termination of the apartheid regime, constituting a major forum for the consolidation of the new multicultural regime.[18] More recently, in Canada, the adoption of an entrenched Charter of Rights and of judicial review of legislation marked a departure from the British tradition of parliamentary supremacy, transforming the role of the Supreme Court and leading to the development of human rights jurisprudence.[19] Within continental Europe, both Belgium and France have recently expanded the powers of their constitutional courts: in 2003, the Belgian Cour d'arbitrage acquired the power to control whether statutes comply with all the fundamental rights and liberties laid down in the Constitution, and in 2007 its name was changed in Cour constitutionnelle, to better reflect its current powers.[20] In France, in 2008, a constitutional reform conferred on higher ordinary courts the power to submit questions to the Conseil constitutionnel concerning the constitutionality of statutes that have already entered into force (*question prioritaire de constitutionnalité*, QPC).[21]

The widespread diffusion of constitutional adjudication has largely contributed to the circulation of legal principles and judicial arguments among constitutional and supreme courts. Courts have become increasingly aware of their changing institutional role, and in recent decades both scholars and constitutional judges have been describing the emergence of 'a global community of courts',[22] 'an ideal constitutional judicial circle',[23] where constitutional and supreme courts frequently 'dialogue' with their foreign counterparts. Especially when 'new issues' or claims of new (or newly recognised) groups come before them, courts learn from the experience of other courts that in the past addressed similar issues and take into account, either explicitly or implicitly, their conclusions and legal reasoning.

[17] M Rosenfeld, W Sadurski and R Toniatti, *Central and Eastern European Constitutionalism a Quarter of a Century After the Fall of the Berlin Wall: Introduction to the Symposium* (2015) 13 *International Journal of Constitutional Law* 119 at 121 (discussing the purchase of the paradigm of 'transitional constitutionalism' in the latest Eastern European scholarship).

[18] See Hirschl, n 16 above, 27 ff.

[19] G Gentili, 'Canada' in T Groppi and MC Ponthoreau (eds), *The Use of Foreign Precedents by Constitutional Judges* (Oxford, Hart Publishing, 2013) 44 ff; D Songer, *The Transformation of the Supreme Court of Canada: An Empirical Examination* (Toronto, Toronto University Press, 2008), 58 ff.

[20] The Court also obtained the power to control whether statutes comply with the principle of legality in fiscal matters and the principle of equal treatment of foreigners. See M de Visser, *Constitutional Review in Europe. A comparative Analysis* (Oxford, Hart Publishing, 2014).

[21] A constitutional reform approved in 2008 amended art 61, s 1 of the French Constitution and introduced an incidental review of legislation through an application referred to the Conseil constitutionnel by the Conseil d'Etat or the Cour de cassation.

[22] AM Slaughter, 'A Global Community of Courts' (2003) 44 *Harvard International Law Journal* 191, 195.

[23] See former President of the Italian Constitutional Court, G Zagrebelsky, 'Corti costituzionali e diritti universali' (2006) *Rivista Trimestrale di Diritto Pubblico* 297 (transl mine).

Reasons explaining the rise of judicial cross-fertilisation and its many ramifications on significant questions such as universalism of human rights and the convergence between common law and civil law legal systems lie mostly outside the purpose of this book. Nonetheless, I argue that both the rise of constitutional adjudication and the reality of transjudicial dialogue have contributed to the circulation of legal arguments among constitutional and supreme courts in cases concerning the recognition of gay and lesbian rights.

At the same time, today judicial cross-fertilisation is also significantly stimulated by a third factor that also contributes to differentiate the present debate over gay rights: the widespread diffusion of global means of mass communication. Easy Internet searches, legal blogs and forums and online law reviews provide real time and worldwide coverage of new constitutional developments about sexual orientation equality issues. Cases circulate rapidly: the Supreme Court's decision on same-sex marriage in *Obergefell v Hodges*,[24] for instance, received great attention in Italy during the debate over the adoption of a law on same-sex civil unions, and activists emphasised that it demonstrated a prevailing trend towards marriage equality in countries of Western constitutional tradition.

Scholarly and political debates over gay rights also attained a global dimension: the harsh confrontation between opponents and proponents of equal marriage ('*mariage pour tous*') in France, for instance, attracted global attention and at the same time provided scholars and movements worldwide with significant teachings about the relationship between courts and legislators in promoting constitutional change.

II. THE AIMS OF THIS BOOK

Against this background, this book aims at analysing, in a comparative perspective, the legal arguments and rationales that constitutional (and supreme) courts developed in their judgments about the rights of gays, lesbians and same-sex couples. I mainly discuss constitutional and supreme court cases, although in many parts I also take into account lower levels of jurisdiction and the ECtHR, showing how litigation before ordinary courts and international bodies paved the way for intervention by supreme and constitutional courts.

Focusing in particular on four main themes (decriminalisation of sexual acts, recognition of same-sex couples as 'families', same-sex marriage and, finally, parental rights) I analyse how courts expounded fundamental rights to liberty, dignity, privacy, equality and non-discrimination of gays and lesbians. The early cases on decriminalisation of sexual acts between consenting adults of the same sex discussed in particular the right of privacy and personal liberty. Later cases focused instead on the 'social dimension' of same-sex relationships, expounding rights of equality, dignity and liberty of same-sex couples.

I analyse differences and analogies in human rights discourses, but I also show the importance that courts attached to arguments of tradition and nature, and how they replied to objections infused with prejudice against same-sex couples.

[24] *Obergefell v Hodges* 135 S Ct 2584 (2015).

In same-sex marriage cases, for instance, all the courts addressed the objection by opponents of same-sex marriage that legal tradition mandates gender difference in marriage. The issue at stake went well beyond the proper definition of marriage: it required the courts to answer the objection that recognition of equal marriage was the consequence of 'a judicial revolution'—ie of judicial activism breaking down traditional and established definitions of family law institutions—and to take a position on the opposite argument, considering recognition of equal marriage as the 'inevitable'[25] result of application of constitutional rights of equality, dignity and privacy.

Claims of recognition of parental rights of gays, lesbians and same-sex couples submitted instead to constitutional courts' arguments of nature: assuming that only the opposite-sex couple can 'naturally' procreate, traditionalists assumed procreation as a determinant of marriage. This objection frequently concealed a bias against gays and lesbians, because it implicitly questioned their aptitude for child-rearing, suggesting that children can adequately be brought up only within a 'traditional' family composed of a mother and father, anchored by the bond of marriage. As in same-sex marriage cases, answering these objections forced the courts to clarify the boundaries of constitutional adjudication and to engage in a dialogue with legislators.

This short account of the subject of this book makes it clear that, in my opinion, constitutional cases cannot be analysed in isolation from the institutional context in which they have been released.[26] As notions such as 'marriage' and 'family' are deeply entrenched in cultural and legal tradition, all the constitutional courts frequently faced the objection that revising traditional family law institutions fell outside judicial powers and that it was instead the duty of legislators to understand and convey into law the prevailing sentiments of public opinion on family law issues. But, at the same time, courts could not avoid providing an answer to the minorities that resorted to them for the assertion and the protection of their fundamental rights, especially when national legislators were unable to break the stalemate and adopt legislative reforms upholding the claims of social movements and minorities.

Therefore, in this book, constitutional cases on gay rights also offer me the opportunity to discuss the role of constitutional and supreme courts in promoting constitutional change and responding to public opinion and minorities' demands. Through a narrative describing the path towards legal recognition of same-sex civil unions or equal marriage in many different jurisdictions, I examine the relationships between some constitutional courts and legislators, arguing that constitutional cases on the rights of same-sex couples both shape and are influenced by the prevailing sentiments of public opinion and politics, in a virtuous circle for the advancement of sexual equality. This has been true even when cases have not resulted in an immediate victory for gays and lesbians and same-sex couples, because courts have nevertheless contributed to the dismantling of prejudice and the creation of legal arguments.

Nonetheless, I do not intend to deny the differences in the role of legislatures and courts in promoting and protecting the human rights of gays and lesbians:

[25] Tribe, 'The Constitutional Inevitability' above n 2.
[26] See, on this underlying assumption, Hirschl, *Towards Juristocracy*, n 16 above.

Parliaments—for instance, as Eskridge stresses—tend to address equality issues 'in smaller steps and only after most voters have come to support or acquiesce in it'.[27] Conversely courts, especially constitutional and supreme courts, usually exercise caution in promoting constitutional change, due to their concern for the consequences of a possible backlash on their legitimacy.

At the same time, constitutional and supreme courts should not be assimilated to lower ordinary courts: in a centralised judicial review system—the prevailing model in Europe—constitutional courts are frequently reluctant to determine radical constitutional changes through their judgments, especially when the issue at stake involves traditional family law institutions. Conversely, lower courts tend to address controversial issues.

I show that the outcome of constitutional litigation also depends on the specific procedural and institutional arrangements governing the judicial review of legislation in each jurisdiction.

III. THE COMPARATIVE METHOD

The extensive case law on sexual orientation equality issues forced me to make a selection of topics and jurisdictions.

As far as the choice of the topics is concerned, this book focuses, as mentioned earlier, on four main themes: the decriminalisation of sexual acts between consenting adults of the same sex (Chapter 2); the recognition of the social value of same-sex relationships and their inclusion within the definition of 'family' (Chapter 3); same-sex marriage—in particular, the role of constitutional courts in promoting marriage equality and their institutional dialogue with legislators (Chapter 4, section I); constitutional courts and the value of tradition in the definition of marriage (Chapter 4, section II); arguments of equality, dignity and liberty in same-sex marriage constitutional cases (Chapter 4, section III); and parental rights of gays, lesbians and same-sex couples and the procreative purpose of marriage (Chapter 5).

In recent decades, many constitutional and supreme courts have been asked to decide on the constitutionality of differences based on sexual orientation in those four fields. Courts have addressed quite similar human rights issues, with a large similarity of arguments put forward by parties and amici curiae.

Nonetheless my choice is not only justified by the simple commonality of subjects and arguments among the cases. The meanings of 'family' and 'marriage', 'parent' and 'spouse' have been left largely undefined in many jurisdictions. For instance, as I illustrate in Chapter 4, most of the constitutions and international documents either do not define marriage in heterosexual terms, or do not mention marriage at all. Definitions are instead mostly expressed in civil codes, family law statutes and judicial precedents, and all those sources of the law contribute, as traditionalists argue, to the longstanding legal tradition of marriage. Against this legal background, courts undertake the difficult task of interpreting vague (or silent) constitutional provisions, and they need to justify their decisions of either endorsing an evolutionary

[27] Eskridge, 'Backlash Politics' n 5 above, 297.

interpretation of marriage and family, or leaving the matter to the discretion of the political branches. Therefore, as illustrated earlier, the four subjects also offer me the opportunity to situate the constitutional cases in a broader terrain and to address issues concerning, for instance, the interpretation of the different sources of law, the role of courts and their relationship with legislators. Cases about the legitimacy of statutes that criminalised sexual intercourse between same-sex adults similarly also involve wider issues, such as the courts' role in preserving 'traditional morality' and the legitimacy of intrusion by courts and the State in the personal lives of citizens.

Although many other interesting issues have been submitted to constitutional courts in the last few years that are equally deserving of the constitutional scholar's attention, I opted for singling out cases related to more specific subjects that are mainly regulated at legislative (or sub-legislative) level, such as employment and housing discrimination, access to assisted procreation and surrogacy, and military service by gays and lesbians.

The selection of the main themes has also influenced the selection of relevant jurisdictions. My attention focuses in particular on the European[28] and extra-European[29] constitutional cases dealing with the four selected themes that have attracted greater scholarly attention in recent years, representing at the same time a model for other courts. Within Europe, in particular, I analyse constitutional and supreme court cases from France, Germany, Italy, Spain and Portugal and from Ireland and the United Kingdom. Outside Europe, I mainly focus on the United States, but in many points also discuss cases from Canadian courts and the South Africa Constitutional Court. Finally, as mentioned earlier, I devote great attention to many judgments of the European Court of Human Rights, which largely contributed to promoting sexual equality in Europe, exerting great influence even outside the Council of Europe. Throughout the book I often look at the experience of my own country, Italy, lagging behind many other democracies of the Western constitutional tradition in sexual orientation equality issues.

The constitutional and supreme court cases I examine in this book are from countries sharing a common constitutional tradition and they expound common values and principles of equality, dignity and liberty.[30] Although the idea of a common tradition can be disputed because no fixed and clear boundary can be drawn among legal traditions,[31] it is at the same time undeniable that, despite their structural differences and their different approaches to sexual equality issues, the selected countries have been following a common path towards the recognition of the human rights and equality of gays and lesbians. This path starts with decriminalisation of sexual acts between persons of the same sex, gets through the legal recognition of same-sex relationships and families and, in more recent times, culminates in same-sex marriage and the right of adoption for same-sex couples.

[28] In particular, France, Germany, Ireland, Italy, Spain, Portugal, United Kingdom.

[29] In particular, Canada, United States of America, South Africa.

[30] On the 'most similar cases' logic in comparative law, R Hirschl, 'The Question of Case Selection in Comparative Constitutional Law' (2005) 53 *American Journal of Comparative Law* 125, 133 ff.

[31] On the complexity of traditions, see P Glenn, *Legal Traditions of the World*, 5th edn (Oxford, Oxford University Press, 2014) 366.

However, I do not intend to suggest that a step-by-step approach should be advisable,[32] but only to argue that, from the perspective of constitutional law, there is a commonality of outcomes that made it possible for the Spanish Constitutional Tribunal, in its same-sex marriage case of 2012, to describe the emergence of 'a new "image" of marriage, gradually becoming more common … which allows us to interpret the idea of marriage, from the point of view of Western comparative law, as a plural conception'.[33]

IV. SOME REMARKS ON COURTS' USE OF FOREIGN PRECEDENTS

In some of the cases I analyse in the book, constitutional courts openly discuss foreign precedents. Sometimes the influence of foreign cases is instead only implicit, due for instance to the style of judicial opinions[34] or, presumably, to the choice of constitutional judges to rely explicitly only on domestic sources of law when issues so deeply entrenched in culture and legal tradition—such as marriage and family—come into consideration.[35]

As judicial cross-fertilisation is a transversal theme emerging throughout the analysis of constitutional cases on sexual orientation equality, it is necessary to premise some remarks on the variety of reasons justifying courts' citations of their foreign counterparts' cases.

In the first place, courts explain their use of foreign citations arguing that they demonstrate the emergence of 'a new idea' of marriage and family or a growing consensus towards the elimination of discriminations based on sexual orientation. The Constitutional Tribunal of Spain, for instance, cited a large number of foreign cases (and legislative materials) that similarly opened marriage to same-sex couples, concluding that they suggested 'a plural image' of marriage.[36] In its judgment on decriminalisation of sexual acts between persons of the same sex,[37] the Constitutional

[32] My choice to follow a path of recognition starting from decriminalisation of sexual acts and culminating in same-sex marriage is merely instrumental to my analysis and not normative. In other words, I am not arguing that a step-by-step approach towards same-sex marriage would have better chances of success in countries (like Italy) that still do not admit it. My choice comes from the observation that this path has been quite common in European and extra-European countries, and that courts, especially constitutional and supreme courts, have been more sympathetic to gay couples seeking the right to marry when claims of equal marriage had been preceded by the recognition of other LGBT rights. I also discuss this point from a different perspective in Ch 4, section I concerning the role of courts in promoting constitutional change.

[33] Case no 198/2012, 6 November 2012, SCT, para 9.

[34] In Italy, for instance, the style of judicial opinion does not admit separate opinions, footnotes or citations of scholarly works. In France, the style of Conseil constitutionnel opinions is quite concise and made up of a list of *Considérant* ('in light of') clauses, sentence-like assertions taking into consideration what the law is. Citation of foreign precedents are quite rare in the German Constitutional Tribunal's cases, although separate opinions sometimes are more open to citing foreign sources than the majority opinions.

[35] For instance citations of foreign cases recur in cases concerning decriminalisation of sexual acts (Ch 2) whereas they are quite rare in cases about 'family' (Ch 3) and same-sex marriage (Ch IV, sections II and III).

[36] Case no 198 of 2012, n 33 above, para 9.

[37] *National Coalition for Gay and Lesbian Equality v Minister of Justice*, Case CCT 11/98, (1998) ZACC 15.

Court of South Africa cited the European Court of Human Rights' landmark decision in *Dudgeon v United Kingdom*,[38] as illustrative of 'a process of change commenced in Western democracies in legal attitudes towards sexual orientation'.[39]

Finally, in *Lawrence v Texas*,[40]—a landmark case of 2003—the Supreme Court of the United States held sodomy law in Texas unconstitutional, overruling *Bowers v Hardwick*,[41] a 17-year-old controlling precedent. Writing for the Court, Justice Kennedy made special note of the ECtHR's ruling in *Dudgeon v United Kingdom*, stressing that this case, released almost five years before *Bowers*, contradicted the premise in *Bowers* that governmental interest in circumscribing personal choice was legitimate or urgent and complied with the values the United States shares with a wider civilisation.[42] He also emphasised that 'other nations ... have taken action consistent with an affirmation of the protected right of homosexual adults to engage in intimate, consensual conduct'.[43]

These examples show that, in cases concerning sexual orientation equality, use of comparative materials, especially of foreign precedents, often plays an evidentiary and confirmatory role. Courts cite foreign cases addressing similar issues in order to demonstrate the existence of a prevailing trend they think should be followed, or to strengthen their conclusion to join the solutions adopted in other jurisdictions.

The South African Constitutional Court, for instance, concluded that the fact that

> a number of open and democratic societies have turned their backs on criminalisation of sodomy in private between adult consenting males, despite the fact that sexual orientation is not expressly protected in the equality provisions of their constitution ... fortify the conclusion ... that the limitation in question in our law regarding such criminalisation cannot be justified under section 36(1) of the 1996 Constitution.[44]

Similar statements can also be found in the Supreme Court of Mexico's case on same-sex marriage, arguing that 'comparative law reveals, both at judicial and legislative level, an evolution in the recognition of the rights of gays, lesbians and same-sex couples, justifying the suppression of the discriminations they suffered in the past'.[45]

By contrast, other constitutional courts have emphasised the lack of a prevailing consensus about same-sex marriage. The decision of some jurisdictions to legally recognise same-sex civil unions instead of opening marriage to same-sex couples supports the courts' conclusions that the issue should be better addressed at legislative level. In 2010, the Italian Constitutional Court, for instance, dismissed same-sex couples' claims, arguing that the decision about how to regulate same-sex relationships pertains to the legislator: in reaching this conclusion the Court relied, inter alia, on comparative law, observing the lack of a unanimous consensus in other

[38] *Dudgeon v UK* (1981) Series A no 45, [1981] EHRR 5.
[39] *National Coalition* n 37 above, para 51.
[40] *Lawrence v Texas* 539 US 558 (2003).
[41] *Bowers v Hardwick* 478 US 186 (1986).
[42] *Lawrence v Texas* n 40 above, 539 US, 576.
[43] ibid.
[44] *National Coalition* n 37 above, para 57.
[45] See *Acción de inconstitucionalidad 2/2010*, 10 August 2010, para 267. See also the Portuguese Constitutional Court in *Acórdão* no 121/2010 (8 April 2010) and the Constitutional Court of Colombia in *Sentencia* C-577/11 at 169.

jurisdictions due to the fact that some countries had opted for opening marriage to same-sex couples, whereas others had introduced same-sex civil unions.[46]

Analogously the Irish High Court, in *Zappone,*[47] cited extensive case law of American and Canadian courts on same-sex marriage, 'dealing with similar definitions of marriage and the assertion of a right to marry requiring a redefinition of the traditional understanding of marriage as is the case in these proceedings', concluding that

> having regard to the clear understanding of the meaning of marriage as set out in the numerous authorities opened to the Court from this jurisdiction and elsewhere, I do not see how marriage can be redefined by the Court to encompass same sex marriage. The Plaintiffs referred frequently in the course of this case to the 'changing consensus' but I have to say the there is little evidence of that. The consensus around the world does not support a widespread move towards same sex marriage.[48]

However, it should also be noted that in other cases, reliance on comparative materials to demonstrate the existence of a common trend on sexual equality issues also serves the courts' purpose to emphasise their efforts to contribute to a common enterprise. This is important, especially for newly established constitutional courts, which are often motivated by the desire to stress the radical changes in their system of government and to place themselves 'in the mainstream of international democratic practice'.[49] The Constitutional Court of South Africa for instance in the *Fourie* same-sex marriage case referred to the ideals of 'a democratic, universalistic, caring and aspirationally egalitarian society',[50] emphasising how 'the contrast between the past which [the Constitution] repudiates and the future to which it seeks to commit the nation is stark and dramatic'.[51]

Finally, comparative law materials offer the courts the opportunity to evaluate the impact of solutions adopted elsewhere. This appears extremely useful when courts are asked to address a new and difficult issue. As former Justice L'Heureax-Dubé of the Supreme Court of Canada wrote:

> Given the similarities of constitutional drafting and sources, one would not be surprised by the new dialogue among judges and lawyers drawing on the expertise and experience of interpreters of similar documents. Moreover, because the legal protection of human rights is a novel phenomenon in many countries, sometimes little or no previous domestic jurisprudence exists to give meaning to the rights, making judgments from elsewhere particularly useful and necessary. Deciding on applicable legal principles and solutions increasingly involves a consideration of the approaches that have been adopted for similar legal problems elsewhere.[52]

[46] See Case no 138 of 2010, para 8.

[47] *Zappone and Gilligan v Revenue Commissioners* [2006] IEHC 404.

[48] ibid.

[49] See the Constitutional court of South Africa in *Coetzee v Government of the Republic of South Africa* 1995 (10) BCLR 1382 (CC), para 51.

[50] *Minister of Home Affairs and Another v Fourie*, Case CCT 60/04, [2005] ZACC 19, para 60.

[51] ibid, para 59.

[52] C L'Heureax-Dubé, 'From Many Different Stones: A House of Justice' (2003) 41 *Alberta Law Review* 659. G Calabresi expounded a similar idea in his concurring opinion in *United States v Then* 56 F 3d 464, 469 (1995).

The use of comparative law, in particular of foreign cases, as an aid to constitutional interpretation in cases concerning the rights of gays and lesbians, is part of a larger trend to judicial cross-fertilisation in constitutional adjudication, which has attracted great scholarly attention in the last few years, as exemplified by the extensive literature on the subject.[53] The general debate has focused on the many different purposes served by the citation of comparative law materials and on the practical difficulties and the theoretical objections surrounding their use in constitutional interpretation.

The analysis of these wider issues, which I have discussed in earlier writings,[54] falls outside the purpose of this book. Nonetheless it is worth remembering, as far as the field of study of this book is concerned, that the citation of foreign cases has stirred a harsh debate, especially in the United States[55]—in the past mainly an 'exporter' of constitutional principles and doctrines—after Justice Kennedy's citation of *Dudgeon* in the text of his opinion of the Court in *Lawrence v Texas*. Justice Scalia, in an impassioned dissenting opinion, labelled the discussion of foreign views—either in order to show that foreign nations have decriminalised same-sex sexual acts or in order to support the opposite argument that others have retained criminal prohibitions on sodomy—as 'meaningless' and 'dangerous dicta since the Court should not

[53] In the last decade, prominent scholars have analysed the use of comparative materials, especially foreign precedents, in constitutional adjudication. See eg G de Vergottini, *Oltre il dialogo tra le Corti. Giudici, diritto straniero, comparazione* (Bologna, Il Mulino, 2010); GF Ferrari and A Gambaro (eds), *Corti nazionali e comparazione giuridica* (Napoli, ESI, 2006); T Groppi and MC Ponthoreau (eds), *The Use of Foreign Precedents by Constitutional Judges* (Oxford, Hart Publishing, 2013); S Choudhry, 'Globalization in Search of Justification: Toward a Theory of Comparative Constitutional Interpretation' (1999) 74 *Indiana Law Journal* 819 (1999) and S Choudhry (ed), *The Migration of Constitutional Ideas* (Cambridge, Cambridge University Press, 2006); P Häberle, *Rechtsvergleichnung im Kraftfeld des Verfassungsstates* (Berlin, Dunker & Humblot, 1992); V Jackson, *Constitutional Engagement in a Transnational Era* (Oxford, Oxford University Press, 2009); B Markesinis and J Fedtke, *Judicial Recourse to Foreign Law. A New Source of Inspiration?* (Routledge, London, 2006); MC Ponthoreau, 'Le recours à l'argument de droit compare par le juge constitutionnel. Quelques problèmes théoriques et techniques' in F Mélin-Soucramanien (ed), *L'interprétation constitutionnelle* (Paris, Dalloz, 2005) 167; AM Slaughter, *A New World Order* (Princeton, Princeton University Press, 2004).

[54] A Sperti, 'United States of America: First Cautious Attempts of Judicial Use of Foreign Precedents in the Supreme Court's Jurisprudence' in T Groppi and MC Ponthoreau (eds), *The Use of Foreign Precedents by Constitutional Judges* (Oxford, Hart Publishing, 2013) 393 and A Sperti, 'Il dialogo tra le corti ed il ricorso alla comparazione nell'esperienza più recente' (2006) *Rivista di diritto costituzionale*, 125 ff (also available in archivio.rivistaaic.it/materiali/anticipazioni/comparazione/index.html).

[55] See *United States v Then* 56 F 3d 464, 468–69 (1995) (Calabresi concurring). See eg B Ackerman, 'The Rise of World Constitutionalism' (1997) 83 *Vanderbilt Law Review* 771; VC Jackson, 'Constitutional Comparison: Convergence, Resistance, Engagement' (2005) 119 *Harvard Law Review* 109; VC Jackson, 'Comparative Constitutional Federalism and Transnational Judicial Discourse' (2004) 2 *International Journal of Constitutional Law (Icon)* 91; VC Jackson, 'Constitutional Dialogue and Human Dignity: States and Transnational Constitutional Discourse' (2004) 65 *Montana Law Review* 15; HH Koh, 'International Law as Part of Our Law' (2004) 98 *American Journal of International Law* 43, 44; P McFadden, 'Provincialism in United States Courts' (1995) 81 *Cornell Law Review* 4; FI Michelman, 'Reflection' (2004) 82 *Texas Law Review* 1737; M Rosenfeld, 'Constitutional Adjudication in Europe and the United States: Paradoxes and Contrasts' (2004) 2 *International Journal of Constitutional Law* 633, 649; Slaughter, 'A Global Community of Courts' n 22 above; E Stein, 'Uses, Misuses—and Nonuses of Comparative Law' (1977) 72 *Northwestern University Law Review* 198; M Tushnet, 'The Possibilities of Comparative Constitutional Law' (1999) 108 *Yale Law Journal* 1225; K Yoshino and M Kavey, 'Immodest claims and Modest Contributions: Sexual Orientation in Comparative Constitutional Law' in M Rosenfeld and A Sajó (eds), *The Oxford Handbook of Comparative Constitutional Law* (Oxford, Oxford University Press, 2012) 1079, 1086 ff.

impose foreign moods, fads, or fashions on Americans'.[56] He contested the majority assumption that *Bowers* had relied on the values of Western civilisation, arguing that the case had 'rather rejected the claimed right to sodomy on the ground that such a right was not 'deeply rooted in [the United States'] history and tradition'.[57] He concluded: 'Constitutional entitlements do not spring into existence because some States choose to lessen or eliminate criminal sanctions on certain behavior. Much less do they spring into existence, as the Court seems to believe, because *foreign nations* decriminalize conduct'.[58]

Some scholars, in commenting on *Lawrence*, analogously argued that the use of foreign materials determines an allocation of decision-making power to foreign bodies lacking democratic legitimacy.[59]

Described by Markesinis and Fedtke as 'an American objection',[60] this critique assumes the use of comparative materials to be a potential threat to democracy and sovereignty. In the debate over the recognition of rights of gays and lesbians it implies an undemocratic exercise of judicial discretion and improper policymaking by constitutional and supreme courts in a field in which they should confine themselves to enforcing only domestic sources, enacted by democratically accountable representatives of the people.

However, this critique appears, in my opinion, too rigid and in some respects misleading. It is too rigid because it implies that comparative sources cannot even be used as a source of inspiration, although courts claim to be expounding domestic principles values and they emphasise the analogies between domestic and foreign sources. The objection is at the same time also misleading, as Markesinis and Fedtke emphasise, because it implicitly assumes that courts are enforcing a *foreign* source.[61] Instead, when a court finds the foreign idea persuasive, the solution it adopts in solving the case becomes part of domestic law.

In cases concerning sexual orientation equality, the strongest objection is instead that one I name, for brevity's sake, the 'cultural objection'. As institutions like 'marriage' and 'family' are deeply entrenched in local legal traditions, culture and history, this objection stresses the risks of an improper or incorrect use of foreign law and the difficulty of importing solutions and ideas conceived in a different social, cultural and legal environment.

This argument has been advanced, for instance, by the government party before the High Court of New Delhi in a case about the legitimacy of India's sodomy statute.[62] The Government stressed in particular that 'social and sexual mores in foreign countries cannot justify decriminalization of homosexuality in India' because 'in western morality standards are not as high as in India'.[63]

[56] *Lawrence v Texas* n 40 above, 539 US, 598 (Scalia dissenting).

[57] ibid.

[58] ibid (emphasis in original).

[59] See especially RA Posner, 'The Supreme Court, 2004 Term: Foreword: A Political Court' (2005) 119 *Harvard Law Review* 31, 84–90; RA Posner, 'No Thanks, We Already Have Our Own Laws: The Court Should Never View a Foreign Legal Decision as a Precedent in Any Way (2004) 7/8 *Legal Affairs*, also available at http://legalaffairs.org/issues/July-August-2004/featureposnerjulaug04.msp.

[60] Markesinis and Fedtke, 'Judicial Recourse to Foreign Law' n 53 above, 157.

[61] Markesinis and Fedtke, 'Judicial Recourse to Foreign Law' n 53 above, 164.

[62] See *Naz Foundation v Government of NCT of Delhi* (2009) 160 Delhi Law Times 277.

[63] *Naz Foundation* n 62 above, para 24.

In *Zappone*, the Irish High Court admitted that foreign 'authorities are interesting in many respects' because 'they are dealing with similar definitions of marriage and the assertion of a right to marry requiring a redefinition of the traditional understanding of marriage as is the case in these proceedings' and 'many of the arguments in those cases put forward on behalf of the proponents of same sex marriage have been relied upon in the arguments in this case also'. Nonetheless it stressed that 'there is a limit to the assistance that can be drawn from them given the different constitutional framework applicable in this jurisdiction but the approach taken to the proposed re-definition of the freedom to marry is of interest'.

Both courts seemed to suggest that relying on foreign sources implied the risk of disregarding the prevailing sentiments of public opinion and the constitutional principles lying at the base of domestic regulation of family law institutions. The Constitutional Tribunal of Spain was probably aware of that objection in its 2012 ruling on same-sex marriage, which after a detailed examination of legal developments in countries 'sharing the same legal culture',[64] cited many surveys showing that 'in Spain there is broad social acceptance of marriage between same-sex couples'.[65]

The legal culture, the Constitutional Tribunal observed:

> is not only based on a literal, systematic or originalist interpretation of the law, but also depends on observing any legally relevant issues of current society. This does not mean that direct regulatory force should be granted to factual issues; the opinions of legal scholars and advisory bodies established by the law; comparative law applicable in neighbouring social and cultural scenarios and—as regards the construction of legal culture in relation to rights—the international activity of States manifested in international treaties; the case-law laid down by international bodies, and the opinions and reports drawn up by competent bodies in the United Nations system, as well as other recognised international authorities.[66]

The Constitutional Tribunal's reply suggested that relying on foreign materials when solving a case concerning the meaning of 'marriage' means neither enforcing foreign sources, nor disregarding domestic culture and legal tradition, but only enlarging the judge's perspective in constitutional interpretation.

This reply to the cultural objection brings to mind an exchange of views between Justice Scalia and Justice Breyer. In a well-known opinion in *Thompson v Oklahoma*, Justice Scalia wrote that 'we must never forget that it is a Constitution for the United States of America that we are expounding'[67] and in *Printz v United States* also argued that 'comparative analysis [is] inappropriate to the task of interpreting a constitution'.[68]

Responding to this objection Justice Breyer wrote that

> of course, we are interpreting our own Constitution, not those of other nations, and there may be relevant political and structural differences between their systems and our own ... But their experience may nonetheless cast an empirical light on the consequences of different solutions to a common legal problem.[69]

[64] Case no 198 of 2012, n 33 above, para 9.
[65] ibid.
[66] ibid (my translation).
[67] *Thompson v Oklahoma* 487 US 815, 868, fn 4 (1988).
[68] *Printz v United States* 521 US 898, 921 fn 11 (1997).
[69] ibid 521 US, 977 (Breyer, dissenting).

I argue that whatever the authoritativeness and the actual pertinence of foreign materials to the solution of the instant case, the courts' final decisions rest always on domestic principles, values and sources of the law. Nonetheless, I do not intend to disregard the relevance of cultural differences: when courts face the delicate task of formulating a definition of 'family' and 'marriage', whose notions are not fixed in time and are also socially constructed, they must devote great attention to analogies and differences among different jurisdictions. Otherwise there is the risk of juxtaposing solutions (or taking into account ideas and principles) adopted in culturally and structurally different environments. The Israeli Supreme Court's ruling in *El Al Israel Airlines v Danielowitz,*[70] concerning the exclusion of a same-sex partner from the possibility of enjoying a free airline ticket, awarded otherwise to married spouses and opposite-sex partners—can be cited as an example of wrong use of comparative materials in constitutional interpretation.[71] In reaching its conclusions, a three-judge panel thoroughly discussed the Canadian human rights cases on sexual orientation equality, disregarding the many differences in local religious feelings between Canada and Israel.

Courts have however usually paid great attention to differences and similarities with other jurisdictions cautioning against a misleading and ill-founded use of foreign materials.

The Constitutional Court of South Africa, in its ruling on same-sex marriage *(Fourie*[72]*)* stressed for instance the difficulty of relying on tradition in constitutional adjudication in South Africa, because the South African Constitution of 1996 'represents a radical rupture with a past based on intolerance and exclusion, and the movement forward to the acceptance of the need to develop a society based on equality and respect by all for all'.[73] The Constitutional Court also emphasised that unlike other jurisdictions, South Africa lacked 'a comprehensive legal regulation of the family law rights of gays and lesbians' and emphasised 'the imperative constitutional need to acknowledge the long history in our country and abroad of marginalisation and persecution of gays and lesbians'.[74]

The Supreme Court of Canada has also consistently stated that although it may undoubtedly benefit from the experience of American and other courts in adjudicating constitutional issues, it is by no means bound by that experience or the jurisprudence it generated. It wrote:

'The uniqueness of the Canadian Charter of Rights and Freedoms flows not only from the distinctive structure of the Charter as compared to the American Bill of Rights but also from the special features of the Canadian cultural, historical, social and political tradition'.[75]

In sum, it can be argued that although courts enrich their arguments and awareness of legal developments looking at other jurisdictions, they always make foreign

[70] *El Al Airlines Ltd v Danilowitz* (1994) 48(5) PD 749.

[71] On the use of foreign materials in *El Al*, see Markesinis and Fedtke, 'The judge as a comparatist' n 53 above, 154.

[72] *Fourie*, n 50 above.

[73] ibid, para 59.

[74] ibid.

[75] *Lavigne v Ontario Public Service Employees Union* [1991] 2 S.C.R. 211, esp 256–58.

ideas and principles their own. At the same time, no court ruling concerning the recognition of the rights of gays and lesbians rests solely on foreign materials. Both the United States Supreme Court in *Lawrence,* and the Spanish Constitutional Tribunal in case no 198 of 2012, for instance, paid careful attention to domestic legal developments (respectively on decriminalisation of sexual acts and same-sex marriage), whereas citations of legal foreign materials played only a secondary role in their arguments.

Although courts should carefully take into account cultural differences when importing foreign solutions or discussing legal arguments and principles expounded elsewhere, cases concerning sexual orientation equality confirm that sometimes the 'cultural objection' can also be raised instrumentally, especially when courts are unwilling to depart from domestic legal tradition in the definition of 'marriage' and 'family'. In other words, the cultural objection can sometimes be advanced to strengthen or to hide critiques of judicial activism and to justify the axiomatic uses of tradition I discuss in Chapter 4.

V. OUTLINE OF THE BOOK

This comparative study of constitutional and supreme court cases on sexual orientation equality[76] starts with *Dudgeon v United Kingdom,*[77] the 1981 ruling of the European Court of Human Rights, which marked a turning point in judicial recognition of the rights of gays and lesbians, putting gay rights at the forefront of legal debate and making them an international issue.

Chapter 2 examines the principles of privacy and liberty the ECtHR expounded in *Dudgeon*, focusing in particular on the construction of homosexuality as an

[76] *A note on terminology:* In order to further define the aims of this book, it is necessary to clarify the meaning of some terms to be used in the following chapters. The word 'sexual orientation' has different meanings, but for purposes of legal analysis, I refer to it in a broad sense, in particular both to the direction of sexual and affectional *attraction* and to emotional-sexual *conduct* in which people actually choose to engage. See, R Wintemute, *Sexual Orientation and Human Rights* (Oxford, Clarendon Press, 1995) 6 ff. Throughout this book I will use the expression 'sexual orientation equality issues' to refer to constitutional issues concerning discrimination on the basis of sexual orientation (whether the discrimination is direct or indirect, as in the case of apparently neutral regulations). I prefer this expression to 'LGBT issues', because the latter has a wider meaning (as it refers also to issues concerning bisexuality and transsexuality, that I do not address in this book) and is also controversial in some respects (sometimes LGBTI or LGBTIQ are suggested as more appropriate variations). The word LGBT appears in this book only when referring to social movements and the community.

As far as constitutional issues concerning discrimination on the basis of sexual orientation in marriage are concerned, as I emphasise in Ch 4, I consider 'equal marriage' the most appropriate term because it implicitly suggests that there is only *one* fundamental and constitutional right to marriage, regardless of people's sexual orientation, and that gays and lesbians are not claiming any special right to marriage. Nonetheless, the expression 'same-sex marriage' also appears in this book because it frequently appears in constitutional courts' cases.

Finally the word 'sex' refers to 'biological' or 'chromosomal' sex. The word 'gender' refers instead to social roles.

I will also use the words heterosexual, homosexual, gay and lesbian to refer to same-sex or opposite-sex sexual orientations and to qualify their acts or relationships. Although I acknowledge that the term 'homosexual' carries a negative acceptation, I use it for the purposes of my analysis only when occurring in judicial discourse.

[77] *Dudgeon v United Kingdom,* n 38 above.

inherent trait of the individual and 'an essentially private manifestation of the human personality'.[78] I analyse the implications of the ECtHR's arguments and the influence these exerted on the constitutional courts and international bodies that—between the end of the 1990s to the early 2000s—addressed similar issues concerning the criminalisation of sexual acts between same-sex consenting adults. In particular, I discuss how courts interpreted the right of privacy, the liberty and dignity of gays and lesbians and I emphasise that the *Dudgeon* legacy lies not only in the right of same-sex couples to engage in consensual sexual conduct as an aspect of individual freedom, but also in the idea that the enforcement of morality cannot be considered a legitimate state interest. In the final part of the chapter I discuss some analogies in the courts' interpretations of the right of privacy, arguing that they perpetuated the 'logic of closet' towards gays and lesbians, delimiting an area of self-determination free from the State's intervention. I finally address the importance of *Dudgeon* as illustrative of a change in legal perspective on sexual orientation equality at a global level.

Chapter 3 focuses instead on the development of a social dimension of same-sex relationships and the rejection of the private–public dichotomy perpetuated by *Dudgeon* and the constitutional cases on decriminalisation of sexual acts. It starts with a premise about the constitutional definition of family as a 'basic social institution' and the 'private/public divide' in some European countries and in common law regulation of family and family relationship. I then focus on the arguments that the ECtHR and some constitutional courts have advanced in order to depart from the traditional definition of 'family' based on gender difference before the recognition of stable same-sex relationships at legislative level. I emphasise that issues concerning the definition of 'family' require courts to take a position between dominant conceptions of family—enforced by laws and supported by a supposed widespread consensus or 'common sense'—and a plural and functional definition of 'family' centred on 'lived lives'. Both approaches raise theoretical objections concerning the proper identification of the essential characteristics of 'family' and bring into question the role of courts and their legitimacy. I conclude this chapter with some remarks on the definition of 'family' in Italian constitutional law, demonstrating how a narrow interpretation of family which excludes same-sex couples has long been advanced by Italian scholarship and courts and how it still, in part, survives after the adoption of law no 76 of 2016, regulating same-sex civil unions.

Chapter 4 focuses on constitutional litigation concerning the recognition of the right to marriage for same-sex couples. This chapter is divided into three sections. Section I focuses on the relationships among courts, legislators and public opinion in the debate over equal marriage for same-sex couples in some significant European experiences (Spain, Portugal, Germany, France and, in some respects, Italy). This digression provides the necessary background for the following comparative analysis of constitutional cases, but at the same time offers me the opportunity to discuss analogies in the role of constitutional courts in promoting constitutional change. As mentioned earlier, constitutional and supreme courts are not the only actors in the debate over sexual equality: I emphasise how they engage in a dialogue with lower

[78] ibid, para 60.

levels of jurisdictions and legislators, providing guidelines, setting deadlines for legislative intervention, clarifying the proper interpretation of the relevant constitutional principles and forging constitutional arguments. I conclude that the general pattern confirms the validity of American scholarship's conclusions on the role of courts in promoting constitutional change, but I also emphasise some peculiarities of European experiences and the differences between constitutional and lower courts ensuing from the specific features of European systems of judicial review of legislation.

Section II of Chapter 4 examines issues concerning the definition of 'marriage' and 'spouse' in constitutional cases about equal marriage. After premising that in most of the jurisdictions, the institution of marriage escapes legal definition, and that constitutions do not mandate gender diversity in marriage, I show that sex difference as a determinant of marriage is mainly inferred from legal tradition. I analyse the different meanings of 'tradition' of opposite-sex marriage in constitutional cases, distinguishing *legal* tradition (which is supported by civil codes, statutes or judicial precedents) from a broader definition of tradition (encompassing religion, morality and culture in a wider sense). I clarify that, in the first place, the legal tradition plays an evidentiary role in same-sex marriage cases: it provides a presumptive (and sometimes conclusive) evidence of the purpose of marriage and its 'essential core'. I discuss the theoretical difficulties raised by the identification of the essential core of marriage in constitutional cases, emphasising how the chance of different outcomes depends on the court's perspective. Then I discuss a second use of tradition in same-sex marriage cases that is related to the identification of 'new' fundamental rights not envisioned in the Constitutional text. This purpose of tradition has been mainly discussed in the United States in cases concerning the judicial interpretation of the Due Process Clause of the XIV Amendment of the Constitution. I argue that although this debate is peculiar to American constitutional law, it casts light on European cases on same-sex marriage, illuminating the nature of tradition and the different normative values it serves in relation to marriage. Finally I focus on progressive interpretations of constitutional clauses on marriage in same-sex marriage cases, discussing courts' efforts to accommodate tradition with 'a new and plural idea' of marriage and, at the same time, to avoid objections of judicial law-making.

Section III of Chapter 4 analyses the arguments of equality, liberty and human dignity that constitutional courts developed in same-sex marriage cases. I start my analysis from equality, emphasising how this principle comes into consideration in same-sex marriage cases both in relation to the 'expressive' value couples and society attach to marriage, and to the rights and responsibilities flowing from marriage. Then I focus on arguments of dignity, emphasising the narrow relationship between dignity, equality and liberty in same-sex marriage cases. The idea of dignity as synthesis of equality and liberty has been thoroughly explored by European constitutional scholarship due also to the influence of German constitutional tradition, but it has been also developed by the United States Supreme Court in recent cases on gay rights. As the concept of dignity is complex and multifaceted, I try to identify its different meanings in same-sex marriage cases: I argue that in the first place, dignity comes into consideration in relation to the sociality of same-sex couples and their aspiration to recognition and respect. Then I address the idea of dignity as equal value of all human beings, arguing that courts frequently rely on this meaning of dignity in order to emphasise the transition of gays, lesbians and same-sex couples into full citizenship. In this respect, equal marriage symbolises the final achievement of same-sex couples in their long-term battle for equality and the end of the 'separate but equal regime'[79] of civil unions. Finally, I discuss use of dignity discourses in relation to liberty and self-determination of all human beings concerning the most intimate and personal life choices. I conclude my analysis with some remarks about the widespread diffusion of dignity discourse which dominates the present human rights adjudication, and I attempt to explain the reasons underlying 'the great success' of dignity even in sexual orientation equality litigation.

In the fifth and final chapter I examine constitutional court and ECtHR cases on the recognition of parental rights of gays, lesbians and same-sex couples. I discuss in particular traditionalists' objection concerning the 'procreative nature' of marriage, showing how courts have contributed to illuminate the many fallacies of this viewpoint. I also explain that the procreation argument has been advanced before constitutional and international courts in order to justify the governmental interest in guaranteeing 'an optimal environment' for children and their right to 'a normal family life'. I discuss this argument in constitutional cases concerning individual adoption, second-parent adoption and joint adoption, demonstrating how courts have usually found in favour of same-sex couples on the basis of principles of equality and the best interests of the child in the instant cases. I argue that, even in countries like Italy that, until recent times, lagged behind in the recognition of the rights of gays and lesbians, the principle of best interest of the child has offered courts a powerful tool for rejecting the idea that the State may better pursue its interest in optimal child-rearing by limiting the right of gays and lesbians to adopt children. In reaching this conclusion courts have not only assessed the reality of family life of same-sex couples and their children, but also contributed to the eradication of prejudices that portrayed gays and lesbians as unfit for parenting.

[79] *Plessy v Ferguson* 163 US 537 (1896).

2

The Private Dimension of Homosexuality: Courts and Decriminalisation of Sexual Acts

I. *DUDGEON v UK* AS A GLOBAL LANDMARK CASE

DUDGEON v UK,[1] a case before the European Court of Human Rights (ECtHR), in 1981 held that Northern Ireland laws, having the effect of making certain sexual acts between consenting adult males criminal offences, were in breach of Article 8 of the European Convention of Human Rights (ECHR). The case marked a turning point in judicial recognition of the rights of gays and lesbians.

As the most remarkable of early ECtHR cases addressing the demands of the gay community, *Dudgeon* promoted the first advancements in sexual equality, 'shaping the terrain of sexual politics across Europe'.[2] The case led to the substantial decriminalisation of sexual activity in the jurisdictions that are part of the United Kingdom, in particular in Northern Ireland, but it is also remarkable because, for the first time, decriminalisation of sexual acts was enforced by a court decision. This achievement resulted in a change in strategy for gay rights movements that started to fight legal discrimination based on sexual orientation also before courts.

Dudgeon had a 'domino effect': it was followed by similar decisions of the ECtHR finding violation of Article 8 in Ireland (*Norris v Ireland*[3]) and Cyprus (*Modinos v Cyprus*).[4] At the same time, *Dudgeon* exerted a profound influence even outside European borders, serving as a landmark case for many constitutional and supreme courts in cases concerning the legitimacy of laws concerning the criminalisation of sexual acts between persons of the same sex.

In 2005, for instance, in *Lawrence v Texas*,[5] the United States Supreme Court declared unconstitutional a Texas statute that made it a crime for two persons of

[1] *Dudgeon v UK* (1981) Series A no 14, (1981) 4 EHRR 149.

[2] P Johnson, '"An Essentially Private Manifestation of Human Personality": Constructions of Homosexuality in the European Court of Human Rights' (2010) 10 *Human Rights Law Review* 67, 69.

[3] *Norris v Ireland* (1988) Series A no 142, (1991) 13 EHRR 186, a case ECtHR defines as 'indistinguishable from the *Dudgeon* case'.

[4] *Modinos v Cyprus* (1993) Series A no 259, (1993) 16 EHRR 485.

[5] *Lawrence v Texas* 539 US 558 (2003).

the same sex to engage in certain intimate sexual conduct. Writing for the Court, Justice Kennedy traced the history of 'sodomy laws' in the United States, arguing that the historical grounds relied upon in *Bowers v Hardwick*[6]—a 17-year-old controlling case—'were more complex than the majority opinion and the concurring opinion indicate'. In order to support his assertion, Justice Kennedy mentioned the Wolfenden Report,[7] which in 1957 had recommended that 'homosexual behaviour between consenting adults in private should no longer be a criminal offence' in Britain, and cited the *Dudgeon* case as an example 'of even more importance'.

'Authoritative in all countries that are members of the Council of Europe ..., the decision'—Justice Kennedy wrote—'is at odds with the premise in *Bowers* that the claim put forward was insubstantial in our Western civilization'.[8] The citation—the first one in the text of an opinion of the Court—raised a heated debate in the United States[9] and was deeply criticised by Justice Scalia in his dissenting opinion. Joined by Chief Justice Rehnquist and Justice Thomas, Scalia contested the majority reliance 'on the values [the United States] share with a wider civilization' and argued that 'constitutional entitlements do not spring into existence because some States choose to lessen or eliminate criminal sanctions on certain behavior. Much less do they spring into existence, as the Court seems to believe, because *foreign nations* decriminalize conduct.'[10]

In recent decades, other constitutional and supreme courts dealing with issues concerning the constitutional legitimacy of statutes that criminalised sexual acts in private between persons of the same sex above the age of consent have referred to the rationale of *Dudgeon v UK*.[11] The South Africa Constitutional Court case in *National Coalition*[12]—a landmark case of 1998—referred to *Dudgeon* as 'indicative of the changes in judicial and social attitudes in recent years'[13] and concluded that statutes prohibiting sexual activities between men violated Articles 9, paragraph 3 (discrimination on the basis of sexual orientation), 10 (human dignity) and 14 (right to privacy) of the South African Constitution of 1996.

In 1994, *Dudgeon* was invoked by Nicholas Toonen, a Tasmanian resident, before the Human Rights Committee of the United Nations. He charged the legitimacy of the Tasmanian Criminal Code that criminalised various forms of sexual contacts between men, including all forms of sexual contacts between consenting adult men in private.[14] The Committee concluded that the charged provisions violated Mr Toonen's right to privacy.

[6] *Bowers v Hardwick* 478 US 186 (1986).

[7] *Report of the Committee on Sexual Offences and Prostitution* ('Wolfenden Report') (London, Her Majesty's Stationery Office, 1957).

[8] *Lawrence v Texas* n 5 above, 539 US, 572.

[9] See above, 11.

[10] *Lawrence v Texas* n 5 above, 539 US, 598 (Scalia J dissenting).

[11] See, eg the Constitutional Court of Ecuador in case no 111-97 TC, 22 November 1997; the Supreme Court of Zimbabwe in *Banana v State* [2000] 4 LRC 621, 29 May 2000; the High Court of Fiji at Suva in *McCoskar and Nadan v State* (2005) FJHC 500; the Court of Appeal of Hong Kong in *Leung v Secretary of Justice* (2006) 4 HKLRD 211 (CA); the High Court of Delhi in *Naz Foundation v Government of NCT of Delhi* (2009) 160 Delhi Law Times 277; the *Sentencia* C-481 of the Constitutional Court of Colombia.

[12] *National Coalition for Gay and Lesbian Equality v Minister of Justice*, Case CCT 11/98, (1998) ZACC 15, 9 October 1998.

[13] *National Coalition* n 12 above, para 42 (Ackermann).

[14] *Toonen v Australia* Communication No 488/1992, UN Doc CCPR/C/50/D/488/1992 (1994).

At the same time, *Dudgeon* influenced legal developments on the regulation of homosexuality in the dependent territories to which the United Kingdom had extended the Convention (Guernsey, Jersey, the Isle of Man, Gibraltar and Bermuda),[15] and had enormous effect on East European legal systems, where the fall of the Soviet Union and the break-up of the Eastern bloc offered an opportunity to join the Council of Europe.[16] Other significant cases on decriminalisation of sexual acts between people of the same sex were released in Ecuador[17] and Fiji.[18]

Although in many jurisdictions decriminalisation of sexual acts was achieved through legislative reforms, *Dudgeon* put the issue at the forefront of legal debate, raising awareness on human rights of gays and lesbians at the international level. In this chapter my purpose is in the first place to analyse the construction of homosexuality *Dudgeon* expounded, and to discuss how the ECtHR forged arguments of liberty and privacy. Then I will analyse the influence the ECtHR's arguments exerted on constitutional courts that have been addressing similar issues in the last decades. I will focus my analysis in particular on the judgments of the United States Supreme Court in *Lawrence v Texas* and of the South Africa Constitutional Court in *National Coalition*. My purpose will be to discuss the legacy of *Dudgeon* but also the arguments of dignity and equality the Courts developed in the cases, influencing legal discourse on sexual orientation for many years to come.

II. *DUDGEON* AND THE RECOGNITION OF HOMOSEXUALITY AS 'AN ESSENTIALLY PRIVATE MANIFESTATION OF HUMAN PERSONALITY'

Mr Dudgeon was a gay resident in Northern Ireland. He was not charged with any offence, but claimed that the mere existence in Northern Ireland of laws[19] which had the effect of making certain sexual acts between consenting adult males criminal offences, caused him 'fear, suffering and psychological distress'. For this reason he alleged that he had suffered 'an unjustified interference with his right to respect for his private life' in breach of Article 8 ECHR, and claimed to be a victim of discrimination on the basis of sex, sexuality and residence, in violation of Article 14 in conjunction with Article 8 ECHR.

The majority adhered to the Commission's opinion and to the Commission's earliest judgments[20] that suggested that criminalisation of sexual acts fell

[15] See R Wintemute, *Sexual Orientation and Human Rights. The United States Constitution, the European Convention, and the Canadian Charter* (Oxford, Clarendon, 1995) 93 ff.

[16] A Hildebrandt, 'Routes to Decriminalization: A Comparative Analysis of the Legalization of Same-Sex Sexual Acts' (2014) 17 *Sexualities* 230, 244 ff.

[17] Case 111-97 TC.

[18] *McCoskar v State* n 11 above.

[19] Offences Against the Person Act 1861 ss 61 and 62 (criminalised buggery and attempted buggery); Criminal Law Amendment Act 1985 s 11 (criminalised gross indecency) and the common law, which criminalised the corruption of public morals and conspiracy to outrage public decency.

[20] *Dudgeon* n 1 above, was the first case to reach the Strasbourg Court after the first cases lodged between 1955 and 1980 when the Commission rejected the claim that the criminalisation of sexual acts between persons of the same sex violated the ECHR. On the first cases as expressive of 'a broader social antipathy towards homosexuality', P Johnson *Homosexuality and the European Court of Human Rights* (Abingdon, Routledge, 2013) 20 ff.

within the ambit of Article 8.[21] However the ECtHR rejected the applicant's complaint that he was subject to greater interference with his private life than are gay men in other parts of the United Kingdom and heterosexuals and lesbians in Northern Ireland itself in violation of Article 14 in conjunction with Article 8:[22] once the ECtHR recognised the existence of a violation of Article 8, it concluded that 'there [was] no useful legal purpose to be served in determining whether [Mr Dudgeon] had in addition suffered discrimination as compared with other persons who [were] subject to lesser limitations on the same right.'[23]

At the same time, the ECtHR did not establish a general principle that sexual orientation discrimination violated the ECHR in the absence of particularly serious reasons justifying it and did not even identify a general concept of 'sexual orientation discrimination'.[24] This solution, although unsatisfying insofar as it prevented the ECtHR from recognising sexual orientation as an illegitimate ground of discrimination,[25] could be interpreted as inspired by the purpose to articulate the reasoning on general considerations concerning all the individuals, instead of focusing on gays and lesbians as a discrete group.

The majority opinion's basic assumption lay instead in the recognition of homosexuality as an 'essentially private manifestation of human personality'.[26] This construction of homosexuality assumed that individuals are entitled to protection under the Convention because of their sexual orientation as an inherent trait of human nature.[27] As Johnson argues, 'acknowledging the congenital nature of the applicant's sexual orientation was foundational to accepting his status as a victim of the criminal law'.[28] The ECtHR emphasised this argument since its introductory statements when, in order to describe the personal circumstances of the applicant, it recounted that Mr Dudgeon 'ha[d] been consciously homosexual from the age of 14'.[29] This argument separated sexual orientation from sexual practices and, for the first time, in contrast with the previous Commission's jurisprudence, placed emphasis on homosexuality as an aspect of personality instead of a 'result of culture'.[30]

It is also significant that no charge against Mr Dudgeon on the basis of his sexual orientation came into consideration in the case. As mentioned earlier, Mr Dudgeon claimed that the fear and distress he suffered in consequence of the existence of Northern Ireland laws made him potentially 'liable to criminal prosecution on

[21] See, eg *WB v Republic of Germany* App n 104/55 (Commission decision, 17 December 1955).
[22] *Dudgeon* n 1 above, para 69.
[23] ibid.
[24] See Wintemute, *Sexual Orientation and Human Rights*, n 15 above, 132.
[25] Five judges out of 19 thought that Article 14 had to be examined. This point was criticised in particular by Judges Evriginis and Garcia de Enterria in their dissenting opinion. Although they assumed that examination of the claim concerning the violation of Article 14 should not prejudice their conclusions on the merits, they argued that the narrow perspective adopted by the majority opinion 'deprive[d] this fundamental provision in great part of its substance and function in the system of substantive rules established under the Convention'.
[26] *Dudgeon* n 1 above, para 60.
[27] See, Johnson, '*Constructions of Homosexuality*' n 2 above, 50 (arguing that this unprecedented statement of the Court has remained axiomatic to the Court's jurisprudence).
[28] ibid.
[29] *Dudgeon* n 1 above, para 32.
[30] ibid, para 15 (J Walsh dissenting).

account of his sexual conduct'.[31] Furthermore, he argued that 'following the search of his house in January 1976, he was questioned by the police about certain sexual activities and that personal papers belonging to him were seized during the search and not returned until more than a year later'.[32]

The majority of the Court admitted that the impugned legislation constituted a continuing interference with the applicant's right to respect for his private life (which includes his sexual life) within the meaning of Article 8. Accordingly the ECtHR held that, on the basis of

> the personal circumstances of the applicant, the very existence of this legislation continuously and directly affects his private life: either he respects the law and refrains from engaging—even in private with consenting male partners—in prohibited sexual acts to which he is disposed by reason of his homosexual tendencies, or he commits such acts and thereby becomes liable to criminal prosecution.[33]

The arguments advanced by the applicant and accepted by the ECtHR can be ascribed to an essentialist view about how sexual categories, such as 'lesbian' and 'gay', should be understood. The idea of the existence of a 'gay essence' has generated a wealth of literature: essentialist theories—demonstrating that homosexuality is an innate feature of the individual that inevitably gives rise to some human experiences and acts—have been in particular contrasted by constructionist theories, aiming at demonstrating that social categories are, to varying degrees, culture-specific and variable from age to age.[34] Thus, whereas essentialism takes for granted that society is composed of individuals who fall into fixed and stable categories (eg, heterosexual, homosexual), constructivists argue that those categories are a socio-historical product, and treat them as unstable, contingent constructs.[35] A detailed examination of these opposite perspectives about the identification of sexual categories falls outside the purpose of this book, but it is useful to observe that in English law, the idea of 'homosexuals' as a distinct, despised social category became part of the political discourse only by the time of the Wolfenden Report in 1957.[36]

The essentialist perspective appears problematic in many respects, as far as it reiterates the idea of a sharp dichotomy between 'homosexuals' and 'heterosexuals'[37] and because there is no necessary consistency between the direction of specific instances of sexual conduct and personal identity, ie the way in which individuals define themselves and their sexual orientation.[38] Even in *Dudgeon*, Judge Walsh expressed

[31] ibid, paras 37 and 60.

[32] ibid, para 38.

[33] ibid, para 41.

[34] For an overview on the longstanding debate between constructionist and essentialist theories about sexual categories, see N Bamforth, *Sexuality, Morals and Justice. A Theory of Lesbian and Gay Rights Law* (London, Cassell, 1997) 74 ff.

[35] See Bamforth, *Sexuality, Morals and Justice*, n 34 above, 76 and S Epstein, 'Gay Politics, Ethnic Identity: the Limits of Social Constructionism' in E Stein (ed), *Forms of Desire: Sexual Orientation and the Social Constructionist Controversy* (New York, Garland, 1990).

[36] Bamforth, *Sexuality, Morals and Justice*, n 34 above, 77.

[37] See M Grigolo, 'Sexualities and the ECHR: Introducing the Universal Sexual Legal Subject' (2003) 14 *European Journal of International Law* 1023.

[38] Wintemute, *Sexual Orientation and Human Rights*, n 15 above, 8.

a clear anti-essentialist view, noting that 'the fact that a person consents to take part in the commission of sexual acts is not proof that such person is sexually orientated by nature in that direction'.[39]

Nonetheless, reliance on traditional essentialist narratives has been useful to make gays' and lesbians' claim recognisable with the framework of ECHR law and to make sexual orientation 'an aspect of humanness that is protectable under the Convention'.[40] Although in *Dudgeon* the ECtHR described homosexuality as a peculiar feature of the individual, the case can be also interpreted as recognising not only gays' and lesbians' specificity but also their commonality as human beings.[41] As Johnson argues, 'ontological claims that sexuality is "inborn" and "natural" have been used because they are conducive to the key epistemological tenets of human rights discourse through which human beings are conceived as individuated "units" in possession of fundamental and universal features common to all humanity'.[42]

In the United Kingdom Government's submissions, the Northern Ireland law was justified by the 'protection of the morals in the sense of moral standards obtaining in Northern Ireland'[43] and 'the protection of the rights and freedoms of others'.[44]

The majority opinion rejected this argument and endorsed the more liberal perspective on the regulation of homosexuality adopted by the English Parliament in the Wolfenden Report, suggesting that the distinction between the two purposes was 'artificial'.[45] It also emphasised that:

> The 'protection of the rights and freedoms of others', when meaning the safeguarding of the moral interests and welfare of certain individuals or classes of individuals who are in need of special protection for reasons such as lack of maturity, mental disability or state of dependence, amounts to one aspect of 'protection of morals'.[46]

Although the ECtHR recognised the legitimacy to take into account 'the moral climate in sexual matters'[47] and the existence of 'a strong body of opposition'[48] in the Northern Irish community, it concluded that 'this cannot of itself be decisive as to the necessity for the interference with the applicant's private life'.[49] The Court also accepted that 'some form of legislation was "necessary" to protect particular sections of society as well as the moral ethos of society as a whole'[50] and did not deny that 'some degree of regulation of male homosexual conduct, as indeed of other forms of sexual conduct, by means of the criminal law can be justified as "necessary in a democratic society"'.[51] Nonetheless, it held that Northern Ireland law—which

[39] *Dudgeon* n 1 above, para 13 (Judge Walsh, partially dissenting).

[40] On the essentialist approach in the ECtHR case law, Johnson, *Homosexuality and the European Court of Human Rights* n 20 above.

[41] See J Butler, *Undoing Gender* (New York, Routledge, 2004), 29–30 (discussing the intelligibility of the 'homosexual subject' and the central tasks of gays and lesbians to demonstrate that their lives are worthy of protection in their specificity and commonality).

[42] Johnson, *Homosexuality and the European Court of Human Rights* n 20 above, 46.

[43] *Dudgeon* n 1 above, para 46.

[44] ibid, para 47.

[45] ibid, para 47.

[46] ibid.

[47] ibid, para 57.

[48] ibid.

[49] ibid, para 59.

[50] ibid, para 49.

[51] ibid.

in contrast to the regulations adopted in other Member States prohibited 'generally gross indecency between males and buggery whatever the circumstances'[52] —could not be considered necessary to accomplish those aims. The Court also relied on statutory developments and public opinion among Contracting States concerning matters of personal morality (a 'European consensus')[53] to support a less deferential treatment of rights violation of gay couples.

As mentioned, the ECtHR's view was influenced by the recommendations of the Wolfenden Report,[54] which was determinative in the repeal of 'sodomy laws' in the United Kingdom in 1967.[55] Although the Wolfenden Committee held that the function of the criminal law was

> to preserve public order and decency, to protect the citizen from what is offensive or injurious, and to provide sufficient safeguards against exploitation and corruption of others, particularly those who are specially vulnerable because they are young, weak in body or mind, inexperienced, or in a state of special physical, official, or economic dependence[56]

it excluded that law should 'intervene in the private lives of citizens, or to seek to enforce any particular pattern of behaviour'.[57]

Accordingly, the Wolfenden Committee emphasised 'the importance which society and law ought to give to individual freedom of choice in action in matters of private morality' and suggested that 'sexual behaviour between consenting adults' in private ought no longer be a criminal offence[58] as it was part of the 'realm of private morality and immorality which is, in brief and crude terms, not the law's business'.[59]

These principles—applied for the most part by the majority in *Dudgeon*[60]—attracted considerable dissent by other members of the Court, who argued that it was 'odd and perplexing ... to underestimate the necessity of keeping a law in force for the protection of morals held in high esteem by the majority of the people'.[61]

Furthermore, following Lord Devlin's theory, which contended that morality is properly the concern of the law,[62] Judge Walsh drew a distinction between

> homosexuals who are such because of some kind of innate instinct or pathological constitution judged to be incurable and those whose tendency comes from a lack of normal sexual development or from habit or from experience or from other similar causes but whose tendency is not incurable[63]

[52] ibid.

[53] See ibid, para 60 ('As compared with the era when that legislation was enacted, there is now a better understanding, and in consequence an increased tolerance, of homosexual behaviour to the extent that in the great majority of the member States of the Council of Europe it is no longer considered to be necessary or appropriate to treat homosexual practices of the kind now in question as in themselves a matter to which the sanctions of the criminal law should be applied').

[54] Wolfenden Report, n 7 above.

[55] Sexual Offences Act 1967.

[56] Wolfenden Report, n 7 above, para 13.

[57] ibid, para 14.

[58] ibid, para 62.

[59] ibid, para 61.

[60] *Dudgeon* n 1 above, paras 60–61.

[61] ibid, para 3 (Zekia J, dissenting).

[62] P Devlin, *The Enforcement of Morals* (Oxford, Oxford University Press, 1965).

[63] *Dudgeon* n 1 above, para 13 (Walsh J, partially dissenting).

and argued that 'sexual behaviour is determined more by cultural influences than by instinctive needs'.[64] Accordingly, he suggested that 'the legal arrangement and prescriptions set up to regulate sexual behaviour are very important formative factors in the shaping of cultural and social institutions'.[65]

These arguments were not only at odds with the Report's view that 'moral conviction ... is not a valid basis for overriding the individual's privacy and for bringing within the ambit of the criminal law private sexual behaviour', but also opposed the majority's interpretation that homosexuality is an innate aspect of personality. The dissenting judges also contended that homosexuality cannot be considered an alternative equivalent to heterosexuality.[66]

III. THE NOTION OF PRIVACY IN *DUDGEON* AND THE PERPETUATION OF THE 'SEXUAL CLOSET'

The idea of homosexuality as an inherent trait of the individual, and the argument that 'the Government right affected by [Northern Irish] legislation protects an essentially private manifestation of the human personality'[67] denoted the ECtHR's choice to focus in *Dudgeon* on a notion of the right of individual privacy referred to the most intimate aspects of life. Although this view could eventually be expounded to imply also a relationship between sexual privacy and right to self-determination, the Court's reliance on an essentialist view of homosexuality as an innate characteristic of the human being prevented the development of an idea of privacy as concerning liberty and self-determination in relation to personal and intimate choices of human life, in a way similar to that expounded by the United States Supreme Court in its cases about the guarantee of liberty under the Fourteenth Amendment.

Notwithstanding that it was control in respect to consensual acts between male adults committed in private that came into consideration in *Dudgeon*, the ECtHR confined the notion of privacy essentially to its *spatial* dimension, implying that private sexual acts were protected as far as they occur in the privacy of homes. The reason which made Northern Irish regulation illegitimate under Article 8 ECHR was not that it interfered with the personal *choices* of the applicant, but that its interference with his private life was not justified under Article 8(2).[68] In particular, as mentioned earlier, the ECtHR argued in the first place that

> The maintenance in force of the impugned legislation constitutes a continuing interference with the applicant's right to respect for his private life (which includes his sexual life) within the meaning of Article 8 par. 1 (art. 8-1). In the personal circumstances of the applicant, the very existence of this legislation continuously and directly affects his private life ...: either he respects the law and refrains from engaging—even in private with consenting male

64 ibid, para 15 (Walsh J, partially dissenting).

65 ibid.

66 ibid, para I (Matscher J, dissenting).

67 ibid, para 60.

68 On the three-stage process the ECtHR followed in *Dudgeon* in order to establish a violation of the right to respect of private life of the applicant, see Wintemute, *Sexual Orientation and Human Rights*, n 15 above, 98 ff.

> partners—in prohibited sexual acts to which he is disposed by reason of his homosexual tendencies, or he commits such acts and thereby becomes liable to criminal prosecution.[69]

Then the ECtHR observed that

> the reasons given by the Government, although relevant, are not sufficient to justify the maintenance in force of the impugned legislation in so far as it has the general effect of criminalising private homosexual relations between adult males capable of valid consent.[70]

As Johnson has emphasised, although

> in designating the private manifestation of homosexual sexuality to be a most intimate aspect of private life the Court can be seen to have taken a significant step away from the idea—exemplified by Wolfenden—that the decriminalization of private homosexual behaviour represented a grudging democratic tolerance for private sexual acts publicly regarded as immoral...[71]

the ECtHR gave support to the idea established at the same time in the Wolfenden Report that 'sexual conduct' must be segregated from the public sphere.[72]

The clear distinction between the public and the private dimensions of homosexuality established in *Dudgeon* was reiterated by the Court in its following cases concerning criminalisation of sexual acts.[73] For example, in *ADT v United Kingdom,*[74] the Court reversed the conviction of a man for acts of gross indecency with four other men in his home. The conviction was based on the contents of some videotapes seized by the police during a search at the applicant's home. Although at that time the Sexual Offences Act 1967 provided that sexual acts in private between consenting adult men were no longer an offence in the United Kingdom, section 1(2) of the Act punished sexual acts done in private if more than two men were present.

The whole reasoning of *ADT* revolved around the definition of privacy and the distinction between the private versus public nature of the sexual acts. Claiming that 'he was prosecuted under a law which prohibits the sexual acts themselves, even though they were carried out in the privacy of the bedroom of his own home',[75] the applicant clarified that 'there was neither organised activity nor any risk of injury in the present case and adds that, had it not been for the prosecution, the videotape would not have been distributed in any real sense whatever'.[76] By contrast, the Government contended that 'where groups of men gather in order to engage in sexual activities, the possibility of such activities being publicised is inevitable, and that this applies all the more where the activities are videotaped'.[77]

[69] *Dudgeon* n 1 above, para 41.
[70] ibid, para 61.
[71] Johnson, *Homosexuality and the European Court of Human Rights* n 20 above, 100.
[72] ibid, 101.
[73] See *Norris v Ireland*, n 3 above, para 3.
[74] *ADT v United Kingdom* ECHR 2000-IX 402.
[75] ibid, para 28.
[76] ibid, para 22.
[77] ibid, para 35.

Concluding in favour of the applicant, the Court unanimously found that given the 'absence of any public-health considerations and the purely private nature of the behaviour', no sufficient reasons justified the maintenance in force of legislation criminalising sexual acts between men in private.[78]

In particular, the Court argued that

> no evidence has been put … to indicate that there was any actual likelihood of the contents of the tapes being rendered public, deliberately or inadvertently. In particular, the applicant's conviction related not to any offence involving the making or distribution of the tapes, but solely to the acts themselves. The Court finds it most unlikely that the applicant, who had gone to some lengths not to reveal his sexual orientation, and who has repeated his desire for anonymity before the Court, would knowingly be involved in any such publication.[79]

As sexual acts fell under the umbrella of ECHR as far as they are expressed in private, *Dudgeon* and the following ECtHR's decisions on criminalisation of sexual acts reiterated the Wolfenden Report's distinction between public and private homosexual behaviour.[80] Assuming that 'exploitation and corruption may be the potential outcome of unregulated homosexual conduct in contexts where consenting adults are not alone … the Court's judgment implicitly legitimized the view that maintaining homosexuality in private was necessary'[81] and that homosexual acts occurring in public should be dealt with by the criminal law.[82]

As Johnson argues, a further consequence of the argument 'that some homosexual acts are protectable under the Convention when they take place in private is its potential to reinforce the social relations of the "closet"'.[83] I will also address the private/public dichotomy and its ramifications in Chapter 3 dealing with family life. Nonetheless, it is worth anticipating that this ideological and socially constructed split has enormous repercussions for what we believe to be the State's responsibility for protecting and assisting individuals and families.[84]

It can be concluded that, by not intervening in so-called 'private matters', the ECtHR took a decision to support the status quo.[85] As Nussbaum has stated, 'the

[78] ibid, para 38.

[79] ibid, para 25.

[80] On the connection between the private/public dichotomy and liberal philosophy in the Wolfenden Committee Report on Homosexual Offences and Prostitution, see K O'Donovan, *Sexual Divisions in Law* (London, Weidenfeld and Nicolson, 1985) 9.

[81] Johnson, *Homosexuality and the European Court of Human Rights* n 20 above, 101.

[82] The Wolfenden Report n 7 above, paras 49–50.

[83] Johnson, *Homosexuality and the European Court of Human Rights* n 20 above, 103–04. See also Wintemute, *Sexual Orientation and Human Rights*, n 15 above, 100 (who also notes that Mr Dudgeon had also complained of the existence in Northern Ireland of the common law offence of conspiracy to corrupt public morals and conspiracy to outrage public decency, arguing that 'they make advocacy of changes in homosexual laws potentially criminal, that explicit association in groups, clubs and societies by homosexual persons could be indictable and that counselling activities are of uncertain legal status'. Wintemute stresses that the Commission said that 'the applicant has not shown that the existence of these offences, which appear by their very nature to concern *public activity* could be said to have affected his private life').

[84] See Ch 3 p 54 ff.

[85] See, for a similar perspective, A Diduck and F Canagas, *Family Law, Gender and the State. Text, Cases and Materials*, 3rd edn (Oxford, Hart Publishing, 2012) 13.

closet ... enabled the politics of disgust, making it possible to portray gay and lesbian as unlike ordinary citizens'.[86] By relying on a clear separation between public and private, the Court's rationale reiterated what was considered as a premise for gay oppression[87] and a form of apartheid.[88]

An implication of this approach lies in the limitation of the protection of family life to the married opposite sex couple. Although neither interference with the applicant's family life nor a stable same-sex relationship came into consideration in *Dudgeon*, in its early cases the ECtHR has been reluctant to regard same-sex relationships as falling within the notion of 'family'.[89] It was to take almost 20 years after *Dudgeon* for the ECtHR to confer protection to homosexuality in the wider social life and, in particular, to recognise that same-sex relationships fall within the definition of 'family' under Article 8 of the European Convention.[90]

Sociological studies of the ECtHR's case law have explained the Court's choice, on the basis of the 'political-moral reluctance' to see same-sex couples as a family on the part of the experts consulted by the Court. Furthermore, scholars have emphasised the ECtHR's tendency to see the family 'as the realm of intergenerational ties, except in the case that a legitimate family tie has been created by birth and/or marriage'.[91] More critically, Johnson highlights that the outcome of *Dudgeon* 'demonstrates the hegemony of heteronormative understanding of family'.[92] As I will clarify in Chapters 3 and 4, when courts—especially constitutional and supreme courts—meet LGBT movements' demands, they usually at the same time endorse (and strengthen) socially accepted notions of sex, marriage and family in their judgments. The Court's early cases confirmed how 'deploying predictive devices',[93] since the early cases on sexual orientation equality, courts have rarely been isolated from their cultural, social and political context.

Sociological studies have suggested in fact that decriminalisation of sexual acts in England—which paved the way to a wave of decriminalisation across Europe during the 1960s and 70s—was triggered by a fundamental cultural change in sexuality induced by prosperity and widespread availability of contraception.[94] This

[86] MC Nussbaum, *From Disgust to Humanity. Sexual Orientation and Constitutional Law* (Oxford, Oxford University Press, 2009) 85.

[87] E Sedwick, *Epistemology of the Closet* (Harmondsworth, Penguin, 1990) 71.

[88] WN Eskridge Jr, *Gaylaw: Challenging the Apartheid of the Closet* (Cambridge MA, Harvard University Press, 1999) arguing that 'so long as they confined their expressions and actions to a mutually protective closet, homosexuals were promised a regime of "separate but equal" safety from witch-hunters'. According to Eskridge, the closet could be 'for gays a refuge from social and legal prosecution and for straights as a means of secluding offensive sexuality and gender-bending, the proverbial skeletons in the closet'.

[89] Wintemute, *Sexual Orientation and Human Rights*, n 15 above, 110 ff. See below, Ch 3 p 64 ff.

[90] *Schalk and Kopf v Austria* ECHR 2010-I 1996. See below, Ch 3 p 65.

[91] L Hart, 'Individual Adoption by non-Heterosexual and the Order of Family Life in the European Court of Human Rights' (2009) 36 *Journal of Law and Society* 536, 538 and 544.

[92] Johnson, *Homosexuality and the European Court of Human Rights* n 20 above, 113.

[93] Y Zylan, *States of Passion: Law, Identity, and Social Construction of Desire* (Oxford, Oxford University Press, 2011) 103.

[94] On the routes to decriminalisation of sexual acts in a comparative perspective, Hildebrandt, 'Routes to decriminalization' n 16 above, 230 ff. See also J Weeks, *Sex Politics and Society. The Regulation of Sexuality Since 1800* (London, Longman, 1989).

culture emphasised individual freedom, but homosexuality was still perceived as a 'social harm', due also to the influence of scientific theories assuming that same-sex orientation could be acquired through experiences during childhood.[95] The private–public dichotomy should therefore be considered a result of these developments: although the gay and lesbian movement was trying to raise public awareness of homosexuality, demanding equal rights in many countries when the *Dudgeon* decision was released, morality concerns were still taken into consideration by legislators, and the notion of family, as I will clarify in Chapter 3, was still interpreted as a social group limited to 'traditional' opposite-sex couples.

IV. *LAWRENCE v TEXAS* AND THE LIBERTY OF ALL INDIVIDUALS IN THEIR PERSONAL RELATIONSHIPS

As Johnson emphasises, the effects of the ECtHR's judgments 'can be considered in terms of the evolution of consciousness they have created through the assertion of the reality of gay and lesbian lives'.[96] The ECtHR's reasoning exerted great influence on constitutional and supreme courts between the end of the 1990s and the early 2000s, which addressed similar issues on criminalisation of sexual acts between people of the same sex.

The Supreme Court of the United States' decision in *Lawrence v Texas* (2003)[97] is probably the most relevant constitutional case that relied on *Dudgeon*'s rationale in order to strengthen its final conclusion that a Texas statute criminalising 'deviate sexual intercourse' between individuals of same sex in the privacy of their home had violated the Fourteenth Amendment of the United States Constitution.

The case came about when the police entered into Mr Lawrence's apartment in Texas, on the basis of a complaint of a 'weapons disturbance' (which was subsequently proved false) by a neighbour, and surprised him engaging in a sexual act with another man. Mr Lawrence and his partner were arrested, held in custody overnight, charged and convicted before a justice of the peace.

By the time of the Supreme Court decision, 36 states of the United States had already repealed 'sodomy laws' through a court decision or a legislative act. As Nussbaum has argued, these repeals were an expression of a general change in American social attitudes. 'Americans were becoming more aware of gays and lesbians as full human beings in families in the workplace, in churches, in the media, in every part of the fabric of American society'.[98] Furthermore, in the other states where laws punishing sexual intercourse between persons of the same sex were still in force, there was a pattern of no enforcement with respect to consenting adults acting in private. Even the state of Texas admitted before the Supreme Court that since 1994 it had not prosecuted anyone under its 'sodomy law'.[99]

[95] Hildebrandt, 'Routes to Decriminalization' n 16 above, 241 ('Law reforms were not about the rights of gays and lesbians but about how to effectively handle a social problem').

[96] Johnson, *Homosexuality and the European Court of Human Rights* n 20 above.

[97] *Lawrence v Texas* n 5 above.

[98] See Nussbaum n 86 above 85.

[99] *Lawrence v Texas* n 5 above, 539 US, 574.

Although the case at issue in *Lawrence*, unlike *Dudgeon*, originated from a conviction, the Supreme Court addressed the case from a more general point of view, suggesting that the mere existence of a law punishing sexual acts was a form of discrimination which might affect gay men's daily lives. Writing for the majority of the Supreme Court, Justice Kennedy emphasised that

> the stigma this criminal statute imposes, moreover, is not trivial. The offense, to be sure, is but a class C misdemeanor, a minor offense in the Texas legal system. Still, it remains a criminal offense with all that imports for the dignity of the persons charged. The petitioners will bear on their record the history of their criminal convictions.[100]

Accordingly, he also observed that

> if protected conduct is made criminal and the law which does so remains unexamined for its substantive validity, its stigma might remain even if it were not enforceable as drawn for equal protection reasons. When homosexual conduct is made criminal by the law of the State, that declaration in and of itself is an invitation to subject homosexual persons to discrimination both in the public and in the private spheres.[101]

It should be emphasised that the *Lawrence* rationale did not revolve around the violation of the principle of equality as sanctioned by the Equal Protection clause of the Fourteenth Amendment of the United States Constitution. *Lawrence* is mostly a liberty case or, in Yoshino's words, 'a liberty case with undertones of equality'.[102] It dealt with the violation of the privacy and the freedom of the *individual* from state interference in sexual intimacy[103] and, unlike *Dudgeon*, it did not have regard to the sexual orientation of the petitioner.[104]

The majority clarified this assumption in the opening statement:

> Liberty protects the person from unwarranted government intrusions into a dwelling or other private places. In our tradition the State is not omnipresent in the home. And there are other spheres of our lives and existence, outside the home, where the State should not be a dominant presence. Freedom extends beyond spatial bounds. Liberty presumes an autonomy of self that includes freedom of thought, belief, expression, and certain intimate conduct. The instant case involves liberty of the person both in its spatial and more transcendent dimensions.[105]

Reliance on more general assumptions can probably be explained in the first place on the basis of Justice Kennedy's intention to achieve a more sweeping result by implying the unconstitutionality of all the state 'sodomy laws', including those (nine out a total of 13) which punished anal sexual intercourse, both between same-sex and opposite-sex participants and were, only apparently, sexual orientation blind.[106]

[100] ibid, 539 US, 575.

[101] ibid, 539 US, 575.

[102] K Yoshino, 'The New Equal Protection' (2011) 124 *Harvard Law Review* 747, 776.

[103] See *Lawrence v Texas* n 5 above, 539 US, 578 ('The Texas statute furthered no legitimate state interest which could justify the statute's intrusion into the personal and private life of the individual').

[104] See Yoshino, 'The New Equal Protection', n 102 above, 776 (arguing that '*Lawrence* was ultimately not a group-based equality case about gays, but rather a universal liberty case about the right of all consenting adults to engage in sexual intimacy in the privacy of their homes').

[105] *Lawrence v Texas* n 5 above, 539 US, 562.

[106] ibid, 539 US, 573. See also below p 36.

Nonetheless, I do not intend to suggest that equality arguments were irrelevant in the majority's reasoning. The Supreme Court emphasised that 'equality of treatment and the due process right to demand respect for conduct protected by the substantive guarantee of liberty are linked in important respects'.[107] However, arguments concerning the potential discrimination suffered by gay men for the mere existence of the sodomy laws, were functional to a reasoning which aimed at demonstrating whether the petitioners were free as adults to engage in a private conduct in the exercise of their liberty.[108]

Observing that 'persons in a homosexual relationship may seek autonomy for these purposes, just as heterosexual persons',[109] the Supreme Court avoided crucial issues concerning the definition of sexual orientation as a illegitimate factor of discrimination deserving strict scrutiny. Consequently, the majority abstained from qualifying gays and lesbians as 'a discrete and insular minority'[110] (a step that, as I will clarify in following chapters,[111] the Court has been unwilling to take even in the more recent cases).

Furthermore, founding its rationale on the liberty of *all* the individuals, the Supreme Court achieved a more sweeping result than it could have obtained through a reasoning centred on the violation of the Equal Protection clause. As Tribe has pointed out, 'the decision's unmistakable heart is an understanding that liberty is centred in equal respect and dignity for both conventional and unconventional human relationships'.

According to the Supreme Court,

> what is truly fundamental ... is not the set of specific acts that have been found to merit constitutional protection, but rather the relationships and self-governing commitments out of which those acts arise, the network of human connection over time that makes genuine freedom possible.[112]

We will return to equality and dignity arguments in cases concerning the rights of gays and lesbian persons in Chapter 4.[113] However it is necessary to emphasise that although concerning similar issues, *Lawrence* and *Dudgeon* approach the cases from different perspectives: whereas *Dudgeon*'s basic idea lay in the recognition of homosexuality as an inherent trait of the human being, *Lawrence* was centred on the liberty of the person from unwarranted interference and 'autonomy of the self'. In this way, unlike the ECtHR, the Supreme Court avoided the binary homosexuality/heterosexuality logic.

[107] ibid, 539 US, 575.
[108] ibid, 539 US, 564.
[109] ibid, 539 US, 574.
[110] *United States v Carolene Products Co* 304 US 144 (1938), fn 4. The footnote—arguing that 'prejudice against discrete and insular minorities' might 'call for a correspondingly more searching judicial inquiry', because such minorities would not be able to protect themselves in the political process—suggested the adoption of different levels of scrutiny and in particular the adoption of a 'heightened scrutiny' for discrimination based on 'suspect classifications' such as on race, age, sex.
[111] See below p 168 ff.
[112] L Tribe, '*Lawrence v Texas*: the "Fundamental Right" That Dare not Speak its Name' (2004) 117 *Harvard Law Review* 1893.
[113] See below p 154 ff.

However both cases reached similar outcomes in implicitly recognising gays and lesbians' commonality with all human beings and both refrained from qualifying sexual orientation as an illegitimate ground of discrimination.[114] My purpose is to focus in the next pages on the notion of privacy the Supreme Court developed in *Lawrence*, in order to analyse differences and analogies with the idea of privacy that the ECtHR expounded in *Dudgeon.*

V. THE 'MULTI-FACETED' NOTION OF PRIVACY IN *LAWRENCE*

In the opening statements of the majority opinion in *Lawrence v Texas*, Justice Kennedy held that 'liberty protects the person from unwarranted government intrusion into a dwelling or other private places'.[115]

In the American constitutional tradition the right of privacy—'at its conceptual core'—is 'the right to freedom for intrusion by the state, especially in one's home'.[116] In the United States, privacy emerged at the end of the nineteenth century essentially as 'the right to be let alone'[117] and it is related to secrecy and to the control of personal information.[118] 'The prime danger, from the American point of view, is that "the sanctity of homes" ... will be breached by government actors'.[119]

Justice Kennedy started his analysis by describing this spatial element of privacy. He emphasised that 'in our tradition the State is not omnipresent in the home' and that 'there are other spheres of our lives and existence, outside the home, where the State should not be a dominant presence'.[120]

However in the United States the idea of privacy as freedom from governmental intrusion is also strictly related to values of liberty and self-determination.[121] In *Eisenstadt v Baird*,[122] for instance, the Supreme Court held that the right of privacy included 'the right of the individual, married or single to be free from unwarranted governmental intrusion into matters so fundamentally affecting a person as the decision whether to bear or beget a child', and in the well-known 1973 abortion case, *Roe v Wade*, the Supreme Court recognised that the 'protection of liberty under the Due Process Clause has a substantive dimension of fundamental significance in defining the rights of the person'.[123]

[114] See for a comparison between *Dudgeon* and American equal protection doctrine, Wintemute, *Sexual Orientation and Human Rights*, n 15 above, 119 ff.

[115] *Lawrence v Texas* n 5 above, 539 US, 562.

[116] JQ Whitman, 'The Two Western Cultures of Privacy: Dignity Versus Liberty' (2004) 113 *Yale Law Journal* 1151, 1161.

[117] See S Warren and L Brandeis, 'The Right to Privacy' (1890) 193 *Harvard Law Review* 220, 195.

[118] C Fried, 'Privacy' (1968) 77 *Yale Law Journal* 475.

[119] Whitman, 'The Two Western Cultures of Privacy' n 116 above, 1162.

[120] *Lawrence v Texas* n 5 above, 539 US, 562.

[121] See *Planned Parenthood of Southeastern Pennsylvania v Casey* 505 US 833 (1992), 847 ('It is a promise of the Constitution that there is a realm of personal liberty which the government may not enter').

[122] *Eisenstadt v Baird* 405 US 438, 453 (1972).

[123] *Roe v Wade* 410 US 113 (1973).

Against this background, Kennedy added in *Lawrence* that 'freedom extends beyond spatial bounds ... Liberty presumes an autonomy of self that includes freedom of thought, belief, expression, and certain intimate conduct'.[124] He emphasised that the instant case 'involv[ed] liberty of the person both in its spatial and more transcendent dimensions'.[125]

It should be noticed that the facts in *Lawrence* shared some similarities with those examined by the Supreme Court in a prior case, *Bowers v Hardwick*,[126] where a police officer entered Hardwick's home and observed him having sex with another adult male in his own bedroom. The conduct was in violation of a Georgia statute that made it a criminal offence to engage in 'sodomy'. The Georgia statute did not distinguish between opposite-sex and same-sex couples, and punished sexual acts whether or not the participants were of the same sex, whereas the Texas statute in *Lawrence* applied only to participants of the same sex.

In his defence, Mr Hardwick asserted that whatever right the State might have to police public sexual practices, conduct occurring in the privacy of home should be protected. However, the majority rejected his argument, arguing that giving constitutional protection to all voluntary sexual conduct between consenting adult in the home would had made it 'difficult ... to limit the claimed right to homosexual conduct while leaving exposed to prosecution adultery, incest, and other sexual crimes even though they are committed in the home.'[127]

The majority in *Lawrence* squarely overruled *Bowers* admitting 'to have previously failed to appreciate the extent of the liberty at stake'.

Justice Kennedy argued that

> To say that the issue in *Bowers* was simply the right to engage in certain sexual conduct demeans the claim the individual put forward, just as it would demean a married couple were it to be said marriage is simply about the right to have sexual intercourse. The laws involved in *Bowers* and here are, to be sure, statutes that purport to do no more than prohibit a particular sexual act. Their penalties and purposes, though, have more far-reaching consequences, touching upon the most private human conduct, sexual behavior, and in the most private of places, the home. The statutes do seek to control a personal relationship that, whether or not entitled to formal recognition in the law, is within the liberty of persons to choose without being punished as criminals.[128]

The multi-faced notion of privacy—as extending beyond spatial privacy and including personal liberty—in *Lawrence* also saved the Supreme Court the criticism that *Dudgeon* attracted for perpetuating the 'logic of the closet'. M Nussbaum, for instance, has praised the Supreme Court's choice to recognise that 'privacy has two aspects, the decisional and the spatial', although she has argued that the opinion should have omitted as irrelevant and misleading any referral to the spatial dimension.[129] Nonetheless Nussbaum has also stressed that 'even with this distinction [between spatial and decisional privacy] ... the opinion goes on to rely on the

[124] *Lawrence v Texas* n 5 above, 539 US, 562.
[125] ibid.
[126] *Bowers v Hardwick* 478 US 186 (1996).
[127] ibid, 478 US, 196.
[128] *Lawrence v Texas* n 5 above, 539 US, 567.
[129] Nussbaum, *From Disgust to Humanity* n 86 above, 85 ff.

spatial notion of privacy at key moments, thus suggesting a constitutional approach that is both overprotective and underprotective'. The relevant issue was instead, in her opinion, one of the interests of other parties: 'No consenting party's rights are being violated and because the conduct took place in seclusion, no nonconsenting party is being subjected to direct offense. That is all that needed to be said. "The home" is a red herring.'[130]

Although in *Lawrence* the majority's reference to 'home' actually gave rise to uncertainty—especially when, for instance, sexual consensual acts could occur in other secluded places—Justice Kennedy could probably not have avoided any reference to 'home'. As mentioned earlier, the American privacy law—although broadened to encompass different situations involving personal autonomy—'always tends to imagine the home as the primary defense, and the state as the primary enemy'.[131]

At the same time, in *Lawrence* the idea of privacy as involving liberty in its 'spatial and more transcendent dimensions'[132] was also connected to the principle of human dignity. Justice Kennedy condemned the stigma that the Texas criminal statute imposed on gay men and its impact on their dignity:

> adults may choose to enter upon this relationship in the confines of their homes and their own private lives and still retain their dignity as free persons. When sexuality finds overt expression in intimate conduct with another person, the conduct can be but one element in a personal bond that is more enduring. The liberty protected by the Constitution allows homosexual persons the right to make this choice.

In Chapter 4 I will illustrate the different meanings of 'dignity' and the widespread reliance on dignity discourse in constitutional cases concerning sexual orientation,[133] but it is necessary to anticipate here that, in its narrowest sense, dignity involves the idea of the inherent worth of all the individuals and is strictly intertwined with the principle of equality whereas, in its relationship with liberty, dignity implies the right to self-determination and autonomy in all personal decisions.[134] Both meanings are present in *Lawrence* although, following the American constitutional tradition,[135] Justice Kennedy mostly emphasised the relationship between autonomy and dignity (sometimes seeming almost to identify them).[136,137]

130 ibid, 88.

131 Whitman, 'The Two Western Cultures of Privacy' n 116 above, 1215. Furthermore, in my opinion, the majority opinion is not entirely focused on 'home' insofar as the spatial dimension of privacy is concerned. As I mentioned above, Justice Kennedy opening statement is quite broad and refers also to the 'other spheres of our lives and existence, outside the home, where the State should not be a dominant presence' (*Lawrence*, n 5 above, 562).

132 *Lawrence v Texas* n 5 above, 539 US, 562.

133 See below, p 154 ff.

134 On the two dimensions of human dignity, R Dworkin, *Is Democracy Possible Here?* (Princeton, Princeton University Press, 2006) 9.

135 See EJ Eberle, *Dignity and liberty: constitutional visions in Germany and in the United States* (Westport CT, Praeger, 2001).

136 Citing *Casey*, n 121 above, Justice Kennedy asserted: 'These matters, involving the most intimate and personal choices a person may make in a lifetime, choices central to personal dignity and autonomy, are central to the liberty protected by the Fourteenth Amendment' (*Lawrence v Texas* n 5 above, 539 US, 574).

137 The Supreme Court's reliance on human dignity and on the right of gays and lesbians not to be demeaned has been criticised as lacking a 'doctrinal hook on which to hang its talk of respect' by Whitman, 'The Two Western Cultures of Privacy' n 116 above, 1214. Against, as I will clarify in Ch 4,

By attaching weight to the relationship between privacy and dignity (in particular in its connection with self-determination), the majority opinion strengthened the idea that criminalisation of private consensual adult sex between persons of the same sex interferes with the private life of all the individuals. As the Texas statute made it a crime only 'to engage in deviate sexual intercourse with another individual of the same sex', the majority arguments seemed to suggest that the holding also applied to a statute punishing sexual acts between persons of different sex.

Justice Kennedy's choice to make the statute invalid as violative of the substantive due process clause with its connections with privacy, dignity and autonomy, turned out to be more sweeping and persuasive than a rationale focused on the violation of the principle of equality and non-discrimination.[138] In justifying why he was not deciding the case on equality grounds,[139] Kennedy affirmed that 'were we to hold the statute invalid under the Equal Protection Clause some might question whether a prohibition would be valid if drawn differently, say, to prohibit the conduct both between same-sex and opposite-sex participants'.[140]

VI. THE LEGACY OF *DUDGEON* IN *LAWRENCE*

Lawrence is also a remarkable case because it rejected the idea that morality could be a constitutional justification for state attempts to regulate sexual conduct occurring in private. For this reason the case represented a significant change in the Supreme Court's view of how the State should regulate sexuality.

In *Bowers v Hardwick*—the 1986 controlling precedent, which the Supreme Court squarely overruled in *Lawrence*— the majority rejected the respondent's argument that 'majority sentiments about the morality of homosexuality should be declared inadequate'[141] to justify the law and was 'unpersuaded that the sodomy laws of some 25 States should be invalidated on this basis'.[142]

By contrast, in *Lawrence*, the Supreme Court admitted that Mr Hardwick's condemnation 'was shaped by religious beliefs, conceptions of right and acceptable behavior, and respect for the traditional family'.[143] Justice Kennedy acknowledged

below p 167 ff, other scholars interpret dignity discourse in recent human rights adjudication as 'a major shift in constitutional doctrine, one that will have ramifications in many cases to come' (see, LH Tribe, 'Equal Dignity: Speaking Its Name' (2015) 129 *Harvard Law Review Forum* 16). See also C McCrudden, 'Human Dignity and Judicial Interpretation of Human Rights' (2008) 19 *European Journal of International Law* 656; E Daly, *Dignity Rights. Courts, Constitutions and Worth of the Human Person* (Philadelphia, University of Pennsylvania Press, 2013), 96 ff; N Rao, 'On the Use and Abuse of Dignity in Constitutional Law' (2008) 14 *Columbia Journal European Law* 201; K Yoshino, 'A New Birth of Freedom?' (2016) 129 *Harvard Law Review* 147.

138 See above p 167 ff.

139 See *Lawrence v Texas* n 5 above, 539 US, 579 ('Rather than relying on the substantive component of the Fourteenth Amendment's Due Process Clause, as the Court does, I base my conclusion on the Fourteenth Amendment's Equal Protection Clause'). Against, see Justice O'Connor' s concurring opinion at 579 ff.

140 *Lawrence v Texas* n 5 above, 539 US, 575.

141 *Bowers v Hardwick* n 126 above 478 US, 196.

142 ibid.

143 *Lawrence v Texas* n 5 above, 539 US, 571.

that 'for many persons these are not trivial concerns but profound and deep convictions accepted as ethical and moral principles to which they aspire and which thus determine the course of their lives'.[144] Nonetheless, he rejected the idea that 'the majority may use the power of the State to enforce these views on the whole society through operation of the criminal law',[145] concluding that the Supreme Court's 'obligation [was] to define the liberty of all, not to mandate our own moral code'.[146] Assuming that enforcement of morality was not a legitimate state interest, the United States Supreme Court rejected the approach that morality could be a proper concern of the law.[147] Justice Kennedy argued: 'The fact that the governing majority in a State has traditionally viewed a particular practice as immoral is not a sufficient reason for upholding a law prohibiting the practice.'[148]

At the same time, he stressed 'an emerging awareness that liberty gives substantial protection to adult persons in deciding how to conduct their private lives in matters pertaining to sex'.[149] Approximately half of the states with laws prohibiting the relevant conduct referenced in the *Bowers* decision had repealed them, and in those states 'where sodomy [was] still proscribed, whether for same-sex or heterosexual conduct, there [was] a pattern of nonenforcement with respect to consenting adults acting in private'.[150]

Against this background, Justice Kennedy emphasised that 'history and tradition are the starting point but not in all cases the ending point of the substantive due process inquiry'.[151] He supported this conclusion mentioning the recommendations of the Wolfenden Report in 1957 and relying on *Dudgeon v United Kingdom*. The citation marks the first time the Supreme Court decided to take into account a foreign case in the text of the opinion of the Court.[152]

He justified his reliance on foreign sources on the basis of the factual similarity and cultural affinity between the cases: *Dudgeon*—he argued—is illustrative of the values the United States share with 'a wider civilization'[153] and 'authoritative in all countries that are members of the Council of Europe [it] is at odds with the premise in *Bowers* that the claim put forward was insubstantial in our Western civilization'.[154]

According to Justice Kennedy, the ECtHR's conclusions in *Dudgeon* demonstrated that the right to engage in consensual same-sex sexual acts 'ha[d] been accepted as an integral part of human freedom in many other countries', but also that 'the

[144] ibid.
[145] ibid.
[146] *Planned Parenthood of Southeastern Pennsylvania v Casey* n 121 above, 850.
[147] See M Nussbaum, *From Disgust to Humanity* n 86 above, 89 (arguing that the Supreme Court's great achievement in *Lawrence* consists in 'a rejection of the politics of disgust so amply evident in *Bowers*, together with the Devlinesque conception of society as dominated by tradition and solidarity, in favour of a politics of humanity that is the heir of John Stuart Mill both in its zealous protection of individual liberty and in its reliance on the ability to imagine a variety of human purposes').
[148] *Lawrence v Texas* n 5 above, 539 US, 577.
[149] ibid, 539 US, 573.
[150] ibid, 539 US, 573.
[151] ibid, 539 US, 572.
[152] See above, Introduction, p 9.
[153] *Lawrence v Texas* n 5 above, 539 US, 576.
[154] ibid, 539 US, 573.

governmental interest in circumscribing personal choice' was not 'somehow more legitimate or urgent'.[155]

These conclusions suggest that *Dudgeon's* legacy lies not only in the recognition of the right to engage in consensual sexual conduct with a person of the same-sex as an aspect of human essence and identity, but also in the idea that the purpose to punish sexual conduct both between same-sex and opposite-sex participants could no longer be justified on the basis of a relevant state interest in criminalising conduct supposed to be 'immoral' or dangerous to society.

In reaching this conclusion, Justice Kennedy relied on *Romer v Evans*,[156] a 1996 post-*Bowers* ruling invalidating an amendment to Colorado's constitution 'which named as a solitary class persons who were homosexuals, lesbians, or bisexual either by "orientation, conduct, practices or relationships" ... and deprived them of protection under state antidiscrimination laws'.[157] He emphasised in particular how *Romer* had held that provision unconstitutional as 'born of animosity toward the class of persons affected' and lacking 'no rational relation to a legitimate governmental purpose'.[158]

The idea that legislation against gays and lesbians could violate the Constitution under the Fourteenth Amendment of the United States Constitution as it is 'born of animosity' towards a particular group of people on the basis of their sexual orientation, is an argument that Justice Kennedy will also develop in future cases concerning same-sex marriage[159] and that should be read in the light of the principle of human dignity that Justice Kennedy has expounded in his opinions in sexual orientation equality cases.[160] However, it is worth noting here that, as in *Dudgeon*—where the ECtHR emphasised how gay men suffered 'the detrimental effects which the very existence of the legislative provisions in question can have on the life of a person of homosexual orientation like the applicant'[161]—in *Lawrence* Justice Kennedy argued against the existence of a legitimate state interest in punishing same-sex sexual acts. He noted that

> if protected conduct is made criminal and the law which does so remains unexamined for its substantive validity, its stigma might remain even if it were not enforceable as drawn for equal protection reasons. When homosexual conduct is made criminal by the law of the State, that declaration in and of itself is an invitation to subject homosexual persons to discrimination both in the public and in the private spheres. ... The stigma this criminal statute imposes, moreover, is not trivial. The offense, to be sure, is but a class C misdemeanor, a minor offense in the Texas legal system. Still, it remains a criminal offense with all that imports for the dignity of the persons charged. The petitioners will bear on their record the history of their criminal convictions.[162]

[155] ibid, 539 US, 576.
[156] *Romer v Evans*, 517 US 620 (1996).
[157] *Lawrence v Texas* n 5 above, 539 US, 574.
[158] See *Romer v Evans*, n 156 above, 571 US, 634.
[159] See eg *United States v Windsor* 133 S Ct 2675 (2013).
[160] See Ch 4, section III, p 159 ff.
[161] *Dudgeon* n 1 above, para 60.
[162] *Lawrence v Texas* n 5 above, 539 US, 575.

When compared to *Dudgeon*, Justice Kennedy's argument is based on different premises, in particular on the principles of dignity and equality of human beings. The ECtHR did not address these principles when discussing the lack of a justification for the interference in the right of privacy of the applicant. Nonetheless both cases demonstrate the courts' attention to the 'collateral consequences' of the very existence of this kind of legislation in the personal sphere of the subjects involved.

In the United States, some scholars and some Justices of the Supreme Court were critical of the Supreme Court's decision to rely on a foreign case and on the European-born principle of human dignity, especially when issues so deeply entrenched in morality, history and culture come into consideration.[163] They stressed that reliance on European materials influenced the Court's judicial methodology because, by concluding that states could justify their intrusion into the personal and private life of the individual, the Supreme Court adopted a standard of review that was close to a European proportionality standard.[164]

Other scholars criticised the novelty of the Court's approach, arguing that it

> may presage a new jurisprudence in which governments are forbidden from doing anything that might convey disapproval of any sexual practices that the Court believes are somehow connected with efforts to define one's own concept of existence, of meaning, of the universe, and of the mystery of human life.[165]

Justice Scalia, in his harsh dissenting opinion, was even more critical of the majority's decision not 'to further the belief of its citizens that certain forms of sexual behavior are "immoral and unacceptable"'.[166] He stressed that the majority's conclusion 'decrees the end of all morals legislation', because 'criminal laws against fornication, bigamy, adultery, adult incest, bestiality and obscenity'[167] could probably not survive the Supreme Court's rational-basis review in the future. He was also especially critical of the majority's quotation of *Dudgeon v United Kingdom* because, in his opinion, the 'emerging awareness' was by definition not 'deeply rooted in this Nation's history and traditions'.[168]

> Constitutional entitlements [he argued] do not spring into existence because some States choose to lessen or eliminate criminal sanctions on certain behavior. Much less do they spring into existence, as the Court seems to believe, because *foreign nations* decriminalize conduct. ... The Court's discussion of these foreign views (ignoring, of course, the many countries that have retained criminal prohibitions on sodomy) is therefore meaningless dicta. Dangerous dicta, however, since this Court ... should not impose foreign moods, fads, or fashions on Americans.[169]

[163] See above, Introduction, p 11 ff.

[164] N Rao, 'On the Use and Abuse of Dignity in Constitutional Law' n 137 above, 241.

[165] See N Lund, JO McGinnis, '*Lawrence v Texas* and the Judicial Hubris' (2004) 102 *Michigan Law Review* 1555, 1583.

[166] *Lawrence v Texas* n 5 above, 539 US, 599.

[167] ibid, 539 US, 590. This is argument is frequently referred to by traditionalists as 'the slippery slope' argument.

[168] ibid, 539 US, 598.

[169] ibid, 539 US, 598 (Scalia dissenting).

At the same time, assuming instead that morality could be a legitimate state interest, Justice Scalia attached great importance to tradition and national history. He noted that, apart from the fact that such an 'emerging awareness' does not establish 'a fundamental right' to engage in sodomy,[170] Justice Kennedy's arguments were factually false because states had continued to prosecute all sorts of crimes by adults 'in matters pertaining to sex', and sodomy laws too had been enforced 'in the past half century'.[171]

Therefore, he stressed that

> social perceptions of sexual and other morality change over time, every group has the right to persuade its fellow citizens that its view of such matters is the best. ... But persuading one's fellow citizens is one thing, and imposing one's views in absence of democratic majority will is something else. ... What Texas has chosen to do is well within the range of traditional democratic action, and its hand should not be stayed through the invention of a brand-new 'constitutional right' by a Court that is impatient of democratic change.[172]

These statements suggest that *Lawrence* is illustrative of a tension that permeates *all* the jurisprudence on the recognition of the rights of gays and lesbians and same-sex couples across different jurisdictions, as far as the reliance on tradition and the role of the constitutional courts in promoting constitutional change over sexual orientation equality are concerned. I will thoroughly discuss reliance on (legal) tradition in sexual equality cases and the many difficulties surrounding its identification in Chapter 4, on same-sex marriage[173] because arguments of tradition assume crucial importance in that field.

As far as the idea of evolving tradition comes into consideration, Justice Kennedy demonstrates how evolving tradition was just malleable in *Bowers*, and in order to prevent a similar objection relied on 'objective benchmarks for evolving tradition'[174] such as state legislative reforms and the experience of Western countries sharing a similar constitutional tradition. Nonetheless, as I will seek to clarify in Chapter 4, the main issue revolves around the identification of the proper *object* of tradition (whether the 'right to engage in sodomy' as in *Bowers*,[175] or the idea that sodomy laws unnecessarily intrude into the private life of individuals, as in *Lawrence*)[176] and its level of generality.

Therefore, since the early cases on sexual orientation equality, the attempts to identify the contents of tradition were influenced by the interpreter's normative choices and tradition could also elide the main argument of the plaintiffs' claim, the violation of their fundamental rights.

170 ibid.

171 ibid. Justice Scalia noted there had been 134 reported cases involving prosecution for consensual, adult, same-sex sexual acts.

172 *Lawrence v Texas* n 5 above, 539 US, 603.

173 See below, Ch 4, section III, esp p 122 ff.

174 WN Eskridge, Jr and ND Hunter, *Sexuality, Gender and the Law* (New York, Foundation Press, 2004) 97.

175 *Bowers v Hardwick* n 126 above, 478 US, 190.

176 *Lawrence v Texas*, n 5 above, 539 US, 565.

VII. THE SUPREME COURT OF SOUTH AFRICA'S CASE IN *NATIONAL COALITION* AND THE INFLUENCE OF *DUDGEON*

Before *Lawrence*, other constitutional and supreme court cases had also referred to *Dudgeon v United Kingdom* when declaring unconstitutional domestic statutes concerning criminalisation of sexual acts between persons of the same sex. Among them, one the most interesting and remarkable cases on decriminalisation of sexual acts is the 1998 Constitutional Court of South Africa's judgment in *National Coalition v Minister of Justice*.[177]

In this case the Constitutional Court addressed the constitutionality of section 20(a) of the Sexual Offences Act 1957, forbidding 'unnatural sex', and of the common law offence of sodomy, which criminalised consensual anal sex between men.[178] Justice Ackerman, writing for a unanimous Court, concluded that sodomy laws were inconsistent with section 9 of the 1996 South Africa Constitution, in particular with § 3, forbidding unfair discrimination on different grounds, including 'sexual orientation':[179]

> Criminalisation of sodomy in private between consenting males is not only a severe limitation of a gay man's right to equality in relation to sexual orientation, because it hits at one of the ways in which gays give expression to their sexual orientation. It is at the same time a severe limitation of the gay man's rights to privacy, dignity and freedom.[180]

Whereas in *Lawrence* the United States Supreme Court framed the issue as being concerned with privacy and freedom of all the individuals, and in *Dudgeon* the ECtHR discussed the violation of the right to respect of the applicant's 'private life' under Article 8(1) ECHR dismissing claims of sexual orientation discrimination, the Constitutional Court's reasoning in *National Coalition* was focused mostly on equality. Justice Ackerman emphasised the discrimination suffered by gay men, reading it in connection to the violation of their dignity, privacy and freedom.

Furthermore, the South Africa Supreme Court's reasoning also revolved around the violation of human dignity, a principle lying at the 'cornerstone of the South African Constitution',[181] which was imported by the German constitutional tradition. *National Coalition*, in particular, embraced an interpretation of dignity as an inherent quality of the individual connected to his community.[182]

[177] *National Coalition for Gay and Lesbian Equality v Minister of Justice*, Case CCT 11/98, 9 October 1998.

[178] Sodomy was defined by the common law as 'unlawful and intentional sexual intercourse *per anum* between human males' (see *National Coalition* n 177 above, para 14).

[179] 1996 Constitution of South Africa s 9 § 1 ('Everyone is equal before the law and has the right to equal protection and benefit of the law') and s 9 § 3 ('The state may not unfairly discriminate directly or indirectly against anyone on one or more grounds, including race, gender, sex, pregnancy, marital status, ethnic or social origin, colour, sexual orientation, age, disability, religion, conscience, belief, culture, language and birth').

[180] *National Coalition* n 177 above, para 36.

[181] ibid, para 28.

[182] See M Herdegen, 'Article 1' in T Maunz and G Dürig (eds), *Grundgesetz. Kommentar* (München, Beck, 2009) 16 but see also C Taylor, 'The Politics of Recognition' in A Gutmann (ed), *Multiculturalism and 'The Politics of Recognition'* (Chicago, Chicago University Press, 1992).

Echoing the German jurisprudence, Justice Ackerman suggested that 'constitutional protection of dignity requires ... to acknowledge the value and worth of all individuals as members of our society'.[183] In the Court's view, laws criminalising sexual acts between individuals of the same sex were unconstitutional because of the stigma they attached to a significant proportion of the population. Furthermore, they had the symbolic effect 'to state that in the eyes of [South Africa's] legal system all gay men are criminals', with the consequence that 'as a result of the criminal offence, gay men are at risk of arrest, prosecution and conviction of the offence of sodomy simply because they seek to engage in sexual conduct which is part of their experience of being human'.[184]

Justice Ackerman also pointed out that 'the case illustrates how, in particular circumstances, the rights of equality and dignity are closely related, as are the rights of dignity and privacy'.[185]

Due to its connection with the principle of human dignity, privacy protects individuals from undue interference from the outside community. In particular, citing a prior Constitutional Court's case, Ackerman noted that

> Privacy recognises that we all have a right to a sphere of private intimacy and autonomy which allows us to establish and nurture human relationships without interference from the outside community. The way in which we give expression to our sexuality is at the core of this area of private intimacy. If, in expressing our sexuality, we act consensually and without harming one another, invasion of that precinct will be a breach of our privacy.[186]

In reaching these conclusions, Justice Ackerman relied extensively on comparative law. He argued in particular that 'the jurisprudence of other open and democratic societies based on human dignity, equality and freedom'[187] also supported his conclusion that 'the enforcement of private moral views of a section of the community, which are based to a large extent on nothing more than prejudice, cannot qualify as ... a legitimate purpose' of the law.[188] He cited in particular *Dudgeon v United Kingdom* and *Norris v Ireland*, as 'indicative of the changes in judicial and social attitudes in recent years'[189] and referred to the legislation of a large number of countries, including Germany, Austria and Brazil, which similarly repealed their legislation on criminalisation of sexual acts in recent years.[190]

These conclusions confirm that the main legacy of *Dudgeon*, outside the Council of Europe's borders, lay in providing an illustrative example of tolerance and recognition of gay men' rights and in the assumption that the enforcement of morality should no longer be considered a legitimate state purpose. Comparative law suggested that 'sodomy laws' were unconstitutional because their only purpose was to criminalise conduct 'which fails to conform with the moral and religious views of a section of society'.[191]

[183] *National Coalition* n 177 above, para 28.
[184] ibid, para 28.
[185] ibid, para 30.
[186] ibid, para 31.
[187] ibid, para 39.
[188] ibid, para 40.
[189] ibid, para 42.
[190] ibid, paras 44 ff.
[191] ibid, para 26.

When compared to foreign cases addressing similar issues, the majority opinion in *National Coalition* was therefore in line with the majority's argument in *Lawrence*, that courts could not enforce their own morality, and had to take into account the widespread support in public opinion for the recognition of gay rights. Arguments concerning the importance of morality (and tradition) are analogously replaced by the idea that courts should take into account prevalent public attitudes and social changes on sexuality. This purpose is extremely relevant for constitutional and supreme courts when, as I will argue in Chapter 4, they aim at promoting constitutional change and forging legal arguments on sexual orientation equality issues.[192]

Nonetheless it should be noted that even in *National Coalition*, this conclusion was divisive. In his concurring opinion Justice Sachs advanced a different view, arguing that 'a State that recognises differences does not mean a state without morality', because the 'Constitution does not debar the State from enforcing morality'.[193] Adhering to a textual approach to constitutional interpretation, he also emphasised that

> what is central to the character and functioning of the state, however, is that the dictates of the morality which it enforces, and the limits to which it may go, are to be found in the text and spirit of the Constitution itself.[194]

VIII. THE RIGHT TO PRIVACY IN *NATIONAL COALITION*: A COMMON THREAD

As a landmark case of its own, *National Coalition* is also interesting for its reliance on the right of privacy for the recognition of the freedom of all the individuals to engage in sexual conduct. Justice Ackerman stated that

> Privacy recognises that we all have a right to a sphere of private intimacy and autonomy which allows us to establish and nurture human relationships without interference from the outside community. The way in which we give expression to our sexuality is at the core of this area of private intimacy.[195]

Nonetheless, when assuming that 'if, in expressing our sexuality, we act consensually and without harming one another, invasion of [our] precinct will be a breach of our privacy', the majority in *National Coalition* shared the idea—also expounded by the ECtHR in *Dudgeon* and the United States Supreme Court in *Lawrence*—that same-sex sexual intercourse was protected as far as it occurred in the privacy of the home.[196]

On the basis of my previous conclusions, I suggest that this can be considered a common thread of the first cases on the recognition of gay rights. Despite the differences in constitutional traditions and social and political contexts, all the cases I have discussed in this chapter seemed to perpetuate the 'logic of the closet' and to reject the idea that same-sex relationships deserve constitutional protection as a

[192] See below, chapter 4, part 1 at 102 ff.
[193] *National Coalition* n 177 above, para 136 (Sachs concurring).
[194] ibid, para 136 (Sachs concurring).
[195] ibid, para 32.
[196] See in particular ibid, paras 29–32.

kind of intimate association (or, in more general terms, as a 'social group'),[197] and that privacy should not be limited to the intimate sphere of the human existence but granted to the individual as a member of the society.

As mentioned earlier, this perspective will be adopted by the constitutional and international courts only in later cases, concerning family rights and equal marriage,[198] but it is interesting to note that Justice Sachs in his concurring opinion in *National Coalition* anticipated instead a different view on the right of privacy. He denied that 'the concept of privacy should be extended to give blanket libertarian permission for people to do anything they like provided that what they do is sexual and done in private',[199] but at the same time, stressed that privacy should not be conceived as 'sealing off from state control what happens in the bedroom'.[200] In his opinion, privacy concerned freedom and self-determination and it had to be taken into account not only as a negative liberty but also for its positive content:

> Just as liberty must be viewed not merely 'negatively or selfishly as a mere absence of restraint, but positively and socially as an adjustment of restraints to the end of freedom of opportunity' so must privacy be regarded as suggesting at least some responsibility on the state to promote conditions in which personal self-realisation can take place.[201]

Stating it in different terms, in Justice Sachs' opinion, 'what is crucial [was] the nature of the activity, not its site'.[202] Therefore, he argued, courts had to recognise the value of the act, regardless of the place where it occurs.[203]

This argument was highly influenced by the German constitutional tradition and in particular by the Kantian view that dignity resides in individuality and in sociality as well.[204] In this perspective, dignity requires not only to protect human personality and personal freedom, but also to promote goods as communal relationships, family and civility. The German Constitutional Tribunal has expounded this view in its cases, emphasising that the Constitution was not framed for individuals alone but also for an organic association of persons expressing its will to leave a common social life grounded on the idea of human dignity.[205]

[197] See eg art 2 of the Italian Constitution (concerning the protection of fundamental rights of individuals and 'social groups').

[198] See below p 56 ff.

[199] *National Coalition* n 177 above, para 118 (Sachs concurring).

[200] ibid, para 116 (Sachs concurring).

[201] ibid, para 116 (Sachs concurring).

[202] ibid, para 117 (Sachs concurring).

[203] Nonetheless, Justice Sachs' argument shares some similarities with Justice Kennedy's opinion in *Lawrence* n 5 above, when he defines his approach as a 'person-centred approach' and rejects the 'formula based position' considering fundamental rights as separate and alternate or ranked in a descending order of value (see para 112). Both from the point of view of the persons affected, as well as from that of society as a whole—he argues—equality and privacy cannot be separated, because they are both violated simultaneously by anti-sodomy laws. In other words, violation of equality and violation of intimacy mutually reinforce each other.

[204] I Kant, *Groundwork of the metaphysics of morals*, transl by M Gregor, introduction by CM Korsgaard (Cambridge, Cambridge University Press, 1997) expounding the idea that 'man and generally any rational being exists as an end in himself, not merely as a means'. See below, Ch 4 p 151.

[205] See 30 BVerfGE 173 (1971) (*Mephisto* case), 5.

Expounding this view, Justice Sachs emphasised that

> the Constitution does not presuppose that a holder of a right is an isolated, lonely and abstract figure possessing a disembodied and socially disconnected self. It acknowledges that people live in their bodies, their communities, their cultures, their places and their times.[206]

Justice Sachs' interpretation of privacy anticipated further developments in the advancement of same-sex couples' rights that I will address in more detail in the following chapters. His view rejected the dual structure—public and private—of privacy, which dominated *Dudgeon* and the other constitutional cases on the criminalisation of same-sex sexual acts, arguing that it 'does not capture the complexity of lived life, in which private and public lives determine each other with the mobile lines between them being constantly amenable to repressive definition'.[207]

The public–private dichotomy is, in Sachs' perspective, the consequence of an impoverished interpretation of the right of privacy which had instead to be regarded as related to autonomy, self-realisation and at the same time to the 'social dimension of the individual' and the equal recognition of the value of all human beings.[208] For this reason, Justice Sachs suggested the importance of taking context into account and he assumed that in constitutional adjudication discrimination should be 'assessed in a larger social, political, and legal context'.[209]

IX. THE 'BOOMERANG PATTERN INFLUENCE' OF *DUDGEON* AT INTERNATIONAL LEVEL

Dudgeon put gay rights at the forefront of legal debate and made them an international issue.

Breaking the legislative stalemate at domestic level, *Dudgeon* led to the adoption of new law which placed Northern Ireland in line with the rest of the United Kingdom in 1983.[210]

At the same time, during the 1980s, many countries legalised sexual acts between consenting adults of the same sex through the adoption of new legislation repealing

[206] *National Coalition* n 177 above, para 117 (Sachs concurring).

[207] ibid, para 110 (Sachs concurring).

[208] ibid, para 115 (Sachs concurring) arguing that 'the depreciated value given in argument to invalidation on the grounds of privacy, treating it as a poor relation of equality, was a result of adopting an impoverished version of the concept of privacy itself. In my view, the underlying assumptions about privacy were doubly flawed, being far too narrow in their understanding, on the one hand, and far too wide in their implications, on the other').

[209] See for instance the Supreme Court of Canada in *Egan v Canada* (1995) 2 SCR 513 (Justice L'Heureux-Dubé dissenting). See also the High Court of Fiji case in *McCoskar v State*, n 18 above, arguing in favour of 'a broad and purposive construction of privacy that is consistent with the recognition in international law that the right to privacy extends beyond the negative conception of privacy as freedom from unwarranted State intrusion into one's private life to include the positive right to establish and nurture human relationships free of criminal or indeed community sanction'.

[210] Homosexual Offences (Northern Ireland) Order 1982, SI 1982/1536 (NI 19).

old sodomy laws or the enactment of new provisions in the penal code.[211] National courts did not play a major role in the process of decriminalisation of sexual acts between adults of the same sex in these countries, but *Dudgeon* set into motion what Keck and Sikkink, in their book on the role of advocacy networks in international politics, define as a 'boomerang pattern of influence'.[212]

They argue that

> it is no accident that rights claims may be the prototypical language of advocacy networks. Governments are the primary 'guarantors' of rights, but also among their primary violators. When a government violates or refuses to recognise rights, individuals and domestic groups often have no recourse within domestic political or judicial arenas. They may seek international connections to express their concerns and even to protect their lives.

In other words, 'where governments are inaccessible or deaf to groups whose claims may nonetheless resonate elsewhere, international contacts can amplify the demands of domestic groups, pry open space for new issues and then echo back these demands into the domestic arena'.[213]

LGBT activists looked at *Dudgeon* as illustrative of a change in legal perspective on homosexuality and followed the same path in order to obtain a judgment in their favor at international level and then promote the advancement of the rights of gays and lesbians within their countries.

In light of *Dudgeon*, in 1988 Mr Norris, a member and chairman of the Irish Gay Rights Movement, successfully filed suit before the ECtHR challenging the same statutory provisions discussed in *Dudgeon*,[214] which were still in force in Ireland (*Norris v Ireland*).[215] As a result, new legislation was then introduced in Ireland in 1993.[216]

In 1993, gay rights activists in Cyprus challenged the provision of the criminal code which criminalised sexual acts between consenting male adults, before the ECtHR. After the ECtHR decision in *Modinos*[217] new legislation was passed in 1998.

[211] Hildebrandt, 'Routes to decriminalization', n 16 above, 242 ff notes that between 1982 and 2010, decriminalisation was achieved in 41 countries around the world. In particular, 'between 1991 and 2003 same-sex acts were decriminalized in 20 former communist or socialist countries, among them the 13 successor states of the Soviet Union and three successor states of Yugoslavia'. In these countries the fall of the Soviet Union was 'an important triggering event for decriminalization, but not so much because democratization provided local gay and lesbian groups with more opportunities to enforce decriminalization but because the break up of the Eastern Bloc offered many countries the chance to become members in western organizations' (ibid, 244–45). Hildbrandt also suggests that in most of the countries decriminalisation was achieved through new legislation or the adoption of a new penal code (30 out of 41), but that *Dudgeon* 'made gay and lesbian rights an international human rights issue which facilitated the decriminalization of same-sex acts and the fight for more far reaching rights during the following three decades' (ibid, 242).

[212] ME Keck and K Sikkink, *Activists Beyond Borders: Advocacy Networks in International Politics* (Ithaca, Cornell University Press, 1998) 13.

[213] ibid.

[214] Offences against the Person Act 1861 and Criminal Law Amendment Act 1885.

[215] *Norris v Ireland* n 3 above.

[216] Criminal Law (Sexual Offences) Act 1993.

[217] *Modinos v Cyprus* n 4 above.

In 1994, Nicholas Toonen, an Australian citizen residing in the state of Tasmania filed suit before the Human Rights Committee established under article 5, paragraph 4, of the Optional Protocol to the International Covenant on Civil and Political Rights, challenging two provisions of the Tasmanian Criminal Code[218] which criminalised various forms of sexual acts between men, including all forms of sexual contacts between consenting adult gay men in private. In particular, Mr Toonen complained that the provisions

> do not distinguish between sexual activity in private and sexual activity in public and bring private activity into the public domain. In their enforcement, these provisions result in a violation of the right to privacy, since they enable the police to enter a household on the mere suspicion that two consenting adult homosexual men may be committing a criminal offence.[219]

Although the provisions were not currently enforced by the judicial authorities in Tasmania, Mr Toonen alleged that they had the effect of attaching a stigma to homosexuality. Mentioning the ECtHR's ruling in *Dudgeon*, he argued that the potential violation of the right of privacy of same-sex couples affected the honour and the reputation of the individuals concerned. At the same time, he argued that, in spite of their gender neutrality, Tasmanian laws against 'unnatural sexual intercourse' were discriminatory because they were mostly enforced against men engaged in same-sex sexual activity.

The Human Rights Committee, in *Toonen v Australia*, gave an interpretation of the right of privacy which shares some similarities with the interpretation of privacy expounded by the ECtHR in *Dudgeon*. Reasoning that the right of privacy 'covers consensual adult sex in private',[220] the Committee concluded that Mr Toonen was victim of a violation of article 17, para 1 of the International Covenant on Civil and Political Rights of 1966 (ICCPR)[221] because 'the continued existence of the challenged provisions ... continuously and directly "interferes" with the author's privacy'.[222] At the same time, the Committee rejected the allegations submitted by Tasmanian authorities that justified the challenged provisions, arguing that moral issues were exclusively a matter of domestic concern. The Committee, however, did not exclude enforcement of morals as a legitimate legislative purpose, but pointed out that the fact that the provisions were not enforced, implied that they could not be deemed essential to the protection of morals in Tasmania.[223]

It should also be noted that, as in *Dudgeon*, the Committee did not consider it necessary to examine whether Mr Toonen was at the same time a victim of discrimination according to art 26 of the ICCPR.[224] Even in this case, equality issues were

[218] Tasmanian Criminal Code, s 122(a) and (c) and s 123.
[219] *Toonen* n 14 above para 3.1.
[220] ibid, para 8.2.
[221] International Covenant on Civil and Political Rights, art 17, para 1 stating that 'No one shall be subjected to arbitrary or unlawful interference with his privacy, family, home or correspondence, nor to unlawful attacks on his honour and reputation'.
[222] *Toonen* n 14 above para 8.2.
[223] ibid, para 8.6.
[224] ibid, para 11.

placed in a secondary position compared to privacy arguments, but the Committee made an important remark when observing that, as far as the identification of factors of discrimination is concerned, 'sex' in articles 2, paragraph 1, and 26 of the ICCPR should be read as also including 'sexual orientation'.[225]

The holdings in *Toonen* and *Dudgeon* provided a great stimulus to the LGBT movements, raising the visibility of gays and lesbians human rights issues internationally. At the same time, soon after *Toonen* it appeared clear that, in order to achieve further results, international litigation could not be disjoined from building a politics of recognition at national level.[226]

Thanks to the growing awareness on sexual orientation issues, in the following years, LGBT movements took up the struggle over decriminalisation of sexual acts even at domestic level. In this chapter I have analysed the circulation of the legal arguments in some constitutional cases of great relevance such as *Lawrence* and *National Coalition* but, as mentioned at the beginning, *Toonen* and *Dudgeon* were also taken into consideration by many other supreme and constitutional courts, which analogously concluded in favour of the protection of individual freedom concerning sexual orientation. The supreme and constitutional courts, which reached an opposite conclusion on sexual equality and right of privacy of gays and lesbians,[227] relied on *Dudgeon* and *Toonen* as well, engaging in a dialogue with their counterparts at international and national level.

I will address in more detail the role of constitutional (and supreme) courts in promoting constitutional change on sexual orientation equality in Chapter 4, focusing in particular on marriage equality.[228] Nonetheless it is worth stressing here that even the first cases discussed in this chapter show how courts, including international courts, have been playing a key role in challenging stereotypes and the 'politics of disgust' against gays and lesbians, but also in promoting the debate on sexual orientation equality issues and forging constitutional arguments of privacy, dignity and equality.

225 ibid, para 8.6.

226 LR Helfer, 'Will the UNHRC Require Recognition of Same-Sex Marriage?' in R Wintemute and M Andenæs (eds), *Legal Recognition of Same-Sex Partnerships* (Oxford, Hart Publishing, 2001) 732, 741 (addressing the implication of *Toonen* in same-sex marriage litigation before the UNHRC and arguing that 'the most effective and lasting legal advances of lesbians and gays will be achieved, not by adopting an aggressive international litigation strategy imposing human rights norms from above, but rather by a selective use of international litigation together with non litigation approaches and active domestic advocacy of sexual orientation issues'.

227 See, eg the Hong Kong Court of First Instance in *Leung*, n 11 above (referring to the ECtHR's definition of privacy in *Dudgeon* (n 1 above, para 123), but also to sexual orientation as included in the notion of 'sex' as a factor of discrimination in *Toonen* (n 14 above, paras 43 ff)). Against, the Supreme Court of Zimbabwe in *Banana*, n 11 above (mentioning *Toonen* and *Dudgeon* but arguing that art 23 of the Constitution of Zimbabwe concerning protection from discrimination on the basis of gender 'does not include an express prohibition against discrimination on the ground of "sexual orientation"').

228 See below, p 140 ff.

3

Out of the Closet: Courts and the Same-Sex Couple as 'Family'

I. DIFFERENT MODELS OF REGULATION OF FAMILY, THE PUBLIC–PRIVATE DICHOTOMY AND THE PURPOSE OF THIS CHAPTER

THE FIRST CASES on sexual equality dealing with criminalisation of sexual acts between people of the same sex—discussed in Chapter 2—focused on recognition of the right to privacy of same-sex couples. I emphasised that the courts' reliance on the right to privacy—interpreted mostly in its spatial dimension, as freedom from interference in the privacy of the home—implied a perpetuation of 'the logic of the closet', strengthening the private and public dichotomy and delimiting an area of self-determination, free of the intervention of the State. Thus, although the European Court of Human Rights' seminal decision in *Dudgeon v United Kingdom*,[1] and other constitutional cases that followed, should be credited for having made gay and lesbian rights an international human rights issue, at the same time they strengthened the idea that same-sex couples and their intimacy deserved protection as far as they remained confined in the privacy of their homes.

The present chapter will look at another remarkable achievement for same-sex couples, the development of the 'social dimension' of their relationships, focusing in particular on the recognition of stable same-sex couples as 'families'. Although in many countries the evolution of the definition of 'family' also resulted in the legalisation and regulation of same-sex relationships, this chapter will keep these achievements distinct, focusing on the contribution of constitutional and international courts to amending 'traditional' definitions of 'family' so as to include the stable same-sex couple.

The notion of 'family' plays an important role in international human rights law. The Universal Declaration of Human Rights describes the family as 'the natural and fundamental group unit of the society', specifying that 'it is entitled to protection by society and the State'.[2]

Article 8 of the European Convention on Human Rights (ECHR) protects the 'right to respect for private and family life',[3] adding that 'there shall be no

[1] *Dudgeon v UK* (1981) Series A no 45, [1981] EHRR 5.
[2] Universal Declaration of Human Rights, GA Res 217 A (III), UN Doc A/810, art 16(3).
[3] European Convention on Human Rights, Art 8(1) ('Everyone has the right to respect for his private and family life, his home and his correspondence').

interference by a public authority with the exercise of the right except such as in the accordance with the law and is a necessary in a democratic society'.[4] Under the ECHR, the protection of family life presupposes the existence of a 'family'[5] and Article 12 of the Convention adds that '[m]en and women of marriageable age have the right to marry and to found a family according to the national laws governing the exercise of this right'.[6]

Most of the national constitutions devote special attention to family, recognising its importance as the core social institution and undertaking to afford it constitutional protection.[7] The national constitutions of France, Finland, Germany, Italy, Luxembourg, Portugal and Spain, for instance, define family in institutional terms, although they conceptualise it in different ways.

Spain[8] and Belgium[9] adopt a constitutional definition of family modelled on Article 8 of the ECHR.[10] The constitutions of Italy,[11] Ireland,[12] Greece[13] and Portugal[14] recognise family as a 'natural institution' or a 'fundamental element of society' and, at the same time, emphasise the narrow relationship between family and marriage.

[4] Art 8(2) which also refers to the interests of 'national security, public safety or the economic well-being of the country, for the prevention of disorder or crime, for the protection of health or morals, or for the protection of the rights and the freedom of others'.

[5] See WA Schabas, *The European Convention on Human Rights. A Commentary* (Oxford, Oxford University Press, 2015) 389 citing *Marckx v Belgium* (1979) 2 EHRR 330, (1979) ECHR 2 para 31.

[6] Art 7 of the Charter of Fundamental Rights of the European Union reproduces the content of Art 8 ECHR, affirming that 'Everyone has the right to respect for his or her private and family life…'. See also Article 9 on the right to marry and build a family.

[7] L Hantrais and MT Letablier, *Families and Family Policies in Europe* (London, Routledge, 2014) 26.

[8] See Art 18(1) of the Spanish Constitution of 1978 ('The right to honour, to personal and family privacy and to the own image is guaranteed') and Art 39(1) ('The public authorities ensure social, economic and legal protection of the family').

[9] Art 22(1) of the Constitution of Belgium affirms that 'Everyone has the right to the respect of his private and family life, except in the cases and conditions determined by the law'.

[10] It should be emphasised that, unlike the constitutions of Italy, Germany and Ireland, mentioned below, the Spanish Constitution disconnects the concepts of family and marriage, and the institutions are regulated by different constitutional clauses (respectively art 39 and art 32). Accordingly, in Spain marriage is not a prerequisite for recognition of the status of family for same-sex couples. See F Jaurena i Salas, ' The Law of Stable Unions of Couples in the Catalonia Autonomous Community of Spain', in R Wintemute and M Andenæs (eds), *Legal Recognition of Same-Sex Partnerships* (Oxford, Hart Publishing, 2001) 505, 515.

[11] Art 29(1) of the Italian Constitution declares that 'The Republic recognises the rights of the family as a natural society founded on marriage'.

[12] Art 41(1) of the Constitution of Ireland declares: 'The State recognises the Family as the natural primary and fundamental unit group of Society, and as a moral institution possessing inalienable and imprescriptible rights, antecedent and superior to all positive law. The State, therefore, guarantees to protect the Family in its constitution and authority, as the necessary basis of social order and as indispensable to the welfare of the Nation and the State'.

[13] Art 9(1) of the Constitution of Greece affirms: 'The private and family life of the individual is inviolable' and art 21(1) adds that 'The family, being the cornerstone of the preservation and the advancement of the Nation, as well as marriage, motherhood and childhood, shall be under the protection of the State'. § 3 of the same article adds that 'The State pledges itself to guard with special care the institution of Marriage, on which the Family is founded, and to protect it against attack'.

[14] See art 26(1) of the Constitution of Portugal, which clarifies that 'Everyone shall possess the right … to protect the privacy of their personal and family life'. Art 36 adds that 'Everyone shall possess the right to found a family and to marry on terms of full equality' and art 67(1) specifies that 'As a fundamental element in society, the family shall possess the right to protection by society and the state and to the effective implementation of all the conditions needed to enable family members to achieve personal fulfilment'. Furthermore, art 67(2) specifies and lists the duties of the state for the protection of family.

For this reason, in these countries the Constitution acts as a 'source of rigidity',[15] prioritising the protection of the traditional family based on opposite-sex marriage. In Italy, for instance, after the end of Fascism that had conceptualised the family as a patriarchal unit, the Constitution of 1948 recognised the value of the family 'as a natural social unit founded on marriage' and on equality between 'husband' and 'wife'. In Germany, Article 6 of the Basic Law (*Grundgesetz*)[16] was designed to protect the institution of marriage, elevating marriage and the family by placing them under 'the special protection of the State'.

These constitutional definitions mainly aim at protecting the institution of 'marriage' rather than the 'family'. The rigidity of the constitutional clauses therefore makes it difficult to adapt family law to the social and cultural changes affecting family. Whereas—as will be clarified in the next chapter—in recent years countries such as Ireland and Germany have been able to circumvent legal constraints in order to afford constitutional protection to same-sex couples, constitutional limitations remain quite rigid in countries like Italy, where they still exert a significant influence on the legal and political debate concerning the recognition and protection of 'new families'.[17]

At the same time, the definition of the family as a 'social institution' at constitutional level implies recognition of a powerful role for the State in the protection and regulation of family relationships. Thus, in these countries, the State plays not only a 'protective role', but also *promotes* the development of family and family relationships. The State is under an *obligation* to establish an environment where the family is able to come into being, survive and flourish. This is exemplified by the constitutional clauses that in Germany, Italy, Spain and Ireland enumerate the duties of the State towards the family[18] and, at the same time, by the large number of statutes which regulate the rights and duties of family members in order to promote public interests such as social stability, protection of morals or procreation.[19] As has been emphasised, 'the State is not only the background where the family is separated and identified as such, but at the same time it is a means of control and the source of regulation of the family as an institution and of family relationships'.[20]

It should be premised that, although 'legal systems are the product of a combination of factors reflecting different national philosophical and religious traditions and

[15] Hantrais and Letablier, *Families and Family Policies* n 7 above, 26.

[16] Art 6(1) German Basic Law (*Grundgesetz*): 'Marriage and the family shall enjoy the special protection of the state'.

[17] See below p 97 ff.

[18] See eg Art 29 ff of the Italian Constitution or art 6 of the German Basic Law (*Grundgesetz*) n 11 and 16 above. It should be also taken into consideration that in Italy and Germany, constitutional clauses concerning family and family relationships are interpreted in connection with the social state principle.

[19] Eg Art 29 of the Italian Constitution—which defines family as a 'natural institution founded on marriage' (§ 1) and also refers to a 'wife' and a 'husband' (§ 2)—deeply influenced the regulation of assisted reproductive technology, which is permitted only for opposite-sex couples, and the regulation of adoption and stepchild adoption, which are open only to married opposite-sex couples. In Germany, as the Constitutional Tribunal frequently emphasised, the legal order exists to instruct its citizens in the moral content of the Basic Law including substantive values pertaining to the nature of life, personhood and family (see eg Abortion Case I (1975) 39 BVerfGE 1 and Abortion II Case (1993) 88 BVerfGE 203).

[20] C Saraceno and M Naldini, *Sociologia della famiglia* (Bologna, Il Mulino, 2013) 221 (translation mine).

the pace and timing of social processes',[21] legal scholars and sociologists distinguish two different models of regulation of family and family relationships at statutory level: a 'civil law model' which can be traced back to the *Code Napoléon* (1804) and which is common to the continental European countries, such as Germany, Italy, Spain, Netherlands and Poland that followed the French civil code in the codification process of the nineteenth century, and a 'common law model' which is prevalent in the Anglo-Saxon tradition.[22]

The civil law model's main feature lies in the adoption of an organic corpus of statutes regulating family members' status and the family relationships (the 'family law'). The basic idea of the French Civil Code, as far as family relationships were concerned, was that family is moulded on the State: a powerful State corresponds to a strongly organised family.[23] The family is therefore structured along vertical lines, with the father exercising parental authority over the children, and marital authority over his wife.

Portalis—the father of the French civil code of 1804—conceived the family as the 'nursery of the State' ('*la pépinière de l'État*'),[24] in which 'private virtues are citizens' virtues'.[25] Therefore, a close relationship was established between family and State, and the family was given a political value, as it was assigned the duty to nurture children into future citizens.

The French *Code Napoléon* therefore clearly exemplifies a government-imposed regulation of family relationships, where 'the public order was founded on the private one, the social order on domestic order and the big nation on the small one'.[26] Meulders-Klein argues that 'the French scholarship and case law—such as those of other European countries whose legislation was inspired by the *Code*—developed an "institutional theory" of family and marriage. "Institutional" because it went beyond individual autonomy in order to achieve a higher goal: the good of the family and, through it, of the social order'.[27]

Although the present features of family law differ significantly from the past and family law is no longer considered part of public law, the constitutional definitions of family as a 'basic social institution' and the connection between family and marriage in some European countries still refer to a heteronormative and 'public' idea of family which can be traced back to the French civil code of 1804.

By contrast, when compared to the French and German experiences and their extensive bodies of rules on the matters of family life, the common law is distinguished by the lack of a unitary and organic regulation of this field of the law.

[21] Hantrais and Letablier, *Families and Family Policies*, n 7 above, 29.

[22] See AM Glendon, MW Gordon and C Osakwe, *Comparative Legal Traditions* (St Paul MN, West Publishing Co, 1994) 278.

[23] V Pocar and P Ronfani, *La famiglia e il diritto* (Bari, Laterza, 2003) 7.

[24] JEM Portalis, *Discours préliminaire du premier projet de Code civil*, 1801 ('*Les familles se forment par le mariage, et elles sont la pépinière de l'État. Chaque famille est une société particulière et distincte dont le gouvernement importe à la grande famille qui les comprend toutes*').

[25] See MT Meulders-Klein 'Individualisme et communautarisme: l'individu, la famille et l'État en Europe occidentale' (1993) 23–24 *Droit et société* 163, 170.

[26] I Théry and C Biet, *La famille, la loi, l'Etat. De la Revolution au code civil* (Paris, Iprimerie Nationale, Ed du Centre George Pompidou, 1989) 118.

[27] Meulders-Klein, 'Individualisme et communautarisme' n 25 above, 170.

In England, there is no statutory definition of family and there is no common law definition either.[28] As it has been emphasised

> the continental lawyer is surprised to discover through the history of the Common Law the almost absence of rules concerning family relationships—with the exception of formation and dissolution of marriage and issues concerning goods (property and inheritance)—as if the notion of family and family ties with their legal effects, did not fall within the realm of the law and were reserved to the 'Poor Laws', rules of public law that assigned to families the duty to take care of poor people.[29]

For this reason, in England, during the Victorian age, family was essentially conceived as 'a moral and religious institution',[30] according to the Puritan ideology.[31] Family was therefore a closed entity, '*une citadelle privée impénétrable à la justice*',[32] until divorce occurred. The common law, it has been said, 'traditionally stays away from interspousal disputes unless and until they reach the divorce court'.[33]

The Victorian ideology conceived family as pertaining to the intimate sphere of the individual.[34] Marriage was related to the private dimension of life, and the family was based on hierarchical relationships founded on fatherhood, with a clear division of labour in household management. In the absence of a formal definition, family was 'about what it does, instead of what it is', according to an idea which is still alive today.[35]

However, even in the common law model, family was not exclusively a matter of private concern.[36] The two realms—the private dimension of family life and the public dimension of economy—were not entirely separate. The public authority was not

[28] A Diduck and F Canagas, *Family Law, Gender and the State. Text, Cases and Materials*, 3rd edn (Oxford, Hart Publishing, 2012) 20. See also *Fitzpatrick v Sterling Housing Association Ltd* [2001] 1 AC 27 (arguing that 'This expression [family] is not a term of art; that is, it is not a technical term with a specific meaning. It is a word in ordinary usage, with a flexible meaning. ... Parliament has left to the courts to determine, in any given case, whether a particular individual falls within the description').

[29] Meulders-Klein, 'Individualisme et communautarisme' n 25 above, 167–68 (author's translation).

[30] Pocar and Ronfani, *La famiglia e il diritto* n 23 above, 11. On the State's intervention in family life during the Victorian age, and on the Elizabethan Poor Laws, K O'Donovan, *Sexual Divisions in Law* (London, Weinfeld & Nicholson, 1985) 14 ff.

[31] D Gittins, *The Family in Question. Changing Households and Familiar Ideologies*, 2nd edn (Houndmills, Macmillan Press, 1993) 43 ff (mentioning the definition of family, according to Puritan doctrines, as 'a "little commonwealth" with the father at head').

[32] Meulders-Klein, 'Individualisme et communautarisme' n 25 above, 168. See, for an analogous and well-known definition in Italian scholarship, AC Jemolo, *La famiglia e il diritto* (Naples, Annali del Seminario Giuridico dell'Università di Catania, 1949) 57, who describes family as 'an island that the sea of law can only lap against' ('*un'isola che il mare del diritto può lambire, ma lambire soltanto*').

[33] MA Glendon, 'Power and Authority in the Family: New Legal Patterns as Reflections of Changing Ideologies', (1975) 23 *American Journal of Comparative Law* 1, 5. See also Meulders-Klein, 'Individualisme et communautarisme' n 25 above, 168 arguing that 'The lack of clear rules concerning filiation and the duties towards the children, even the legitimate ones, considered as moral instead of legal obligations; the absence of formal duties concerning material support between ancestors and descendants, the liberty to make will ... seem equally surprising' (author's translation). On the view that family and marriage should be left alone, as long as conflict does not cause breakdown, O'Donovan, *Sexual Divisions in Law* n 30 above, 13.

[34] Gittins, *The Family in Question* n 31 above, 43.

[35] Diduck and Canagas, *Family Law, Gender and the State* n 28 above, 26.

[36] MC Regan, *Family Law and the Pursuit of Intimacy* (New York, New York University Press, 1993) 10.

uninterested in the realm of private and family life: as sociological and legal studies illustrate, both common and civil law systems in Western tradition were concerned with the interests of the middle class because of the narrow relationship between family and property. 'The French code designed the family according to capitalistic organisation, and the common law adopted a similar approach in its idea of family as a spiritual and affective community and the assignment of specific roles to husband and wife'.[37]

The private/public dichotomy—whose origin lies in the liberal philosophy[38] and which was perpetuated by nineteenth-century liberal thought[39]—'relates to the boundaries of law'[40] and has enormous repercussions for what we believe to be the State's responsibility for protecting and assisting families. It marks the opposition between the realm of legitimate public regulation and the realm of freedom from intrusion, personal autonomy and private choice.[41]

In other words,

> the public/private divide functions ideologically to draw boundaries around what properly constitutes the subject of politics and what is considered the legitimate scope of political claims. ... These boundaries, which are shifting, serve to limit arbitrarily the reach of liberal ideals such as democracy, equality, justice and liberty.[42]

English critics of the private/public divide tend to place family in the first realm and to oppose it to the public and the market as realms of public regulation, although the two spheres, as mentioned above, are not completely separate. On the contrary, in civil law countries—especially those whose constitutions, as mentioned earlier, adopt an institutional idea of family—constitutional law is much more concerned with the regulation of family and family relationships. I assume in this book that the definition of the boundary between the private and the public dimension of family life by the law enshrines values in legal and social policy that explain governmental choices concerning the notion and the function of family and the relationships among family members.

[37] Pocar and Ronfani, *La famiglia e il diritto* n 23 above, 13.

[38] See O'Donovan, *Sexual Divisions in Law* n 30 above, 8. The author recalls the seventeenth-century tradition as represented by Locke, who posited a distinction 'between reason and passion, knowledge and desire, mind and body', arguing that 'this leads to a split between the public sphere in which individuals prudently calculate their own self-interest and act upon it, and a private sphere of subjectivity and desire'.

[39] O'Donovan, *Sexual Divisions in Law* n 30 above cites John Stuart Mill and his feminist work *On the Subjection of Women*, in order to emphasise the continuation of the private/public split.

[40] O'Donovan, *Sexual Divisions in Law* n 30 above, 3.

[41] See N Rose, 'Beyond the Public/Private Division: Law, Power and the Family' (1987) 14 *Journal Law and Society* 61, 64 arguing that 'The division between public and private is traced back in political and social philosophy at least as far as Aristotle's distinction between *polis* and *oikos* and up to the natural rights theories of John Locke. However, in the eighteenth and nineteenth centuries the distinction is reposed in terms of the division between home and market. It is given a philosophical foundation in the liberal political philosophy of J.S. Mill and his followers, with the opposition between the realm of legitimate public regulation and the realm of freedom from intrusion, personal autonomy and private choice'.

[42] Diduck and Canagas, *Family Law, Gender and the State* n 28 above, 15 (citing L Phillips, 'Tax Law and Social Reproduction: The Gender of Fiscal Policy in the Ade of Privatization' in J Fudge and B Cossman (eds), *Privatization, Law and the Challenge of Feminism* (Toronto, University of Toronto Press, 2002)).

Although this book doesn't have the purpose of discussing the sociological literature on the private/public spheres of the family, I agree with the theory that the private/public dichotomy is not a naturally occurring social phenomenon but, rather is socially constructed[43] and that constitutional law regulation of family is influenced by this social construction.[44] As it has been emphasised, 'the very definitions of what "family" is, or what is right or wrong with it is a legal matter'.[45] The boundary between the private and the social dimension of homosexuality is, in my perspective, ideological and, as Gittins emphasises, 'this ideology changes over time but nonetheless is presented as something universal. For the past few decades this ideal has been of a young, married, heterosexual, white, middle-class couple with two children.'[46]

In the following pages I will analyse the arguments through which the ECtHR and some constitutional courts have departed from the 'traditional' definition of 'family' or 'spouse' in order to give legal recognition to same-sex families. The cases I will discuss take into consideration stable same-sex relationships which were not recognised by the law, due to the lack of a regulation of same-sex civil partnership at the time of the cases. The decision to focus on cases released before the introduction of civil partnerships at legislative level, is due to the fact that the acknowledgement at legislative level of the sentimental value of the relationship between two persons of the same sex—and the regulation of the legal consequences of their formal bond—necessarily brings about the recognition of its value as 'family'. The choice of regulating same-sex partnerships and equating them (totally or partially) with heterosexual marriage, in other words, makes the issue of the definition of the stable same-sex couple as 'family' worthless.[47] On the contrary, when the stable same-sex

[43] Diduck and Canagas, *Family Law, Gender and the State*, n 28 above, 16 and also Rose, 'Beyond the public/Private Division' n 41 above, 61.

[44] See O'Donovan, *Sexual Divisions in Law* n 30 above, 3 (arguing that 'law is not only central to concepts of private and public, and to the division between the two, but also plays an important part in the construction of that division').

[45] For this perspective, Diduck and Canagas, *Family Law, Gender and the State* n 28 above, 17 and Rose, 'Beyond the Public/Private Division' n 41 above, 65 (arguing that 'like *laissez faire* in relation to the market, the idea that the family can be private in the sense of outside public regulation is a myth').

[46] Gittins, *The family in question* n 31 above, 2.

[47] Under EU law eg the notion of 'family member' is strictly related to a legally recognised bond between the partners. Under EU Directive 2004/38 art 3 para 2(a), regulating the right of citizens of the Union and their family members to move and reside freely within the territory of the Member States, a 'family member' means the EU citizen's spouse and the partner in a registered civil partnership (in addition to direct descendants and dependent parents and grandparents). However this provision applies when 'the host Member State treats registered partnerships as equivalent to marriage' and covers registered partnerships formed within an EU Member State. When these conditions do not apply, the partner will not properly fall with the definition of 'family member', but can still be considered 'part of the family' because art 3, s 2(b), includes among the beneficiaries 'the partner with whom the Union citizen has a durable relationship, duly attested'. In this case, however, the partner will not enjoy 'an automatic right of entry and residence in the host Member State' but his/her request will be examined by the host Member State 'on the basis of its own national legislation, in order to decide whether entry and residence could be granted to such persons, taking into consideration their relationship with the Union citizen or any other circumstances, such as their financial or physical dependence on the Union citizen'. As has been emphasised by Diduck and Canagas, *Family Law, Gender and the State* n 28 above, 28, the EU definition of 'family' arguably still follows the 'old model', 'premised on the traditional and increasingly exclusive notion of the legally married, nuclear and economically functional model' (see also H Salford, 'Concepts of Family Under the EU Law: Lessons From the ECHR' (2002) 16 *International Journal of Law, Policy and the Family* 410, 411).

couple lives in the limbo that precedes its legal recognition, the attribution to partners of some rights (such as tenancy rights) at judicial level can only be achieved through a redefinition of the 'traditional' and normative idea of family and the adoption of a pluralistic notion of family.

In the following pages I will address the passage, at judicial level, from a 'private' dimension towards a 'public' and social dimension of same-sex relationships. I aim at analysing the arguments through which the constitutional courts moved from the recognition of the rights of gays and lesbians within the sphere of private life and personal autonomy to the acknowledgment of their rights and value as 'families'. This passage requires elucidating the ideological premises which lie beneath the legal definition of 'family'.

II. THE SUPREME COURT OF CANADA AND THE INADEQUACY OF 'UNEXAMINED CONSENSUS' IN THE DEFINITION OF 'FAMILY'

In 1993, the Supreme Court of Canada was the first constitutional court to address the issue of the acknowledgement of same-sex couples as *families*.[48] The case arose when a federal government employee, Brian Mossop, took a day off to attend the funeral of the father of the man he described as his lover. The two men had known each other for over 10 years and resided together in a jointly owned and maintained home. The day after the funeral, Mr Mossop applied for bereavement leave pursuant to the collective agreement governing the terms of his employment. The employer, the Treasury Board, refused his application, arguing that, although the collective agreement provided for up to four days' leave upon the death of a member of an employee's 'immediate family' and this term included the 'common-law spouse', it should be intended as restricted to a person of the opposite sex.

Before reaching the Supreme Court, the case was discussed before the Human Rights Tribunal,[49] which concluded in favour of Mr Mossop and held that the complainant had suffered a discriminatory treatment in violation of section 2 of the 1983 Canadian Human Rights Act.[50] According to the Tribunal, the issue at stake revolved around the interpretation of the notion of 'family status'. For this reason, it identified the fundamental question as being whether the denial of a bereavement leave was based on the prohibited ground of 'family status'. On the basis of a purposive interpretation of the Canadian Human Rights Act, the Tribunal found that the legislator did not aim at promoting certain types of status instead of others, and that Mr Mossop and his partner could fit within the scope of 'family status'.

[48] *Canada v Mossop* (1993) SCJ No 20.

[49] *Canada v Mossop*, Canadian Human Rights Tribunal (1989), 10 CHRR D/6064.

[50] Canadian Human Rights Act, RSC, 1985, c H-6. In particular s 2 states: '2. The purpose of this Act is to extend the laws in Canada to give effect, within the purview of matters coming within the legislative authority of Parliament, to the principle that every individual should have an equal opportunity with other individuals to make for himself or herself the life that he or she is able and wishes to have, consistent with his or her duties and obligations as a member of society, without being hindered in or prevented from doing so by discriminatory practices based on race, national or ethnic origin, colour, religion, age, sex, marital status, *family status*, disability or conviction for an offence for which a pardon has been granted' (emphasis added).

The Federal Court of Appeal reversed the Tribunal's conclusion, arguing that the word 'family' did not include a same-sex relationship.[51] The Federal Court of Appeal suggested that 'sexual orientation' and not 'family status' was the real ground of discrimination at stake, and that the former was not included among the prohibited grounds of discrimination listed in section 3 of the Act.[52]

The Supreme Court (5-4) finally dismissed Mr Mossop's appeal because the general question raised was one of statutory interpretation and as such it was a question of law over which the Federal Court of Appeal had jurisdiction.

However, the majority was not unanimous in identifying the legal issue raised by the case. According to three justices,[53] the case basically involved a discrimination based on sexual orientation: they argued that when in 1983 the Parliament included the notion of 'family status' in the Act, it had refused at the same time to include 'sexual orientation' among the prohibited grounds of discrimination. By contrast, the other two justices in the majority[54] focused only on the interpretation of the notion of 'family status' and suggested that 'while the Act should be interpreted generously with a view to effecting its purpose, neither ordinary meaning, context, nor purpose indicates a legislative intention to include same-sex couples within "family status"'.

Canada v Mossop is mostly regarded for Justice L'Heureux-Dubé's comprehensive and detailed dissenting opinion. Starting from the assumption that 'human rights legislation has a unique quasi-constitutional nature, and that it is to be given a large, purposive and liberal interpretation',[55] Justice L'Heureux-Dubé argued that the case should be phrased as relating to the interpretation of the 'family status' in section 3 of the Act. In particular, she suggested that 'nothing in the textual context, indicate[d] that the protection of the Act is to be extended only to certain types of legally validated families': 'On the contrary the term "family status" suggest[ed] a broader protection that would prohibit discrimination against individuals on the basis of the internal structuring of their families'.[56]

For this reason, Justice L'Heureux-Dubé concluded in favour of an evolutionary and purposive interpretation of the Act. In her opinion the nature itself of a legislative text—and its differences from a Constitution—suggested the opportunity to read section 2 of the Act's reference to 'family status'[57] according to the so-called 'living tree doctrine'. She argued:

> Even if Parliament had in mind a specific idea of the scope of 'family status', in the absence of a definition in the Act which embodies this scope, concepts of equality and liberty which appear in human rights documents are not bounded by the precise understanding of those who drafted them. Human rights codes are documents that embody fundamental principles,

[51] *Canada v Mossop*, Federal Court of Appeal, [1991] 1 FC 18.

[52] S 3(1) ('For all purposes of this Act, race, national or ethnic origin, colour, religion, age, sex, marital status, family status, disability and conviction for which a pardon has been granted are prohibited grounds of discrimination').

[53] In particular see the opinion of Chief Justice Lamer and of Justices Sopinka and Iacobucci in *Canada v Mossop*, n 48 above.

[54] ibid, opinion of Justices Iacobucci and La Forest.

[55] ibid, para 94 (L'Heureux-Dubé dissenting).

[56] ibid, para 104.

[57] ibid, para 108.

> but which permit the understanding and application of these principles to change over time. These codes leave ample scope for interpretation by those charged with that task. The 'living-tree' doctrine, well understood and accepted as a principle of constitutional interpretation, is particularly well suited to human rights legislation. The enumerated grounds of discrimination must be examined in the context of contemporary values, and not in a vacuum. As with other such types of legislation, the meaning of the enumerated grounds in s. 3 of the Act is not 'frozen in time' and the scope of each ground may evolve.[58]

At the same time, Justice L'Heureux-Dubé's dissenting opinion is very interesting as it drew upon deep and interesting sociological arguments that deserve a detailed analysis. She moved from the idea that narrow and textual interpretation of 'family' are based on an implicit and preconceived idea of family. The logic of 'unexamined consensus'—she argued—'leads many to feel that the term "family" in fact has a plain meaning'.[59]

She challenged the validity of this assumption, arguing that the 'unexamined consensus' is proved inadequate when one is required to define the concepts that are embedded in the term 'family' in the context of 'family status'.[60] In other words, according to Justice L'Heureux-Dubé's interpretation, the 'unexamined consensus' could not be regarded as a satisfactory means of interpretation simply because a unanimous interpretation of 'family' does not exist. As there is 'no consensus as to the boundaries of family', family status 'may not have a sole meaning,' but rather 'varied meanings depending on the context or purpose for which the definition is desired'.[61]

> Those who support a formalistic or more restrictive meaning for the term family point out that there is a dominant conception of family that has been traditionally enforced by laws and social custom. The form taken by this dominant conception is commonly referred to as the traditional family. It is widely understood that the traditional family is one composed of a married man and woman and their children.[62]

But the formalist and traditional idea is not the only conception of family.[63] Justice L'Heureux-Dubé also illustrated other definitions of family: some of them looked at what a family does (for instance, sharing resources or responsibility, values and goals),[64] others took into account not only the purposes of the family but also other essential features such as the personal commitment and attachment among family members.[65] Therefore, she argued, whatever the definition of family, it 'invariably results in exclusion'.[66]

[58] ibid, para 109.
[59] ibid, para 114.
[60] ibid, para 114.
[61] ibid, para 117.
[62] ibid, para 115.
[63] ibid, para 116.
[64] Justice L'Heureaux-Dubé mentioned eg the definition of family suggested by the American Home Economics Association (AHEA) that defines a family as 'two or more persons who share resources, share responsibility for decisions, share values and goals, and have commitments to one another over time'. *Canada v Mossop* n 48 above, para 116.
[65] Justice L'Heureaux-Dubé cited eg the definition of family suggested by KG Terkelsen, 'Toward a Theory of the Family Life Cycle' in E Carter and M McGoldrick (eds), *The Family Life Cycle: A Framework for Family Therapy* (1980), 21 at 23.
[66] *Canada v Mossop* n 48 above, para 116.

Family, in her opinion, had a plural meaning and it was more appropriate to talk about 'families'. She emphasised that families can take different forms and 'it is important to recognize that there are differences which separate as well as commonalities which bind. The differences should not be ignored, but neither should they be used to de-legitimize those families that are thought to be different'.[67]

In rejecting a traditional notion of family, Justice L'Heureux-Dubé shared the Tribunal's factual and functional approach: she looked at the common problems which all families face[68] and, at the same time, took into consideration the values that all the families have in common, arguing that 'non-traditional family forms may equally advance true family values'.[69]

In other contexts, such as in feminist legal scholarship, the functional approach to defining families has been described as progressive and centred on 'lived lives'. 'Not coincidentally, therefore, many of the proponents of functional family approaches in relationship law are feminist and progressive scholars, who embrace the idea of dynamic change in law to reflect changing social practices'.[70] As Millbank stresses, 'functional family claims hold that those who function as a committed interdependent relationship require—and implicitly deserve—legal protections, regardless of their sex, or restrictive formal indicia of status such as marriage, or ability to marry'.[71]

Problems arise, however, when functionalists are asked to clarify what the essential elements and purposes of a family are. Justice L'Heureux-Dubé in *Mossop* was aware of this difficulty and remembered that the Tribunal took into consideration a long list of variables that was neither exhaustive nor determinative. None of the variables, she argued, was in fact necessarily present in any given family.

The cluster of variables include elements which differ greatly from each other, ranging from objective elements ('the existence of a relationship of some standing in terms of time and with the expectation of continuance, self-identification as a family, holding out to the public of the unit as a family')[72] to subjective variables ('an emotional positive involvement, sexual union') and to properly functional elements that look at 'what a family does' (eg 'raising and nurturing of children, caregiving to children or adults, shared housework, internal division of life-maintenance tasks, co-residence, joint ownership or joint use of property or goods, joint bank accounts',[73] etc).

[67] ibid, para 130.

[68] *Canada v Mossop* n 48 above, para 131 ('Though not all people structure their family relations in the same manner, it is clear that there are common problems. Today, families of all descriptions are subject to pressures that are often shattering. Changes in the economy mean that most families feel that they need the wages of two adult workers. At the same time, families must often care for the young, elderly, and ill, with little help from the larger community. Although these problems are shared by all forms of families, they are further exacerbated in families whose legitimacy is called into question. Given these pressures and responsibilities, it would seem that it is in society's interest to improve conditions to enable families to function as best they can, free from discrimination.')

[69] *Canada v Mossop* n 48 above, para 132.

[70] ibid, para 156.

[71] J Millbank, 'The Role of Functional Family in Same-Sex Family Recognition Trends' (2008) 20 *Child & Family Law Quarterly* 155.

[72] *Canada v Mossop* n 48 above, para136.

[73] ibid.

Commentators have argued that functionalists are only establishing a different model of family as the norm, and that they are requiring families to comply with it. This objection was for instance advanced in the United States in the early 1990s, when, analogously, some courts moved from a formal approach to a functional approach in the definition of 'family'.[74] In particular, it has been objected that 'as its name suggests, functionalism requires that all alternative families resemble traditionally recognized relationships in function, if not in precise form'.[75]

Functionalists could probably argue that the indeterminacy of the essential elements of a 'family' prevents this objection. Nonetheless, doubts persist regarding the re-emergence of an 'unexamined consensus' and of a preconceived model of family. In *Canada v Mossop*, for instance, Justice L'Heureux-Dubé cautioned that 'the requirement that a couple hold themselves out to the public as a couple may not, perhaps, be appropriate to same-sex couples, who still often find that public acknowledgement of their sexual orientation results in discriminatory treatment'.[76]

Justice L'Heureux-Dubé's extensive dissenting opinion aimed to reply to the objection. Her answer, however, in my opinion, did not seem to adequately address the core of the issues. She noted that the functional method cannot be considered arbitrary, and basically argued that its most important point of strength lay in its flexibility.

> Every method has its drawbacks. A functional approach offers distinct advantages over a more formalistic approach which systematically excludes all but a specific form of relationship. Further, it provides an objective yet flexible standard, which allows for a more accurate recognition of a greater number of family groupings which share characteristics which are thought to be essential in specific contexts. It does not mandate that certain variables must be present, nor dictate the weight of any given variable. In different contexts, different variables will have more, less or perhaps even no weight. However, the weight of any given variable can only be determined in the specific context. The functional approach has the additional attraction of being a well-rounded test which, by incorporating a greater number of factors, may assist a tribunal in making determinations as to whether or not a family exists for a given purpose. This approach provides guidance to tribunals, yet retains a strong element of flexibility. As society's understanding of family relationships continues to develop and evolve, this approach will allow such a definition to remain more readily adaptable to the realities of families in specific contexts. Although there are other approaches, the choice made by the Tribunal was certainly not unreasonable.[77]

Therefore, whereas a formalistic approach is proved inadequate to satisfy the needs of 'real life', the functional approach can also be criticised for being a case-by-case approach. The lack of precise standards gives courts a great deal of discretion to determine whether a couple falls within the definition of family. At the same time, the

[74] See eg *Braschi v Stahl Associates*, 74 NY 2d 201 (1989).

[75] 'Note: Looking for a Family Resemblance: the Limits of the Functional approach to the Legal Definition of Family' (1991) 4 *Harvard Law Review* 1640, 1653 (holding also at 1654 that 'Because functionalism gives judges no specific guidance on the importance to be given to various characteristics of relationships, it does not ensure that courts will confer legal family status on nontraditional relationships unless they resemble traditional families in every detail').

[76] *Canada v Mossop* n 48 above, para 138.

[77] ibid, para 139.

functional approach denies couples any certainty about their legal status.[78] Justice L'Heureux-Dubé, in particular, admitted that 'the complexity of the term [family status] militates against [the] conclusion' that Mr Mossop and his partner 'or any other couple, would come within "family status" for all purposes or in all contexts'.[79]

These remarks raise the objection whether, by advancing ad hoc solutions, the functional approach is replacing the heteronormative idea of family embedded in the constitutional clauses and statute law with a different ideology of family, based on judges' personal perspective.

In the following pages of this chapter I aim at analysing how the ECtHR and other domestic (supreme) courts departed from a formalistic definition of family and how they addressed the difficulties involved in the adoption of a different interpretation of the 'family'. However, before analysing the developments at Council of Europe's level, a premise on the distinction between private life and family life in early ECtHR cases (and its consequences) is needed.

III. 'PRIVATE LIFE' v 'FAMILY LIFE' IN THE EUROPEAN COURT OF HUMAN RIGHTS' EARLY CASES

As P Johnson emphasises, the systematic failure of the European Court to consider a wide range of issues relating to same-sex relationships under family life in its early case law 'has not been accidental'.[80] In his opinion, it is the consequence of the adoption of a heteronormative and ideological notion of family interpreted in connection with marriage and the opposite-sex couple. In *Mata Estevez v Spain*,[81] for instance, the European Court addressed the legitimacy of the refusal to award a survivor's pension to a partner in a same-sex relationship. The ECtHR upheld the provision under the privacy limb of Article 8, noting that 'the Spanish legislation relating to eligibility for survivors' allowances does have a legitimate aim, which is the protection of the family based on marriage bonds'.[82]

At the same time, from an interpretative point of view, the ECtHR's reliance on the right of privacy under Article 8 was 'the direct result of the Court's deliberate

[78] See Note, 'Looking for a Family Resemblance' n 75 above, 1653.

[79] *Canada v Mossop* n 48 above, para 141.

[80] P Johnson, *Homosexuality and the European Court of Human Rights* (Abingdon, Routledge, 2013) 113.

[81] *Mata Estevez v Spain* ECHR 2001-VI.

[82] ibid, 5. A similar argument was reiterated in *Manenc v France* App no 66686/09 (ECtHR, 21 September 2010). Furthermore, in *EB v France* App no 43546/02 (ECtHR, 22 January 2008) the applicant, a woman in a stable relationship with another woman, alleged that she suffered discrimination based on sexual orientation by being denied a single parent adoption. She maintained that the denial was based on her 'lifestyle', in particular on her sexual orientation. She did not claim 'a right to adopt', which did not exist, nevertheless she argued that she had suffered a violation of Art 14 (Prohibition of discrimination) of the European Convention in conjunction with Art 8, both with regard to 'private life'—since it concerned the creation of a new relationship with another individual—and 'family life', since she was denied the opportunity of a family life. The European Court of Human Rights concluded that the applicant suffered a violation of her right to private life, but did not address her claim concerning the violation of her right to family life. The case will be analysed below, p 185 ff.

reading of Article 8 to separate the rights associated with "private" and "family" life'.[83] As Johnson argues, 'this approach has allowed [the Court] to challenge the view that the phrase "private and family life" establishes a right to a sphere of existence that is defined by familial relationship'.[84] Therefore, distinguishing the notion of 'family life' from the concept of 'private life', in its early cases the European Court succeeded in keeping the idea of family (and its heteronormative premises) separate from the sphere of personal autonomy. This is quite evident if we consider that after *Dudgeon v UK*,[85] the European Court endorsed the idea that

> it [would] be too restrictive to limit the notion of 'private life' to an 'inner circle' in which the individual may live his own personal life as he chooses and to exclude therefrom entirely the outside world not encompassed within that circle. Respect of private life must also comprise to a certain degree the right to establish and develop relationships with other human beings.[86]

In other words, although the European Court described 'a zone of interaction between a person and others, which even in a public context, may fall within the scope of "private life"',[87] in its early cases it included same-sex relationships in such a wide notion of privacy, reserving instead the protection of family bonds to the traditional, married and opposite-sex couple. Such an approach can be traced back to the previous Commission's case law that analogously endorsed an interpretation of family 'in strictly heterosexual terms'.[88]

As clarified in Chapter 2, no family issue came into consideration in *Dudgeon*.[89] Nonetheless, the ECtHR apparently rejected Judge Walsh's view, suggesting that sexual privacy is protected only within marriage. In particular in his partially dissenting opinion, he wrote:

> Paragraph 1 of Article 8 (art. 8-1) provides that 'everyone has the right to respect for his private and family life, his home and his correspondence'. There is no suggestion that any point relating to family life arises in this case. Therefore the complaint is in reality one to a claim of right to indulge in any homosexual activities in the course of his private life and, presumably, in private.[90]

At the same time Judge Walsh clarified that

> Outside marriage there is no such compelling interest of privacy which by its nature ought to prevail in respect of such activities. It is to be noted that Article 8 (1) of the Convention speaks of 'private and family life'. If the *ejusdem generis* rule is to be applied, then the provision should be interpreted as relating to private life in that context as, for example, the

[83] Johnson *Homosexuality and the European Court of Human Rights* n 80 above, 113.
[84] ibid.
[85] *Dudgeon v UK* n 1 above.
[86] *Niemietz v Germany* (1992) Series A no 251-B, (1992) ECHR 80 para 29.
[87] Schabas, *The European Convention on Human Rights* n 5 above, 370. See also *ADT v United Kingdom* ECHR 2000-IX,(2000) ECHR 402.
[88] Johnson, *Homosexuality and the European Court of Human Rights* n 80 above, 114 (mentioning eg a separate opinion annexed in the Commission's report in *X v United Kingdom* (1981) ECHR 6), but see also R Wintemute, *Sexual Orientation and Human Rights: The United States Constitution, the European Convention, and the Canadian Charter* (Oxford, Clarendon Press, 1995) 110 ff.
[89] See above, p 28 ff.
[90] *Dudgeon v UK* n 1 above, para 7 (Judge Walsh, partially dissenting).

> right to raise one's children according to one's own philosophical and religious tenets and generally to pursue without interference the activities which are akin to those pursued in the privacy of family life and as such are in the course of ordinary human and fundamental rights. No such claim can be made for homosexual practices.[91]

In *Karner v Austria*[92] the ECtHR held that the narrow interpretation of the Austrian legislation concerning residential tenancy was in violation of Article 14 (Prohibition of discrimination) in conjunction with Article 8, because it did not enable a lease to pass to a same-sex partner of the deceased, such as to a 'life companion' in an opposite-sex relationship. Although the case concluded in favour of same-sex couples, the ECtHR left open the issue of interpretation of privacy and family life under Article 8, focusing only on the concept of 'home'. The ECtHR reiterated the idea that the 'protection of family in the traditional sense' can be considered 'in principle a weighty and legitimate reason which might justify a difference in treatment';[93] nonetheless, it should also be noted that it emphasised that

> this aim [protection of traditional family] ... is rather abstract and a broad variety of concrete measures may be used to implement it. In cases in which the margin of appreciation afforded to member states is narrow, as [is] the position where there is a difference in treatment based on sex or sexual orientation ... it must also be shown that it was necessary to exclude persons living in a homosexual relationship from the scope of application of section 14 of the Rent Act in order to achieve that aim.[94]

This argument was strengthened in *Kozak v Poland*,[95] where the ECtHR rejected the Government's argument that a differential treatment between same-sex and different-sex couples in the succession to the deceased partner's tenancy was justifiable under the ECHR as a measure designed to protect the traditional family.

Karner and *Kozak* dealt with long-term same-sex relationships not formalised in a civil union or in any other legally recognised bond. Although the ECtHR considered them equivalent to an opposite-sex de facto relationship, the affection and intimacy and long-term commitment between the partners were not considered sufficient for their explicit inclusion within the notion of 'family'. Nonetheless, it should be noted that in *Kozak* the ECtHR emphasised that

> given that the Convention is a living instrument, to be interpreted in the light of present-day conditions ... the State, in its choice of means designed to protect the family and secure, as required by Article 8, respect for family life must necessarily take into account developments in society and changes in the perception of social, civil-status and relational issues, including the fact that there is not just one way or one choice in the sphere of leading and living one's family or private life.[96]

[91] *Dudgeon v UK* n 1 above, paras 24–25 (Judge Walsh, partially dissenting).

[92] *Karner v Austria* (2004) 38 EHRR 24. Cp *Mata Estevez v Spain* (dec) ECHR 2001-VI.

[93] *Karner v Austria* n 92 above, para 40.

[94] ibid, para 41. For a reading in positive terms of this paragraph of the ECtHR's ruling, R Wintemute, 'From "Sex Rights" to "Love Rights": Partnership Rights as Human Rights', in N Bamforth (ed), *Sex Rights. The Oxford Amnesty Lectures 2002* (Oxford, Oxford University Press, 2005) 186, 195. A more critical interpretation of the case, as 'avoiding the issue of family life', has been expressed by Johnson, *Homosexuality and the European Court of Human Rights* n 80 above, 117.

[95] *Kozak v Poland* [2010] ECHR 280.

[96] ibid, para 98.

Wintemute has offered a persuasive explanation of the ECtHR's choice to focus in its early cases, on 'sex rights' (ie on discrimination against LGBT individuals because of their actual or presumed same-sex sexual activity, or their undergoing gender reassignment) and to exclude 'the love rights' of same-sex partners (ie legal recognition and equal treatment of relationships between LGBT individuals and their partners).[97] He wrote that the progression from the recognition of the rights falling in the first stage to those falling in the second

> requires society to acknowledge that there is more to the lives of LGBT individuals than a search for sexual pleasure, or a need to change their physical appearance and dress. Rather, they have the same human capacity as heterosexual and non-transsexual individuals to fall in love with another person, to establish a long-term emotional and physical relationship with them and potentially to want to raise children with them. When they choose to do so, they will often want the same opportunities as heterosexual individuals to be treated as a couple, as 'spouses', as 'partners', as 'parents', as a 'family'.[98]

The choice of the ECtHR to focus, in its early cases, on the privacy limb of Article 8 ECHR had several consequences. In the first place, as illustrated in Chapter 2, the 'logic of the closet' hid the gays and lesbians as couples, depriving them of their social visibility, pushing the social dimension of their relationships into the background.[99] At the same time, same-sex couples were not recognised as holders of 'collective rights' or 'group rights' or 'associative rights'.

It is interesting to note that a similar approach can be traced in the United States Supreme Court's early jurisprudence on privacy and self-determination concerning sex and contraception. Although the American cases took into consideration different-sex relationships, the Supreme Court's reliance on the right of privacy similarly cast a shadow on the *couple* as holder of constitutional rights.

In 1967, in *Griswold v Connecticut*,[100] for instance, the Supreme Court held a statute which forbade the use of contraceptives (and made their use a criminal offence) to be unconstitutional. The majority declined to base the opinion of the Court on the substantive due process doctrine and argued that the Bill of Rights clauses protected individuals' privacy interest. They recognised 'a penumbra of privacy', or zone where privacy is protected from governmental intrusion.[101] According to the Supreme Court, the 'penumbra of privacy' included the right of married couples to use contraceptives.

Further developments since *Griswold* extended the right to privacy even to unmarried persons. In *Eisenstadt v Baird*[102] (1972) the Supreme Court invalidated a statute that permitted the distribution of contraceptives only to married couples and by registered pharmacists and physicians. According to the Supreme Court's majority, the statute discriminated against unmarried couples, since the constitutionally protected

97 Wintemute, 'From "Sex Rights" to "Love Rights"', n 94 above, 191 ff.
98 ibid, 191.
99 See above, p 28 ff.
100 *Griswold v Connecticut* 381 US 479 (1965).
101 ibid, 461 ff.
102 *Eisenstadt v Baird* 405 US 438 (1972).

right of privacy inhered in the individual, not the marital couple. Writing for the Supreme Court, Justice Brennan wrote:

> It is true that ... the right of privacy in question inhered in the marital relationship. Yet the marital couple is not an independent entity with a mind and heart of its own, but an association of two individuals each with a separate intellectual and emotional makeup. If the right of privacy means anything, it is the right of the *individual*, married or single, to be free from unwarranted governmental intrusion into matters so fundamentally affecting a person as the decision whether to bear or beget a child.[103]

As M Nussbaum argued, although in the United States there is a long tradition of recognising a set of liberty interests in the area of intimate association, the rights pertaining to family and marriage were 'understood to be decisional rights of the individuals'[104] until recent times.[105]

Finally, arguments on privacy and self-determination hide the intimate mutual love and affection that can bind two individuals of the same sex as well as an opposite-sex couple. As will be clarified in more details in the following pages, mutual respect, affection and long-term commitment are conceived as the essential elements of *family* and as typical features of the relationship of husband and wife. The exclusion of same-sex partnerships from the protection that the ECtHR assigned to a family was therefore a consequence of the concealment of those elements that might entitle an individual to be, in the common judgement of society, the member of a 'family'.[106]

IV. *SCHALK AND KOPF v AUSTRIA* AND RECOGNITION OF THE SAME-SEX COUPLE AS 'FAMILY'

The 2010 European Court of Human Rights' decision in *Schalk and Kopf v Austria*[107] marked a radical change of perspective from the early cases centred on the right of privacy.

The applicants, a same-sex couple, alleged that they were discriminated against on the basis of their sexual orientation under Article 14 taken in conjunction with Article 8 ECHR since, before the entry into force of the Registered Partnership Act

[103] ibid, 453.

[104] M Nussbaum, *From Disgust to Humanity. Sexual Orientation and Constitutional Law* (Oxford, Oxford University Press, 2009) 74.

[105] For the recognition of a right to intimate association as a right of the same-sex *couple*, see eg *Obergefell v Hodges* 576 US (2015), 14 (opinion of the Court). See below, p 142 ff.

[106] Nonetheless, in early 2000 a change of perspective on the recognition of same-sex couples as families gained momentum at international level. The United Nations Committee of Human Rights—which, as mentioned in Chapter 2, in its 1994 ruling in *Toonen v Australia*, Communication No 488/1992, UN Doc CCPR/C/50/D/488/1992 (1994) had already held that the Tasmanian laws banning all sexual activity between men were in breach of the right of privacy under Art 17, para 1 of the International Covenant on Civil and Political Rights of 1966 (ICCPR)—concluded in *Edward Young v Australia*, Communication No 941/2000, UN Doc CCPR/C/78/D/941/2000 (2003), that Australia had violated Art 26 of the Covenant for having denied to a partner in a same-sex relationship a survivor pension benefit on the ground that he did not meet the definition of dependant, whereas this right was granted to both unmarried and married different-sex partners.

[107] *Schalk and Kopf v Austria* ECHR 2010-I, (2010) ECHR 1996. See also for a similar argument, *PB and JS v Austria* App no 18984/02 (ECtHR, 22 July 2010).

in Austria,[108] they were denied the right to marry or to have their relationship recognised by law.[109]

Although, pending the trial, the Registered Partnership Act provided same-sex registered partners with the status of spouses in various fields of the law,[110] the European Court concluded that the case required examination on the merits. It noted that 'a rapid evolution of social attitudes towards same-sex couples had taken place in many member States'[111] of the Council of Europe that had introduced new legislation in order to give legal recognition to same-sex relationships.

Against this background the ECtHR emphasised that

> it is artificial to maintain the view that, in contrast to a different-sex couple, a same-sex couple cannot enjoy 'family life' for the purposes of Article 8. Consequently the relationship of the applicants, a cohabiting same-sex couple living in a stable *de facto* partnership, fell within the notion of 'family life', just as the relationship of a different-sex couple in the same situation would.[112]

The ECtHR had affirmed in its previous cases about opposite-sex relationships that 'the protection of "family life" presupposes the existence of a family'.[113] This raises the issue about what essential elements of family same-sex and opposite-sex families have in common. In *Schalk and Kopf* the Court adopted a quite narrow definition of family relating to the same-sex couple that, as Bamforth has emphasised, had the potential to give rise to ambiguities. He has stated these in clear terms:

> The 'family life' finding in *Schalk* related simply to a long-standing same-sex couple living together and sharing resources. No real guidance was offered as to the characteristics which a couple must display in order to count as a 'family' rather than merely a 'private' relationship. For example, would only very stable, long-standing couples count? What might be said about the not unusual situation in which a couple enjoys a stable and long-standing relation but the partners do not cohabit?[114]

At the same time, the European Court's reliance only on cohabitation and stability did not pay adequate attention to the bond of love and affection between the partners. Although *Schalk and Kopf* was a case concerning the recognition of mutual

[108] The Registered Partnership Act (*Eingetragene Partnerschaft-Gesetz*), Federal Law Gazette (*Bundesgesetzblatt*) vol I, no 135/2009, entered into force on 1 January 2010.

[109] At the same time, the couple alleged that the authorities' refusal to allow them to contract marriage amounted to a violation of Art 12 (right to marriage). Issues concerning the recognition of the right to marry will be analysed in the following chapter.

[110] The registered partnership was open only to same-sex couples. Partners were accorded the same status as married couples in inheritance law, labour, social and social insurance law, fiscal law, the law on administrative procedure, the law on data protection and public service, passport and registration issues, as well as the law on foreigners. The main differences between the married opposite-sex couple and the same-sex civil partnership concerned parental rights (because, unlike married couples, registered partners were not allowed to adopt a child, nor was stepchild adoption permitted) and access to artificial procreation.

[111] *Schalk and Kopf v Austria* n 107 above, para 93.

[112] ibid, para 94.

[113] Schabas, *The European Convention on Human Rights* n 5 above, p 389, citing *Marckx v Belgium* (1979) ECHR 2 para 31.

[114] N Bamforth, 'Families but not (yet) marriages? Same-sex partners and the developing European Convention "margin of appreciation"' (2011) 23 *Children & Family Law Quarterly* 128, 137.

commitment—besides the enjoyment of economic right[115]—between same-sex partners, the ECtHR did not take into consideration the sentimental elements of a union that could dispel some of the doubts about its definition.

Compared to the Supreme Court of Canada's approach in *Canada v Mossop*, discussed above, it is possible to note that although sometimes the ECtHR's cases oscillate between the adoption of formal and informal factors in the definition of family,[116] in *Schalk and Kopf* the Court seemed to prefer realism and to look at the existence of de facto close family ties between same-sex partners.[117]

The adoption of a 'reality test' was certainly favoured by the fact that the text of Article 8 of the European Convention refers to family *life* and not to family *relationship*. Whereas the Supreme Court of Canada was required to interpret the notion of 'family status', the ECtHR was able to assess the reality of same-sex couples without taking into consideration issues concerning the nature of bond between the partners and its legal effects.

Although its realistic approach is different from either a formalistic definition of family or from a functional approach, the ECtHR still refers to a notion of family modelled on the opposite-sex couple. The conclusion that same-sex couples are family as far as they are living in stable de facto partnership is in fact still based on a comparison with the 'traditional' couple as the starting point for a 'family'.[118]

V. FROM THE 'PERCEPTION OF THE ORDINARY MAN' TO A FUNCTIONAL DEFINITION OF 'FAMILY': THE *FITZPATRICK* CASE

In the common law tradition where—as clarified—'there is no statutory definition of family and there is really no common law definition either',[119] the idea of an implicit and presumed notion of family has been the starting point of judicial reasoning when courts have been called upon to determine whether the stable same-sex relationship can be subsumed under the concept of 'family'.

In English law, the importance of 'common sense' and the perception of the 'ordinary man' is illustrated by the 1985 decision in *Harrogate Borough Council v Simpson*.[120] The Court of Appeal (of England and Wales) was asked to decide whether a woman who had lived with the deceased secure tenant in a lesbian relationship for some years qualified for succession to the tenancy, for the purposes of the Housing Act 1980.[121] Section 50(3) of the Act clarified that 'A person is a member of another's family [within the meaning of this chapter] if he is his spouse, parent, grandparent, child, grandchild, brother, sister, uncle, aunt, nephew or niece... or if they live together as husband and wife'. Ms Simpson argued that her lesbian

[115] See *Schalk and Kopf v Austria* n 107 above, paras 11 and 12.

[116] See *Marckx v Belgium* n 113 above, but cp *van den Heijden v Netherlands* App no 42857/05 (ECtHR, 3 April 2012).

[117] Schabas, *The European Convention on Human Rights* n 5 above, 389.

[118] For a similar approach see *PB and JS v Austria* App no 18984/02 (ECtHR, 22 July 2010).

[119] Diduck and F Canagas, *Family Law, Gender and the State* n 28 above, 21.

[120] *Harrogate Borough Council v Simpson* [1985] 17 HLR 205.

[121] Housing Act 1980 c. 51.

relationship with the deceased tenant was similar to living as husband and wife, because they shared a household in a permanent, monogamous, faithful, sexual and loving relationship.[122]

The Court dismissed the appeal, arguing that she could be not considered a family member according to a literal interpretation of the section 50(3) of Act and on the basis of the common perception of the concept of 'spouse'. In particular, Watkins LJ wrote:

> [Counsel for the plaintiffs] contends that, if Parliament had wished homosexual relationships to be brought into the realm of the lawfully recognised state of a living together of man and wife for the purpose of the relevant legislation, it would plainly have so stated in that legislation and it has not done so. I am bound to say that I entirely agree with that. I am also firmly of the view that it would be surprising in the extreme to learn that public opinion is such today that it would recognise a homosexual union as being akin to a state of living as husband and wife. The ordinary man and woman ... would in my opinion not think even remotely of there being a true resemblance between those two very different states of affairs.[123]

Ewbank J agreed that same-sex relationship did not fall with the traditional notion of a 'family', and he stressed that heterosexuality was an essential feature of the family. 'The essential characteristic of living together as husband and wife, in my judgment, is that there should be a man and a woman and that they should be living together in the same household.'[124]

The common perception of 'family' comes into consideration again in the seminal case of *Fitzpatrick v Sterling Association Ltd.*[125] The case—concerning private sector tenancies[126]—arose when a tenant, a man living in a stable same-sex relationship, applied to take over the tenancy after the death of his partner who was the 'original tenant'. He claimed that the their 'longstanding, close, loving and faithful, monogamous' relationship made him 'a spouse' of the deceased under the Rent Act 1997[127] because he had been living with the tenant 'like husband and wife'.[128]

[122] See S Harris-Short and J Miles, *Family Law: Text, Cases and Materials* (Oxford, Oxford University Press, 2011) 38.

[123] *Harrogate Borough Council v Simpson* n 120 above, 210.

[124] ibid. Subsequently, Ms Simpson applied to the European Commission of Human Rights arguing that the denial of her right to succeed to the tenancy violated her rights under Arts 8 and 14 of the ECHR. However, her case was declared inadmissible by the Commission (*Simpson v United Kingdom* App no 11716/85 (ECommHR, 1986)) that did not recognise that Simpson had a 'family life' with the deceased partner. The Commission therefore concluded that 'the difference in treatment between the applicant and somebody in the same position whose partner had been of the opposite sex can be objectively and reasonably justified'.

[125] *Fitzpatrick v Sterling Association Ltd* [2001] 1 AC 27.

[126] The main difference with *Horrowgate Borough Council v Simpson* n 120 above lays in the fact that the Rent Act 1977, although amended on two occasions, left the notion of 'family' undefined.

[127] Rent Act 1977, as amended by the Housing Act 1988, s 39(2), Sch 1, paras 2(2), 3(1), Sch 4, Pt I, paras 2, 3.

[128] Sch 1, para 2(2) to the Rent Act 1977 as amended by the Housing Act 1988: 'A person who was living with the original tenant as his or her wife or husband shall be treated as the spouse of the original tenant'.

Alternatively, the appellant alleged that he was 'a member of the original tenant's family' under the Rent Act 1977.[129]

A unanimous House of Lords dismissed Mr Fitzpatrick's appeal on the ground concerning his qualification as a 'spouse' under the Rent Act 1977. As Lord Slynn emphasised in his opinion, 'although the Rent Act was amended in 1988 in order to include as a "spouse" a person living with the original tenant "as his or her wife or husband", this 'prima facie mean[t] a man and a woman'. Nonetheless, the majority concluded that the appellant was entitled to take over the contract as a member of the tenant's family.

As in *Canada v Mossop*, the issue is a matter of interpretation. However, whereas in *Mossop* the interpretative issue concerned the words 'family status', in *Fitzpatrick* it dealt with the word 'family'. This made the issue before the House of Lords easier in some respects because, as Lord Clyde argued, the definition of 'family status' can be narrower than the notion of 'family'.[130] At the same time, sociological arguments can be more easily advanced when the evolution of 'family' comes into consideration.

However, as Lord Slynn and Lord Nicholls pointed out, 'family is not a term of art'.[131] It is 'a word that ... does not have a readily recognisable meaning'[132] because the meaning of 'family' 'depends upon the context in which it is being used'[133] and the Parliament 'left it to the courts to determine, in any given case, whether a particular individual falls within the description'.[134]

For this reason, they argued, the 'ordinary meaning test' gives uncertain guidance. At the same time, as Lord Clyde wrote, even the formalistic approach that identifies the family with the legal bond should be rejected:

> it is now far from being a significant criterion for the existence of a family unit. While it remains as a particular formalisation of the relationship between heterosexual couples, family units may now be recognised to exist both where the principal members are in a heterosexual relationship and where they are in a homosexual or lesbian relationship.[135]

This reasoning leads to the crucial issues at stake: what are the essential characteristics of a 'family' and does the same-sex stable relationship satisfy them? Lord Clyde framed the issue in clear terms:

> The problem in the present case is to determine what, short of blood or marriage, may evidence the common bond in a partnership of two adult persons which may entitle the one to be in the common judgment of society a member of the other's family.[136]

[129] Sch 1, para 3(1) to the Rent 1977 Act: 'Where paragraph 2 above does not apply, but a person who was a member of the original tenant's family was residing with him in the dwelling-house at the time of and for the period of two years immediately before his death then, after his death, that person or if there is more than one such person such one of them as may be decided by agreement, or in default of agreement by the county court, shall be entitled to an assured tenancy of the dwelling-house by succession'.

[130] *Fitzpatrick v Sterling Association Ltd* n 125 above, 53 (Lord Clyde). *Cf*, for a different interpretation, Lord Hobhouse's remarks at 73.

[131] *Fitzpatrick v Sterling Association Ltd* n 125 above, 35 (Lord Slynn) and 41 (Lord Nicholls).

[132] ibid.

[133] ibid, 45 (Lord Nicholls).

[134] ibid, 41 (Lord Nicholls).

[135] ibid, 52 (Lord Clyde).

[136] ibid, 51. *Cf* Lord Slynn's opinion who asks this question looking instead at what was Parliament's purpose (at 38).

The House of Lords' arguments suggested that a functional approach in the identification of family should be preferred. Looking at Parliament's purpose, Lord Slynn emphasised that, when the first tenancy succession provision was enacted in section 12(1)(g) of the Increase of Rent and Mortgage Interest (Restrictions) Act 1920, 'the hallmarks of the relationship were essentially that there should be a degree of mutual interdependence, of the sharing of lives, of caring and love, of commitment and support'.[137]

Lord Nicholls noted instead that 'the legislation [sought] to provide a measure of protection for members of a family who are sharing their lives together as a single family in one home'.[138] This implied that neither blood relation nor procreation were necessary to qualify a relationship as a family. Therefore, he argued,

> A man and woman living together in a stable and permanent sexual relationship are capable of being members of a family for this purpose. Once this is accepted, there can be no rational or other basis on which the like conclusion can be withheld from a similarly stable and permanent sexual relationship between two men or between two women. Where a relationship of this character exists, it cannot make sense to say that, although a heterosexual partnership can give rise to membership of a family for Rent Act purposes, a homosexual partnership cannot. Where sexual partners are involved, whether heterosexual or homosexual, there is scope for the intimate mutual love and affection and long-term commitment that typically characterise the relationship of husband and wife. This love and affection and commitment can exist in same sex relationships as in heterosexual relationships. In sexual terms a homosexual relationship is different from a heterosexual relationship, but I am unable to see that the difference is material for present purposes. As already emphasised, the concept underlying membership of a family for present purposes is the sharing of lives together in a single family unit living in one house.[139]

Finally Lord Clyde paid more attention to functional elements of family than to features such as mutual affection and household. He argued:

> It seems to me that essentially the bond must be one of love and affection, not of a casual or transitory nature, but in a relationship which is permanent or at least intended to be so. As a result of that personal attachment to each other, other characteristics will follow, such as a readiness to support each other emotionally and financially, to care for and look after the other in times of need, and to provide a companionship in which mutual interests and activities can be shared and enjoyed together. It would be difficult to establish such a bond unless the couple were living together in the same house. It would also be difficult to establish it without an active sexual relationship between them or at least the potentiality of such a relationship. If they have or are caring for children whom they regard as their own they would make the family designation more immediately obvious, but the existence of children is not a necessary element. Each case will require to depend eventually upon its own facts.[140]

In sum, the Lords shared the idea that the common sense of family 'is now about what it does, rather than what it is'.[141] However, as Donovan and Diduck have

[137] ibid, 38 (Lord Slynn).
[138] ibid, 41 (Lord Nicholls).
[139] ibid, 44.
[140] ibid, 51 (Lord Clyde).
[141] Diduck and Canagas, Family Law, Gender and the State n 28 above, 26.

clarified, when compared to 'traditional' notion of 'family', it is quite clear that their definitions of family 'remain[ed] within an ideal in which conjugality and the privatisation of care and dependency are central. In this way, law's model is still the private, heterosexual, traditional family'.[142]

Nonetheless, it should be noted that the House of Lords did not address this issue. At the same time it did not discuss the other objection concerning the discretional nature of the newly suggested ideology of family lying behind its conclusions. The Lords basically argued that the concept of family was not changed, but that it 'is not fixed once and for all the time'.[143] In other words, as Lord Slynn emphasised, 'it is not the meaning [of family] which has changed but that those who are capable of falling within the words have changed'.[144]

In this way the House of Lords' majority succeeded in preventing further critical remarks, that the case rationale was departing from the Parliament's intention when the Act was enacted.[145] Accordingly, the case conclusion appeared like the solution to a matter of fact: Lord Nicholls for instance stressed that when Parliament amended the Rent Act in the Housing Act 1988, extending the remit of surviving tenants, 'was not expressing a view, either way, on the morality of such relationships'.[146] Lord Clyde added that the solution was in accord with the purpose of legislation but at the same time, in a short passage summarising the basic issue that came into consideration in the case, he referred to the definition of family 'in the common judgement of society'.[147] Therefore, in his opinion, the definition of family was still that of ordinary people, not the Court's.

VI. SAME-SEX COUPLES AS 'SPOUSES' IN *GHAIDAN v GODIN-MENDOZA*

Although in *Fitzpatrick* the House of Lords ruled in favour of the stable same-sex couple, concluding that it fell within the definition of 'family', it was still reluctant to reject the idea that there should be a biological sex difference between two partners 'living together as husband and wife'.

Nonetheless, once the legislation[148] has gone beyond marriage in order to extend its benefits even to marriage-like unmarried relationships, the issue of the legitimacy of the exclusion of stable same-sex couples becomes inevitable. When the rights descending from marriage are granted even to the cohabiting and stable couple regardless of the formal bond of marriage, it becomes clear that the legislative intention is to encourage a kind of relationship for its specific features and functions.

[142] ibid, but *cf* L Glennon, '*Fitzpatrick v Sterling Housing Association Ltd:* An Endorsement of the Functional Family?' (2000) *International Journal of Law, Policy and the Family* 226, 237 (who notes how 'this involved a limited equalization').

[143] *Fitzpatrick v Sterling Association Ltd* n 125 above, 37 (Lord Slynn, citing *Gammans v Ekins* [1950] 2 KB 328).

[144] ibid, 39.

[145] ibid, 46 (Lord Nicholls).

[146] ibid.

[147] ibid, 51 (Lord Clyde).

[148] Rent Act 1977 Sch 1, s 2(2).

The issue concerning the interpretation of the word 'spouse' is therefore only apparently about marriage: the question is whether, for the purposes of law, gender or biological sex have to be considered a typical feature of the stable relationship between unmarried partners.

This question was addressed by the House of Lords in another seminal case, *Ghaidan v Godin-Mendoza*[149] in 2004. Although the essential issue was different, it bore many analogies to the cases discussed in the previous pages.

The claim was almost identical to that heard by the House of Lords in *Fitzpatrick*. The defendant lived in a stable, permanent same-sex relationship for 30 years with his partner who was the protected tenant. On his partner's death, in 2001, the defendant claimed to be entitled to succeed to the tenancy of the flat as the surviving spouse of the original tenant within paragraph 2 of Schedule 1 to the Rent Act 1977. As the Human Rights Act 1998 had become operative, Mr Godin-Mendoza alleged that, pursuant to section 3, it was possible to give effect to Schedule 1, paragraph 2(2) of the Rent Act 1977 in a way that was compatible with the ECHR and the ECtHR's case law. Otherwise, the possibility for the survivor in a same-sex couple to succeed, in competition with other members of the original tenant's 'family', only to the less advantageous assured tenancy under paragraph 3, amounted to a discrimination on the basis of sexual orientation, contrary to Article 14 ECHR, in conjunction with Article 8. The ECtHR, in *Salgueiro v Portugal*[150] had in fact affirmed for the first time that 'sexual discrimination' fell within Article 14 ECHR.

In possession proceedings, the judge concluded that Mr Godin-Mendoza was entitled to an assured tenancy of the flat by succession as a member of the original tenant's family within paragraph 3(1) of that Schedule. The Court of Appeal reversed concluding that since Parliament had 'swallowed the camel of including unmarried [opposite-sex] partners within the protection given to married couples, it is not for this Court to strain at the gnat of including such partners who are of the same sex as each other'.[151] Accordingly, it argued that the words 'as his or her wife or husband' in Schedule 1 had to be interpreted as meaning 'as if they were his or her wife or husband', allowing the appellant to succeed to a statutory tenancy.

On appeal, the House of Lords upheld the Court of Appeal's decision and concluded that Mr Godin-Mendoza had to be considered a 'spouse' for the purposes of the Rent Act 1977.

Baroness Hale's opinion captured the core of the issue: she stressed that 'everything which has been suggested to make a difference between the appellant and other surviving partners comes down to the fact that he was of the same sex as the deceased tenant. It is the decisive factor.'[152] Nonetheless, she denied that the roles of husband and wife were still defined by gender: she argued that they are 'interchangeable' and 'there is thus no difficulty in applying the term "marriage-like" to same sex relationships'.[153] Therefore the issue turned on the identification of the relevant

[149] *Ghaidan v Godin-Mendoza* [2004] 2 AC 557.
[150] *Salgueiro da Silva Mouta v Portugal* ECHR 1999-IX, [1999] ECHR 176.
[151] *Mendoza v Ghaidan*, [2003] HLR 35, para 35.
[152] *Ghaidan v Godin-Mendoza* [2004] 2 AC 557, 606.
[153] ibid, 609 (Baroness Hale).

factors of a 'marriage-like relationship' that, as Baroness Hale admitted, 'is not easy'. She suggested that 'what matters most is the essential quality of the relationship, its marriage-like intimacy, stability and social and financial interdependence'.[154]

If 'homosexual couples can have exactly the same sort of interdependent couple relationship as heterosexuals can', a different treatment in the enjoyment of tenancy rights will result in a illegitimate discrimination, based on sexual orientation. She also argued:

> Sexual 'orientation' defines the sort of person with whom one wishes to have sexual relations. It requires another person to express itself. Some people, whether heterosexual or homosexual, may be satisfied with casual or transient relationships. But most human beings eventually want more than that. They want love. And with love they often want not only the warmth but also the sense of belonging to one another which is the essence of being a couple. And many couples also come to want the stability and permanence which go with sharing a home and a life together, with or without the children who for many people go to make a family. In this, people of homosexual orientation are no different from people of heterosexual orientation.[155]

The implications of the House of Lords' conclusions in *Ghaidan* have been of great relevance. The case paved the way for further recognition of same-sex couples' rights in other fields of the law[156] and, as has been stated, it was 'arguably the strongest sign of the increasingly insignificant role of gender in marriage-like and parental relationships'[157] before the adoption of the Civil Partnership Act 2004[158] in the United Kingdom. At the same time, the opinions are very interesting even for their strong reliance on arguments concerning the recognition of equality and dignity of same-sex couples.

However, as far as the main subject of this chapter is concerned, it should be noted that the model is still the opposite-sex couple. The same-sex unmarried couple does not deserve protection per se, ie for its own features or because it is, in itself, the expression of the fundamental needs and rights of the individual, but inasmuch as it resembles the 'traditional couple'.[159] 'Homosexuals', Baroness Hale argued, 'cannot hold themselves out as legally married, but they can if they wish present themselves to the world as if they were married'.

[154] *Ghaidan v Godin-Mendoza* n 152 above, 607–08 (Baroness Hale).

[155] ibid, 606 (Baroness Hale).

[156] Eg Baroness Hale mentions the implications of *Ghaidan v Godin-Mendoza* on adoption. On the ramifications of the Court of Appeal's decision see E Hitchings, '*Mendoza v Ghaidan*: Two Steps Forward, One Step Back' (2003) 15 *Family Law Quarterly* 313, 322.

[157] E Thomlinson, 'Same-Sex Relationships: Going with the Grain or Judicial Vandalism?' 2004 63 *Cambridge Law Journal* 577, 579.

[158] Civil Partnership Act 2004.

[159] See also *Ghaidan v Godin-Mendoza* n 152 above, 607–08 ('Homosexual couples can have exactly the same sort of inter-dependent couple relationship as heterosexuals can. Sexual "orientation" defines the sort of person with whom one wishes to have sexual relations. It requires another person to express itself. Some people, whether heterosexual or homosexual, may be satisfied with casual or transient relationships. But most human beings eventually want more than that. They want love. And with love they often want not only the warmth but also the sense of belonging to one another which is the essence of being a couple. And many couples also come to want the stability and permanence which go with sharing a home and a life together, with or without the children who for many people go to make a family. In this, people of homosexual orientation are no different from people of heterosexual orientation.').

The other majority members shared a similar perspective: Lord Nicholls, for instance, after stressing that neither marriage nor parenthood are a precondition of security of tenure for the survivor,[160] argued that 'all that remains, as the essential feature [for a succession to tenancy under paragraph 2] is the cohabitation of the heterosexual couple'. Accordingly, he concluded that

> the reason underlying this social policy, whereby the survivor of a cohabiting heterosexual couple has particular protection, is equally applicable to the survivor of a homosexual couple. A homosexual couple, as much as a heterosexual couple, share each other's life and make their home together. They have an equivalent relationship.[161]

Although *Ghaidan* dealt with an issue which is different from the qualification of same-sex couples as 'families' (that is the main object of the present chapter), my purpose was to emphasise here that the identification of same-sex partners as 'spouses' meets in conclusion similar objections. Although the word 'spouse' is conceived as a generic term, independent from the presence of a formal bond of marriage, the old definition can be replaced by another one that is analogously ideological and modelled on the 'traditional heterosexual' couple.

VII. SOME FINAL REMARKS AND A FIRST CONCLUSION

A similar approach can also be traced in other constitutional cases addressing the issue of the qualification of gays and lesbians as 'spouses'. Although these cases are less rigorous than those illustrated above, because they blur the distinction between 'family' and 'spouses', they deserve some attention because they confirm the courts' propensity to use functional arguments in the definition of familiar relationships and to avoid the controversial issues surrounding the adoption of definitions still modelled on the 'traditional heterosexual' couple.

In 1999 the Constitutional Court of South Africa was asked to decide whether it was unconstitutional for immigration law to facilitate the immigration into South Africa of the spouses of permanent South African residents but not to afford the same benefits to gays and lesbians in stable same-sex life relationship with South African residents. The case, *National Coalition v Minister of Home Affairs*[162] concerned, in particular, the constitutionality[163] of

> section 25(2) of the Aliens Control Act, 1991[164] that enable[d] preferential treatment to be given to a foreign national applying for an immigration permit who [was] 'the spouse … of a person permanently and lawfully resident in the Republic', but not to a foreign national

[160] *Ghaidan v Godin-Mendoza* n 152 above, 567 (Lord Nicholls).

[161] ibid, 568, but see also 603–04 (Lord Rodger, arguing that 'the reason underlying this social policy, whereby the survivor of a cohabiting heterosexual couple has particular protection, is equally applicable to the survivor of a homosexual couple. A homosexual couple, as much as a heterosexual couple, share each other's life and make their home together. They have an equivalent relationship.').

[162] *National Coalition for Gay and Lesbian Equality v Minister for Home Affairs*, (CCT10/99) [1999] ZACC 17; 2000 (2) SA 1.

[163] Constitution of the Republic of South Africa Act, Act 108 of 1996, in particular s 9 (right to equality) and s 10 (right to dignity).

[164] Aliens Control Act, Act 96 of 1991.

> who, though similarly placed in all other respects, [was] in a same-sex life partnership with a person permanently and lawfully resident in the Republic.[165]

Writing for the Court, Justice Ackermann clarified that 'the starting point is to enquire what the nature of such family life is in the case of spouses'. Relying extensively on comparative law materials,[166] he defined marriage as a '*consortium omnis vitae*'[167] which 'creates a physical, moral and spiritual community of life' and concluded:

> Gays and lesbians in same-sex life partnerships are as capable as heterosexual spouses of expressing and sharing love in its manifold forms including affection, friendship, eros and charity. They are likewise as capable of forming intimate, permanent, committed, monogamous, loyal and enduring relationships; of furnishing emotional and spiritual support; and of providing physical care, financial support and assistance in running the common household. They are individually able to adopt children and in the case of lesbians to bear them. In short, they have the same ability to establish a *consortium omnis vitae.* Finally, and of particular importance for purposes of this case, they are capable of constituting a family, whether nuclear or extended, and of establishing, enjoying and benefiting from family life which is not distinguishable in any significant respect from that of heterosexual spouses.[168]

In 1994 the Supreme Court of Israel adopted an (apparently) different approach in a case (*El-Al Israel Airlines v Danielowitz*)[169] involving a flight attendant, in a stable relationship with another man, who was denied a free ticket for his spouse. Under the collective agreement, the free ticket was given 'to a companion recognized publicly as the employee's husband/wife'.

Writing for the majority, Justice Barak held that 'not giving the respondent a free ticket for his same-sex companion amounted to discrimination, since a distinction on the basis of the difference between a heterosexual and a homosexual relationship was unjustified in the context of employee benefits'. However, Justice Barak declared himself unwilling to enquire into the nature of the relationship and the similarities between the stable same-sex couple and the heterosexual one. He wrote:

> the question ... is not whether one relationship (a life of sharing and harmony between persons of opposite sexes) is different on any criteria from the other relationship (a life of sharing and harmony between persons of the same sex). As stated, I am prepared to assume that in various social contexts this difference does indeed exist. The question that we must ask is whether the difference in the relationship is relevant to the issue before us. The 'issue before us' is the social unit, the life of sharing and harmony that justify, in El-Al's opinion, giving a benefit to a (permanent) employee in the form of an aeroplane ticket which will enable him to take with him the person with whom he cohabits. In this respect, the difference between

[165] *National Coalition v Minister of Home Affairs* n 162 above, para 16.

[166] See in particular ibid, para 54.

[167] This definition, which is frequently mentioned in South African family law, traces back to the Roman tradition, in particular to the definition of marriage formulated by the jurist Modestinus who defined '*nuptiae*' as 'a union between a man and a woman, a partnership for life involving divine as well as human law' ('*nuptiae sunt coniuctio maris et feminae et consortium omnis vitae, divini et humani iuri communicatio*', Dig 23.2.1).

[168] *National Coalition v Minister of Home Affairs* n 162 above, para 53.

[169] *El-Al Israel Airlines v Danielowitz*, HCJ 721/94.

> a life of sharing between persons of different sexes and a life of sharing between persons of the same sex is clear and blatant discrimination.[170]

The rationale of the case is not completely clear because, in my opinion, the Court's conclusion rests however on a comparison between the two relationships and on the assumption that both have in common 'a life of sharing' in which gender is not determinative.[171] Nonetheless, the *El Al* case—like the South Africa Supreme Court's case mentioned above—reveals the Court's lack of attention to the issues involved in the qualification of the stable same-sex relationship as 'family' (or 'spouse').

These cases, although different from the other constitutional cases discussed in the beginning of this chapter, confirm the courts' propensity to qualify same-sex couples as 'family' only through assimilation with the opposite-sex couple. Such an approach, as emphasised, is receptive of a heteronormative idea of family still modelled on the opposite-sex couple and, at the same time, it does not recognise that the same-sex couple deserves constitutional protection for its own value.

The following chapter, on same-sex marriage, will show how the rejection of binary logic—based on the comparison between 'homosexuals' and 'heterosexuals'—will be achieved in constitutional law cases by giving due prominence to the dignity of same-sex couples.

VIII. A DIGRESSION ON A NARROW INTERPRETATION OF 'FAMILY'

The cases analysed in the previous pages addressed the claims of recognition of same-sex couples whose union was not formalised due to the absence of a regulation of same-sex civil partnerships at the relevant time. Courts were unanimous in concluding that changes in the structure of family might be in part a response to social changes, and that the definition of 'family' was capable of adapting to such changes. Accordingly, they felt it necessary to depart from the traditional and normative definition of 'family' (based on marriage and gender difference) in order to meet the demands for recognition of same-sex couples.

As the House of Lords wrote in *Fitzpatrick*,

> the concept of the family has undergone significant development during recent years, both in the United Kingdom and overseas. Whether that is a matter for concern or congratulation is of no relevance to the present case, but it is properly part of the judicial function to endeavour to reflect an understanding of such changes in the reality of social life.[172]

By describing the law's role 'as reflecting and assisting actual families' experiences and needs',[173] the courts mostly opted for a functional definition of 'family', looking, as clarified earlier, at what 'a family does'.

[170] ibid, para 16.

[171] Furthermore, Justice Kedmi, in his dissenting opinion, assimilated the concepts of 'family' and 'couple' (see eg para 3 where he emphasises that, for the purposes of the collective agreement, 'recognized companions are not a "married"' couple but they do constitute a "couple" and a "family"').

[172] *Fitzpatrick v Sterling Association Ltd* n 125 above, 51.

[173] Millbank, 'The Role of Functional Family' n 71 above, 156.

Against the prevailing trend, the Italian legal system has provided a more narrow interpretation of the concept of 'family' which in my opinion still survives, at least in part, after the enactment of law no 76 of 2016, regulating same-sex civil unions.

As mentioned at the beginning of this chapter, Article 29 of the Italian Constitution of 1948 describes 'family' as a 'natural institution founded on marriage' (§ 1) and also refers to a 'wife' and a 'husband' (§ 2) when it formulates the principle of equality between the spouses. During the debates over the adoption of the Constitution, the 'natural institution' formula emerged as a compromise between the Catholic political forces, which wanted the adoption of a definition of 'family', and the liberal and the left-wing parties, which instead advocated a 'neutral' recognition of family rights at constitutional level.[174] The 'natural institution' formula was finally chosen because it adhered to the concept of family as an already existing institution, which precedes the state and which the legislator can only partially regulate.

Shortly after Italy's Constitution came into force, this interpretation was expounded by a branch of legal scholarship that emphasised, for instance, the duration and the purpose of marriage. By contrast, other scholars endorsed the idea that the notion of family was not frozen, but was flexible, and that it was the duty of the state to guarantee and promote family taking into account social developments and the actual structure of family relationships.[175] Furthermore, as Bonini Baraldi has emphasised,[176] Article 2 of the Italian Constitution refers to the principle of 'social solidarity' and this implies—according to some commentators—that the obligation to provide a regulation of same-sex couples—recently reiterated by the ECtHR in *Oliari v Italy*[177]—should be read as a manifestation of solidarity.

Nonetheless, the dominant argument is that Article 29 of the Italian Constitution draws a sharp distinction between marriage and de facto families and this idea has been expounded by a part of Italian scholarship, even in order to mark a separation between the family—founded on 'heterosexual' marriage—and non-families. Whereas marriage and the family founded on marriage fall under Article 29 of the Constitution, 'unmarried cohabitation is considered by many as a way for the individual to realise his or her personality'.[178] Against this background, same-sex couples are considered as falling under the protection of Article 2 of the Constitution, which 'guarantees the inviolable rights of the person, both as an individual and in the social groups where human personality is expressed'.

This view has been endorsed also by the Italian Constitutional Court, which has been reluctant to dismiss the distinction between 'family'—as related to marriage—and the 'social formation'. In 2000 for instance, it emphasised the distinction between

[174] See AC, II, 957 ff, session of 17 April 1947.

[175] For a general overview of the interpretations of the definition of family as a 'natural institution founded on marriage' in Italian law, see F Caggia and A Zoppini, *Articolo 29* in R Bifulco, A Celotto, and M Olivetti (eds) *Commentario alla Costituzione*, vol 1 (Torino, Utet, 2006) 601 ff.

[176] See M Bonini Baraldi, 'Family vs solidarity. Recent epiphanies of the Italian reductionist anomaly in the debate on de facto couples' (2008) 4 *Utrecht Law Review* 175, 181.

[177] *Oliari v Italy* [2015] ECHR 752.

[178] For an overview of these positions and their implications for same-sex unions, see Bonini Baraldi, 'Family vs solidarity', n 176 above, 179. See also M Bonini Baraldi, *La famiglia de-genere* (Sesto S Giovanni, Mimesis, 2010).

cohabitation and the matrimonial tie, arguing in favour of the adoption at legislative level of a separate regime, and argued that such a distinction is prescribed by Article 29 of the Constitution where it imposes 'the duty to protect individual affective relationships, but at the same time the duty to protect the family institution based on stability of relationship'.[179]

The Italian Constitutional Court reiterated this interpretation even in its 2010 ruling on same-sex marriage.[180] I will thoroughly analyse this case in the following chapter,[181] but as far as it is relevant here, it should be emphasised that the Constitutional Court defined the same-sex couple as a 'social formation' having the right 'to live freely their condition as a couple' under Article 2 of the Constitution.[182] Nonetheless the Court emphasised at the same time that same-sex relationships 'cannot be regarded as homogeneous with marriage' because, on the basis of a long-established legal tradition, marriage is a heterosexual institution. At the same time, the Court has implicitly reserved the word 'family' to the married opposite-sex couple, also mentioning, as I will clarify in Chapter 5, its 'potential procreative purpose'.[183]

The Italian Constitutional Court has reiterated this view in a more recent ruling[184] when concluding in favour of a married opposite-sex couple in which the husband underwent gender reassignment surgery and who had been automatically divorced under the Italian law on transsexualism.[185] The Court argued, in particular, that Italian regulation of gender reassignment was unconstitutional 'insofar as it does not make it possible for the couple's relationship to survive in the form of a civil partnership'. The Court, in other words, acknowledged the value of the union and pressed the Parliament to enact appropriate legislation in order 'to afford adequate protection to the rights and duties of the couple', but cautioned that the legislator could not solve the issue by opening marriage to same-sex couples, because Article 29 of the Italian Constitution implicitly reserves marriage to the opposite-sex couple.

These narrow interpretations have also informed the long-term debate over the adoption of a statute on same-sex civil unions. They can be traced in the wording of

[179] Case no 352 of 2000, 25 July 2000 (transl mine).

[180] Case no 138 of 15 April 2010.

[181] See below p 115 ff.

[182] In particular Art 2 of the Italian Constitution of 1948 states that 'The Republic recognises and guarantees the inviolable rights of the person, both as an individual and in the social groups where human personality is expressed'. Art 3, s 1, states that 'all citizens have equal social dignity and are equal before the law, without distinction of sex, race, language, religion, political opinion, personal and social conditions'.

[183] Case no 138, n 180 above, para 9. See Ch 5 p 178.

[184] Case n 170 of 11 June 2014.

[185] In particular, in an opposite-sex heterosexual and married couple the male spouse underwent gender reassignment surgery, transitioning as a trans woman. Later she was legally recognised as such according to the Italian law on transsexualism (Legge 14 aprile 1982, no 164). However the couple discovered that their marriage was automatically dissolved under the statute, because Italy does not recognise same-sex marriage. The couple, considering the 'imposed divorce' to be a violation of their fundamental rights under the Constitution and the ECHR, asked to the courts to be allowed to remain married. The courts denied such a right, arguing that same-sex marriage was not admitted in the legal system, but submitted the issue to the Constitutional Court for a final decision on the legitimacy of the 'imposed divorce' under the Constitution.

the recent law no 76, which was finally signed into law in May 2016.[186] Article 1(1) of the law, for instance, defines the civil union as 'a specific social group' under Article 2 of the Constitution in order to implicitly mark the distinction from marriage and traditional family. At the same time, the law carefully avoids in many parts using the words 'family' when referring to the civil union, using instead the words 'parts of the union', or referring to their 'common needs' (Article 1(11)), their 'common life' (Article 1(7)a) and their 'common last name' (Article 1(10)). Nonetheless the word 'family'—translating an Italian idiom—while 'pushed out of the door, comes in from the window': the law clarifies that partners jointly decide the line of their 'familiar life' (Article 1(12)). This unique mention of family marks, although timidly, a radical change of perspective.[187]

It should also be emphasised that law no 76 of 2016 also reiterates the idea—expounded even by the Court of Cassation in 2000—that 'stability' is a principal feature of heterosexual unions crowned by marriage. In particular it has removed, with regard to the parties to civil unions, the 'duty of faithfulness' that article 143 of the Civil Code still imposes on married couples. Although many commentators argue—and I share their opinion—that this is an outdated legal duty, whose breach does not affect, for instance, the suitability of the married couple to adopt a child, it has been also interpreted in a wider sense, as imposing a duty to mutual support between spouses. It has therefore mostly a symbolic value and its exclusion for same-sex couples has as its only purpose the attachment of an unconstitutional stigma to same-sex relationships and to demean their dignity as a couple.[188]

[186] Law no 76 of 20 May 2016.

[187] See M Gattuso, 'Cosa c'è nella legge sulle unioni civili: una prima guida' (2016) *Articolo29.it*.

[188] On the duty of faithfulness in the Italian law on same-sex civil unions, see below, Ch 4, section III, p 147.

4

Same-Sex Marriage: Judicial Revolution or Constitutional Inevitability?

I. COURTS AND CONSTITUTIONAL CHANGE

A. From Civil Partnerships to Same-Sex Marriage: Courts, Constitutional Change and Judicial Backlash

THE JUDICIAL DEFINITION of same-sex couples as 'families' and the recognition to them of some rights of the unmarried opposite-sex couples—illustrated in Chapter 3—has been a piecemeal and incremental change, but it has contributed to the LGBT movement's struggle for the introduction, at legislative level, of registered civil partnerships and then, of the right to marry.

In Canada, Justice L'Heureux Dubé's dissent in *Mossop*[1] has been influential, for instance in the 1995 case of *Egan v Canada*.[2] Although a narrow majority dismissed Mr Egan's claim, arguing that the definition of 'spouse' could not be interpreted as including the partner in a same-sex relationship and, consequently, denied him the old age security and income supplements he might otherwise have received under the Old Age Security Act,[3] the Supreme Court of Canada unanimously considered 'sexual orientation' to be an illegitimate ground of discrimination under Article 15 of the Canadian Charter of Rights and Freedoms.[4]

Egan has been a pivotal case in itself in Canadian constitutional case law: it led to a sequence of relevant judicial decisions through the late 1990s in which same-sex couples were made equal to common law spouses.[5] In 1999, in particular, in *M v H*[6] Canada's Supreme Court held that the failure to provide stable lesbian and gay couples with the same legal rights and duties accorded to unmarried cohabiting opposite-sex couples, in case of breakdown of the relationships, amounted to illegitimate discrimination under the Canadian Charter of Rights.

[1] *Canada v Mossop* (1993) SCJ No 20.

[2] *Egan v Canada* [1995] 2 SCR 513.

[3] Old Age Security Act, RSC 1970, s 2 ('spouse') defining couples as relationships of 'opposite sex'.

[4] Canadian Charter of Rights and Freedoms 1982, c.11, s 15. In particular, although the majority of the Supreme Court considered that the Old Age Security Act 1970 violated s 15 of the Charter, it concluded that the infringement was justified under s 1 of the Charter as 'demonstrably justified in a free and democratic society'.

[5] *Rosenberg v Canada* (1998) 158 DLR (4th) 664; *M v H* [1999] 2 SCR 3. For a detailed analysis of the impact of *Canada v Mossop* and its aftermath, see J Millbank, 'The Role of Functional Family in Same-Sex Family Recognition Trends' (2008) 20 *Child & Family Law Quarterly* 155, 159 ff.

[6] *M v H* [1999] 2 SCR 3.

Writing for the Supreme Court, Justice Cory concluded that

> The exclusion of same-sex partners from the benefits of s. 29 of the [Family Law] Act[7] promotes the view that M, and individuals in same-sex relationships generally, are less worthy of recognition and protection. It implies that they are judged to be incapable of forming intimate relationships of economic interdependence as compared to opposite-sex couples, without regard to their actual circumstances. Such exclusion perpetuates the disadvantages suffered by individuals in same-sex relationships and contributes to the erasure of their existence. The human dignity of individuals in same-sex relationships is violated by the impugned legislation.[8]

M v H has been, in turn, a powerful stimulus for further achievement of same-sex couples' rights: although this case affected only the province of Ontario, it stimulated the adoption of new legislation at provincial and federal level extending to same-sex partners the rights and obligation afforded to common law opposite-sex couples.[9] Furthermore, as Eskridge contends, not only did this decision not provoke a backlash, but it inspired new marriage equality lawsuits that resulted in rulings by the Provincial Courts of Ontario, Quebec and British Columbia recognising the right to marriage to same-sex couples under the Charter.[10] In 2005 they were followed by the enactment of new legislation at federal level extending the right to marriage to same-sex couples.[11]

The present chapter—divided into three sections—focuses on the legal arguments in same-sex marriage cases and their circulation among constitutional and supreme courts. As the main title suggests, all the courts have been facing a similar issue: whether recognition of equal marriage is the consequence of 'a judicial revolution', ie of judicial activism breaking with traditions and established definitions of the institution of marriage, or whether equal marriage is—in Tribe's words—'a constitutional inevitability',[12] ie a development that stems, almost automatically, from the principles of equality, dignity and privacy and their application in former cases about the rights of gays and lesbians.

Before addressing this issue and discussing the arguments of equality, dignity, privacy the constitutional courts expounded in their cases, I think it is necessary to focus on the interactions among courts, legislators and public opinion in some significant European jurisdictions that culminated in the introduction of same-sex marriage

[7] Family Law Act 1990, c F3, s 29 ('spouse').

[8] *M v H*, n 5 above, para 73.

[9] For a detailed analysis of the developments at legislative level after *M v H*, see N Bala and R Jaremko Bromwich, 'Context and Inclusivity in Canada's Evolving Definition of the Family' (2000) 16 *International Journal of Law, Policy and the Family*, 145, 161.

[10] WN Eskridge Jr, 'Backlash Politics: How Constitutional Litigation Has Advanced Marriage Equality in the United States' (2003) 93 *Boston University Law Review* 275, 288–89. The cases which Eskridge refers to are: *Hendricks v Quebec* (2004) 238 DLR 4th 577 (Can Que.CA); *EGALE Canada, Inc v Canada* (2003) 13 BCLR 4th 1 (Can BC CA); *Halpern v Canada* (2003) 65 OR 3d 161 (Can Ont CA).

[11] Civil Marriage Act 2005, c 33 (Can). For an interesting account of these developments, see also R Wintemute, 'Sexual Orientation and the Charter: The Achievement of Formal Legal Equality (1985–2005) and Its Limits' (2004) 49 *McGill Law Journal* 1143.

[12] LH Tribe, 'The Constitutional Inevitability' of Same-Sex Marriage (2012) 71 *Maryland Law Review* 471.

(or of other frames of recognition substantially equal to marriage). This digression will provide the necessary background information for the following comparative analysis and offer me the opportunity for discussing some analogies among different constitutional systems in their path towards equal marriage.

The Canadian experience I briefly summarised above exemplifies 'the powerful impact of a social, or functional, definition of the family on legislative and constitutional development, as well as … the synergy of legislation and constitutional litigation once a functional definition of the conjugal relationship has generally been accepted by lawmakers'.[13] For this reason, it illustrates how the role of the courts (especially constitutional courts) in constitutional change cannot be properly evaluated without taking into consideration their dialogue with national legislators, public opinion and LGBT movements.

United States constitutional scholarship has deeply investigated the role of courts in constitutional change since landmark cases such as *Brown v Board of Education*[14] on desegregation, or *Roe v Wade*[15] on abortion. Some of those scholarly works have shown that courts are typically in tune with public opinion and help promoting legislative change. According to Eskridge, 'constitutional litigation has significantly advanced the cause of marriage equality, but that such litigation advances the cause only if litigators minimize the risk of significant backlash'.[16] By contrast, in the rare cases in which courts have released groundbreaking decisions on the rights of gays and lesbians contrary to the prevailing public opinion and the dominant political orientation, their conclusions raised a powerful local backlash and went almost unheard. In 1993, in *Baehr v Lewin*,[17] the Hawaii Supreme Court was the first Supreme Court to conclude that the exclusion of homosexual couples from marriage amounted to a discrimination subject to strict scrutiny under the state constitution. As Eskridge argues, the strong negative response, at political and social level, to *Baehr* 'set off a firestorm of anti-gay legislation in other states and at the national level with the enactment of the Defense of Marriage Act in 1996'.[18]

Nonetheless, in Eskridge's opinion, the fierce reaction to *Baehr* at state and federal level taught LGBT movements a valuable lesson: they realised that they needed 'a flourishing and successful politics of recognition in place before mounting any new campaign' and used constitutional litigation 'as a focal point for grass-roots mobilization'.[19] Activists became aware that the courts' intervention is more effective after politics and social movements themselves had created a substantially favourable environment for their intervention. Eskridge remembers, for instance, the relationship between the recognition of gay couples as families and the LGBT community's demands for parental rights and the introduction of same-sex civil unions,

[13] G. Blumberg, 'Legal Recognition of Same-sex Conjugal Relationships: The 2003 California Domestic Partner Rights and Responsibilities Act in Comparative Civil Rights and Family Law Perspective' (2004) 51 *UCLA Law Review* 1555, 1583.

[14] *Brown v Board of Education of Topeka* 347 US 483 (1954).

[15] *Roe v Wade* 410 US 113 (1973).

[16] Eskridge, 'Backlash Politics' n 10 above, 278.

[17] *Baehr v Lewin* 74 Haw 530, 852 P.2d 44 (1993).

[18] Eskridge, 'Backlash Politics' n 10 above, 284.

[19] Eskridge, 'Backlash Politics' n 10 above, 285.

arguing that, 'for the second-parent adoption and domestic partnership measures activists emphasized the social fact of lesbian and gay families and argued that they were productive enough to justify some kind of state recognition'.[20]

Eskridge suggests that a similar strategy has proved to be successful in other states of the US: in 1999, in Vermont—where the LGBT community had already achieved some considerable successes at legislative level[21]—the Supreme Court held in *Baker v State*[22] that the exclusion of lesbian and gay couples from family law benefits and duties violated the state constitution but left to the legislature the decision on how to remedy it. Although there was a great deal of public opposition to this compromise, the Vermont legislature introduced 'a new institution for same-sex couples and invested these "civil unions" with all the legal rights and duties of marriage'.[23] Later efforts to repeal the law or to amend the state constitution in order to prohibit same-sex marriage failed.[24]

Like Vermont, Massachusetts is an example of the advancement of the rights of gays and lesbians in a fertile environment for gay marriage litigation. As early as 1989, Massachusetts had prohibited discrimination based on sexual orientation in the financial system, public and private employment, union practices, housing and public accommodation. In 1992, state employees were allowed to register as domestic partners 'for purposes of bereavement leave and visitation rights in state prisons and hospitals'. In 1993 the Massachusetts Judicial Supreme Court ruled in favour of second-parent adoption by same-sex couples.[25] In 1999, the same Court granted joint custody rights to a lesbian woman after the ending of her relationship with the child's biological mother.[26]

Against this background, in 2003 the Judicial Supreme Court released a landmark case, *Goodridge v Department of Public Health*[27] holding the restriction of marriage to opposite-sex couples unconstitutional under Massachusetts' state constitution. The case, as *Baker* in Vermont, gave rise to fierce opposition, especially in some political environments, but, as Eskridge emphasises, 'the fact is that same-sex marriage survived in Massachusetts'.[28]

[20] WN Eskridge Jr, *Equality Practice. Civil Unions and the Future of Gay Rights* (New York, Routledge, 2002) 46.

[21] In particular, the state legislature had not only repealed its consensual sodomy law, but had also outlawed sexual orientation discrimination in the workplace and public housing and had codified the state Supreme Court's decision allowing two persons of the same sex to jointly adopt children. See Eskridge, 'Backlash Politics' n 10 above, at 285.

[22] *Baker v State* 744 A 2d 864 (Vt 1999).

[23] Eskridge, 'Backlash Politics' n 10 above at 286.

[24] ibid. For a detailed account on Vermont's creation of Civil Unions and its background, M Strasser, *On Same-Sex Marriage, Civil Unions and the Rule of Law. Constitutional Interpretation at the Crossroads* (Westport, Praeger, 2002).

[25] *Adoption of Tammy* 416 Mass 205, 619 NE 2d 315 (1993).

[26] *ENO v LMM* 429 Mass 824, cert denied 528 US 1005 (1999).

[27] *Goodridge v Department of Public Health* 440 Mass 309 (2003).

[28] Moving from a distinction among the different kinds of opposition on the basis of their intensity, Eskridge, 'Backlash Politics' n 10 above, 302 ff argues that *Goodridge*, n 27 above, stirred a less severe backlash than *Baehr*, n 17 above, in Hawaii. The fact that same-sex marriage survived in Massachusetts, although 'a large minority, perhaps even a majority, of Massachusetts citizens felt intensely and personally that the decision was wrong for them and for the state', was in his opinion due to 'a marked decline in the politics of disgust' in Massachusetts because increasing numbers of Americans were becoming

In more recent years other scholars have reached similar conclusions on the role of courts in promoting legal and social change in the United States,[29] extending their theories also to the debate over same-sex marriage. Their writings, as Eskridge's scholarly works, similarly subject to a strong critique the theory, proposed by Rosenberg and other theorists,[30] who by contrast affirm that courts cannot determine significant social reform and that constitutional litigation is counterproductive in the struggle for sexual orientation equality due to legislative backlash. Moving from cases such as *Baehr* and *Goodridge*, Rosenberg in particular argues that

> same-sex marriage proponents had not built a successful movement that could persuade their fellow citizens to support their cause and pressure political leaders to change the law. Without such a movement behind them, winning these court cases sparked an enormous backlash. They confused a judicial pronouncement of rights with the attainment of those rights. The battle for same-sex marriage would have been better served if they had never brought litigation, or had lost their cases.[31]

Conversely, critics of the backlash theory stress that courts contribute to social change, even when activists lose their battles before them[32] and that struggle over the courts helps change public opinion and forges new constitutional understandings,[33] laying the foundations for further achievements.[34] Although usually court cases, especially at supreme court level, polarise conflict more than legislative acts, neither the courts nor the Congress in the United States 'change net support for the underlying constitutional issue it is deciding'.[35] At the same time, judicial backlash arises

familiar with committed same-sex couples. He also points out that 'the reaction to *Goodridge* was more intense in other states and at the national level, where the politics of disgust still retained a constituency and gay people were less acceptable' (at 302). Against, MJ Klarman, *From the Closet to the Altar. Courts, Backlash and the Struggle for Same-Sex Marriage* (Oxford, Oxford University Press, 2013) ch 5.

[29] On the 'Court-caused' backlash narrative on abortion, see L Greenhouse and R Siegel, 'Before (and After) *Roe v. Wade*' (2011) 120 *Yale Law Journal* 2028.

[30] Backlash theorists identify the Supreme Court as the cause of polarising conflict and imagine backlash as arising in response to the Supreme Court's counter-majoritarian role. See MJ Klarman, 'Brown and Lawrence (and Goodridge)' (2005) 104 *Michigan Law Review* 431, 459 ff; MJ Klarman, *From the Closet to the Altar* n 28; GN Rosenberg, 'Courting Disaster: Looking for Change in the Wrong Place' (2006) 54 *Drake Law Review* 795; GN Rosenberg, *The Hollow Hope: Can Courts Bring About Social Change?*, 2nd edn (Chicago, Chicago University Press, 2008). For a similar perspective see JS Schacter, 'Sexual Orientation, Social Change and the Courts' (2006) 54 *Drake Law Review* 861; JS Schacter, 'Courts and the Politics of Backlash: Marriage Equality Litigation Then and Now (2009) 82 *Southern California Law Review* 1153, 1217 ff.

[31] Rosenberg, 'Courting Disaster' n 30 above, 814.

[32] G Torres, 'Some Observations on the Role of Social Change on Courts' (2006) 54 *Drake Law Review* 895, 900 ff.

[33] This argument has been suggested to me by R Siegel. On the subject, I had the opportunity to attend a seminar she gave at the European University Institute in Fiesole (Italy) in April 2016.

[34] G Torres, 'Some Observations on the Role of Social Change on Courts', n 32 above, for instance argues that although *Brown v Board of Education*, n 14 above, did not put an end to racial desegregation, it helped to change the culture towards racism and laid the foundations for the adoption of the Civil Rights Act of 1964. Similarly, he points out, LGBT victories did not put an end to sexual discrimination, but changed the culture.

[35] D Fontana and D Braman, 'Judicial Backlash or Just Backlash? Evidence From a National Experience' (2012) 112 *Columbia Law Review* 731, 735.

with different levels of intensity, depending on the institutional context[36] and cannot be necessarily 'invoked as the sole and sufficient cause of political polarization'.[37]

I argue that the American debate about courts and judicial backlash can help to illuminate also the progression to the right to marriage for same-sex couples in European countries. Although my purpose is not to formulate a theory of the role of courts in promoting constitutional and social change, I think that it is necessary to offer a historical account of the path towards equal marriage in some of the European countries I analyse in this book. This historical narrative will afford me the opportunity to emphasise the relationships among courts, legislators and, in some respects, social movements and public opinion, and to assess the role of European constitutional courts in the path toward sexual orientation equality in Europe, although relevant achievements (like equal marriage) have mainly been the result of legislative reforms.

Constitutional and supreme courts are only one of the actors of the debate over sexual equality: they frequently engage in a dialogue with national legislators, providing guidelines and setting deadlines for their intervention or clarifying the interpretation of the relevant constitutional principles that should be implemented at legislative level. At the same time, in countries like the United States—where judicial review is decentralised and concrete (in that it is exercised pursuant to ordinary litigation) and the Supreme Court is a court of general jurisdiction, courts address claims originating from civil society and stimulated by LGBT movements. Similar considerations apply to countries adopting a model of judicial review of legislation, such as Italy and Portugal, where the power to hold parliamentary laws unconstitutional is centralised, but constitutional issues are referred to the constitutional court by ordinary (civil, criminal and administrative) courts within a case pending before them.[38] The historical account will also offer me the opportunity to clarify that some of the differences in the role of constitutional courts in advancing the cause of sexual orientation equality in European countries stem from the specific features of their model of judicial review of legislation.

[36] On the distinction between backlash and 'normal politics', see Eskridge, 'Backlash Politics' n 10 above, at 278.

[37] See Greenhouse and Siegel, 'Before (and After) *Roe v. Wade*' n 29 above, 2034, focusing on the struggle over abortion before *Roe v Wade* and showing how conflict over abortion escalated through the interaction of other institutions even before the Court ruled. Furthermore, Eskridge, 'Judicial Backlash' n 10 above at 299 suggests that concern with judicial activism is not always the real motivation behind reactions qualified as judicial backlash. He says that judicial backlash 'was, at best, a secondary motivation for DOMA, the most sweeping anti-gay measure in American history' arguing that 'there is every reason to believe that a marriage recognition law passed by the Hawaii Legislature would have had similar consequences in Washington DC, as the Hawaii Supreme Court's decision in *Baehr*'.

[38] On the different systems of judicial review, see M Cappelletti, *Judicial Review in the Contemporary World* (New York, Bobbs-Merrill Co, 1971); M de Visser, *Constitutional Review in Europe. A Comparative Analysis* (Oxford, Hart Publishing, 2014); A Stone Sweet and M Shapiro, *On Courts, Politics and Judicialization* (Oxford, Oxford University Press, 2002); J Ferejohn and P Pasquino, 'Constitutional Adjudication: Lessons from Europe' (2003–04) 82 *Texas Law Review* 1671. See also VC Jackson and M Tushnet, *Comparative Constitutional Law*, 2nd edn (New York, Foundation Press, 2006); N Dorsen, M Rosenfeld, A.Sajó and S Baer, *Comparative Constitutionalism. Cases and Materials* (St Paul MN, West Publishing Company, 2003).

B. The Path Towards Equal Marriage: On the Dialogue Between Courts and Legislators in Some European Countries

i. Spain (2005)

Spain was the first Southern European country to introduce same-sex marriage,[39] and the third in Europe after Belgium and the Netherlands. Equal marriage (*matrimonio igualitario*) was in particular introduced by law no 13 of 2005[40] which emended the Spanish Civil code (art 44, sec 2)[41] in order to extend the right to marry to same-sex couples with the same rights and obligations of opposite-sex couples.

It should be premised that the Spanish Constitution of 1978 (art 32, sec 1) explicitly confers the right to marry to a 'man' and a 'woman'.[42] In 1994, the Constitutional Tribunal held that constitutional protection of marriage is reserved to the different-sex couple and denied that, in the absence of a statutory regulation of same-sex relationships, same-sex couples could be treated the same way as married couples for the purposes of the survivor benefits (ATC 222/1994).[43] Nonetheless, the Constitutional Tribunal emphasised that 'this interpretation has not prevent[ed] the legislative power establishing a system of equalisation so that same-sex relationships can enjoy the full rights and benefits of marriage'.

Although the Constitutional Tribunal clarified that only the Spanish Parliament could introduce same-sex marriage, the 1994 case paved the way for the adoption at local level of regulation of same-sex partnerships. In the following years, the seven Autonomous Communities enjoying the largest powers to legislate on civil matters and family law[44] passed statutes regulating opposite-sex and same-sex partnerships. As Martín Casals[45] points out, although in the beginning the main

On the incidental system of judicial review and in particular on the differences and analogies between the American and the Italian models of judicial review of legislation, see generally A Pizzorusso, 'Italian and American Models of the Judiciary and of Judicial Review of Legislation: A Comparison of Recent Tendencies' (1990) 38 *American Journal of Comparative Law* 373.

[39] See MM Sánchez, *Matrimonio homosexual y Constitución* (Valencia, Editorial Tirant lo Blanch, 2008); T Fidalgo de Freitas and D Tega 'Judicial Restaint and Political Responsability: A Review of the Jurisprudence of the Italian, Spanish and Portuguese High Courts on Same-Sex Couples' in D Gallo and L Paladini and P Pustorino (eds), *Same-Sex Couples before National, Supranational and International Jurisdictions* (Heidelberg, Springer, 2015) 287, 299 ff.

[40] *Ley 13/2005, de 1 de julio, por la que se modifica el Código Civil en materia de derecho a contraer matrimonio* (Act 13/2005, of 1 July, amending the Civil Code on the regulation of the right to marry).

[41] Art 1 of Ley 13/2005 adding a sec 2 to Art 44 of the Spanish Civil code of 1889 (stating that 'marriage will have the same requisites and effects whether both spouses are of the same or different sex').

[42] Spanish Constitution of 1978, art 32 sec 1 ('Men and women have the right to marry with full legal equality').

[43] *Auto no 222/1994 de Tribunal Constitucional, Sección 1ª, 11 de Julio de 1994* (hereinafter ATC 222/1994) holding in particular that 'in the same way as de facto cohabitation between a heterosexual couple, a partnership between persons of the same biological sex is not a legally regulated institution, nor is its establishment embodied in a constitutional right; quite the opposite to marriage between a man and a woman, which is a constitutional right (Article 32.1), generating *ope legis* a plurality of rights and duties').

[44] See art 149 of the Spanish Constitution regulating the distribution of legislative powers between the State and the Autonomous Communities and sec 1(8) reserving the *relaciones jurídico-civiles relativas a las formas de matrimonio* ('the private legal relationships about the forms of marriage') to the State.

[45] For a detailed account of these developments in the Spanish Autonomous Communities, M Martín Casals, 'Same-Sex Partnerships in the Legislation of Spanish Autonomous Communities' in K Boele-Woelki

concern of local legislators was the introduction of opposite-sex partnerships, 'the cause of same-sex partnership gained ground in only a few years', especially in progressive Catalonian society. The Catalan Parliament adopted the Stable Unions of Couples Act in 1998,[46] setting a model for the parliaments of Spain's other six 'historical territories'. The Catalonian Act was rapidly followed by similar statutes adopted by the Autonomous Communities of Aragón (1999),[47] Navarre (2000),[48] the Balearic Islands (2001),[49] Valencia (2001),[50] Basque Country (2003)[51] and Galicia (2006).[52]

It is interesting to note that during the same period the other Autonomous Communities without legislative powers on private law also adopted statutes on unmarried couples:[53] 'such a legislation [was] very often rather thin in substance, since it deal[t] with very limited areas of public law open to the intervention of the Autonomous Communities, such as public housing, benefits for civil servants' families, social rights and tax law'.[54]

Some scholars questioned the legitimacy of these regulations under the constitutional distribution of legislative powers.[55] However they trod a path: they helped to penetrate the idea of constitutional illegitimacy of differences between same-sex and different-sex couples in Spanish society and politics, paving the way to equal marriage.

At the political level the Spanish Socialist Party (PSOE) included marriage on its agenda on 2000, but the first bills introduced in the Spanish Parliament (*Cortes Generales*) were defeated.[56] During the campaign for the 2004 general elections,

and A Fuchs (eds), *Legal Recognition of Same-Sex Couples in Europe* (Cambridge, Intersentia, 2003) 58 ff.

[46] *Ley 10/1998* on stable unions of couples (*Unions estables de parella*). The Catalonian Act basically equalised different-sex and same-sex partnerships; a few differences concerned inheritance rights, joint adoption and step-child adoption. See F Jaurena i Salas, 'The Law of Stable Unions of Couples in the Catalonia Autonomous Community of Spain', in R Wintemute and M Andenæs (eds), *Legal Recognition of Same-Sex Partnerships* (Oxford, Hart Publishing, 2001) 505.

[47] *Ley 6/1999, de 26 de marzo, de las Cortes de Aragón, relativa a Parejas estables no casadas* (Act 6/1999, on unmarried stable couples).

[48] *Ley Foral 6/2000, de 3 de julio, para la igualdad jurídica de la parejas estables* (Act 6/2000, of 3 July, on legal equality of stable couples).

[49] *Ley 18/2001, de 19 de diciembre, de Parejas estables* (Act 18/2001, of 19 December, on stable couples).

[50] *Ley 1/2001, 6 de abril, por la que se regulan las uniones de hecho* (Act 1/2001, of 6 April, regulating de facto unions). The legislative powers of Valencia on these fields of the law have been however questioned on constitutionality grounds.

[51] *Ley 2/2003, de 7 de mayo, reguladora de la parejas de hecho* (Act 2/2003, of 7 May, regulating de facto couples).

[52] *Ley 2/2006, de 14 de junio, de derecho civil de Galicia* (Act 2/2006, of 14 June, on civil law of Galicia).

[53] Madrid (2001), Asturias (2002), Andalusia (2002), Castile and León (2002), Extremadura (2003), Basque Country (2003), Canary Islands (2003), Cantabria (2005), Galicia (2008), La Rioja (2010), Ceuta (1998) and Melilla (2008).

[54] C Gonzales Beilfuss, 'All or Nothing: the Dilemma of Southern Jurisdictions', in K Boele-Woelki and A Fuchs (eds), *Legal Recognition of Same-Sex Relationships in Europe. National, Cross-Border and European Perspectives*, 2nd edn (Cambridge, Intersentia, 2012) 46. See also Martín Casals, 'Same-Sex Partnerships' n 45 at 65 ff.

[55] On the legitimacy of these regulations under art 149, sec 1, 8 of the Spanish Constitution (fn 42) see ME Rodriguéz Martinez, *La legislación autonómica sobre uniones de hecho. Revisión desde la Constitución* (Valencia, Editorial Tirant lo blanch, 2003).

[56] Martín Casals, 'Same-Sex Partnerships' n 45 above at 57.

the PSOE supported the legalisation of same-sex marriage. The party's manifesto aimed at amending the civil code in order to open marriage to same-sex couples and to grant gays and lesbians full social and legal equality.[57] After the Socialist Party won an unexpected and sweeping victory at the general elections (three days after the Madrid bombings), the new Prime Minister Zapatero declared the Government's intention to honour that promise, stating that 'the moment has finally arrived to end once and for all the intolerable discrimination that many Spaniards suffered because of their sexual orientation'.[58]

In June 2005, law no 13 was approved with a vote in Congress overriding the veto of the Senate. The Act adds a new paragraph to article 44 of the Civil Code, stating that 'marriage will have the same requisites and effects when both spouses are of the same or different sex'.[59] The Act eliminates all references to the sex of spouses in the Civil Code and permits joint adoption for married same-sex couples.[60]

Although at the time over 60 per cent of the Spanish population favoured the introduction of equal marriage, the adoption of law 13/2005 provoked a backlash at political and social level, especially from Catholic political forces, traditionalist segments of civil society and civil servants in charge of the Civil Registry Service (*Registros Civiles*).[61] The centre right-wing MPs (*Partido Popular*, Popular Party) lodged a complaint with the Constitutional Tribunal arguing that same-sex marriage substantially altered the nature of marriage enshrined in article 32 of the Spanish Constitution and violated the constitutional principle of protection of family and children (article 39). Nonetheless, this complaint caused division within the same political party.

The Constitutional Tribunal delivered its judgments only in 2012 (case no 198/2012),[62] at the conclusion of the seven years of Socialist-led government, putting an end to the waiting and uncertainty for more than 20,000 same-sex couples who since 2005 had concluded marriage ceremonies. Before the case was released, almost 77 per cent of Spaniards supported gay marriage. Even the leader of the Popular Party—who won the 2011 elections—adopted a more nuanced position than in the past, indicating 'his intention to await the judgment of the Constitutional Tribunal and then respond according to the view prevailing in Spanish society'.[63]

The main arguments advanced by the majority of the Constitutional Tribunal will be thoroughly discussed in the following sections of this Chapter but it is necessary to anticipate here that, on the basis of a progressive interpretation of the Constitution, the majority held that same-sex marriage neither impaired the protection of the individual right to marry, nor violated the institutional guarantee of marriage that

[57] 'Merecemos una España mejor, Programma electoral, Elecciones generales 2004' available at *web.psoe.es*, p 32.

[58] Discurso de investitura del candidato a la Presidencia del Gobierno, José Luis Rodriguéz Zapatero, Congreso de los Diputados, 15 de abril 2004 available at *estaticos.elmundo.es*.

[59] Ley 13/2005, art 1 amending art 44 of the Civil Code.

[60] ibid, art 7 amending art 175 of the Civil Code.

[61] B Rodríguez Ruiz, 'Matrimonio, género y familia en la Constitución Española: Transcendiendo la familia nuclear' (2011) 91 *Revista española de derecho constitucional* 69, 76.

[62] Case no 198/2012, 6 November 2012, SCT.

[63] Gonzales Beilfuss, 'All or nothing' n 54 above, 44.

(following the German constitutional tradition) dictates that the legislator must seek to preserve the fundamental features of marriage.[64]

It has been argued that the Tribunal's delay in releasing its judgment was probably due to its intention to minimise backlash.[65] Choosing not to step into the political and social debate about same-sex marriage, the Constitutional Tribunal favoured political intervention, leaving it to the political branches of government to respond to the claims coming from the open and tolerant Spanish society.

Nonetheless the role of the Constitutional Tribunal in advancing the rights of same-sex couples before the adoption of law no 13/2005 should not be underestimated: as early as 1994 the Tribunal's conclusion in favour of an equalisation between marriage and same-sex unions revealed an openness towards the rights of gays and lesbians that was quite uncommon among constitutional and supreme courts at that time. In particular, as it has been emphasised, although ATC 222/1994

> held that the principle of heterosexuality was constitutional it did not conclude that passing gender neutral marriage legislation was unconstitutional. In fact ATC 222/1994 underlined that legislator had broader options. One could reasonably say that this decision left open the possibility of later declaring a same-sex marriage statute constitutionally forbidden, constitutionally mandated or constitutional possible. Nonetheless, ATC 222/1994 seemed to follow the last option by stating that although opposite sex marriage was constitutionally guaranteed, the legislature had a broad margin of action.[66]

At the same time, in a short passage of the decision, the Constitutional Tribunal suggested the idea of separation between marriage and family, holding that the Parliament was free to extend social security rights to 'familiar bonds'.[67] In this way, the Constitutional Tribunal expounded a constitutional principle that will be the premise for future recognition of the right of marriage regardless of gender and sexual orientation.

ii. Portugal (2010)

Compared to other constitutional systems, Portugal offers an example of intense dialogue and narrow cooperation between the constitutional court and the legislator.

Unlike the Spanish Constitution, which refers explicitly to spouses' sex, the Portuguese Constitution of 1976 states that 'everyone shall have the right to found a family and to marry',[68] and defines 'sexual orientation' as an illegitimate ground of discrimination.[69] Nonetheless the original version of the Civil Code (adopted

[64] Constitutional Tribunal, Case no 198, 6 November 2012 para 9.

[65] See De Freitas and Tega, 'Judicial Restraint and Political Responsibility' n 39 above, 304 stressing that 'the decision was not taken by one or two votes: there was a clear majority outvoting the dissenters which shows that the cause of the delay was not an internal impasse'.

[66] JML Villaverde, 'And the Story comes to an End: the Constitutionality of Same-Sex Marriages in Spain' in M Sáez (ed), *Same Sex Couples—Comparative Insights on Marriage and Cohabition* (Heidelberg, Springer, 2015), 13, 32.

[67] ATC 222/1994, n 43, para 2. See, for the case law on the relationship between marriage and family prior to 1994, Villaverde, 'And the Story comes to an End', n 66 above, 31.

[68] Constitution of the Portoguese Republic of 1976, art 36, para 1.

[69] ibid, art 13, para 2 ('No one shall be privileged, favoured, prejudiced, deprived of any right or exempted from any duty on the basis of ... sexual orientation').

10 years before the Constitution) referred to marriage as involving the opposite-sex couple.[70]

Homosexuality was decriminalised in Portugal in 1982 and same-sex de facto unions (*união de facto*) were legalised in 2001.[71] Anti-discrimination laws were implemented in many fields of the law,[72] but a first attempt to introduce same-sex marriage was defeated in Parliament in 2008.

In 2009, the Constitutional Tribunal was asked to decide on same-sex marriage for the first time (case no 359/2009):[73] two women lodged an appeal against the decision of the Registrar of Births, Marriages and Death to reject their request to marry. The couple argued that the Civil Code's definition of marriage was unconstitutional, and referred the issue of constitutional legitimacy to the Constitutional Court.[74] The question submitted to the Constitutional Court was whether under the Portuguese Constitution the legislator had a duty to open marriage to same-sex couples.[75] After an extensive examination of the comparative case law and legislation on same-sex marriage, a narrow majority of the Tribunal concluded that there was no constitutional obligation to open marriage to same-sex couples. The Tribunal found that marriage was not a frozen institution, and that the Portuguese Constitution provided a broad definition on marriage; nonetheless, it suggested that constitutional clauses did not require the legislator to open marriage to same-sex couples, and that equal marriage could not be introduced through a Constitutional Tribunal judgment.[76]

Politics quickly followed the guiding principles suggested by the Constitutional Tribunal. Only seven months later, the Parliament voted law no 9/2010,[77] a five-article statute amending the definition of marriage in the Civil Code (but reserving joint adoption to the opposite-sex married couple).

[70] Civil Code of 1966, art 1577 ('marriage is a contract between two persons of different sex'). See, for a general introduction on the Portuguese legal framework on family and marriage issues, de Freitas and Tega, 'Judicial Restraint and Political Responsibility' n 39 above, 304 ff.

[71] *Lei no 7/2001 de 11 de Maio, Adopta medidas de protecção das uniões de facto* (Law no 7/2001 of 11 May, adopting protection measures on de facto unions), in part art 1, sec 1 (which states that the purpose of the law is to regulate de facto unions, regardless of the sex of the partners).

[72] *Decreto no 9/XI da Assembleia da República resultou da aprovação da Proposta de Lei no 7/XI* (*Diário da Assembleia da República*, II série A, n.º 18XI/1, de 22/12/2009) aiming at 'removing the legal barriers to the implementation of de fact uions between people of the same sex'.

[73] Tribunal Constitucional, case no 359/2009 (9 July 2009).

[74] The Constitutional Tribunal in Portugal is the final instance of concrete judicial review. According to art 280 para 1 § b of the Constitution, an 'Appeal may be made to the Constitutional Court against court rulings: ... b) That apply any rule, the unconstitutionality of which has been raised during the proceedings in question'. For a general overview of the judicial review of legislation in Portugal see generally A Cortes and C Violante, 'Concrete Control of Constitutionality in Portugal: A Means Towards Effective Protection of Fundamental Rights' (2011) 29 *Pennsylvania State International Law Review* 759.

[75] Case no 359 of 2009 n 73 above, para 9.

[76] Commenting on the case, some scholars argued that in case no 359/2009, n 73 above, the Constitutional Tribunal 'seems to presuppose that [for art 13, sec 2 of the Constitution on the principle of non-discrimination] to be fully effective, ordinary law [ie the Civil Code] would have been modified in accordance to it'. See de Freitas and Tega, 'Judicial Restraint and Political Responsibility' n 39 above, 306.

[77] *Lei no 9/2010 de 31 de Maio, Permite o casamento civil entre pessoas do mesmo sexo* (Law no 9/2010 of 31 May permitting the civil marriage between persons of the same sex).

The President of the Republic, Mr Cavaco Silva, challenged the law before the Constitutional Tribunal before signing it.[78] The Court held the law constitutional (case no 121/2010),[79] stressing this time that the Portuguese Constitution did not prohibit same-sex marriage.

The arguments adopted by the Tribunal will be thoroughly analysed in the following section of this chapter. It is worth observing here that the Tribunal reiterated that Article 67 of the Constitution assumes a broad definition of family, and that Article 36 does not define marriage as the union between persons of different sex, but assigned to the legislator 'the duty to preserve the connection between law and social reality'.[80] The Tribunal also stressed that marriage is a concept devoid of any fixed meaning, and clarified that it 'refers to the communion of life between two persons, celebrated by means of an official act and with legally binding effects, which is free and not subject to any condition or deadline'.[81]

It is interesting to observe that the close coordination between the judiciary and the legislator in the advancement of same-sex couples' rights in Portugal did not reflect a widespread support for equal marriage on the part of the general public. Several studies emphasised that in 2010 a large majority of the Portuguese population did not approve same-sex marriage.[82] Furthermore, a study revealed that, two years after its introduction, the rate of disapproval towards same-sex marriage surprisingly had increased in Portugal, contrary to the position in other countries after same-sex marriage legislation had been passed.[83]

Since a need to comply with the expectations of a progressive public opinion cannot explain the introduction of same-sex marriage in Portugal, it is possible to infer that, by introducing it, the political elite wanted to demonstrate the country's ability to adopt modern and advanced legislation on human rights,[84] after its undemocratic past.[85] However it is also important to note that the issue of same-sex marriage did not provoke a violent backlash in the population or in Catholic organisations. Portugal was facing a major economic crisis at the time when same-sex marriage was passed, so probably the Government and the population decided that it was better to move on.

[78] Under art 278 para 1 of the Portuguese Constitution, the President of the Republic may ask the Constitutional Tribunal to conduct a prior review of the constitutionality of any law that is sent to him for enactment.

[79] Constitutional Tribunal, case no 121/2010 (8 April 2010).

[80] Case no 121, n 79, para 22.

[81] ibid.

[82] See AM Brandao and TC Machado, 'How Equal is equality? Discussions about same-sex marriage in Portugal' (2012) 15 *Sexualities* 662, 667 (concluding that 'Portugal continued to be one of the most conservative countries of Southern Europe'); M Hooghe and C Meeusen, 'Is Same-Sex Marriage Legislation Related to Attitudes Toward Homosexuality? Trends in Tolerance of Homosexuality in European Countries Between 2002 and 2010' (2013) 10 *Sexuality Research and Social Policy* 258. An ILGA Europe survey (released in May 2015) titled 'Attitudes towards marriage equality in 51 countries' (www.old.ilga.org) showed that 49 per cent of the Portuguese population supported equal marriage.

[83] Hooghe and Meeunsen, 'Is Same-Sex Marriage Legislation Related to Attitudes' n 82 above, 264.

[84] ibid, 265.

[85] It may be noted that same-sex marriage was introduced early in countries such as Spain, South Africa and Portugal, that had recently experienced an undemocratic past.

This clearly emerged in the statements of the President of the Republic: when signing the law, the President mentioned 'divisions among the Portuguese population', and suggested that Parliament should adopt a different legal solution to address such 'a sensitive issue' (as had happened in other countries with the introduction of civil partnerships). Nonetheless, he chose to promulgate the law in order to leave the political powers free to face more pressing problems.

From a comparative constitutional law perspective, it is possible to qualify the Portuguese experience as an example of trust in the political branches of government and, as was emphasised in journalistic sources, an example of a commitment 'to the will of the law'.[86] Such an idea was also shared by the Constitutional Tribunal when expressing its deference to the democratically elected powers in the solution of sensitive and divisive issues: the majority concluded that 'especially when there is not a solution that is widely accepted as legitimate by the legal community, the Parliament has the power to choose and decide'.[87]

iii. France (2013)

A debate on legal recognition of same-sex relationships in France began at the end of the 1980s, when progressive political parties and LGBT movements inspired the first parliamentary bills for the regulation of same-sex civil unions[88] in order to address the pressing needs of the gay community, at that time deeply touched by the spread of Aids.

These proposals were defeated in the National Assembly. Similarly, the first attempts to achieve recognition of the rights of same-sex couples at judicial level—through an extensive interpretation of 'concubinage' (cohabitation) under Article 8 of the European Convention on Human Rights (ECHR)—failed.[89]

In 1999 the National Assembly approved a statute regulating the *pacte civil de solidarieté* (PaCS, 'civil solidarity pact').[90] The passage of PaCS law met fierce opposition from French religious associations and the right-wing political parties. In an official speech, President Jacques Chirac declared that the institution of PaCS 'denaturalise[d] marriage' and 'alter[ed] the founding values of the family'. French public opinion was divided: in 1998 only 49 per cent of the French population supported same-sex marriage, but 67 per cent considered homosexuality as 'normal'.

[86] See F Bruni, 'One Country's Big Gay Leap', *International New York Times*, 9 October 2011, p SR3.

[87] Case no 121/2010 n 79 above, para 22.

[88] For a detailed account of the proposals that preceded the introduction of PaCS in 1999, see generally D Borrillo 'The "Pacte Civil de Solidarité" in France: Midway Between Marriage and Cohabitation', in R Wintemute and M Andenæs (eds), *Legal Recognition of Same-Sex Partnerships* (Oxford, Hart Publishing, 2001) 475, 476 ff.

[89] In *Secher v Air France*, 11 July 1989, *Bulletin civil* 1989, V, 311 n 514 the Cour de Cassation denied that art 515 sec 8 *Code Civil* on concubinage (de facto unions) could be extended to same-sex de facto couples and stated that cohabitation between partners outside marriage 'can only concern a couple consisting of a man and a woman'. Such a conclusion was reiterated by the Cour de Cassation in 1997 (*Vileva v Weil*, 17 December 1997, *Bulletin civil* 1997, III, 151, no 225). See on the case law prior to the passage of the PaCS law, Borrillo 'The Pacte Civil de Solidarieté' n 88, 477.

[90] *Loi n° 99-944 du 15 novembre 1999 relative au pacte civil de solidarité.*

Even the Socialist Party and the Prime Minister Lionel Jospin expressed only cautious support for the initiative, preferring not to introduce a government bill.[91]

The PaCS is defined by the law as a 'contract concluded by two adult persons of the same or different sex in order to organise their joint life'.[92] It is considered as a hybrid between marriage and cohabitation, 'situated somewhere in the no-man's land between status and contract'.[93] PaCS are open to both different and same-sex couples, regardless of the nature of their bond or the existence of a sexual relationship.[94] The statute does not provide a definition of 'joint life' and does not make any reference to the '*pacsée* couple' as 'family'. Partners that enter a PaCS accept to give each other mutual material support.[95] They enjoy some of the rights of married couples (such as joint taxation, tenancy rights, bereavement right, some inheritance rights, preferential treatment in case of job transfer for civil servants). However, the law does not permit either joint or stepchild adoption.

On the day of the passage of the PaCS bill, deputies and senators of the right filed an appeal to the Conseil constitutionnel, the French Constitutional Court, claiming its unconstitutionality, but the Court rejected the appeal (case 419/1999).[96] The case provided the Conseil the occasion to clarify, albeit timidly,[97] the differences between marriage and PaCS under constitutional fundamental principles. The Court clearly stated that a PaCS is different from marriage[98] and argued that its introduction neither violated the 'fundamental principles of the laws of Republic'[99] nor affected the protection of marriage for the fact of acknowledging some of the rights descending from marriage to the '*pacsée* couple'.[100] Furthermore the Conseil constitutionnel suggested that the PaCS did not violate constitutional principles concerning the protection of family and children.[101]

Although, as mentioned, the law did not provide a definition of 'joint life', the Conseil constitutionnel seized the opportunity to break the silence on the issue: the *vie commune* ('common life'), it said

> does not cover only a community of interests and it is not limited to the requirement of cohabitation between two people; ... the joint life ... implies, in addition to a common place

[91] 'Borrillo, The "Pacte Civil de Solidarieté"' n 88 above, 482, citing a *Le Monde* headline which says that 'Socialists are ashamed of the PaCS'.

[92] Art 1 amending art 515(1) *Code Civil.*

[93] I Curry-Summer, 'A Patchwork of Partnership: Comparative Overview of Registration Schemes in Europe', in K Boele-Woelki and A Fuchs (eds), *Legal Recognition of Same-Sex Couples in Europe* (Cambridge, Intersentia, 2003) 71, 76.

[94] Even cousins may conclude a PaCS. PaCS is however forbidden between relatives of direct line of descent and between brothers and sisters.

[95] *Code Civil*, art 514(4).

[96] Case no 99-419 DC (9 November 1999).

[97] This is also due to the style of constitutional cases, which is very concise and made up of a list of *considérant* ('in light of') clauses, sentence-like assertions taking into consideration what the law is.

[98] Case no 99-419, n 96, *considérant* no 67 (*'le pacte civil de solidarité est un contrat étranger au mariage'*).

[99] Fundamental principles of the laws of the Republic have been 'constitutionalised' by the Conseil constitutionnel in a famous case (Décision no 71–44 DC of 16 July 1971). In this judgment the Conseil held unconstitutional a law adopted by the Parliament under the indeterminate concept of the 'fundamental principles of the law of the Republic' that are incorporated into the Constitution by the preamble.

[100] Case no 99-419, n 96 above, *considérant* no 59.

[101] ibid, *considérant* no 81.

> of residence, a life as a couple. This is why the legislator specifies conditions for the PaCS to be valid which are similar to those of marriage, ... such as the existence of familiar bonds and the conditions concerning the violation of the obligation of fidelity.[102]

Although 'life as a couple' (*vie de couple*) was merely supposed and not required by the PaCS law,[103] the decision implied that joint life required a sexual and affective life between the partners. These conclusions of the Conseil constitutionnel forged the further debate on same-sex marriage defining the boundaries between the judicial and the legislative powers in the interpretation of open statutory clauses.[104] The Conseil constitutionnel was still reluctant to qualify the couple as a 'family',[105] 'nevertheless, as narrow as the grounds of the judgment [were], the decision remain[ed] a form of acceptation of same-sex relationships and sexuality at the apex of the French judicial hierarchy'.[106]

The PaCS law was a success: a year after the approval of law no 944 of 1999, 70 per cent of French citizens declared themselves 'favourable' to the PaCS and more than half of them supported the introduction of equal marriage.[107]

In December 2004, the French Government took into consideration the possibility of expanding the rights granted in PaCS law. French LGBT groups considered this a tactic for postponing same-sex marriage. Nonetheless the idea of equal marriage began to take shape in French political debate: the same year, MP Noël Mamère, mayor of Bègles (a commune of Bordeaux) and an LGBT activist, celebrated a marriage between two men.[108] The celebration was intended to spark off a public debate on same-sex marriage and to bring the issue before France's highest ordinary court, the Cour de Cassation. In 2007 the Cour declared the marriage void,[109] stating that marriage in French law 'is only the union between a man and a woman'.[110]

102 ibid, *considérant* no 26.

103 See AM Lecis Cocco Ortu, 'Le unioni di persone dello stesso sesso in Francia: dai PaCS alla sentenza sul mariage homosexual' (2011) 2 *Ianus* 213, 222. See also G Charbonneau and FJ Pansier, 'Et in Terra Pacs. Commentaire du Pacte civil de solidarité créé par la loi du 14 novembre 1999 et à la lumière de la décision du Conseil constitutionnel' (1999) 323–24 *Gazette du Palais* 2.

104 At the same time, the Conseil constitutionnel rejected the arguments of the claimants who submitted that the absence of clear rules on the definition of 'joint life' amounted to a violation of Parliament's prerogatives in favour of the judiciary and the Government's regulatory powers. The Conseil constitutionnel confirmed the constitutional legitimacy of legislative choices and stated that courts have the power of interpretation of the vague definitions (*réserve d'interprétation*) that is justified on the basis of legal certainty and institutional balance. See P Reyniers, 'Same-Sex Couples in France and Belgium: the Resilient Practise of Judicial Deference' in D Gallo and L Paladini and P Pustorino (eds), *Same-Sex Couples before National, Supranational and International Jurisdictions* (Springer, Heidelberg, 2015) 249, 252.

105 Recognition of same-sex couples as 'families' was achieved only in a more recent decision of the Conseil constitutionnel, concerning equal marriage. See n 120 below.

106 Renyniers, 'Same-Sex Couples in France and Belgium' n 104 above, 252.

107 WF Edmiston and A Duménil, *La France contemporaine* (Boston, Heile Cencage, 2009) 151.

108 He was responding to a call by D Borrillo and D Eribon in the *Manifeste pour l'égalité des droits* ('Manifesto for equal rights'), published on *Le Monde*, 16 March 2004 (www.lemonde.fr) asking for mayors to celebrate marriages between people of the same sex, as had happened in San Francisco.

109 Cour de Cassation, case no 511, 13 March 2007.

110 The case was also brought before the European Court of Human Rights, which recently released its final judgment (*Chapin and Charpentier v France* (2016) ECHR 504). The ECtHR held that there was no violation of Art 12 (right to marriage) in conjunction with Art 14 (prohibition of discrimination), and no violation of Art 8 (right to private and family life) in conjunction with Art 14. The Court reiterated its finding in *Schalk and Kopf v Austria* ECHR 2010-I, (2010) ECHR 1996 that there is no obligation under the ECHR on contracting states to open marriage to same-sex couples. Nonetheless the ECtHR noted that law no 404 of 2013 opened marriage to same-sex couples on equal terms to different-sex couples.

Two years later, the Conseil constitutionnel—through the newly established procedure for the priority preliminary rulings (*question prioritaire de constitutionnalité*, QPC)[111]—confirmed the Cour de Cassation's conclusions.[112] The Conseil constitutionnel was asked to decide on the constitutionality of the provisions of the Code civil[113] that conferred marriage only to heterosexual couples. With a reasoning that shares some similarities with the 'living law doctrine' (*dottrina del diritto vivente*) expounded by the Italian Constitutional Court,[114] the Conseil constitutionnel moved from the established interpretation of marriage given by the Cour de Cassation affirming that the institution of marriage has traditionally been referred to the opposite-sex couple. Nonetheless, as the ordinary meaning of marriage is based on the civil code, the Conseil argued that the legislator had the power to amend the legislation in order to open the institution of marriage to same-sex couples. In other words, the Conseil seemed to suggest that the Constitution did not prohibit equal marriage, but that it could not be introduced by the means of judicial review of legislation.[115]

The Conseil constitutionnel's conclusions put equal marriage on legislative agenda. In 2011 the Socialist Party submitted a first proposal for the introduction of same-sex marriage to the National Assembly,[116] but it was rejected. By that time public opinion was largely in favour of same-sex marriage and F Holland, the Socialist Party candidate, included equal marriage and adoption for same-sex couples among his party's commitments during the campaign for the 2012 general elections.

After the Socialist Party's victory, the Minister of Justice introduced a bill for *Mariage pour tous* in the National Assembly. The purpose of the bill, the Government declared, was not to change the existing legal regime of marriage, but 'to open the institution of marriage—with its rights and duties—to same-sex couples'.[117] The core of the proposal was the definition of marriage: it aimed at amending article 143 of the Civil Code, stating that 'marriage is contracted by two persons of different sex or of the same sex'. The law also granted same-sex couples joint adoption 'with the same conditions established for different-sex couples'.

Although 63 per cent of the French population supported equal marriage and 49 per cent supported the right to adoption for married same-sex couples, the bill was voted into law (*loi* 2013-404)[118] only after more than 140 hours of heated

[111] A constitutional reform approved in 2008 amended art 61, sec 1 of the French Constitution and introduced an incidental review of legislation through an application referred to the Conseil constitutionnel by the Conseil d'Etat or the Cour de Cassation.

[112] Case no 2010-92 QPC, 28 January 2011.

[113] Code civil, art 75 and 144.

[114] See D Rousseau, 'L'art italien au Conseil constitutionnel: les décisions de 6 et 14 octobre 2010' (2010) *Gazette du Palais* 12. On the 'doctrine of living law' C Severino, *La doctrine du droit vivant* (Paris, Economica-PUAM, 2003).

[115] Case no 92 of 2010, n 112, considérant no 9. See *Cahiers du Conseil constitutionnel*, no 32, 2 (www.conseil-constitutionnel.fr).

[116] Bill no 586, introduced by MP P Bloche.

[117] *Compte rendu du Conseil des ministers*, 7 November 2012.

[118] *Loi n° 2013-404 du 17 mai 2013 ouvrant le mariage aux couples de personnes de même sexe*, in particular art 13 that adds art 6–1 *Code civil* ('Marriage and filiation through adoption produce the same effects, rights, and obligations provided by legislation, with the exception of those provided for in Book I, Title VII, of this Code, regardless whether the spouses or parents are of different sex or same sex').

debates, with massive rallies and violence across the country. As sociological studies confirmed, such a strong reaction probably cannot be explained only by religious attitudes:[119] France, 'a secular Republic' according to Article 1 of the French Constitution, with a diverse population, experienced in fact the largest demonstrations in decades.

As happened for law no 944 of 1999 on PaCS, some members of the National Assembly and Senators referred the text to the Conseil constitutionnel before it was signed into law. The Conseil constitutionnel confirmed the constitutionality of the law,[120] rejecting all the allegations. The case was in line with the 2011 judgment[121] although the Conseil constitutionnel took a more explicit stance on the nature of marriage and filiation of same-sex couples. It argued that although the legislature had the power to regulate same-sex marriage according to constitutional principles, gender difference was not a 'natural' feature of marriage according to the traditions of the Republic and was not mandated by 'the fundamental principles of the law of the Republic'.[122] In other words, according to the Conseil constitutionnel, opening marriage to same-sex couples did not violate the fundamental right to marriage because it did not impinge on the liberty of different-sex couples.[123]

The arguments adopted will be analysed thoroughly in the following section of the present chapter, but it is worth noting that the Conseil constitutionnel took a firm stance in recognising the power of Parliament to regulate sensitive social issues (*questions de société*).[124] At the same time, the Conseil constitutionnel made a fundamental contribution to the definitive dismissal of trite arguments like the 'natural character of heterosexuality',[125] the 'bilinear nature of filiation based on sexual alterity'[126] and the children's 'right to a normal family life'.[127]

In the year following the passing of law n 404 of 2013, more than 7,000 same-sex marriages were celebrated in France, giving a new lease of life to the declining

[119] Hooghe and Meeusen, 'Is Same-Sex Marriage Legislation Related to Attitudes' n 82 above, 258 who also emphasise the role played by strong veto players like conservative parties.

[120] Decision no 2013-669 DC of 17 May 2013.

[121] Reyniers, 'Same-Sex Couples in France and Belgium' n 104 above, 254.

[122] Case no 2013-669 DC, n 120 above, *considérant* no 21 ('Considering that the republican tradition cannot be properly invoked in order to assert that a legislative text which is at odds with it breaches the Constitution unless that tradition has given rise to a fundamental principle recognised by the laws of the Republic within the meaning of the first recital of the Preamble to the 1946 Constitution (Préambule); that, whilst republican legislation prior to 1946 and subsequent legislation until the enactment of the Law referred have considered marriage as a union between a man and a woman, this rule, which does not affect fundamental rights and freedoms, national sovereignty or the organisation of public authorities cannot amount to a fundamental principle recognised by the laws of the Republic within the meaning of the first recital of the 1946 Preamble; that moreover, the objection alleging that marriage is "naturally" the union of a man and a woman must in any case be rejected').

[123] Case no 2013-669 DC, n 120 above, *considérant* no 3.

[124] ibid, *considérant* no 22 ('the difference between couples comprised of a man and a woman and same-sex couples no longer justified the fact that the latter could no longer attain the status and legal protection associated with marriage; that it is not for the Constitutional Council to substitute its appraisal for that of the legislator regarding the assessment of this difference in circumstances in relation to marriage'). But see B Mathieu, 'Decision du Conseil constitutionnel sur le mariage homosexuel', in *bertrandmathieu.over-blog.com*.

[125] Case no 2013-669 DC, n 120 above, *considérant* no 21.

[126] ibid, *considérant* no 56.

[127] ibid, *considérant* no 49 ff.

institution of marriage. 'Marriage equality has also hastened the pace at which gay and lesbian people are assimilating into wider French society'.[128] Although—as clarified earlier in this book[129]—French private law tradition considers family and intimate relationships as matters of private law, the synergy between the legislative and judicial interventions and the struggle over them, contributed to the neutralisation of arguments that previously had made gay and lesbian families remain in the closet.

iv. Germany (2001)

After an account of the role of constitutional courts in the introduction of same-sex marriage in some other European countries, it is useful to devote some attention to the regulation of same-sex relationships issues in Germany.

The German model—that grants special protection to marriage and yet regulates same-sex legal unions with rights similar to marriage—is frequently referred to as a 'separate but equal' or 'double track' model. It shares many similarities with the Austrian and Swiss regulation of same-sex relationships[130] and served as an example to several Latin American and East European countries and, more recently, to Italy.[131] At the same time, Germany is an interesting exemplification of dialogue and confrontation between courts and legislator in the advancement of the rights of gays and lesbians. Although the constitutional clause on marriage operates as a factor of rigidity,[132] this has not prevented the German legislator providing increasing protection to same-sex relationships, in response to a stimulus of the Federal Constitutional Tribunal (Bundesverfassungsgericht).

Marriage and family in Germany enjoy a special constitutional protection. Article 6 of the Basic Law of 1949 (*Grundgesetz*) states that 'family and marriage shall enjoy the special protection of the State',[133] and Article 2(1) recognises everyone's 'right to free development of personality'.[134] However there is no definition of 'marriage' at constitutional and statutory level: neither the German civil code (*Bürgerliches Gesetzbuch*, BGB) nor the old Law on Marriage (*Ehegesetz*)[135] define marriage in heterosexual terms, although many civil code provisions refer to 'the husband' and 'the wife'.[136]

[128] L Hoare, 'France's gays are assimilating. What comes next?' in *Slate.com* (10 August 2015).

[129] See above, Ch 3 p 52.

[130] G Repetto, 'At the Crossroads Between Privacy and Community: the Legal Status of Same-Sex Couples in German, Austrian and Swiss law' in D Gallo and L Paladini and P Pustorino (eds), *Same-Sex Couples before National, Supranational and International Jurisdictions* (Heidelberg, Springer, 2015) 263.

[131] Law no 76 of 20 May 2016 (civil unions).

[132] Above p 51.

[133] German Basic Law 1949 (*Grundgesetz*), art 6(1).

[134] German Basic Law 1949, art 2(1) ('Everyone has the right to free development of his personality insofar as he does not violate the rights of others and offend against the constitutional order or against morality').

[135] Law on marriage (*Ehegesetz*, EheG) 1946. The Act was repealed in 1998.

[136] R Schimmel and S Heun, 'The Legal Situation of Same-Sex Partnership in Germany: An Overview' in R Wintemute and M Andenæs (eds), *Legal Recognition of Same-Sex Partnerships* (Oxford, Hart Publishing, 2001) 575, 583.

The Federal Constitutional Tribunal's case law defines Article 6 of the Basic Law as 'a value-setting fundamental norm'.[137] The right to marriage is conceived as having an 'objective value' (*objective Wertentscheidungen* or *Grundsatznormen*): it operates as a 'general policy directive'[138] because, according to the German Constitutional Tribunal, 'human rights not only influence the state-citizen relationship but also, by establishing a value system, ... other areas of law, for example the interpretation of private law rules effective between citizens'.[139]

Longstanding Constitutional Tribunal case law holds that Article 6 of the Basic Law acknowledges a classic fundamental basic right 'designed specifically to protect the private spheres of marriage and the family against the coercive influence of the State',[140] in contrast with the total dominance of the State (*Allstaatlichkeit*) under National Socialism.[141] The right to marriage protects 'the independence and self-determination of persons' in the sphere of personal relationships (*Abwehrrecht*).

At the same time, Article 6 of the Basic Law establishes a guarantee of marriage and family as basic social institutions, resulting in the so-called 'institutional guarantee' (*Institutgarantie*). As repeatedly clarified by the Constitutional Tribunal, 'in this capacity, [Art 6] safeguards the essential structure of marriage and the family'.[142] This implies that the legislature cannot abandon marriage altogether and must provide a legal framework allowing people to marry and to organise their life as a couple. At the same time, the State must promote marriage by suitable measures.[143] As in Spanish constitutional case law,[144] the institutional guarantee argument plays a crucial role in the legal discourse over gay and lesbian rights, same-sex unions and equal marriage being conceived as potentially affecting the institution of marriage.

Against this background, in its early cases, the Constitutional Tribunal endorsed a notion of marriage as 'the union of one man and one woman within an all-embracing, and in principle, indissoluble community of life'.[145] Marriage and family, it argued, represented 'the nucleus of every human community'[146] and could not be compared to any other personal and intimate bond.

Attempts to regulate same-sex unions were made in the early 1990s when German LGBT movements prompted litigation before family courts in order to stimulate the debate over same-sex marriage. The action did not receive public support and only

[137] 6 BVerfGE 55 (1957) (Joint Income Tax Case), D.II.2 translated by DP Kommers and RA Miller, *The Constitutional Jurisprudence of the Federal Republic of Germany* (Durham, Duke University Press, 2012).

[138] Repetto, 'At the Crossroads Between Privacy and Community' n 130 above, 266.

[139] A Sanders, 'Marriage, Same-Sex Relationship, and the German Constitution' (2012) 13 *German Law Journal* 911, 917.

[140] ibid.

[141] Art 6 follows the tradition of the Weimar Constitution of 1919 (art 119 ff). See R Gröschner, 'Ehe und Familie, Elternrecht, Mutterschutz, uneheliche Kinder (Artikel 6)' in H Dreier (ed), *Grundgesetz Kommentar*, 2nd edn, vol 1 (Tubingen, Mohr Siebeck, 2004) 750, para 756 ff.

[142] 6 BVerfGE 55 (1957). See also 31 BVerfGE 58 (1971) (*The Spanish Marriage case*).

[143] Sanders, 'Marriage, Same-Sex Relantionship, and the German Constitution' n 139 above, 917.

[144] See above p 88 ff.

[145] 53 BVerfGE 224 (1980) (Civil Divorce case); 10 BVerfGE 59 (1959), para 66. Nonetheless, the Constitutional Tribunal clarified that Art 6, sec 1 protects a secularised notion of marriage as developed during the 19th century that demands a civil rather than a religious ceremony. See Sanders, 'Marriage, Same-Sex Relationship, and the German Constitution' n 139 above, 919.

[146] 6 BVerfGE 55 (1957).

a single district court affirmed the applicability of family law provisions to same-sex relationships.[147] This holding was quashed on appeal.[148]

In 1993, a three-justice chamber of the First Senate of the Constitutional Tribunal took into consideration the first complaint of a same-sex couple, who claimed that denial of the right to marriage to same-sex couples violated the Basic Law. The First Senate dismissed the appeal, concluding that 'according to the structural principles guaranteed by Article 6, which fall outside the legislature's discretion, the constitutional protection of marriage is mainly aimed at a legal safeguard for partners to found a family with children'.[149] Such an approach implied that the common law marriages and unmarried couples did not fall under the protection of Article 6.[150] Nonetheless, the judgment seemed to indicate that the legislature might grant an equal treatment to 'forms of social life similar to marriage' in certain specific situations.[151]

At that time, the Constitutional Tribunal was still not prepared to confer upon same-sex couples the right to marry. However, the 1993 case 'noted the hindrances these couples faced relative to persons united in marriage'.[152] In the early 2000s this acknowledgement, along with growing demands by the LGBT community, led the left-wing Government to support the introduction of civil partnerships, despite the fierce opposition of large segments of the population and religious groups.[153] In 2001, in particular, the Bundestag passed the Civil Partnerships Act[154] legalising same-sex civil unions (*eingetragene Lebenspartnerschaft*, literally 'life partnership'). In order to maintain a proper distinction with the institution of marriage,[155] the Act opted for a 'parallel' regulation of civil unions: the legal consequences of the registered partnership were mostly based on the legal consequences of marriage, but civil partners were not allowed to adopt children, were treated as single persons as far as inheritance and tax law were concerned, and had no right to a partner's pension in the event of that person's death.

The *Länder* (state) governments of Bavaria and Saxony immediately challenged the Act before the Constitutional Tribunal on several grounds. In particular they

[147] AG Frankfurt/Main, (1993) NJW 940. See Schimmel and Heun, 'The Legal Situation' n 136 above, 585.

[148] LG Frankfurt/Main, (1993) NJW 1998.

[149] Case No 1 BvR 640/93, Oct 4, 1993, 1993 NJW 3058. See Gröschner, 'Ehe und Familie' n 141, 774 and fn 145.

[150] Nonetheless this kind of union is constitutionally protected under Art 2(1) of the Basic Law concerning the right to free development of personality and the general freedom of action (*allgemeine Handlungsfreitheit*).

[151] See Kommers and Miller, *The Constitutional Jurisprudence of the Federal Republic of Germany* n 137 above, 499.

[152] ibid.

[153] The German Government was headed by Chancellor Gerhard Schröder and composed by a coalition between the Social Democrats and the Green Party. For a detailed account of the political struggle over the Civil Partnership Act 2001, see Repetto, 'At the Crossroads Between Privacy and Community', n 130 above, 270.

[154] Act on the Termination of the Discrimination of Same-Sex Couples: Civil Partnerships (*Gesetz zur Beendigung der Diskriminierung gleichgeschlechtlicher Gemeinschaften: Lebenspartnerschaften*) of 16 February 2001 (Federal Law Gazette, *Bundesgesetzblatt*, BGBl I, 266).

[155] On the necessity to preserve a 'principle of distance' (*Abstandsgebot*) between marriage and civil unions, see 105 BVerfGE 313(2002), paras 19–20.

contended that it was not consistent with the protection of marriage and the family required by Article 6 of the Basic Law because it undermined the duty of the State to promote marriage. In a long-awaited case of 2002 (the 'civil partnerships case'),[156] the Constitutional Tribunal confirmed the constitutionality of the civil unions, arguing that they are basically different from marriage and do not compete with it.[157] However, the Court remarked again that 'marriage is inherently heterosexual'[158] and declined the invitation to elevate civil unions to the level of dignity of marriage under Article 6.[159]

It is interesting to observe that, as far as the relationship among the Constitutional Tribunal, the legislator and the public opinion were concerned, the 2002 case emphasised that

> the Basic Law itself contains no definition of marriage, but presupposes it as a special form of human cohabitation. The realisation of the constitutional protection of marriage therefore needs a legal provision that structures and restricts what form of partnership enjoys the protection of the Constitution. Here, the legislature has considerable freedom of drafting in determining the form and content of marriage. The Basic Law guarantees the institution of marriage not in the abstract, but in the form that corresponds to current prevailing opinions, which are expressed definitively in the statutory provisions. However, in shaping marriage, the legislature must take into account the essential structural principles that follow from the application of Article 6(1) of the Basic Law to marriage as it is actually encountered in connection with the nature of the fundamental right guaranteed as a freedom and in connection with other constitutional norms.[160]

In other words, the Tribunal said that the content of marriage (as 'the union of one man with a woman') 'has stood the test of time despite social change and the concomitant changes of its legal structure and been shaped by the Basic Law'.[161] In commenting on the judgment, German scholarship emphasised the 'dilemma' of a circular reasoning in this argument[162] insofar as it seemed to suggest that public opinion and statutory provisions influence the interpretation of marriage in

[156] 105 BVerfGE 313 (2002).

[157] ibid, para 103 ('Such a danger might exist if the legislature created another institution in competition with marriage, with the same function, and, for example, gave it the same rights and lesser duties, so that the two institutions were interchangeable. Such interchangeability, however, is not associated with the registered civil partnership. It cannot enter into competition with marriage, if for no other reason that that the group of persons for whom the institution is intended does not overlap with the group of married persons. The registered civil partnership, because of this difference, is also not marriage with a wrong label, as is assumed in the two minority votes, but something different from marriage. Its different nature does not result from its name, but from the circumstance that not man and woman, but two persons of the same sex can create a union in the registered civil partnership' (official transl)).

[158] ibid, para 79.

[159] ibid, para 88 ('This protection does not cover the institution of the registered civil partnership. The fact that the 88 partners are of the same sex distinguishes it from marriage and at the same time constitutes it. The registered civil partnership is not marriage within the meaning of Article 6(1) of the Basic Law. It grants rights to same-sex couples. In this way, the legislature takes account of Article 2.1 and Article 3.1 and 3.3 of the Basic Law, by helping these persons to better develop their personalities and by reducing discrimination' (official transl)).

[160] ibid, para 87.

[161] ibid.

[162] See Gröschner, 'Ehe und Familie', n 141 above, 36.

Article 6, and at the same time this clause is binding on the legislature. As Sanders has pointed out,

> a constitutional interpretation that is bound by the meaning of marriage as defined in family law would prevent constitutional law from exerting any meaningful influence on the law below it. In addition, if marriage is interpreted in this manner, this means that constitutional law would, in effect, impose no restrictions on the legislature. Moreover, the courts and legislature are undoubtedly influencing public opinion on marriage, but in turn, public opinion itself is what influences legislation and, according to the Constitutional Tribunal, the constitutional understanding of marriage.[163]

However, the importance of the civil partnership case of 2002 lay in the interpretation of the constitutional mandate to promote and support marriage that, the Tribunal said, does not imply that the legislator should treat other relationships less favourably.[164] By remarking the differences between marriage and same-sex unions and by leaving the latter in the hands of the legislator, the Constitutional Tribunal arguably devalued the constitutional meaning of same-sex relationships, but at the same time 'weakened the criticism against registered partnerships as a "lesser marriage" which ... could have imperilled the autonomy and persistence of [civil partnerships]'.[165]

This argument provided the constitutional framework for a further enlargement of rights and guarantees to same-sex couples: in 2004 the Civil Partnerships Act of 2001 was amended in order to include stepchild adoption and the divorce rules which had been excluded in 2001 for political reasons.[166] At the same time, after 2002, the Constitutional Tribunal has been reinforcing the equalisation of civil partnerships to marriages stating in recent cases that every person has a constitutional right[167] to establish a relationship with a partner of the same or of different sex and to secure it respectively with a civil partnership or a marriage.[168] In 2009, in a case concerning the unequal treatment of marriage and civil partnership with regard to the right of widow's pension,[169] the Tribunal concluded that this discrimination lacks 'a special factual ground of justification that goes beyond the abstract promotion of marriage'.[170] It held that

> The mere reference to the requirement of protecting marriage does not justify such a differentiation. For the authority to give favourable treatment to marriage over other ways of life ... does not give rise to a requirement contained in Article 6.1 of the Basic Law to disadvantage other ways of life in comparison to marriage. It cannot be constitutionally justified to derive from the special protection of marriage a rule that other partnerships are to be structured in a way different from marriage and to be given lesser rights.[171]

[163] Sanders, 'Marriage, Same-Sex Relationship, and the German Constitution', n 139 above, 919.

[164] 105 BVerfGe 313, n 156 above, para 103.

[165] Repetto, 'At the Crossroads Between Privacy and Community', n 130 above, n 273.

[166] Registered Life Partnership Law (Revision) Act, 2004 (*Gesetz zur Überarbeitung des Lebenspartnerschaftsrechts*).

[167] The constitutional right to establish a relationship with a partner of the same or different sex is protected under Art 1(1) and Art 2(1), concerning respectively the right to dignity and the right to the free development of personality.

[168] 115 BVerfGE 1 (2005), paras 53–54. (*Transsexuals case III*).

[169] 124 BVerfGE 199 (2009).

[170] ibid, para 106.

[171] ibid, para 105.

More recent cases have declared other differences of treatment unconstitutional, leading to a fuller equalisation between marriage and civil partnership: in 2009 the Tribunal eliminated the differences in inheritance taxes[172] and in 2010 it declared unconstitutional the inequalities in respect of taxes on purchase of real estate[173] and benefits for married civil servants.[174] Finally, the Constitutional Tribunal addressed differences concerning parental rights of same-sex couples in a civil partnership: in 2013 the Tribunal overturned the ban on the so-called 'successive adoption', making it possible for a same-sex partner to become parent of their partner's adoptive child (*Sukzessivadoption*).[175] The Court clearly states that same-sex couples can raise a child as well as married opposite-sex couples and that no scientific study supports an opposite conclusion.[176] Nonetheless in 2014 the Tribunal dismissed on procedural grounds a request from a Berlin district court (Amtsgericht Berlin-Schöneberg) to declare the ban on joint adoption unconstitutional.[177]

Civil partnerships now confer rights nearly equal to those of married couples. The only difference lies in joint adoption and, as Sanders emphasises, 'in their names and prestige'.[178] The road towards the introduction of equal marriage is now open[179] and has the support of 65 per cent of the German population.[180] The Constitutional Tribunal has repeatedly emphasised the importance that social opinion has on the concept of marriage, arguing, since its first case on same-sex couples in 1993, that a change of marriage as a consequence of a change of the prevailing sentiments of public opinions is possible.

C. The Different Roles of Constitutional and Ordinary Courts in Promoting Equal Marriage in Europe

The foregoing account of the path towards equal marriage in some European countries affords the opportunity to make some final remarks on the roles of constitutional

172 ibid.

173 126 BVerfGE 400 (2010).

174 2 BvR 855/06 (2007) (First Chamber of the Second Senate).

175 133 BVerfGE 5 9 (2013). Before this ruling, in consequence of the 2004 Act amending of the Civil Partnership Act of 2001, a same-sex partner could only adopt their partner's biological child (stepchild adoption). See below, Ch 5 p 174 ff.

176 133 BVerfGE 59 n 175 above, para 80. The Constitutional Tribunal gave the Parliament a deadline (June 2014) to amend the legislation on adoption. The law was approved in May 2014, Law for the Execution of the Judgment of the Constitutional Tribunal on Successive Adoption for Civil Partners (*Gesetz zur Umsetzung der Entscheidung des Bundesverfassungsgerichts zur Sukzessivadoption durch Lebenspartne*) of 26 June 2014, *Federal Law Gazette, Bundesgesetzblatt*, BGBl 2014, I, no 27.

177 (2014) 2 BvL 2/13.

178 AEH Sanders, 'When, if not Now? An Update on Civil Partnership in Germany' (2016) 17 *German Law Journal* 487, 507.

179 In 2013 and in 2015 two initiatives were proposed by five *Länder* and were approved by the Bundesrat (German lower House): the first was defeated by the Bundestag (the German upper House) whereas, at the time of writing, the second case was still pending but the governing coalition had blocked consideration of the bill in the Legal Affairs Committee.

180 INSA poll published by *Bild* on 2 June 2015.

and ordinary courts in promoting legislative reform and validating public opinion and the claims of social movements.

Whereas European legislators, which are politically accountable, have been taking steps in the advancement of same-sex couples rights that are consistent with public opinion, or have ruled in favour of same-sex marriage when a strong backlash was unlikely to occur due to the distinctive features of the political national landscape (as in Portugal),[181] the courts are placed in a more difficult position. They are called upon to respond to the minorities that resort to them seeking to assert and protect their fundamental rights. As Eskridge emphasises, 'for a minority whose members [are] socially disparaged and politically toxic, courts [are] virtually the only forums where minority group members can seek decent treatment from the state'.[182] Furthermore, in the civil law tradition, principles regulating the burden of proof imply that courts cannot refuse to adjudicate and are obliged to release a judgment that supports, totally or partially, the case of one of the parties (prohibition of *non liquet*).[183]

However, the European experience makes clear that constitutional and supreme courts should not be assimilated to lower ordinary courts: in a centralised judicial review system—the prevailing model in Europe[184]—constitutional courts are more reluctant to determine radical constitutional changes through their judgments, especially when the issue at stake involves an institution so entrenched in culture, history and tradition as marriage.

Conversely, lower courts are more responsive to changing social claims, first of all because they are closer to the public and, in comparison with constitutional courts, are less concerned with the prospect of backlash that could undermine their own legitimacy.

[181] See above p 91 f.

[182] Eskridge, 'Backlash Politics' n 10 above at 282.

[183] The term *non liquet* originates in Roman law and it means 'it is not clear'. It refers to the case in which a competent court does not release a judgment for the absence of a suitable law, the vagueness of the rule, or the injustice of the legal results. Therefore, the prohibition of *non liquet* means that the judge must necessarily reach a decision using all the legislative and interpretative means available. This principle was codified in the French Civil Code of 1805 (*Code Napoléon*), art 4 stating that 'A judge who refuses to give judgment on the pretext of legislation being silent, obscure or insufficient, may be prosecuted for being guilty of a denial of justice.' This clause overturned the 18th-century French tradition where in case of doubt the judge was obliged to turn to the legislator (ie the King) who would then issue a declaration of his will *(référé au législatif)*. See J Gilissen, 'Le Probleme des Lacunes du Droit dans l'Evolution du Droit Medieval et Moderne', in C Perelman (ed), *Le Probleme des Lacunes en Droit* (Bruylant, 1968) 197; A Pizzorusso, *Sistemi giuridici comparati* (Milano, Giuffrè, 1998) 232. Similar principles were codified in the Prussian Civil Code of 1794 and are followed in modern civil codes (see eg art 12 of *Preleggi* (Provisions on the law in general) of the Italian Civil Code of 1942; Swiss Civil Code of 1907 art 1(2).

It should be noticed that the *non liquet* duty should be distinguished from the 'political question doctrine', whose equivalents can be found in procedural rules of European constitutional courts (see, for instance art 28 of law no 87 of 11 March 1953 on the functioning of the Italian Constitutional Court, stating that 'judicial review of legislation excludes any evaluation of political nature and any check on the exercise of discretionary powers of the Parliament).

[184] On the classification of judicial review systems and the differences between the American system and the system adopted by some European countries, see n 38 above. On the peculiar features of the centralised system of judicial review, V Ferreres Comella, 'The European Model of Constitutional Review of Legislation: Toward Decentralization'? (2004) 3 *International Journal of Constitutional Law* 461.

Furthermore, it should be remembered that in centralised systems of judicial review, ordinary courts have a duty to interpret the law in conformity with the constitution. This means that before referring a question to the constitutional court, which only has the power to set aside an unconstitutional statute, the ordinary judges are expected to look for an interpretation that will preserve its validity.[185] This implies that, as the Italian Constitutional Court has emphasised repeatedly since 1996, 'laws are not declared unconstitutional illegitimate because it is possible to give them an unconstitutional interpretation, but because it is not possible to give them a constitutional interpretation'.[186] Some courts—such as the Spanish, the Italian and the German constitutional courts—are very rigorous in this regard and explicitly require that the referring court explains in its reference the reasons why it is not possible to construe legislation in conformity with the Constitution; otherwise the preliminary reference will be dismissed as inadmissible.

Scholars have argued that this duty to construe legislation in conformity with the Constitution is enlarging the constitutional role and responsibilities of ordinary judges and is propelling the European centralised model toward decentralisation.[187] As Stone Sweet writes, 'ordinary judges enhance their own autonomy. In this way, both legislative intent and the alleged monopoly of the constitutional court on constitutional interpretation are subverted, enhancing the importance of the ordinary law courts as lawmakers in their own right'.[188]

On the contrary, especially in countries like Italy that do not have a direct constitutional complaint procedure, and whose citizens are not even allowed to lodge a complaint to the constitutional court, constitutional courts can make use of the technique of constitutionally conforming interpretation to avoid direct confrontation with the political branches of government. As Lamarque points out when discussing the role of the Italian Constitutional Court,'it wants to exercise the well-known "passive virtues" typical of a supreme court that is attributed with the power to review the constitutionality of law, but finds itself operating in a system with a very strong political power'.[189]

Italy is illustrative of the different approach to sexual orientation equality issues between a very cautious constitutional court and more responsive ordinary

[185] In Spain this obligation is laid down in *Ley Orgánica 6/1985*, of 1 July, art 5, sec 3 (*Ley Orgánica del Poder Judicial*) which clarifies that the judge should not refer an issue to the Constitutional Tribunal if it is possible to interpret the statute in such a way as to make it comply with the Constitution. In Italy and Germany, the constitutional courts are required to attempt to engage in a constitutionally conforming interpretation, on pain of the preliminary reference being rejected as inadmissible. See M de Visser, *Constitutional Review in Europe. A Comparative Analysis* (Oxford, Hart Publishing, 2014) 377.

[186] Case no 356 of 14 October 1996. See E Lamarque, 'Interpreting Statutes in Conformity with the Constitution: The Role of the Italian Constitutional Court and Ordinary Judges' (2010) 1 *Italian Journal of Public Law* 91. See also V Barsotti, PG Carozza, M Cartabia and A Simoncini, *Italian Constitutional Justice in Global Context* (Oxford, Oxford University Press, 2015) 219 ff.

[187] Comella, 'The European Model' n 184 above, 463; T Groppi,'The Italian Constitutional Court: Towards a Multi-level system of Judicial Review?' (2008) 3 *Journal of Comparative Law* 1000; Lamarque 'Interpreting Statutes' n 186 above, 118.

[188] A Stone Sweet, 'The Politics of Constitutional Review in France and Europe' (2007) 5 *International Journal of Constitutional Law* 69, 91.

[189] Lamarque, 'Interpreting Statutes' n 186 above, 114.

courts: before May 2016, when Italy's Parliament approved the first regulation of same-sex partnerships,[190] Italy was the last major European country not to formally recognise same-sex relationships. In 2010, some lower courts made the first attempts to promote sexual orientation equality by referring to the Constitutional Court the issue of constitutionality of the articles of the Civil Code on marriage 'insofar as they do not allow same-sex couples to conclude marriage'. They argued that Article 29 of the Italian Constitution does not define marriage in heterosexual terms and it neither prohibits nor permits same-sex marriage. Accordingly, they asked the Constitutional Court to fill the legislative gap and to eliminate illegitimate discrimination against same-sex couples, by removing unconstitutional references to gender in the civil code.[191]

The Constitutional Court dismissed the case (case no 138 of 2010),[192] arguing that the lower courts were looking for a legislative regulation of same-sex marriage that could not be obtained through a judicial case. Same-sex unions—the Constitutional Court clarified—require a detailed regulation at legislative level. Therefore, the Court urged the Parliament to intervene 'according to its time-scales, procedures and limits set by the law'.[193] At the same time, the Constitutional Court rejected the constitutional issues on substantial grounds, moving from an originalist interpretation of 'marriage' in Article 29 of the Italian Constitution. The Court's basic argument—which will be discussed more deeply below[194]—is that concepts of 'marriage' and 'family' are not 'fixed' because they are endowed with the flexibility of constitutional principles; nonetheless, a progressive interpretation cannot go so far as to impinge upon the core of Article 29 that refers to marriage being of a different-sex couple.[195]

Against such a hard-line position of the Constitutional Court,[196] in the last few years Italian lower ordinary courts have instead been promoting constitutional change through a constitutionally conforming interpretation of statutes and a progressive reading of constitutional clauses on marriage and family.[197] At the same time

[190] Law no 76 of 2016.

[191] The issue of constitutionality is therefore quite similar to that one submitted to the Constitutional Court in Portugal in case no 359 of 2009, n 73 above.

[192] Constitutional Court case no 138 of 15 April 2010. For an accurate analysis of the case in Italian scholarship on this judgment, see R Romboli, 'Il diritto "consentito" al matrimonio ed il diritto "garantito" alle coppie omosessuali in una pronuncia in cui la Corte dice "troppo" e "troppo poco"', in (2010) *Giurisprudenza costituzionale* 1629 ff.

[193] Case n 138 of 2010 n 192, para 8.

[194] See below p 115 ff.

[195] See De Freitas and Tega, 'Judicial Restraint and Political Responsibility' n 39 above at 291 ff.

[196] The Italian Constitutional Court reiterated an originalist interpretation of Art 29 of the Italian Constitution on marriage in case no 170 of 11 June 2014 (concerning the compulsory divorce of a opposite-sex couple after the husband's gender reassignment surgery).

[197] See, eg Tribunal of Milan, case no 9965/11 of 13 June 2011 (recognising the right of a homosexual partner to compensation following the death of the partner); Tribunal of Reggio Emilia, ordinance of 13 February 2012; Court of Appeal of Milan, Labour Section, Judgment no 7176/12 of 29 March 2012 (same-sex partner's right to be covered under the employed partner's medical insurance); Tribunal of Grosseto, case of 3 April 2014 and case 17 February 2015 (refusal to register a same-sex marriage unlawful); Court of Appeal of Turin, case of 29 October 2014 (registration of birth for two mothers); Tribunal of Palermo, decree of 13 April 2015 (right of a child to maintain a relationship with his social parent after divorce); Tribunale dei Minorenni di Roma (Rome Juvenile Court), case of 30 July 2014, case of

they have frequently stressed the importance of reading constitutional principles of marriage and family in the light of Articles 8 and 12 ECHR, an argument that the Constitutional Court rejected in 2010, refusing to engage in a dialogue with international case law. This 'progressive' approach has also been followed in several cases concerning parenting rights of same-sex couples.[198]

Furthermore, courts and ordinary courts are placed in a different position as far as the legal consequences of their judgments on the rights of gays and lesbians are concerned: in the groundbreaking judgment in *Oliari v Italy*[199] of 2015 (condemning Italy under Article 8 ECHR for the lack of any kind of recognition of same-sex unions), the ECtHR stressed that, although Italian national courts have repeatedly upheld the need to ensure protection for same sex-unions and to avoid discriminatory treatment', they make their findings only on a case-by-case basis.[200] Conversely, in a centralised system of judicial review, constitutional cases—totally or partially repealing a piece of legislation—have an *erga omnes* effect and can be considered analogous to a binding source of the law.[201]

These evaluations—and the consequent concern of the Court for its own legitimacy—have probably been behind the Italian Constitutional Court's choice not to interfere with the exercise of discretionary powers of the Parliament. But as mentioned above, mostly European constitutional courts have been analogously reluctant to anticipate legislative reforms: in France and in Portugal, for instance, the constitutional courts dismissed the first cases on same-sex marriages before the introduction of equal marriage at legislative level,[202] whilst the same courts later concluded in favour of same-sex marriage, when Parliaments had passed legislative reforms extending this right to same-sex couples. This makes it possible to argue that, although even constitutional courts take into account the prevailing sentiments

22 October 2015 and case of 23 December 2015 (on stepchild adoption); Court of Appeal of Milan, case of 16 October 2015 (registration of foreign stepchild adoption); Court of Appeal of Naples, case of 30 March 2016 (mutual adoption of the biological children of a same-sex couple married in France). See also Court of Cassation, decision no 4184 of 15 March 2012 and decision no 2400 of 9 February 2015 (concluding that lack of recognition of equal marriage is not incompatible with the applicable domestic and international system of human rights, but holding that such same-sex marriage concluded abroad can no longer be considered 'void' and urging the Parliament to adopt a regulation).

[198] These developments will be analysed thoroughly in Ch 5.

[199] *Oliari v Italy* [2015] ECHR 752.

[200] *Oliari v Italy* n 199 above, para 170.

[201] The *erga omnes* (ie applicable to all, absolute) effect of judgments declaring the unconstitutionality of the referred legislation is due to the fact that in European centralised systems of judicial review, issues are mostly submitted to constitutional courts by a public authority (the government, members of parliament, or courts), whereas in the United States, constitutional cases are mostly binding on the parties of the case. See L Favoreau, 'Constitutional review in Europe', in L Henkin and AJ Rosenthal (eds), *Constitutionalism and Rights: The Influence of the United States Constitution Abroad* (New York, Columbia University Press, 1989). Nonetheless this assertion is controversial in relation to certain instances involving judicial review in France. See Dorsen and Rosenfeld and Sajó and Baer, *Comparative Constitutionalism. Cases and Materials* n 38, 138 above. On the binding and *erga omnes* effect of constitutional court cases in a centralised system of judicial review and on their nature of sources of law, see A Pizzorusso, *Delle fonti del diritto* (Bologna, Zanichelli, 1977) 274 ff. Against, see R Guastini, *Le fonti del diritto. Fondamenti teorici* (Milano, Giuffrè, 2010) 374 ff.

[202] *Conseil constitutionnel*, case no 419/99, n 96 above and case no 92/2010, n 112 above; Portugal Constitutional Tribunal, case no 359/2009, n 73 above.

in public opinion, concerns for the consequences of the case of their legitimacy are probably decisive, especially in civil law countries and in centralised systems of judicial review.

Nonetheless, although in Europe same-sex civil unions and marriage are mostly the result of legislative reforms, a similarity among the Canadian, the United States and the European paths towards equal marriage should be emphasised: it lies in the contribution that the lower courts as well as the constitutional/supreme courts have made to elevating sexual orientation equality issues on the public agenda. As Eskridge suggests, 'when courts validate equality claims by same-sex couples, as they increasingly have done in the last decade, they raise marriage equality higher up on the public agenda'.[203] In recent years European lower courts, as well as the more influential constitutional courts, have been bringing sexual orientation equality issues to public attention: as illustrated earlier, in the mid-2000s in France, for instance, lower courts and local authorities promoted the debate on the passage from PaCS to equal marriage; in Italy, courts have repeatedly broken the silence of political parties and authorities on the rights of gays and lesbians; in Germany, as early as the 1990s, courts stimulated a debate on same-sex union rights.

Furthermore, as happened in the United States, courts have been playing a key role in challenging stereotypes and the 'politics of disgust': by including same-sex couples within the definition of 'family' or by describing with greater details the normalcy of same-sex couples' life with their children, courts have contributed to de-emphasising many prejudices against homosexuality. As mentioned above, in 1993 in Germany the first Senate of Constitutional Tribunal drew attention on the difficulties that same-sex couples face in comparison with married couples.[204] Even in Italy, the Constitutional Court emphasised the right of same-sex couples to 'live freely as a couple' in 2010, and its admonitions to the legislature to introduce regulation in order to regulate same-sex unions in 2010 and in 2014, as well as the many judgments of ordinary courts on parental rights of gay couples, contributed to the passage, in Eskridge's words, from 'backlash politics' to 'identity politics', ie a rhetoric motivated by identity-based concerns.[205]

Courts' role in promoting public debate on sexual orientation equality issues is not limited to judgments resulting in a victory for gays and lesbians. Most of the early European cases mentioned in the previous pages rejected same-sex couples' claims (Germany,[206] France,[207] Italy,[208] Spain,[209] Portugal).[210] Nonetheless, especially constitutional courts' decisions and the debate surrounding them, helped to forge arguments against and in favour of same-sex couples' rights.[211] As I will clarify

[203] Eskridge, 'Backlash Politics' n 10 above, 310.

[204] On the effects of the 1993 judgment of the first Senate on same-sex marriage, see above p 99.

[205] Eskridge, 'Backlash Politics' n 10 above, 300.

[206] See Case No 1 BvR 640/93 but also the ordinary courts cases mentioned in n 147 above.

[207] Case 419/1999 n 96.

[208] Case no 138 of 2010, n 192 above.

[209] ATC 222/1994, n 43 above.

[210] Case no 359 of 2009, n 73 above.

[211] See Siegel n 33 above.

in the following pages, objections concerning for instance the procreative purpose of marriage, the 'natural' character of heterosexuality or the unsuitability of same-sex couples for rearing children have been dismissed and weakened by the courts, and they almost entirely no longer form part of the rhetoric against homosexuality.

However, in spite of its unsatisfactory outcome, early litigation resulted in a long-term success for LGBT movements: the Spanish Constitutional Tribunal refused in 1994 to extend to same-sex relationships the constitutional protection of marriage. Nonetheless, the rationale of the case paved the way for the adoption of regulations of same-sex unions at local level and, as clarified above,[212] the Constitutional Tribunal's openness towards an equalisation of marriage at legislative level helped to penetrate the idea of the 'normalcy' of same-sex relationships. In Portugal, the Parliament introduced same-sex marriage just a few months after the Constitutional Tribunal's judgment in case no 359 of 2009: the case rejected the claims of a lesbian couples, but at the same time suggested to the legislator and to LGBT movements that constitutional clauses did not prohibit same-sex marriage.[213] As early as 1993 the German Constitutional Tribunal analogously played a key role in the advancement of same-sex couples' rights.[214] In France, although in 1999 the Conseil constitutionnel displayed an initial reluctance to qualify same-sex couples as 'families',[215] it recognised the importance of same-sex relationships and sexuality. Its arguments, as clarified above, forged the further debate on same-sex marriage and defined the boundaries between the judicial and the legislative powers in the interpretation of open statutory clauses.[216] In Italy, case no 138 of 2010—that rejected a couple's claims on the basis of an originalist interpretation of marriage—provided clear instructions for the adoption of a regulation of same-sex civil unions based on the German model. The Court's statements have been accurately taken into consideration by the Italian Parliament in the debate on the 2016 statute on same-sex civil unions.[217]

These examples demonstrate that what mattered most in the European countries analysed in this chapter was not the outcomes of the judgments, but the subtle instructions that courts—especially constitutional courts—provided to legislators, social movement and even public opinion. They gave implicit (sometimes explicit)[218] directions for further litigation, paved the way for legislative reforms and helped forge the constitutional arguments that could successfully support further claims. As M Nussbaum emphasises, 'as some States experiment with same-sex marriage, some others try civil unions, and some others recognize same-sex marriages legally contracted elsewhere, people will learn more about the institution, and democratic

[212] See above p 86 ff.
[213] See above at 90 ff.
[214] See above at 99.
[215] Case no 419/1999, n 96 above.
[216] See above at 95.
[217] Law no. 76 of 20 May 2016 (Civil Unions).
[218] See for instance case no 138 of 2010, n 192 above, para 4.2 (providing instructions to lower courts on which kind of constitutional issues on the rights of same-sex couples the Constitutional court will probably admit in the future).

preferences are highly likely to change. None of that would have started, however, had at least some state courts not had the daring to read their constitutions with a courageous and unbiased eye'.[219]

Furthermore, as the courts—especially the highest courts—both influence and are influenced by the prevailing sentiments in public opinion and politics, in my opinion this process will result in a 'virtuous cycle' in which each single achievement leads to a further advancement towards sexual equality.[220]

I would like to reiterate that this conclusion does not imply my support for a step-by-step approach by LGBT movements.[221] In the last few years each country has addressed same-sex marriage at a different pace and in different ways, depending on the intensity of disgust-based backlash, but also—as the experiences of Portugal and Italy make clear—on the distinctive features of the political landscape,[222] its receptiveness to civil rights reforms.[223] My purpose is basically to emphasise that experience shows that in civil law countries, with a centralised system of judicial review, it is difficult to resort to constitutional courts in the hope of bringing about a radical change in the regulation of institutions like marriage and family, deeply entrenched in historical and cultural traditions. In conclusion, the general pattern confirms the validity of American scholarship's theories suggesting that courts' intervention is more effective after politics and social movements themselves have created a substantially favourable environment for their intervention.

II. ARGUMENTS IN SAME-SEX MARRIAGE CASES: TRADITION v CONSTITUTIONAL CHANGE

A. The Argument of Tradition in Constitutional Cases. Introductory Remarks

The first constitutional hurdle that courts face in same-sex marriage cases lies in the legal definition of 'marriage'. Either considering marriage as a 'contract' or as a 'legal relationship' or, finally, as an institution,[224] the issue revolves around whether sex difference should be assumed as the defining criterion of the marital bond.

Since this question involves the interpretation of the relevant constitutional clauses (or of the statutory texts and precedents) on marriage, most of the courts have

[219] M Nussbaum, *From Disgust to Humanity. Sexual Orientation and Constitutional Law* (Oxford, Oxford University Press, 2009) at 161-2.

[220] See *Lewis v Harris* 188 NJ 415, 462 (2008) ('Although courts can ensure equal treatment, they cannot guarantee social acceptance, which must come through the evolving ethos of a maturing society. Plaintiffs' quest does not end here. Their next appeal must be to their fellow citizens whose voices are heard through their popularly elected representatives.')

[221] See Introduction p 8.

[222] Above p 89 ff.

[223] Eg in Italy, the opportunity of a 'step-by-step' approach towards equal marriage has been fiercely rejected by a part of LGBT movements, who reasonably argue that their final goal is the introduction of equal marriage. Accordingly they have deeply criticised the 2016 Act regulating same-sex civil unions on the basis of the 'German model', claiming that it replicates a 'separate but equal' logic.

[224] On the basic difference between marriage as a 'contract' or as a 'legal institution', see K O'Donovan, *Sexual Divisions in Law* (London, Weinfeld & Nicholson, 1985) 133–34.

usually addressed it before engaging in a detailed analysis of the fundamental rights involved. For this reason, in my opinion, a comparative analysis of same-sex marriage cases should start from investigating the different ways in which courts have framed the relevance of sex difference in the definition of 'marriage'.[225]

It should be premised that, as far as the wording of constitutional texts is concerned, most of the constitutions neither explicitly define 'marriage' nor explicitly mention sex or gender difference as a prerequisite to marriage. Some constitutions (such as the German Basic Law,[226] the Italian,[227] the Portuguese[228] and the Greek[229] Constitutions) only refer to the institution of marriage in order to emphasise its narrow relationship with the family and to accord both of them constitutional protection. Other constitutional texts (like the French Constitution of 1958 and the United States federal Constitution) do not even explicitly include the right to marriage within their bill of rights. Finally, other constitutions (for instance, the Spanish Constitution)[230] state that 'men' and 'women' have the right to marry and to found a family (although they do not explicitly require that they must marry each other).

The last formula follows the text of international documents: Article 16 of the Universal Declaration of Human Rights 1948 similarly provides that 'men and women … have the right to marry and to found a family', Article 23(2) of the International Covenant on Civil and Political Rights (ICCPR) of 1966 states that 'the right of men and women of marriageable age to marry and to found a family shall be recognized',

[225] I do not take into consideration in this chapter wider issues concerning the difference of *biological* or *chromosomal* sex as a determinant of marriage. As early as in the 1960s, this issue was addressed by constitutional and supreme courts in cases in which one of the spouses had undergone gender reassignment surgery. See *Corbett v Corbett (otherwise Ashley)* [1970] 2 WLR 1306 (concluding that for the purposes of marriage the law should adopt the chromosomal, gonadal and genital tests, and if all three were congruent, determine sex accordingly, ignoring any operative intervention had to be considered of the sex assigned at birth) and *Goodwin v United Kindgom* ECHR 1996-II, [1996] ECHR 16 (concluding that the UK's position on immutability of gender and the inability of transsexuals to marry people of the same biological sex amounted to a violation of Arts 8 and 12 of the ECHR). The European Court of Human Rights case was followed by *Bellinger v Bellinger* [2003] UKHL 21, in which the House of Lords issued a declaration of incompatibility of s 11(c) of the Matrimonial Causes Act 1973. In the United Kingdom the issue is now governed by the Gender Recognition Act 2004.

In Germany, similar issues have been addressed by the Constitutional Tribunal as early as in 1978, in the *Transsexual I* case 88 BVerfGE 87 (recognising a right to 'gender self-identification'). In 2008, in the *Transsexual V* case, 121 BVerfGE 175, the First Senate of the Constitutional Tribunal struck down a provision of the German Gender Transsexual Act 1980 (*Transsexuellengesetz*) that recognised an approved gender change only if the person involved was unmarried. See also (2011) 128 BVerfGE 109 (holding that juridical recognition of transsexual people may not be made conditional upon genital surgeries).

In Italy, gender reassignment is governed by Law no 164 of 14 April 1982. In 2014 (case no 170 of 2014, the 'compulsory divorce case') the Constitutional Court declared this law partially unconstitutional as far as it requires the automatic dissolution of the marriage of a spouse who had undergone a gender reassignment surgery. See also Corte di Cassazione, case no 15138 of 2015 (concluding that surgery is not necessary to juridical recognition of gender).

[226] Art 6(1) German Basic Law (*Grundgesetz*). See above, Ch 3 n 16.

[227] Art 29(1) of Italian Constitution of 1948 above, Ch 3 n 19.

[228] Art 36(1) of the Portuguese Constitution above, Ch 3 n 14.

[229] Art 21(1) and (3) of the Greek Constitution above, Ch 3 n 13.

[230] Constitution of Spain of 1978, art 32. See above, n 42. See also, outside Europe, the 1988 Constitution of Brazil (art 226(3)).

and the terms of Article 12 of the European Convention on Human Rights (ECHR) are almost identical.[231]

As constitutions usually do not explicitly define marriage as an opposite-sex institution, references to 'man' and 'woman', 'husband' and 'wife' are mostly expressed in civil codes, statutes and judicial precedents. In the civil law tradition, sex-difference in marriage dates back to the Roman definition of marriage[232] and is confirmed by the use of gender-specific language in the provisions of the European civil codes regulating marriage.[233] Marriage between persons of the same sex was accordingly considered invalid.[234]

In the common law tradition, the judicial definition of marriage most commonly referred to was established by Lord Penzance in *Hyde v Hyde and Woodmansee*,[235] a nineteenth-century case stating that marriage 'as understood in Christendom' is 'the voluntary union for life of one man and one woman with the exclusion of all others'. This definition—whose Victorian heritage traces back to Western church and canon law[236]—was put in statutory form by section 11(c) of the Matrimonial Causes Act 1973.[237] It has not been directly overruled, and continued in force until the introduction of same-sex marriage in 2013.[238]

In Canada the impediment to marriage for same-sex couples was established by the common law rule formulated by Lord Penzance in *Hyde v Hyde*, because provincial statutory law does not impose sex diversity as determinant of marriage.[239]

[231] Art 12 ECHR states that 'Men and women of marriageable age have the right to marry and to found a family, according to the national laws governing the exercise of this right'.

[232] According to the formal definition by Modestinus, 'Nuptiae sunt coniuctio maris et feminae et consortium omnis vitae, divini et humani iuris communicatio' (Dig 23, 2, 1).

[233] See eg former art 144 of the French Code Civil (on the age for contracting marriage for men and women); arts 107 and 108 of the Italian Civil Code of 1942 (on the celebration of marriage, which refers to the spouses' declaration of intent to be joined as 'husband' and 'wife'); art 1416 ff of the German Civil Code (BGB) (on marital property, referring to a 'wife' and 'a husband'). In Spain, criticism against same-sex marriage has been based on old legal texts, such as the Provisional Act of Civil Marriage of 1870 (*Ley de Matrimonio Civil*), the Civil Code of 1889 or the Act of Civil Marriage of 1932 (*Ley de Matrimonio Civil*), and even on medieval texts such as *Las Siete Partidas* or *Las Decretales*, in order to emphasise that marriage involves procreation and heterosexuality.

[234] In Italy eg a marriage celebrated between two persons of the same sex has been repeatedly considered 'non-existent' by the ordinary courts. Nonetheless the Corte di Cassazione, the highest Italian civil and criminal court, in a recent case (no 4184 of 15 March 2012) concluded that due to the evolution of international law and the growing consensus towards same-sex unions, the registration of a same-sex marriage celebrated abroad should be denied not due to its non-existence but because same-sex marriages are 'unsuited to give rise to any legal effect' due to the lack of a regulation of same-sex marriage in the Italian legal system. See de Freitas and Tega, *Judicial Restraint and Political Responsibility*, n 39 above, 296 ff. In Germany a marriage between people of the same sex is analogously considered *Nichtehe*, ie as no marriage came into existence. For similar issues concerning the recognition of same-sex marriages celebrated abroad in the German legal system, see D Martiny, 'Private International Law Aspects of Same-Sex Couples under German Law' in K Boele-Woelki and A Fuchs (eds), *Legal Recognition of Same-Sex Relationships in Europe. National, Cross-Border and European Perspectives* (Cambridge, Intersentia, 2012) 189, 197.

[235] *Hyde v Hyde and Woodmansee* [1886] L Rev 1 P &D 130.

[236] A Diduck and F Canagas, *Family Law*, and F Canagas, *Family Law, Gender and the State. Text, Cases and Materials*, 3rd edn (Oxford, Hart Publishing, 2012) 43.

[237] Matrimonial Causes Act 1973.

[238] Marriage (Same Sex Couples) Act 2013, ch 30.

[239] For a detailed examination of the common law rule regarding marriage in the Canadian legal system, *Halpern v Canada*, [2003] OJ No 2268, para 35 ff; *Layland v Ontario* (Minister of Consumer

In the United States, as early as the end of the nineteenth century, the Supreme Court acknowledged the heterosexual and monogamous nature of marriage[240] and upheld the states' power to reserve the marital status to opposite-sex couples.[241] In 1976 the New Jersey Superior Court argued that despite winds of change, 'there was almost a universal recognition that a lawful marriage requires the performance of a ceremonial marriage of two persons of the opposite sex, a male and a female".[242] More recently, sex difference in marriage has been reiterated by the well-known definition of 'marriage' and 'spouses' adopted by the Defence of Marriage Act 1996 (DOMA)[243] whose primary justification was identified by proponents as the protection of tradition.[244] At state level, with the exception of Massachusetts, every state law in the past defined marriage in heterosexual terms.[245] Even in the state of Washington—where the marriage statute refers to 'persons' instead of to 'a man' and 'a woman'—courts assumed the 'heterosexual nature' of marriage.[246]

In South Africa the exclusion of same-sex couples from marriage was stated in the common law as early as in 1905[247] and was reiterated in the Marriage Act of 1961 which provides the formula for the celebration of marriage referring to the will of the spouses 'to take each other as husband and wife'.[248]

At international level, in *Joslin v New Zealand*,[249] the UN Human Rights Committee held that New Zealand had not violated human rights under the ICCPR

and Commercial Relations) (1993) 14 OR (3d) 658 (Ont Div Ct) and *Hendricks v Québec (Procureur général)* [2002] RJQ 2506, para 87; *EGALE Canada, Inc v Canada* (2003) 13 BCLR 4th 1 (Can BC CA), para 102 (arguing that 'In order to find that Parliament has the power to define same-sex relationship as marriage, the word "marriage" in s 91 (26) [Constitution Act, 1867] must be construed to mean a legal relationship between two persons regardless of sex or to include marriage like relationships. There is nothing to suggest that "marriage" in s 91 (26), was used in any context other than its legal context as understood in 1867, namely a monogamous, opposite-sex relationship'.

240 *Reynolds v United States* 98 US 145 (1878).

241 *Baker v Nelson* 409 US 810 (1972). See MA Glendon, *The Transformation of Family Law. State, Law and the Family in the United States and Western Europe* (Chicago, Chicago University Press, 1989) 50.

242 *MT v JT* 140 NJ Super 77 (1976), 83–84.

243 See 1 US Code § 7 (Definition of 'marriage' and 'spouse') as amended in 1996 by the Defense of Marriage Act (DOMA) (which stated that 'in determining the meaning of any Act of Congress, or of any ruling, regulation, or interpretation of the various administrative bureaus and agencies of the United States, the word "marriage" means only a legal union between one man and one woman as husband and wife, and the word "spouse" refers only to a person of the opposite sex who is a husband or a wife'). The definition was declared unconstitutional by the Supreme Court in *Windsor v United States* 133 SCT 2675 (2013).

In Canada, at federal level, the only statutory reference to a definition of marriage is found in s 1(1) of the Modernization of Benefits and Obligations Act 2000 which provides: 'For greater certainty, the amendments made by this Act do not affect the meaning of the word "marriage", that is, the lawful union of one man and one woman to the exclusion of all others'.

244 See Note, 'Litigating the Defense of Marriage Act: The Next Battleground for Same-Sex Marriage' (2004) 117 *Harvard Law Review* 2684, 2696–98.

245 See for a detailed analysis of the relevant statute law at state level, *Lewis v Harris* 88 NJ 415 (2006), 437 fn 11.

246 *Singer v Hara*, 11 Wn.App. 247, 522 P.2d 1187 (1974). See Glendon, *The Transformation of Family Law*, n 241 above, 50.

247 *Mashia Ebrahim v Mahomed Essop* 1905 TS 59, 61.

248 *Marriage Act*, no 25 of 1961, s 30(1).

249 *Joslin v New Zealand*, Communication no 902/1999, UN Doc A/57/40 at 214 (2002).

because Article 23 referred to 'men' and 'women' instead of using more general terms like "every human being", "everyone" and "all persons".

> Use of the term 'men and women' [the Committee argued] rather than the general terms used elsewhere in Part III of the Covenant, has been consistently and uniformly understood as indicating that the treaty obligation of States Parties stemming from Article 23, paragraph 2, of the Covenant is to recognize as marriage only the union between a man and a woman wishing to marry each other.[250]

Sex difference as an essential determinant of marriage comes into consideration within different arguments against same-sex marriage. It is the premise for asserting the procreative nature of marriage.[251] It also reminds of the idea of 'nature' in sexual relationships and, finally is considered as supported by historical and legal tradition. In the present chapter my purpose is to focus mainly on the last point in order to analyse how constitutional and supreme courts have addressed the binding value of legal tradition in the definition of marriage.

However, it should be premised that frequently both tradition and nature are taken into account by equal marriage opponents and it is difficult to distinguish clearly between the two arguments. This is exemplified by Justice Ormrod's statements in *Corbett v Corbett*, the 1970 judgment concerning the legal meaning of 'man' and 'women' for the purposes of marriage:

> Sex is clearly an essential determinant of the relationship called marriage because it is and always has been recognised as the union of man and woman. It is the institution on which the family is built, and in which the capacity for natural heterosexual intercourse is an essential element. It has, of course, many other characteristics, of which companionship and mutual support is an important one, but the characteristics which distinguish it from all other relationships can only be met by two persons of opposite sex.[252]

Nature and tradition are instead distinct concepts, and objections based on them move from different assumptions. The idea that only different-sex marriage is 'natural' appeals in particular to a basic aversion to homosexuality as 'against nature'. For this reason, such an argument can be traced back to a 'politics of disgust': in the United States, for instance, the backlash raised by the early cases on same-sex marriage, like *Baehr v Lewin*[253]—the 1993 judgment of the Supreme Court of Hawaii, stating that state's exclusion of same-sex couples from civil marriage violated the state constitution—was thoroughly soaked in the 'rhetoric of disgust'. As Eskridge clearly demonstrates in its writings, in the early 1990s, many Americans were emotionally upset at the idea that giving marriage rights to 'disgusting homosexuals' would result in the sacrifice of 'traditional marriage'.[254] When moral disapproval against homosexuality gradually disappeared—due also to federal Supreme Court

[250] *Joslin* n 249 above, para 8.2.
[251] See Ch 5 at 176.
[252] *Corbett v Corbett* n 225 above, 105–06.
[253] *Baehr v Lewin* 74 Haw 530, 852 P 2d 44 (1993).
[254] WN Eskridge, 'Backlash Politics: How Constitutional Litigation Has Advanced Marriage Equality in the United States' (2003) 93 *Boston University Law Review* 275, 297.

cases like *Lawrence v Texas*,[255] which 'helped shape the trajectory of debate'[256]—arguments based on the 'natural' meaning of marriage gradually disappeared from judicial rhetoric and were replaced by new and more respectful arguments for rejecting marriage equality claims.[257]

By contrast, the argument of sex-difference as a determinant of 'traditional' marriage appeals to history. In this perspective the essential elements of marriage are inferred from the axiomatic presumption of 'what marriage is and has always been'. The persuasiveness and the coherence of such an argument will be thoroughly discussed in the following pages, but it worth anticipating that those arguing that same-sex marriage is against tradition assume history as a proof of validity, and dismiss any need of evidence to demonstrate the consistency of tradition over time. At the same time, traditionalists frequently resort to generic references to the Judaeo-Christian tradition or to Roman law in order to presume the existence of marriage in its basic form from time immemorial.[258]

The reason why 'naturalness' is frequently called in aid to tradition, and why it is difficult to set the two arguments apart, is that both of them take into account the *effects* of the passage of time on the institution of marriage. In Michel de Montaigne's words, 'what we call against nature is in fact against custom. The laws of conscience which we say stem from nature, stem from custom. It is custom that makes impossible for us things which are not in themselves impossible.'[259] What is considered 'natural' in marriage is therefore supposed to be supported by constant usage. On the other hand, tradition represents judgments made in the past by those who framed the original meaning of marriage. As the Supreme Court of Canada pointed out in its 2004 reference judgment on same-sex marriage, 'customs are apt to develop into traditions which are stronger than law and remain unchallenged long after the reason for them has disappeared'.[260]

> A law's longevity suggests it has been time tested. A political community has likely retained a law over many years or generations because it has proven useful. Deferring to tradition thus involves deferring to the experience, judgment, and wisdom of prior generations Moreover, adhering to traditions may serve predictability and reliance interests. To the extent people develop expectations and structure their lives based on current laws, especially laws whose longevity suggests their likely continuance, abandoning such laws may cause a certain degree of social and economic disruption. Finally, respecting traditions can reinforce a sense of shared social identity and heritage, either within discrete cultural or religious communities or in the nation as a whole.[261]

[255] *Lawrence v Texas* 539 US 558 (2003).

[256] Eskridge, 'Backlash Politics' n 254 above, 297.

[257] For a deep insight on the role of United States federal and state courts in shaping the debate on same-sex marriage, RB Siegel, 'Foreword: Equality Divided' (2013) 127 *Harvard Law Review* 9, 83 ff.

[258] See, eg case no 138 of 15 April 2010 of the Italian Constitutional Court relying on 'a consolidated concept of marriage dating back thousands of years'. Against, the Supreme Court of Canada in *Reference Re Same-Sex Marriage* [2004] 3 SCR 698, 2004 SCC 79, para 25.

[259] Michel de Montaigne, *Essais*, Livre II, Chapitre 30.

[260] *Reference Re Same-Sex Marriage*, n 258 above, para 25.

[261] K Forde-Marzui, 'Tradition as Justification: The Case of Opposite-Sex Marriage' (2011) 78 *University of Chicago Law Review* 281, 285.

Furthermore, as Scheffler emphasises, 'traditions may themselves be ... regarded as valuable repositories of human knowledge, experience, creativity and achievement'.[262]

B. What is 'Tradition'?

i. Legal Tradition and the Difficult Identification of an 'Essential Core' of Marriage

As the institution of marriage escapes legal definition and is deeply entrenched in local history and culture, 'tradition' comes into consideration in same-sex marriage cases in different meanings. My purpose is to focus on the value of *legal* tradition, but it should be clarified that in same-sex marriage cases and in the arguments of those who are flatly opposed to equal marriage, tradition also encompasses religion and culture in its wider sense.[263]

Courts whose purpose is to emphasise the separation between Church and State and the secularism of the State, have addressed the value of tradition with reference to its legal contents (although not even legal tradition is totally immune from the influence of the dominant religion). In this respect legal tradition is inferred not only from constitutional clauses, relevant statutes (or articles of the civil codes), judicial precedents, custom, but also from the established legal scholarship on marriage.

The Italian Constitutional Court, for instance, in case no 138 of 2010 on same-sex marriage, observed that 'all legislation governing the institution contained in the Civil Code and in special legislation postulates the difference in sex of the married couple against the backdrop of "a consolidated concept of marriage dating back thousands of years"'.[264] The Court also recalled that, according to the Court of Cassation,[265] 'the difference in sex of the married couple is one of the minimum indispensable prerequisites for the existence of a marriage' and that academic literature had reached the same conclusion, concluding that 'any same-sex marriage will be void'.[266]

Against this background, the Italian Constitutional Court argued that the unbroken tradition of the sex difference in marriage supported an originalist interpretation of Article 29 of the Constitution (on marriage and family).[267] In particular, it concluded that

> As is clear from the *travaux preparatoires* [the debates on the adoption of the Constitution], the question of homosexual unions remained entirely unaddressed within the debate conducted within the Assembly, even though homosexuality was by no means unknown.

[262] S Scheffler, *Equality and Tradition. Questions of Value in Moral and Political Theory* (Oxford, Oxford University Press, 2010) 293.

[263] See below p 119 ff.

[264] Italian Constitutional Court, case no 138 of 2010, n 258 above, para 6.

[265] Court of Cassation, judgments no 7877, sez I Civ, of 9 June 2000, no 1304 of 22 February 1990 and no 1808 of 20 May 1976.

[266] Case no 138 of 2010, n 258 above, para 6.

[267] Art 29(1) of the Italian Constitution states that 'the Republic recognises the family as a natural society founded on marriage'.

> When drafting Article 29 of the Constitution, the delegates discussed an institution with a precise articulation and which was regulated in detail under civil law. Therefore, absent any different references, the inevitable conclusion is that they took account of the concept of marriage defined under the Civil Code which entered into force in 1942 and which, as noted above, specified (and still specifies) that married couples must be comprised of persons of the opposite sex.[268]

It is interesting to note that the Italian Constitutional Court defined this conclusion as 'inevitable' although Article 29 of the Italian Constitution does not provide any definition of marriage and in particular is silent on spouses' sex. Furthermore, the Civil Code, the main source of the law from which the Constitutional Court inferred the legal tradition of opposite-sex marriage, is not only subordinate to the Constitution (and should accordingly be interpreted in light of constitutional clauses, and not vice versa) but was also adopted before the 1948 Constitution came into force.[269]

Although the Constitutional Court was probably aware of this interpretative flaw,[270] it clearly stated that the original meaning of the constitutional clause 'cannot be set aside through interpretation, because to do so would not involve a simple re-reading of the system or the abandonment of a mere interpretative practice, but rather the implementation of a creative interpretation'.[271] Accordingly, the Court concluded that 'it must therefore be reasserted that the provision [Article 29 of the Constitution] did not take into account homosexual unions, but rather intended to refer to marriage within the traditional meaning of that institution'.[272]

Legal tradition was considered deeply also by the Irish High Court in *Zappone and Gilligan v Revenue Commissioners*,[273] a 2006 case, concluding that 'marriage was understood under Article 41 of the 1937 Constitution [*Bunreacht na hÉireann*][274] to be confined to persons of the opposite sex'. According to the High Court, this conclusion was supported lastly by a 2003 Supreme Court divorce case[275] and by the Civil Registration Act 2004,[276] which 'sets out what was previously the common

[268] Case no 138 of 2010, n 258 above, para 9.

[269] For a detailed analysis of case no 138 of 2010, see A Sperti, *Omosessualità e diritti. I percorsi giurisprudenziali ed il dialogo globale delle Corti costituzionali* (Pisa, Pisa University Press, 2013).

[270] The Constitutional Court argues that the originalist interpretation of Art 29(1) of the Constitution is confirmed by para 2 of the same article establishing the principle of the moral equality of the married couple. According to the Court this clause aims at guaranteeing equal dignity to the wife and rights within the marital relationship and therefore implicitly refers to the opposite-sex marriage. See case no 138 of 2010, n 258 above, para 9.

[271] ibid.

[272] ibid.

[273] *Zappone and Gilligan v Revenue Commissioners* [2006] IEHC 404, [2008] 2 IR 417.

[274] See Irish Constitution of 1937 (*Bunreacht na hÉireann*), Art 41 stating that '1. The State recognises the Family as the natural primary and fundamental unit group of Society, and as a moral institution possessing inalienable and imprescriptible rights, antecedent and superior to all positive law. 2. The State, therefore, guarantees to protect the Family in its constitution and authority, as the necessary basis of social order and as indispensable to the welfare of the Nation and the State.' Article 41(3) provides that 'The State pledges itself to guard with special care the institution of marriage, on which the family is founded, and to protect it against attack'.

[275] *T v T* [2003] I.L.R.M. 321. On the actual relevance of this citation to the issue at stake, J Ennis, 'Marriage: Redefined and Realigned with Bunreacht na hÉireann' (2010) 1 *Irish Journal of Legal Studies* 29, 33 ff.

[276] Civil Registration Act 2004 (no 3).

law exclusion of same-sex couples from the institution of marriage'. Therefore, writing for the High Court, Justice Dunne held that 'the definition of marriage to date has always been understood as being opposite sex marriage' and concluded that

> having regard to the clear understanding of the meaning of marriage as set out in the numerous authorities opened to the Court from this jurisdiction and elsewhere, I do not see how marriage can be redefined by the Court to encompass same sex marriage.[277]

It is interesting to observe that both the Italian Constitutional Court and Irish High Court reached similar conclusions arguing that marriage is not 'a frozen institution' and that the Constitution is 'a living instrument'.[278] Analogously in 2009, the Portuguese Constitutional Tribunal held that 'the fact that article 36, section 1 of the Constitution[279] does not explicitly define "marriage"' means that it did not intended to call into question its common definition, rooted in the community and followed by the Civil code, as 'a contract between two persons of different sex'.[280] Nonetheless, the Tribunal clarified that 'the reception of the historical meaning of marriage' did not imply that marriage is 'a petrified concept' because the Constitution neither prohibited nor mandated same-sex marriage.[281]

Thus, how did constitutional courts justify their originalist interpretations of constitutional clauses supported by legal tradition, when the institution of marriage—as they admitted—has undergone substantial changes? Their answer is that legal tradition actually safeguards the 'essential core' of the institution of marriage, which according to the Italian and the Irish courts should be precisely identified in difference of sex between the spouses. The Italian Constitutional Court, in particular, clarified that constitutional interpretation 'cannot go so far as to impinge upon the core of the constitutional clause on marriage'.[282] Therefore, it held, the meaning of marriage could not be changed through interpretation, because this would imply a re-reading of marriage[283] and a radical change

[277] *Zappone and Gilligan v Revenue Commissioners* n 273 above, [2008] 2 IR 417, 505.

[278] See Italian Constitutional Court, case no 138 of 2010, n 258 above, para 9 ('it is true to say that the concepts of family and marriage cannot be considered to have been "crystallised" with reference to the time when the Constitution entered into force, because they are endowed with the flexibility that is inherent within constitutional principles, and are therefore be interpreted taking account not only of the transformations within the legal system, but also the evolution of society and customs'); Irish High Court, *Zappone v Revenue Commissioners*, n 273 above ('It cannot be said that this is some kind of fossilized understanding of marriage. I fully appreciate the changes have been made; indeed, some far reaching changes have been made to the institution of marriage as it was understood in 1937... I accept that the Constitution is a living instrument').

[279] See above, at p 190.

[280] Tribunal Constitucional, case no 359/2009 (9 July 2009), para 10.

[281] ibid, para 14.

[282] Case no 138 of 2010, n 258 above, para 9.

[283] See also for an analogous conclusion, the Portuguese case no 359 of 2009, n 280 above, para 14. All the Courts differentiated the instant cases. According to Justice Dunne—who delivered the opinion of the Irish High Court in *Zappone*, n 273 above—the case did not involve the recognition of an 'unenumerated right' because the right to marriage is 'undoubtedly not an express right but is clearly implicit from the terms of article 41 [of the Irish Constitution]'. The Portuguese Constitutional Tribunal and the Italian Constitutional Court argued instead that in the instant cases the petitioners did not ask them to remove an unconstitutional limitation to the exercise of the right to marry, but to add a new feature of the right of marriage that is not mandated by domestic Constitutions.

of its real meaning corresponding 'to a social and historical datum, made stable by positive law'.[284]

The idea of binding value of the legal tradition concerning the essential core of marriage was rejected by the Supreme Court of Canada in its 2004 reference judgment regarding the constitutional validity of same-sex marriage. Some interveners argued before the Supreme Court that although the Constitution is 'capable of growth and expansion within its natural limits', 'these natural limits ... preclude same-sex marriage'. The Supreme Court replied to this objection, suggesting that 'the natural limits argument can succeed only if its proponents can identify an objective core of meaning, which defines what is natural in relation to marriage. Absent this, the argument is merely tautological'.[285] Nonetheless the Supreme Court acknowledged that there are 'competing opinions of what the natural limits of marriage may be' but that 'the only objective core which the interveners ... agree is "natural" to marriage is that it is the *voluntary union* of two people to the exclusion of all others'.[286]

As Diduck and Kaganas comment on the case, 'while some may argue that accepting monogamous union as natural is problematic, the point here is that the Supreme Court acknowledged that there may be differing views about a state of affairs or even an entity that is purported to be "natural"'.[287]

The difficulty in identifying the essential core of marriage, and the possibility of very different interpretive outcomes, depending on the interpreter's perspective, are exemplified by the Spanish Constitutional Tribunal's judgment on same-sex marriage (case no 198 of 2012). Although, as mentioned, Article 32 of the Spanish Constitution of 1978 refers to 'a man' and 'a woman', the Constitutional Tribunal suggested that the clause's original intent and essential core lies in the 'wish to secure the equality of men and women, without going into other matters'.[288] Nonetheless, the Constitutional Tribunal observed that this

> does not mean that [Article 32] implicitly accepted marriage between persons of the same sex or that it excluded this possibility. ... If strictly and literally interpreted, Article 32 CE only identifies the holders of a right to marry, not the other spouse, although, we must insist, systematically speaking it is clear that this does not mean that there was a wish in 1978 to extend the exercise of this right to homosexual unions.[289]

The Spanish Constitutional Tribunal upheld the constitutionality of same-sex marriage on the basis of a progressive interpretation of the Constitution.[290] As far as the legal tradition was concerned, the majority framed the issue of the identification of the traditional core of marriage as revolving around whether marriage will 'still be recognisable as marriage' once opened to same-sex couples. The Tribunal answered

[284] I Massa Pinto and C Tripodina, 'Sul come per la Corte costituzionale le "unioni omosessuali non possono essere ritenute omogenee al matrimonio". Ovvero tecniche argomentative impiegate per motivare la sentenza 138/2010' (2010) *Diritto Pubblico*, n 1–2, 471.

[285] *Reference Re Same-Sex Marriage*, n 258 above, para 27.

[286] ibid (emphasis added).

[287] Diduck and F Canagas, *Family Law*, n 236 above, 54.

[288] Spanish Constitutional Tribunal, case no 198/2012 of 6 November 2012, para 8.

[289] ibid.

[290] Case no 198 of 2012, n 288 above, para 9.

this question affirmatively, arguing that the 'institutional guarantee of marriage'[291] was not breached by the introduction of equal marriage.

> The institution of marriage remains in terms which are totally recognizable as regards the image that current Spanish society has of marriage. Notwithstanding its evident changes, it is an affective unit that generates a bond, or a form of mutual assistance between two persons that hold the same status within this institution and who voluntarily decide to join to establish a common family life plan, agreeing to the rights and duties inherent to the institution and expressly manifesting this through the formalities foreseen by law. Thus, equality between spouses, a free will to enter into marriage with a person of one's own choice and a manifestation of this wish are the essential characteristics of marriage, already present in the Civil Code before it was reformed in 2005, and which are still recognised in the new institution established by the legislator.[292]

The Portuguese Constitutional Tribunal's judgment was quite explicit in remarking the ambiguities in the identification of the essential meaning of marriage. Although, as mentioned above, it finally upheld a traditional view of marriage, the majority opinion suggested that this conclusion is influenced by the interpreter's point of view:

> if you understand marriage as a social institution ... with the relatively stable meaning of a union between man and woman, and such a definition is in particular based on its procreative purpose, it might make sense to reserve marriage to heterosexual couples. On the contrary, only if we adopt a notion of marriage as a purely private relationship between two adults, without any reference to reproduction, the exclusion of gay couples would emerge as necessarily discriminatory.[293]

I will clarify in the following pages how discretion in the identification of a central core of marriage can be explained in the light of the interpreter's view on the normative value of tradition.

ii. Cultural and Religious Tradition, its Indeterminacy and the Vicious Cycle that Perpetuates Discrimination

The foregoing paragraphs have illustrated how the practical identification of the contents of tradition can give rise to controversial interpretative results. Perplexities concerning in particular the discretionary selection of the elements identifying the legal tradition of marriage increase whenever tradition comes into consideration in its broader meaning and its contents are enlarged to encompass religion, morality and culture in the wider sense. I will illustrate in this section how tradition, especially

[291] The 'institutional guarantee' of marriage has been deeply analysed by the German Constitutional Tribunal cases on art 6(1) of the Basic Law (*Grundgesetz*). See 10 BVerfGE 59 (1959), 66–67. In 2002, in its judgment on the constitutionality of the Civil Partnership Act (105 BVerfGE 313) the Constitutional Tribunal similarly stressed that 'part of the content of marriage, as it has stood the test of time despite social change and the concomitant changes of its legal structure and been shaped by the Basic Law, is that it is the union of one man with one woman to form a permanent partnership, based on a free decision and with the support of the state ... in which man and woman are in an equal partnership with one another ... and may decide freely on the organisation of their cohabitation' (para 87). The Tribunal concluded that 'marriage as an institution is not affected by the Civil Partnership Act' (para 89).

[292] ibid.

[293] Case no 359 of 2009, n 280 above, para 14.

when detached from any connection with positive law, contributes to perpetuating discriminatory social practices. Furthermore, even in this context, the selection of the proper content of tradition masks the real normative issue, concerning the role tradition ought to play in judicial analysis.

United States state case law on differences grounded on race in marriage is illustrative of how judicial rhetoric can be caught up in a vicious cycle of religious/cultural arguments, legal tradition and discrimination. As Forde-Marzui explains, 'the historical use of tradition to justify racial discrimination ... reveals how tradition has been used to justify laws originally founded on religious beliefs'.[294] For instance, in order to justify the constitutional legitimacy of Virginia's anti-miscegenation law, 'the lower court in *Loving v Virginia* wrote that "Almighty God created the races white, black, yellow, malay and red, and he placed them on separate continents. The fact that he separated the races shows that he did not intend for the races to mix"'.[295] Furthermore, Forde-Marzui adds,

> nor were religious justifications for racism limited to the South. Massachusetts, for example, defended its antimiscegenation law as fulfilling the "Infinite Wisdom of God's design". Similarly, Pennsylvania justified antimiscegenation laws as preserving the arrangement required by the "order of Divine Providence".[296]

Corbett v Corbett, the 1970 High Court judgment concerning the legal meaning of 'man' and 'women' for the purposes of marriage,[297] provides another unequivocal evidence of how an axiomatic use of tradition may contribute to perpetuating and even reinforcing social roles. Once he had defined marriage as inherently heterosexual, Judge Ormrod went on to clarify 'what is meant by the word "woman" in the context of marriage' and concluded that biological criteria should be determinant, because

> even the most extreme degree of transsexualism in a male or the most severe hormonal imbalance which can exist in a person with male chromosomes, male gonads and male genitalia cannot reproduce a person who is naturally capable of performing the essential role of a woman in marriage.[298]

The acknowledgement of the value of the religious tradition of opposite-sex marriage is also recurrent in some same-sex marriage cases. A well-known example is the Minnesota Supreme Court's judgment in *Baker v Nelson*:[299] in order to argue that the United States Constitution does not protect 'a fundamental right' for same-sex couples to get married, the state Supreme Court held that 'the institution of marriage as a union of a man and a woman ... is as old as the book of Genesis'.[300]

Similar arguments were expounded in other state courts' cases in the early 2000s concluding that the limitation of marriage to opposite sex couples is constitutional.

[294] Forde-Marzui, 'Tradition as Justification', n 261 above, 327.
[295] See *Loving v Virginia* 388 US 1, 3 (1967).
[296] Forde-Marzui, 'Tradition as Justification', n 261 above, 327.
[297] *Corbett v Corbett*, n 225 above, 218.
[298] ibid, 48. On the use of tradition in this case, see Diduck and Canagas, 'Family law', n 236 above, 54 ff.
[299] *Baker v Nelson*, 291 Minn 310, 191 NW 2d 185 (1971).
[300] ibid, 191 N.W.2d 185, 186.

In *Lewis v Harris*,[301] for instance, the New Jersey Superior Court relied on the 'common understandings of the religious and social foundations of marriage that limit the institution to members of the opposite sex' in order to conclude that 'marriage between members of the same sex has no historical foundation or contemporary societal acceptance and therefore is not constitutionally mandated'.[302]

The plaintiffs—seven same-sex couples that had applied for marriage licences—argued that reliance on a tradition of opposite-sex marriage amounted to a 'circular reasoning'. The majority overturned this argument arguing that 'plaintiffs' reasoning proceeds along the same kind of circular path that they accuse the State of following':

> Plaintiffs start with the premise that there is no difference between a 'compelling and definitive expression of love and commitment' between members of the same sex and a marriage between members of the opposite sex, and then argue from this premise that the State has failed to carry its burden of justifying the limitation of the institution of marriage to a man and a woman. But the significant difference between these arguments is that the State's argument is grounded on historical tradition and our nation's religious and social values, while plaintiffs' argument is based on nothing more than their own normative claim that society should give unions between same-sex couples the same form of recognition as marriages between members of the opposite sex.[303]

In this passage, religious/cultural arguments and legal tradition mutually reinforce each other and an axiomatic use of tradition is regarded as sufficient to support the court's conclusion against same-sex marriage. As I will better clarify below, such a use of tradition elides the main argument of the plaintiffs' claim—the discrimination against same-sex couples—with the practical effect that the Court's rationale reinstates discrimination without even addressing it.[304]

However not all the courts accorded similar deference to tradition and its religious underpinnings. South African constitutional case law has been following an opposite approach. It should be premised that in South Africa, the Constitution does not explicitly refer to the right to marry[305] and the Constitutional Court, since 1996 (First Certification case)[306] held that

> families are constituted, function and are dissolved in such a variety of ways, and the possible outcomes of constitutionalising family rights are so uncertain, that Constitution-makers appear frequently to prefer not to regard the right to marry or to pursue family life as a fundamental right that is appropriate for definition in constitutionalised terms. This avoids questions that relate to the history, culture and special circumstances of each society.[307]

[301] *Lewis v Harris* 378 NJ Super 168 (2005).

[302] ibid, 185 (also arguing that 'Our leading religions view marriage as a union of men and women recognized by God,... and our society considers marriage between a man and woman to play a vital role in propagating the species and in providing the ideal environment for raising children').

[303] *Lewis v Harris*, n 301 above, 187.

[304] On the tautological nature of a legal reasoning based on tradition as a value in itself, see also below n 432 and accompanying text.

[305] South Africa Constitution of 1996. A definition of marriage as based on sex-difference was instead expressed in the common law and statute law. See n 247 above and accompanying text.

[306] *Certification of the Constitution of the Republic of South Africa*, 1996, in *Re Ex parte Chairperson of the Constitutional Assembly 1996*, 1996 (4) SA 744 (CC); 1996 (10) BCLR 1253 (CC).

[307] *Certification of the Constitution*, n 306 above, para 99.

In 2005, in *Fourie*[308] same-sex couples asked the Court to clarify whether the law denies equal protection to and discriminates unfairly against same-sex couples by not including them in the provisions of the Marriage Act 1961.[309] By contrast, the State and amici contended that even if the Marriage Act 1961 and the common law definition of marriage were under-inclusive, the remedy was not to be found in radically altering the law of marriage which, by its very nature and as historically evolved, was concerned with opposite-sex relationships. The answer, they said, was to provide appropriate alternative forms of recognition to same-sex family relationships.[310] They also pointed out that 'to disrupt and radically alter an institution of centuries-old significance to many religions, would accordingly infringe the Constitution by violating religious freedom in a most substantial way'. In support they mentioned passages in the Old and New Testaments describing marriage as a sacred institution ordained of God.[311]

The Constitutional Court dismissed these arguments, stating that 'religious sources of the law may not appropriately be relied upon by a court'[312] and concluded that 'acknowledgement by the State of the right of same-sex couples to enjoy the same status, entitlements and responsibilities as marriage law accords to heterosexual couples is in no way inconsistent with the rights of religious organisations to continue to refuse to celebrate same-sex marriages'.[313] As far as the role of the Constitutional Court was concerned, Justice Sachs also clarified that 'what matters is for the Court to ensure that [amicus curiae opposing same-sex marriage] be protected in his right to regard his marriage as sacramental, to belong to a religious community that celebrates its marriages according to its own doctrinal tenets, and to be free to express his views in an appropriate manner both in public and in Court. Further than that the Court could not be expected to go'.[314]

C. The Debate on Unenumerated Rights in the United States and its Teachings on the Normative Value of Tradition

In the cases analysed above, the legal and religious tradition plays 'an evidentiary role' for the identification of a common shared and established meaning of marriage. Same-sex marriage opponents argue that tradition represents 'time-tested wisdom and cultural identity' and that altering it may result in unintended and irreversible consequences. In their opinion, 'the longevity of opposite-sex marriage at least counsels patience, some caution, for society to accustom itself to such fundamental

[308] *Minister of Home Affairs and Another v Fourie*, Case CCT 60/04, [2005] ZACC 19, 1 December 2005.
[309] *The Marriage Act* (no 25 of 1961).
[310] *Fourie* n 308 above, para 83.
[311] *Fourie* n 308 above, para 93.
[312] ibid. ('Whether or not the Biblical texts support his beliefs would certainly not be a question which this Court could entertain'.)
[313] ibid, para 98.
[314] ibid, para 93.

reform'.[315] Therefore, tradition provides 'a presumptive, or even conclusive, evidence of intent, which is dispositive'.[316]

Another (although always evidentiary) use of tradition in same-sex marriage cases is related to the identification of 'new' fundamental rights not envisioned in the Constitutional text.[317] This role of tradition has been developed by the United States Supreme Court within its case law on the interpretation of the Due Process Clause of the Fourteenth Amendment.[318] From this perspective, tradition is conceived 'as an opportunity to enlarge the universe of protected freedoms by supplementing enumerated rights with rights that have developed over time, through traditional recognition'.[319] As early as 1933 the United States Supreme Court stated in fact that the Due Process Clause protects those liberties, which are 'so rooted in the traditions and conscience of our people as to be ranked as fundamental'.[320]

However, Supreme Court justices have been interpreting this role of tradition in the identification of unenumerated rights in different ways. Some extreme positions attached too great weight to the fixed and limiting value of tradition[321] whereas, on the opposite, some others Justices disregarded its importance in the identification of new rights.[322] Two more nuanced and flexible approaches to due process traditionalism were articulated by Justice Harlan in his dissent in *Poe v Ullman*[323] and by the majority in *Washington v Glucksberg*.[324]

The first approach—which Yoshino describes as 'an open-ended common law approach'[325]—recognises the dynamic and evolving nature of tradition and assumes that 'due process has not been reduced to any formula; its content cannot be determined by reference to any code'.[326] In his dissenting opinion in *Poe* Justice Harlan argued in favour of 'a balanced methodology that weighted individual liberties against governmental interest in a reasoned manner'.[327] He held that 'each new claim to Constitutional protection must be considered against a background of Constitutional purposes, as they have been rationally perceived and historically developed'.[328] In his opinion, tradition should be conceived as a source of guidance

[315] Forde-Marzui, 'Tradition as Justification', n 261 above, 284–85.

[316] RL Brown, 'Tradition and Insight' (1993) *Yale Law Journal* 177, 185.

[317] ibid, 200.

[318] United States Constitution, XIV Amendment ('[N]or shall any State deprive any person of life, liberty, or property, without due process of law').

[319] Brown, 'Tradition and Insight', n 316 above, 201.

[320] *Snyder v Massachusetts* 291 US 97, 105 (1933). See also, *Griswold v Connecticut* 381 US 479, 493 (1965) (Douglas concurring).

[321] For a general analysis about the more radical approaches, see KT Bartlett, 'Tradition As Past And Present In Substantive Due Process Analysis' (2012) 62 *Duke Law Journal* 535. A more rigid view attaching great weight to tradition for the identification of unenumerated rights under the Due Process Clause has been advanced by the conservative Justices of the Supreme Court. See eg Justice Scalia's dissenting opinion in *Lawrence v Texas*, 539 US 558 (2003).

[322] The view that rejects the value of tradition in constitutional interpretation arguing that it is 'steeped in the prejudices and superstitions of a time long past' was advanced by Justice Brennan in his dissenting opinion in *Michael H v Gerald D* 491 US 110, 141 (1989).

[323] *Poe v Ullman* 367 US 497 (1961).

[324] *Washington v Glucksberg* 521 US 702 (1997).

[325] K Yoshino, 'A New Birth of Freedom?' (2016) 129 *Harvard Law Review* 147, 150.

[326] *Poe v Ullman*, n 323 above, 367 US, 543.

[327] ibid.

[328] ibid, 544.

in the development of constitutional doctrine, without offering determinacy on any issue because 'there is no mechanical yardstick, no mechanical answer'.[329] This does not imply that courts are free to disregard tradition or to revise it. Tradition operates as a real constraint.[330] 'A decision ... which radically departs from [tradition] could not long survive, while a decision which builds on what has survived is likely to be sound'.[331]

The second approach—defined as 'a more closed-ended formulaic approach'[332]—was articulated by the majority in *Glucksberg*. The Supreme Court argued in this case that to be recognised as a due process liberty, a right had to be 'objectively, deeply rooted in this Nation's history and tradition ... and implicit in the concept of ordered liberty such that neither liberty nor justice would exist if they were sacrificed'.[333] In the case the Supreme Court also asked for a 'careful description' of the asserted fundamental right arguing that 'history, legal traditions, and practices ... provide the crucial "guideposts for responsible decision-making"'.[334]

It should be noted that, as Yoshino clarifies,[335] *Glucksberg* did not coin these formulations. In *Bowers v Hardwick*[336]—the 1986 case that upheld the Georgia sodomy law and was later overruled by *Lawrence v Texas*[337] in 2003—the Supreme Court similarly referred to tradition and to the formulation relating to 'the concept of ordered liberty'. The Supreme Court dismissed as 'at best, facetious'[338] a claim of historical support for the claimed right and concluded that it did not satisfy either.[339]

In recent decades, a large number of scholarly works has thoroughly explored each of the four approaches, taking position on their limits and points of strength.[340] My purpose is not to address this debate in detail, but to demonstrate how reliance on tradition in order to support (or reject) the identification of an unenumerated 'right to same-sex marriage' raises controversial and objectionable results close to

[329] ibid. Nonetheless, Justice Harlan contended that 'the vague contours of the Due Process Clause do not leave judges at large. We may not draw on our merely personal and private notions and disregard the limits that bind judges in their judicial function. Even though the concept of due process of law is not final and fixed, these limits are derived from considerations that are fused in the whole nature of our judicial process ... These are considerations deeply rooted in reason and in the compelling traditions of the legal profession' (*Poe*, n 323 above, 544–45).

[330] Bartlett, 'Tradition As Past And Present', n 321 above, 565.

[331] *Poe v Ullman*, n 323 above, 367 US, 542 (Harlan, J, dissenting).

[332] Yoshino, 'A New Birth of Freedom?', n 325 above, 149.

[333] *Washington v Glucksberg*, n 324 above, 521 US, 721.

[334] ibid. The majority also took position on the Justice Souter's approach which relied on Justice Harlan's dissent in *Poe*. See ibid 721–72.

[335] Yoshino, 'A New Birth of Freedom?', n 325 above, 152.

[336] *Bowers v Hardwick* 478 US 186 (1986).

[337] *Lawrence v Texas*, n 321 above.

[338] *Bowers v Hardwick*, n 336 above, 478 US, 194.

[339] However, as Yoshino argues ('A New Birth of Freedom?', n 325 above, 152), the Supreme Court in *Bowers v Hardwick*, n 336 above, did not clearly articulate the standard of review, and failed to clarify whether both the tests had to be met. By contrast, 'in making the two requirements conjunctive, *Glucksberg* [n 324 above] made the tradition inquiry inescapable'.

[340] See, JM Balkin, 'Tradition, Betrayal, and the Politics of Deconstruction' (1990) 11 *Cardozo Law Review* 1613; CR Sunstein, 'Due Process Traditionalism' (2008) 106 *Michigan Law Review* 1543; R Post and R Siegel, 'Originalism as Political Practice: The Right's Living Constitution' (2006) 75 *Fordham Law Review* 545.

those concerning the use of tradition for the identification of the core meaning of 'marriage' according to an originalist interpretation of constitutional clauses. Even in this context, the basic issue similarly revolves around the proper role that tradition ought to play in the judicial interpretation.

The Supreme Court has taken legal tradition into account since its early cases on criminalisation of consensual sexual acts between persons of the same sex. Those cases, discussed in Chapter 2, reveal that—as in the European and South African cases—use of tradition is influenced by the outcome that the interpreter intends to achieve.

In *Bowers v Hardwick*, as shown in Chapter 2, the Supreme Court relied on tradition in order to demonstrate that proscriptions against acts of consensual sodomy 'have ancient roots'.[341] Writing for the Court, Justice White identified a longstanding tradition of sodomy laws in all 50 states, some of them dating back to the end of the eighteenth century.[342] Against this background he concluded for the constitutionality of the Georgia sodomy statute, stating that 'the Court is most vulnerable and comes nearest to illegitimacy when it deals with judge-made constitutional law having little or no cognizable roots in the language or design of the Constitution'.

In 2003 the Supreme Court in *Lawrence v Texas* addressed a similar issue.[343] Writing for the Court, Justice Kennedy assumed that 'history and tradition are the starting point but not in all cases the ending point of the substantive due process inquiry'. He discussed at length how history shows that sodomy laws were directed at both same-sex and different-sex sexual intercourses and concluded that the *Bowers'* court had erroneously inferred the existence of a longstanding legislative tradition against same-sex sexual conduct. He, conversely, emphasised that historical references show 'an emerging awareness that liberty gives substantial protection to adult persons in deciding how to conduct their private lives in matters pertaining to sex'.[344]

He argued:

> The longstanding criminal prohibition of homosexual sodomy upon which *Bowers* placed such reliance is as consistent with a general condemnation of nonprocreative sex as it is with an established tradition of prosecuting acts because of their homosexual character. Far from possessing 'ancient roots', American laws targeting same-sex couples did not develop until the last third of the 20th century. ... Thus, the historical grounds relied upon in *Bowers* are more complex than the majority opinion and the concurring opinion by Chief Justice Burger there indicated. They are not without doubt and, at the very least, are overstated. The *Bowers* Court was, of course, making the broader point that for centuries there have been powerful voices to condemn homosexual conduct as immoral, but this Court's obligation is to define the liberty of all, not to mandate its own moral code.[345]

The different outcome of the research into the very same tradition (the proscription against same-sex acts) illustrates how difficult it is to identify which practice should be the one legitimated and relied upon in interpreting the Constitution in the

[341] *Bowers*, n 336 above, 478 US, 192.
[342] ibid, 193–94.
[343] *Lawrence v Texas*, n 321 above. The case has been analysed in Chapter 2 p 30 ff.
[344] ibid, 539 US, 572.
[345] ibid, 539 US, 571.

face of conflicting traditions.[346] In those cases results differed depending on what the interpreter was looking for: whereas Justice White took into account the mere existence of a legal tradition of sodomy laws, Justice Kennedy examined the same statutes in more detail, looking at how they were implemented and to whom they were directed.[347] He finally reached the conclusion that 'the historical grounds relied upon in *Bowers* are more complex than the majority opinion and the concurring opinion by Chief Justice Burger indicate. Their historical premises are not without doubt and, at the very least, are overstated'.[348]

Yoshino argues that Justice Kennedy's 'history seemed somewhat beside the point—the absence of a robust history militating against a right is not the same as the presence of a robust history militating for it. But the gratuitousness of the analysis only underscores the force of the imperative to reason from history'.[349]

In the United States the critique concerning the identification of the contents of tradition is related to a second serious objection, dealing with the selection of the proper level of generality of the unenumerated right (to be confirmed by tradition).[350] As mentioned earlier, in *Glucksberg*, the Supreme Court asked for a 'careful description' of the asserted fundamental right. As, after *Glucksberg*, the Supreme Court focused more on tradition than on the requirement concerning the concept of 'ordered liberty',[351] frequently the identification of the right at stake and the search for the tradition supporting it, have become intertwined.[352] Yet the choice of the proper level of generality, at which the Court construes the claim, determines the outcome.[353]

The Supreme Court cases on the criminalisation of same-sex sexual acts exemplify this difficulty. In *Bowers v Hardwick*[354] the Supreme Court clarified that 'the issue presented is whether the Federal Constitution confers a fundamental right upon homosexuals to engage in sodomy'.[355] By contrast, in his dissenting opinion, Justice Blackmun argued that the case was about 'the most comprehensive of rights and the right most valued by civilised men, "namely, the right to be let alone"'.[356] In *Lawrence*, instead, Justice Kennedy formulated the right of the petitioners

[346] See Brown, 'Tradition and Insight', n 316 above, 203.
[347] *Lawrence v Texas*, n 321 above, 539 US, 568 ff.
[348] ibid, 539 US, 571.
[349] Yoshino, 'A New Birth of Freedom?', n 325 above, 152.
[350] See LH Tribe and MC Dorf, 'Levels of Generality in the Definition of Rights' (1990) 57 *University of Chicago Law Review* 1057.
[351] Yoshino, 'A New Birth of Freedom?', n 325 above, 152.
[352] Nonetheless the two inquiries are theoretically distinct and they do not necessarily reinforce each other: in *Lawrence v Texas*, n 321 above, eg the Supreme Court took into account the tradition directed against same-sex sexual conduct in order to overturn its conclusions in *Bowers v Hardwick*, n 336 above, but at the same time discussed how 'laws and traditions in the past half century ... show an emerging awareness that liberty gives substantial protection to adult persons in deciding how to conduct their private lives in matters pertaining to sex' (*Lawrence v Texas*, n 321 above, 572). Only the last part of the majority's enquiry aims at supporting the asserted autonomy of the individual in personal choices concerning sex.
[353] Yoshino, 'A New Birth of Freedom?', n 325 above, 155.
[354] *Bowers v Hardwick*, n 336 above.
[355] ibid, 478 US,190.
[356] ibid, 478 US, 199.

as concerning the ability 'to engage in the private conduct in the exercise of their liberty under the Due Process Clause of the Fourteenth Amendment to the Constitution'.[357] He also criticised the Court's 'failure to appreciate the extent of the liberty at stake'[358] in *Bowers*, stating that

> To say that the issue in *Bowers* was simply the right to engage in certain sexual conduct demeans the claim the individual put forward, just as it would demean a married couple were it to be said marriage is simply about the right to have sexual intercourse.[359]

As Tribe and Dorf emphasise,[360] the majority's descriptive choice clearly affected the Court's conclusions. They argue:

> the majority and the dissenters in *Hardwick* argue over how abstractly to describe the right at issue. The majority describes the right narrowly, the dissent broadly. These alternative descriptions evidently reflect the fact that the majority and dissent have reached different conclusions as to whether Hardwick's behavior is constitutionally protected. As such, we might view them as shorthand for the holding and the dissent. Yet the characterizations are the starting points for the analysis. Because the majority and dissent ask different questions, it is not surprising that they give different answers.[361]

The Supreme Court's landmark judgment on same-sex marriage, *Obergefell v Hodges*,[362] confirms how crucial the level of generality of the asserted claim is. The respondent asserted that the petitioners did not seek to exercise the right to marry but rather a new and non-existent 'right to same-sex marriage'.[363] Writing for the Court, Justice Kennedy rejected this argument and framed the issue as concerning the general 'right to marriage' instead of a more specific 'right to same-sex marriage'. He held that 'four principles[364] and traditions … demonstrate that the reasons marriage is fundamental under the Constitution apply with equal force to same-sex couples'.[365] Invoking *Poe*[366] directly,[367] he also argued that traditions 'guide and discipline' the Court's inquiry 'without allowing the past alone to rule the present'.[368]

[357] *Lawrence v Texas*, n 321 above, 539 US, 565.

[358] ibid, 539 US, 567.

[359] ibid.

[360] Tribe and Dorf, 'Levels of Generality', n 350 above, 1058 (arguing that 'The more abstractly one states the already-protected right, the more likely it becomes that the claimed right will fall within its protection'). See also WN Eskridge, Jr and ND Hunter, *Sexuality, Gender and the Law* (New York, Foundation Press, 2004) 97.

[361] Tribe and Dorf, 'Levels of Generality', n 350 above, 1066.

[362] *Obergefell v Hodges* 135 S Ct 2584 (2015).

[363] Brief for Respondent n 14-556 at 8.

[364] *Obergefell*, n 362 above, 135 S Ct, 2599. The four principles Justice Kennedy invoked in order to argue that marriage is a fundamental right were the following: the right to personal choice regarding marriage is inherent in the concept of individual autonomy; the right to marry is fundamental because it supports a two-person union unlike any other in its importance to the committed individuals; the right to marry safeguards children and families and thus draws meaning from related rights of childrearing, procreation, and education; marriage is a keystone of our social order. The arguments will be analysed in the following section of this chapter and in Chapter 5.

[365] ibid.

[366] *Poe v Ullman*, n 323 above.

[367] On the majority's explicit reliance on *Poe* and on the differences between *Lawrence* and *Obergefell* as far as use of tradition is concerned, Yoshino, 'A New Birth of Freedom?', n 325 above, 163 ff.

[368] *Obergefell*, n 362 above, 135 S Ct, 2598.

By contrast, in his dissenting opinion, Justice Alito emphasised that according to *Glucksberg*, '"liberty" under the Due Process Clause should be understood to protect only those rights that are "deeply rooted in this Nation's history and tradition"',[369] adding that 'it is beyond dispute that the right to same-sex marriage is not among those rights'.[370] Relying on tradition (conceived as cultural tradition), Justice Alito also emphasised that the majority's

> understanding of marriage, which focuses almost entirely on the happiness of persons who choose to marry, is shared by many people today, but it is not the traditional one. For millennia, marriage was inextricably linked to the one thing that only an opposite-sex couple can do: procreate.[371]

Justice Kennedy replied to this objection in clear terms:

> *Glucksberg* did insist that liberty under the Due Process Clause must be defined in a most circumscribed manner, with central reference to specific historical practices. Yet while that approach may have been appropriate for the asserted right there involved (physician-assisted suicide), it is inconsistent with the approach this Court has used in discussing other fundamental rights, including marriage and intimacy. *Loving* did not ask about a 'right to interracial marriage'; *Turner* did not ask about a 'right of inmates to marry'; and *Zablocki* did not ask about a 'right of fathers with unpaid child support duties to marry'. Rather, each case inquired about the right to marry in its comprehensive sense, asking if there was a sufficient justification for excluding the relevant class from the right.[372]

If both the selection of the contents of tradition and the definition of the appropriate level of generality are influenced by the interpreter's value choices, the essential question turns out to be whether it is possible to discover a neutral method of constitutional interpretation that relies on tradition safeguarding judicial neutrality.

Before attempting to answer this question, it is useful to remember that in *Michael H v Gerald D*,[373] Justice Scalia addressed the problem of discretionary judicial powers and tried to solve it arguing that the courts should rely 'on the most specific level at which a relevant tradition protecting, or denying protection to, the asserted right can be identified'.[374] He justified this assertion, noting that 'general traditions provide such imprecise guidance' and 'they permit judges to dictate rather than discern the society's views'.[375]

Commenting on the case, Tribe and Dorf dismissed Justice Scalia's solution as ill-founded. They speculate that it shifts the problem of abstraction from the realm of legal precedent to that of historical precedent and that 'the extraction of fundamental rights from societal traditions is no more value-neutral than the extraction of fundamental rights from legal precedent'.[376] Furthermore, they observe that 'there

369 ibid, 135 S Ct, 2641(Alito dissenting, citing *Washington v Glucksberg*, 521 US, 720–21).
370 ibid.
371 ibid.
372 ibid, 135 S Ct, 2602 (citing, *Loving v Virginia* n 295 above; *Zablocki v Redhail* 434 US 374 (1978); *Turner v Safley* 482 US 78 (1987). On this passage of the majority opinion, see Yoshino, 'A New Birth of Freedom?', n 325 above, 165.
373 *Michael H v Gerald D* 491 US 110 (1989).
374 *Michael H v Gerald D*, n 373 above, 91 US, 127, fn 6.
375 ibid.
376 Tribe and Dorf, 'Levels of Generality', n 350 above, 1086.

is no universal metric of specificity against which to measure an asserted right'.[377] By contrast, the two authors have suggested an opposite approach, which—they argue—does not eliminate judicial value choice, although it does limit it considerably:[378] taking as point of departure Justice Harlan's observation in *Poe*[379] that 'the search for unenumerated rights should proceed by interpolation and extrapolation from the enumerated rights', they assume that the Constitution is a living text and that courts should look for general principles when faced with a case of first impression.

Nonetheless, they argue, the call for more abstract principles encounters textual limits: 'requiring that fundamental rights be connected to the constitutional text provides one check on the tendency of judges to choose a level of abstraction to suit their own subjective preferences'.[380] In other words, new rights should be consistent with enumerated rights. Tribe and Dorf also suggest placing 'precedent and historical tradition on a more or less equal footing'.[381] 'Applying this method not just to the clauses of the Bill of Rights but also to the Supreme Court's precedents'—they argue—a typical judicial opinion should 'distinguish between essential and non-essential facts' so that 'judges trained in the method of the common law can generalize from prior cases without merely imposing their own values'.[382]

Although even this issue is peculiar to the American debate over unenumerated rights and the interpretation of the Ninth and Fourteenth Amendments of the American Constitution, in my opinion it may cast light on the normative use of tradition in European same-sex marriage cases. However, there are some differences that should not be neglected: in continental Europe, constitutional texts mention the right to marry in general terms (eg, Spain and Germany) or implicitly refer to marriage in the articles granting protection to family (eg, Italy and Ireland). Compared to the United States' courts, European courts are accordingly asked to decide whether same-sex marriage falls under the protection of a general clause. This implies that opponents to same-sex marriage do not argue that same-sex couples ask for an unenumerated 'right to same-sex marriage': they instead suggest that a same-sex couple's claim 'does not involve a simple re-reading of the Constitution' but a creative (and therefore forbidden) interpretation.[383] Conversely, in the United States, the

[377] ibid. I will discuss their further objection concerning the judicial responsibility to protect individual rights (and how reliance on tradition perpetuates discrimination against same-sex couples) in the following pages.

[378] See Tribe and Dorf, 'Levels of Generality', n 350 above, 1103.

[379] *Poe v Ullman*, n 323 above.

[380] See Tribe and Dorf, 'Levels of Generality', n 350 above, 1099. This implies, eg, that 'liberty' cannot be taken at a high level of abstraction to include kleptomania because the 'the Constitution's repeated references to 'property' pretty squarely foreclose any argument that there is a fundamental right to deprive another of her property'.

[381] ibid, 1103.

[382] ibid, 1059.

[383] See for instance the Italian Constitutional Court in case no 138 of 2010, n 258 above, and the Portuguese Constitutional Tribunal reasoning in case no 359 of 2009, n 280 above. See also the Irish High Court in *Zappone and Gilligan v Revenue Commissioners* n 273 above, [2008] 2 IR 417, 505, emphasising that 'there is a difference between an examination of the Constitution in the context of ascertaining unenumerated rights and redefining a right which is implicit in the Constitution and which is clearly understood. In this case the court is being asked to redefine marriage to mean something which it has never done to date. ... The right to marry contained in the Constitution is undoubtedly not an

issue is whether under the Constitution, the Supreme Court's cases and tradition it is possible to enlarge the meaning on the unenumerated fundamental right to marriage and to describe it in 'a comprehensive sense' (as Justice Kennedy clearly states in *Obergefell*) or whether both historical tradition and the circumstance that the Constitutional text 'says nothing about a right to same-sex marriage' suggest a narrower interpretation, which in particular precludes the recognition of an unenumerated 'right to same-sex marriage' as distinguished by the traditional right to marriage (as Justice Alito contends).[384]

These differences should not be neglected, but both approaches focus on the legitimacy of an addition to the constitutional text, which impinges on the essential and traditional meaning of marriage.

Both Justice Scalia's and Professors Tribe and Dorf's approaches assume a specific idea on the nature of tradition, its relationship with the past and the future, and how fixity should be balanced with change. As Scheffler writes in a fascinating essay on the normativity of tradition,[385]

> participation in a tradition has a backward-looking as well as a forward-looking dimension. If, in the forward-looking dimension, one seeks to ensure the survival of what one values, then in the backward-looking dimension, one sees oneself as inheriting values that have been preserved by others. One is heir to, and custodian of, values that have been handed down by those who went before.[386]

It is commonplace that the participation in a tradition enables people to feel part of something that is larger than themselves. In order to give content to this idea, Scheffler argues that 'in its forward-looking dimension participation in a tradition diminishes the perceived significance of one's death, while in the backward-looking dimension it enhances the perceived significance of one's life'.[387]

All same-sex marriage cases illustrate Scheffler's argument that

> it would be a mistake to think of any tradition as completely fixed and invariant. On the contrary, all traditions change over time and new generations always find ways to modify and traditional legacy in light of changing circumstances and outlooks. Fixity in one area of

express right but is clearly implicit from the terms of Article 41. It is not a case where the court requires to ascertain a previously unenumerated right as the right to marry falls squarely within the terms of the Constitution.'

[384] *Obergefell*, n 362 above, 135 S Ct, 2640 Alito dissenting (arguing that 'the Constitution says nothing about a right to same-sex marriage, but the Court holds that the term "liberty" in the Due Process Clause of the Fourteenth Amendment encompasses this right. Our Nation was founded upon the principle that every person has the unalienable right to liberty, but liberty is a term of many meanings. For classical liberals, it may include economic rights now limited by government regulation. For social democrats, it may include the right to a variety of government benefits. For today's majority, it has a distinctively postmodern meaning. To prevent five unelected Justices from imposing their personal vision of liberty upon the American people, the Court has held that "liberty" under the Due Process Clause should be understood to protect only those rights that are "deeply rooted in this Nation's history and tradition". And it is beyond dispute that the right to same-sex marriage is not among those rights. ... For today's majority, it does not matter that the right to same-sex marriage lacks deep roots or even that it is contrary to long-established tradition.').

[385] Scheffler, *Equality and Tradition*, n 262 above, 287.

[386] ibid, 305.

[387] ibid.

> practise and belief may go hand-in-hand with significant change in other areas. In general every tradition must strike a balance between continuity and change.[388]

I argue that the two approaches balance continuity and change in different ways. Justice Scalia's idea of the normative value of tradition emphasises its backward-looking dimension and its fixity over time. This leads him to identify very specific features of the asserted right.

Conversely, Tribe and Dorf's approach, although analogously assuming the double dimension of tradition, strikes the balance between continuity and change in favour of the latter and emphasises the forward-looking dimension of traditional rules. This perspective leads them to abstract from the specific features of the asserted right and to identify its essential and general traits, the only ones that could make it possible to the legal tradition to adapt to novel circumstances and evolving social convictions.

In *Obergefell*, the majority's and the dissenters' approaches mirror similar differences when articulating the contents of tradition and its normative value in relation to marriage. By placing emphasis on the forward-looking dimension of tradition, the majority's argument implies the identification of a general 'right to marriage'; conversely, the adoption of a more fixed idea of tradition brings about the recognition of more narrow and specific rights, based on spouses' personal qualities. As Balkin argues, these opposite perspectives also reveal a 'different view about human knowledge and moral growth'.[389]

In my opinion the first approach is more persuasive. Although—as Tribe and Dorf also admit[390]—philosophical objections can be raised against a theory of essential properties, their approach assumes that 'as a practical matter, however, law must proceed from the assumption that judges can tell the difference between the essential and the trivial in reading and applying prior decisions'. At the same time, they emphasise, 'recognizing such distinctions in a principled manner is, after all, the essence of legal judgment'.[391]

In conclusion, the American debate on same-sex marriage and unenumerated rights helps to illuminate how the attempts to identify an essential core of marriage are influenced by choices concerning the normative value of tradition and the interpreters' view about the essence of constitutional adjudication. The Italian and the Irish cases excluding that same-sex marriage falls within the protection of the constitutional clauses of marriage, for instance, implicitly assume a backward-looking

388 ibid, 307.

389 J Balkin, 'Obergefell and Tradition' in *Balkinization*, 28 June, 2015 (available at *balkin.blogspot.com*). Roberts, Scalia and especially Alito—Balkin writes—'view tradition as the accumulated wisdom of previous generation' and for this reason they conclude that 'we should not disturb the judgements of previous generations because … we view matters from a very narrow perspective—our own lifetimes—and therefore if we try to make significant changes based on contemporary judgements and reasons we are likely to produce unintended and undesirable consequences, as well as destroying institutions of long-standing'. By contrast, Justice Kennedy 'regards the evolution of tradition as beneficially shaped by increases in knowledge and understandings'. He frequently speaks of 'new insight', and 'enhanced understandings' that should properly be incorporated in constitutional traditions, altering, according to Balkin, what tradition means to us today.

390 Tribe and Dorf, 'Levels of Generality', n 350 above, 1098.

391 ibid, 1106.

interpretation of tradition and emphasise the fixity of traditional core of marriage in order to support an originalist interpretation of constitutional clauses. By contrast, the Canadian Supreme Court (objecting to the idea of a 'natural meaning' of marriage but suggested that what all the theses in favour and against equal marriage have in common is the idea that marriage is a 'voluntary union' between two persons)[392] and the Spanish Constitutional Tribunal (that concluded that opening marriage to same-sex couples does not impair 'the institutional guarantee' of marriage as a voluntary bond between two persons)[393] identify the abstract and essential features of marriage. The Belgian Cour d'Arbitrage went even further when in 2004 it concluded in more general terms that, according to the legislature which only has the power to regulate family law, marriage has the 'main purpose of establishing an enduring life union between two persons'.[394]

From this perspective, spouses' personal features (race, sex, gender, sexual orientation) lose their importance in comparison with other determinants like affection and sentimental bond and with purposes of stability and public recognition. This 'new image of marriage' does not appear to conflict with the traditional idea of marriage.

D. The Normative Value of Tradition and the Risk of a 'Circular Reasoning'

The normative value of tradition can be justified by a variety of reasons. Scheffler, for instance, argues that traditions provide guidance for future actions or express individual loyalty not only to the values embodied by the tradition but also to the community that adhered to the tradition in the past.[395] At the same time, traditions may themselves be seen as valuable because they are 'repositories of human knowledge, experience, creativity and achievement'.[396]

In same-sex marriage cases, courts do not devote great space to arguments justifying their reliance on tradition. The main argument to support an interpretation of the constitutional clauses based on tradition is—as mentioned—that opening the institution of marriage to same-sex couples does not imply a 'regular' interpretation of constitutional clauses, but 'a re-reading' of marriage that exceeds the courts' interpretative powers.[397] Justification of the normative value of tradition lies therefore in its stability and in loyalty to the constitutional arrangement: the Italian and Portuguese constitutional courts for instance, suggest that opening marriage to same-sex couples implies an aggrandisement of judicial power in violation of legislative prerogatives.

[392] *Reference Re Same-Sex Marriage*, n 258 above, para 27.

[393] Case no 198 of 2012, n 288 above, para 8.

[394] Cour d'Arbitrage, case no 159/2004 of 20 October 2004, para B.4.6. In 2003 Belgium became the second country in the world to legalise same-sex marriage. The Act of 13 February 2003, in particular, amended the Civil Code in order to open marriage to same-sex couples.

[395] See Scheffler, *Equality and Tradition*, n 262 above, 290 ff (identifying seven reasons behind the normative force of tradition: convention, habit, wisdom, guidance, value, loyalty and integrity).

[396] Scheffler, *Equality and Tradition*, n 262 above, 293.

[397] See n 283 above and accompanying text.

Nonetheless, whenever reliance on tradition is justified only by the value of tradition in itself, the argument amounts to a circular reasoning. The Irish High Court's reasoning in *Zappone*, for instance, illustrates that it is tautological to maintain that marriage must remain a heterosexual institution because that is what it has been historically. Writing for the High Court, Justice Dunne states that 'the definition of marriage to date has always been understood as being opposite sex marriage' and then she elaborates:

> How then can it be argued that in the light of prevailing ideas and concepts that definition be changed to encompass same sex marriage? Having regard to the clear understanding of the meaning of marriage as set out in the numerous authorities opened to the Court from this jurisdiction and elsewhere, I do not see how marriage can be redefined by the Court to encompass same sex marriage.

Furthermore, as illustrated by the 2005 New Jersey Superior Court judgment in *Lewis v Harris*,[398] the reasoning that 'marriage between members of the same sex has no historical foundation or contemporary societal acceptance and therefore is not constitutionally mandated' is not only circular but also sidesteps the entire analysis and the claim concerning the discrimination suffered by same-sex couples.[399] As the Ontario Court of Appeal emphasised in *Halpern v Canada*,[400] 'it is the opposite-sex component of marriage that is under scrutiny. The proper approach is to examine the impact of the opposite-sex requirement on same-sex couples to determine whether defining marriage as an opposite-sex institution is discriminatory'.[401]

In the last decade, other courts in the United States and Canada have rejected arguments of tradition as tautological, adding that they fail to address the core issue of discrimination. In *Varnum v Brien*,[402] for instance, the Supreme Court of Iowa wrote that

> when a certain tradition is used as both the governmental objective and the classification to further that objective, the equal protection analysis is transformed into the circular question of whether the classification accomplishes the governmental objective, which objective is to maintain the classification. In other words, the equal protection clause is converted into a 'barren form of words' when 'discrimination ... is made an end in itself'.
>
> Opposite-sex marriage, however, is the classification made under the statute, and this classification must comply with our principles of equal protection. Thus, the use of traditional marriage as both the governmental objective and the classification of the statute transforms the equal protection analysis into the question of whether restricting marriage to opposite-sex couples accomplishes the governmental objective of maintaining opposite-sex marriage.
>
> This approach is, of course, an empty analysis. It permits a classification to be maintained 'for its own sake'.[403]

[398] *Lewis v Harris* n 301 above.
[399] ibid, 185.
[400] *Halpern v Canada* [2003] OJ No 2268, 65 OR (3d) 161.
[401] ibid, para 71.
[402] *Varnum v Brien* 63 N.W.2d 862 (2009).
[403] ibid, 63 NW 2d, 898 (quoting *Truax v Raich* 239 US 33, 41 (1915)). See also, for similar conclusions, *Goodridge v Department of Public Health* 440 Mass 309, 332 (2003); *Hernandez v Robles* 7 NY 3d 338, 385 (2006).

I will address issues concerning the equality claims of same-sex couples in the following section of the present chapter. However it should be noted that these quotations suggest that the justifications of reliance on tradition must be external to tradition itself and that they cannot be found in the idea of a natural or traditional difference of same-sex couples.

The Italian Constitutional Court in 2010 and the Portuguese Constitutional Tribunal in 2009 were probably aware of the risk of this interpretative flaw when they shifted the issue from a 'self-referential' normative value of tradition to separation of powers and to the limits of constitutional adjudication. Nonetheless it is interesting to observe that a tautological use of tradition resurfaces when the Italian Constitutional Court dismisses the claim of a violation of the principle of equality arguing that 'homosexual unions cannot be regarded as homogeneous with marriage'.[404]

Justice Kennedy's opinion of the Court in *Obergefell* contains the firmest and clearest statement against a tautological reliance on tradition in its backward-looking dimension. Suggesting that previous cases did not deal with 'specific' rights to marriage, but with 'the right to marry in its comprehensive sense'[405] and assuming that traditional practices change over time, he emphasises: 'If rights were defined by who exercised them in the past, then received practices could serve as their own continued justification and new groups could not invoke rights once denied.'[406]

E. Progressive Interpretations of Constitutional Clauses on 'Marriage' and Separation of Powers Concerns

In the previous pages I focused on the different uses of tradition for supporting an originalist interpretation of the constitutional clauses (or of the common law definition of marriage) in same-sex marriage cases. Now I would like to turn my attention to the arguments advanced by constitutional and supreme courts in order to expound progressive interpretations of constitutional clauses on marriage.

The Canadian Supreme Court[407] and the Spanish Constitutional Tribunal[408] gave the most salient statements of the evolving nature of marriage and the forward-looking dimension of the legal tradition of marriage.

Assuming, in a more general perspective, that the theory of 'frozen concepts' runs against the most fundamental principles of constitutional interpretation, these courts defined the Constitution as 'a living tree' that, by way of progressive interpretation, accommodates and addresses the realities of modern life.[409] The Canadian Supreme Court argued that only a large and liberal interpretation assures 'the continued relevance and, indeed, legitimacy' of the Constitution.[410] The Spanish Constitutional

[404] Case no 138 of 2010, n 258 above, para 9.
[405] See above n 372 and accompanying text.
[406] *Obergefell*, n 362 above, 135 S. Ct, 2602.
[407] *Reference Re Same-Sex Marriage*, n 258 above.
[408] Case no 198 of 2012, n 288 above.
[409] See, *Reference Re Same-Sex Marriage*, n 258 above, para 22; case no 198 of 2012, n 288 above, para 9.
[410] *Reference Re Same-Sex Marriage*, n 258 above, para 23.

Tribunal held that it is a duty of public powers, in particular of the legislator and of the Spanish Constitutional Tribunal itself, to update the Constitution in order to 'endow the rules with a content enabling their reading in light of modern-day issues and the needs of current society' and 'to build up legal culture, to the extent that the law is treated as a social phenomenon that is linked to the reality in which it is implemented'.[411] Otherwise, the Spanish Constitutional Tribunal argued, 'there is the risk of an unfulfilled Constitution'.[412]

Delivering the opinion of the Constitutional Tribunal, Justice Perez Tremps placed the judiciary and the legislator on an equal footing in the effort of adapting the Constitution to the changing reality of family relationships: 'The Court cannot remain aloof from social reality'.[413] Although this argument might appear similar to Justice Kennedy's remarks in *Obergefell* that 'individuals need not await legislative action before asserting a fundamental right' and courts 'are open to injured individuals who come to them to vindicate their own direct, personal stake in our basic charter',[414] the Spanish Constitutional Tribunal's assertions rest entirely on separation of powers arguments. The idea that the Constitutional Tribunal must answer to changing social needs was in fact influenced by the circumstance that the Spanish Parliament had already adopted a regulation of same-sex marriage when Justice Tremps was writing. Law no 13 of 2005 had already been in force for more than seven years, and 'quantitative data in official statics ... confirm[ed] ... a broad social acceptance of marriage between same-sex couples'.[415]

Nevertheless, Justice Perez Tremps did not conclude that same-sex marriage is mandated by the Constitution: he said only that it is 'constitutionally possible'.[416]

Separation of powers concerns similarly suggested to the Canadian Supreme Court the conclusion that 'read expansively', the word 'marriage' in section 91(26) of the Constitution Act 1867 did not exclude the legislative authority of the Parliament of Canada from regulating same-sex marriage.[417] At the same time, the Supreme Court was silent on whether this change is required under the principle of equality enshrined by section 15(1) of the Canadian Charter of Rights and Freedoms.[418]

[411] Case no 198 of 2012, n 288 above, para 9.

[412] ibid.

[413] ibid. Nonetheless, writing for the majority, Justice Perez Tremps cautions that 'this does not mean that direct regulatory force should be granted to factual issues'.

[414] *Obergefell*, n 362 above, 135 SCt, 2605–06.

[415] Case no 198 of 2012, n 288 above, para 9.

[416] See JML Villaverde, 'And the Story come to an End: the Constitutionality of Same-Sex Marriages in Spain' in M Sáez (ed), *Same Sex Couples—Comparative Insights on Marriage and Cohabition* (Heidelberg, Springer, 2015) 13, 39.

[417] *Reference Re Same-Sex Marriage*, n 258 above, paras 17–19.

[418] ibid, para 45. It is interesting to observe that the European Court of Human Rights, in *Schalk and Kopf v Austria* ECHR 2010-I, (2010) ECHR 1996, states that 'it would no longer consider that the right to marry enshrined in article 12 must in all circumstances be limited to marriage between two persons of the opposite sex' (§ 61). However the ECtHR leaves the decision of whether to allow same-sex marriage to Contracting States. In that respect, the Court stresses the importance of the 'deep-rooted social and cultural connotations' of marriage in European countries and argues that 'it must not rush to substitute' the legal provisions of 'national authorities who are best placed to assess and respond to the need of the society'. As P Johnson, *Homosexuality and the European Court of Human Rights* (Abingdon, Routledge, 2013) argues, 'this privileging of "traditional" heterosexual marriage can be seen as the defensive behaviour of the Court which ... sought the safe harbour of heteronormativity'.

These cases confirm my remarks on the different role of constitutional and ordinary courts in the advancement of the rights.[419] In particular, they suggest that Constitutional or Supreme Courts that were asked to decide on the legitimacy of new regulations of marriage which were already in force, usually endorsed liberal interpretations of the Constitution emphasising the flexible meaning of 'marriage' and the forward-looking dimension of tradition. Conversely, constitutional courts that were asked to intervene before their national legislators, adopted more conservative views relying on the fixed and backward-looking value of tradition.

In Canada, when the Supreme Court released its ruling in *Reference Re Same-Sex Marriage* on the federal draft bill on same-sex marriage, previous court judgments by the superior provincial courts of Ontario, Quebec and British Columbia[420] had already held the restriction of marriage to opposite-sex couples to be discriminatory under the Canadian Charter of Rights of Freedoms.[421] Furthermore, the Ontario Court of Appeal judgment in *Halpern v Canada*[422] had made same-sex marriage possible throughout the Province of Ontario.[423]

The Portuguese constitutional judgment of 2010 is illustrative of a similar trend: as clarified earlier, in 2009[424] the Constitutional Tribunal admitted that marriage was not 'a petrified institution' but it refused to call into question the common definition of marriage as 'a contract between two persons of different sex'.[425] In 2010, when Parliament had just passed law no 9 of 2010 opening marriage to same-sex couples, the same court reiterated that marriage has a flexible meaning but found the 'essential core' of marriage in its being 'a relationship based on a communion of life between two persons, established by a free, unconditional and binding act'.[426] Accordingly, the Constitutional Tribunal argued that 'it [was] a duty of the legislator to preserve the necessary connection between law and social reality'[427] and, similarly to the Constitutional Tribunal of Spain and the Supreme Court of Canada, concluded that Article 36 of the Portuguese Constitution did not forbid the opening of marriage to same-sex couples:

> The limit of intangibility of the essential core [of marriage] is not violated by the elimination of sex diversity between spouses. Indeed, whereas the establishment of communion of life between two people is a structural feature of marriage—without which marriage is deprived of its essential characteristics—the same cannot be said of the sexual diversity

[419] See above, section I p 102 ff.

[420] See n 9 above and accompanying text.

[421] Canadian Charter of Rights and Freedoms, ss 1, 2(a), 15(1).

[422] *Halpern v Canada* n 400 above, 382.

[423] The Superior Courts of Ontario (in *Halpern v Canada (Attorney General)* 95 CRR (2d) 1 (Ontario Superior Court, 12 July 2002)), Quebec (*Hendricks v Quebec* [2002] RJQ 2506 (Quebec Superior Court, 6 September 2002)) and British Columbia (*Barbeau v British Columbia* 2003 BCCA 251 (Court of Appeal for BC, 1 May 2003) stayed their declarations of invalidity, in order to give the federal government the opportunity to consider legislative responses but the Ontario Court of Appeal judgment in *Halpern v Canada*, n 400 above, took effect immediately, making same-sex marriage possible throughout the Province of Ontario. The case put more pressure on the federal government, which just one month after the case submitted a draft bill to the Supreme Court.

[424] Case no 359 of 2009 n 280 above, 70.

[425] See n 73 above and accompanying text.

[426] Case no 121 of 2010 n 79 above, para 22.

[427] ibid.

> between the persons … Sex difference would be essential if the purpose of marriage were the procreation of biologically common children, but the this purpose is neither constitutionally nor legally mandated. … The communion of life between two people, in a presumably endless lifetime of mutual support and sharing is also available to same-sex couples who want to join themselves before the State and be recognized as such by their community.[428]

F. 'A New Image of Marriage' and Judicial Cross-Fertilisation

Constitutional courts have been very cautious in relying on foreign materials in same-sex marriage cases. This is probably due to pressing concerns about their own legitimacy: the 'separation of powers anxiety' that I discussed in the foregoing pages leads the courts to rely on domestic sources when addressing issues concerning an institution like marriage, deeply entrenched in national culture, history and tradition. At the same time, arguments of tradition—which are given special prominence is same-sex marriage cases—rest entirely on the analysis of domestic sources of law.

Nonetheless, whenever the prevailing sentiments on the idea of marriage are taken into account, constitutional courts have been relying extensively on foreign legal developments at legislative and judicial level in order to support their departure from the traditional definition of marriage in heterosexual terms. Comparative law plays an evidentiary role in order to demonstrate not only that marriage, as mentioned above, is not 'a frozen concept', but also the existence of a growing consensus at global level on 'the integration of same-sex marriages into the current idea of marriage'.[429]

In its case no 198 of 2012, for instance, the Constitutional Tribunal of Spain carried out a detailed comparative analysis in order to demonstrate that many other countries—sharing, the Tribunal says, 'the same legal culture'—have been opening up 'the traditional notion of marriage' to same-sex couples. The Tribunal in particular found 'a consolidated equivalence' of legal solutions in various western legal systems', which—starting with the Netherlands in 2000—have been introducing same-sex marriage in recent decades. It also took into account legislative developments in many European countries, in several states within the United States and Canada and in Latin America. Against this background, the Tribunal argued that was possible to assume 'a new "image" of marriage, gradually becoming more common, though not totally standard as of now, which allows us to interpret the idea of marriage, from the point of view of Western comparative law, as a plural conception'.[430]

As mentioned in the previous pages, Justice Perez Tremps—who delivered the opinion of the Tribunal—focused on 'determining to what extent marriage between persons of the same sex [was] integrated in [Spanish] legal culture, thereby resorting to the components of this culture'.[431] I addressed issues concerning the cultural

[428] ibid.
[429] Case no 198 of 2012, n 288 above, para 9.
[430] ibid.
[431] ibid.

objection to judicial cross-fertilisation in same-sex marriage cases in the introduction to this book, but it is worth reiterating here that for the Constitutional Tribunal, cultural and traditional elements in marriage did not preclude the Court from taking into account foreign authorities. Justice Perez Tremps argued that, as illustrative of a wider 'legal culture', comparative materials supported the conclusion that 'the possibility of homosexual marriage ... falls within the portrayed image of marriage as an institution'.[432]

At the same time, Justice Perez Tremps emphasised that legal developments occurring in foreign countries mirror changes in social perception of marriage at domestic level. Noting that even 'quantitative data in official statistics confirm that in Spain there is broad social acceptance of marriage between same-sex couples', he concluded that the essential core of marriage has in fact not been affected by the opening of marriage to same-sex couples.[433] Marriage, he argued, is defined as 'a community of affection which generates a bond of mutual aid between two persons who are equal within this institution and who freely decide to join a common project of family life by giving their consent and expressing it expressly according to the established formalities'.[434] Therefore, he held, neither the institutional guarantee of marriage, nor the individual right to marry were impaired by law no 13 of 2005.

Even the Portuguese Constitutional Court, in its 2010 judgment on the constitutional legitimacy of the reform of the civil code, which opened marriage to same-sex couples, relied extensively on comparative law in order to support an evolutionary interpretation of the constitutional clause on marriage: noting that issues concerning the recognition of same-sex unions have been thoroughly debated in many countries belonging to 'the same space of civilization and culture',[435] the Constitutional Tribunal observed that, especially in judicial review of legislation, 'it might be useful to know what is happening in other legal experiences, especially in order to infer common legal principles'.[436]

After a detailed discussion of the European Court of Justice and the European Court of Human Rights cases (which are binding on Portugal, as a Member State of the respective international organisations),[437] the Constitutional Tribunal provided a detailed account of the different legislative solutions adopted by many European and American countries in order to regulate same-sex unions (same-sex marriage or civil partnerships).[438] Finally, the Tribunal analysed the most relevant constitutional

[432] ibid.

[433] Case no 198 of 2012 n 280 above, para 10 (arguing that 'The changes have not affected its content or harmed he right to marry held by heterosexuals, given that the challenged Law does not make any material amendment in the legal provisions governing the requirements and effects of civil marriage between opposite-sex persons').

[434] Case no 198 of 2012, n 288 above, para 9.

[435] Tribunal Constitucional, Case no 121/2010, n 79 above, para 7.

[436] ibid.

[437] In my opinion, reliance on international materials (cases and legislation) should not be considered equal to foreign law. Although there are different perspectives on the relationship between international and domestic law, international law should not be treated as foreign law for the purposes of constitutional interpretation. On this issue, see A Sperti, 'United States of America: First Cautious Attempts of Judicial Use of Foreign Precedents in the Supreme Court's Jurisprudence', in T Groppi and MC Ponthoreau (eds), *The Use of Foreign Precedents by Constitutional Judges* (Oxford, Hart Publishing, 2013) 393, 397–98.

[438] Case no 121 of 2010 n 435 above, para 13 ff.

cases on same-sex marriage, from *Baehr v Lewin*[439]—the 1993 decision of the Hawaii Supreme Court—to the German constitutional cases on registered civil partnerships (*Eingetragene Lebenspartnerschaft*),[440] to the South Africa Constitutional Court's judgment in *Fourie*.[441]

Against this background, and citing the South Africa Constitutional Court's conclusions in *Fourie*,[442] the Portuguese Constitutional Court argued that although 'it is reasonable to conclude that ... according to international law documents marriage is between a man and a woman' this definition is only 'descriptive of an assumed reality, rather than prescriptive of a normative structure for all time'.[443] Assuming that marriage is 'an open concept', the Constitutional Tribunal concluded that 'it is up to the legislator to understand and to convey into law to prevailing public sentiments on this issue'.[444]

Furthermore, foreign cases and legislation have been taken into account by the Supreme Court of Canada in its 2004 reference case on same-sex marriage[445] in order to support an evolutionary interpretation of 'marriage', by the Israel Supreme Court in *Ber-Ari*,[446] a ruling on the registration of same-sex marriages concluded in foreign countries, and by South American constitutional courts in their cases on the reforms of domestic civil codes that opened marriage to same-sex couples.[447]

The High Court of Ireland in *Zappone*[448] adopted a traditionalist interpretation of marriage, while also admitting that foreign authorities 'are interesting in many respects', because 'they are dealing with similar definitions of marriage and the assertion of a right to marry requiring a redefinition of the traditional understanding of marriage'.[449] Nonetheless, writing for the Court, Justice Dunne asserted that 'there is a limit to the assistance that can be drawn from [foreign authorities] given the different constitutional framework applicable in [Irish] jurisdiction'. Accordingly he dismissed the plaintiffs' arguments 'to the effect that the definition of marriage as understood in 1937 require[d] to be reconsidered in the light of now prevailing

[439] *Baehr v Lewin* 74 Haw 530, 852 P 2d 44 (1993).
[440] 105 BVerfGE 313(2002) (Civil Partnership Act case).
[441] *Minister of Home Affairs and Another v Fourie*, Case CCT 60/04 [2005] ZACC 19.
[442] *Fourie* n 441 above.
[443] Case no 121 of 2010, n 435 above, para 21, citing *Fourie* n 441 above, para 100.
[444] ibid, para 22.
[445] See eg the Supreme Court of Canada in *Reference Re Same-Sex Marriage* n 258 above, para 25 (arguing that recognition of same-sex marriage in several Canadian jurisdictions as well as two European countries belies the assertion that the notion of marriage is fixed).
[446] HCJ 3045/05, *Ben-Ari v The Director of the Population Administration in the Ministry of the Interior*.
[447] See *Freire Alejandro v GCBA* (expte no 34.292/09), *Juzgado en lo Contencioso Administrativo y Tributario No 15 de la Ciudad Autónoma de Buenos Aires*, 10 November 2009 (discussing same-sex marriage in many European countries and in Canada and South Africa); Supreme Court of Justice of Mexico, *Acción de Inconstitucionalidad 2/2010*, 10 August 2010 (analysing laws and judicial decisions concerning same-sex marriage and same-sex unions in the Netherlands, Belgium, Spain, Norway, Sweden, Portugal, United States, Canada, South Africa); Constitutional Court of Colombia in *Sentencia* C-577/11, 26 July 2011 (holding art 113 of the Civil Code unconstitutional because it limited marriage to opposite-sex couples and relying extensively on comparative law (para 4.5.3.1.1)). See also the Supremo Tribunal Federal of Brasil in *Ação direta de inconstitucionalidade* 4.277, 5 May 2011.
[448] *Zappone*, n 273 above.
[449] See *Zappone*, n 273 above, the Court's conclusions.

standards and conditions'.[450] At the same time, the Court concluded that 'the consensus around the world does not support a widespread move towards same-sex marriage'.[451]

III. ARGUMENTS IN SAME-SEX MARRIAGE CASES: EQUALITY, LIBERTY AND HUMAN DIGNITY

A. Equality and Diversity in the Present Debate over Civil Rights

The present debate over civil rights poses something of a paradox.

On one side, it is possible to describe a general trend towards equality and assimilation: protection of civil rights, as demonstrated by increasing recognition of the rights of gays, lesbians and same-sex couples is spreading and it is possible to describe a general convergence of courts and legislators towards similar models and standards of protection. At the same time, constitutional cases on the rights of gays and lesbians focus on ideals of dignity, equality and liberty: constitutional and supreme courts' arguments sound in a universal registry.

On the other side, the fight for civil rights does not 'serve only the cause of equality, but also the "diversity-within-equality"'.[452] Assimilation and diversity proceed along parallel paths, because globalisation of civil rights includes not only claims of equality but also demands of liberty and the natural aspiration of different groups and cultures to preserve their own identities. New forms of identity politics within all liberal democracies 'complicate and increase century old tensions between the universalistic principles ushered in by the American and French Revolutions and the peculiarities of nationality, ethnicity, religion, gender, race and language'.[453]

This trend towards particularism is exemplified by the enlarging list of prohibited grounds of discrimination in international documents: whereas Article 14 of the European Convention on Human Rights declares that

> the enjoyment of the rights and freedoms ... shall be secured without discrimination on any ground such as sex, race, colour, language, religion, political or other opinion, national and social origin, association with a national minority, property, birth or other status,

[450] ibid.

[451] ibid. ('Having regard to the clear understanding of the meaning of marriage as set out in the numerous authorities opened to the Court from this jurisdiction and elsewhere, I do not see how marriage can be redefined by the Court to encompass same sex marriage. The Plaintiffs referred frequently in the course of this case to the "changing consensus" but I have to say the there is little evidence of that. The consensus around the world does not support a widespread move towards same-sex marriage. There has been some limited support for the concept of same sex marriage as in Canada, Massachusetts and South Africa together with the three European countries previously referred to but, in truth, it is difficult to see that as a consensus, changing or otherwise. In this jurisdiction, as recently as 2004, s. 2(2)(e) of the Civil Registration Act was enacted. That Act sets out what was previously the common law exclusion of same sex couples from the institution of marriage. Is that not of itself an indication of the prevailing idea and concept in relation to what marriage is and how it should be defined? I think it is.').

[452] MR Ferrarese, *Il diritto al presente* (Bologna, Il Mulino, 2002) 160.

[453] S Behnabib, *The Claims of Culture: Equality and Diversity in the Global Era* (Princeton, Princeton University Press, 2002) 1.

the more recent Article 21 of the European Union Charter of Fundamental Rights—the counterpart of Article 14 of the ECHR—enlarges this list including ethnic and social origin, genetic features, belief, disability, age and sexual orientation.

In the United States, Carozza emphasises the existence of 'an inherent tension in international human rights law' between upholding a universal understanding of human rights and 'respecting the diversity and freedom of human cultures'.[454] Yoshino also discusses the 'pluralist anxiety' spreading across the United States, 'as an apprehension of and about its demographic diversity'[455] arguing that it 'has transformed civil rights' because demands from 'new kinds of people and newly visible kind of people' are stimulating change in American constitutional jurisprudence, 'signal[ling] the end of equality doctrine'.[456]

My purpose in the present chapter is to analyse arguments of equality, difference-within-equality, liberty and dignity in same-sex marriage cases. I will start my analysis from equality discourse in same-sex marriage cases in order to emphasise how the legal debate mostly revolves around the implications of equality in terms of dignity of same-sex couples. Then I will address in more detail the different meanings that constitutional and supreme courts attach to dignity in same-sex marriage cases and their narrow relationship with equality and liberty. Lastly, taking my cue from Yoshino's and Carozza's remarks and the many scholarly works that in recent years have analysed the reasons behind the widespread use of dignity discourse in human rights adjudication, I will attempt to clarify the different purposes that dignity discourse serves in same-sex marriage cases.

B. Equality and its Implications in Same-Sex Marriage Cases

The scholarly and political debate on same-sex marriage is framed in the language of equality.

In recent years, for instance, it has been argued (and I also assume in this book) that 'equal marriage' should be a more appropriate label for the institution. 'Equal marriage' makes reference to the equal allocation of rights and benefits to all married couples, regardless of spouses' sexual orientation, gender or biological sex. At the same time, 'equal marriage' suggests that there is only *one* right to marriage, and that the LGBT community is not looking for a 'new' or a special right, but just for the removal of an old discrimination restricting access to marriage to opposite-sex couples.[457] By contrast, the expression 'gay marriage' has recently been interpreted as conveying a sense of inferiority.

[454] PG Carozza, 'Subsidiarity as a Structural Principle of International Human Rights Law' (2003) 97 *American Journal of International Law* 1.

[455] K Yoshino, 'The New Equal Protection' (2004) 124 *Harvard Law Review* 747.

[456] Yoshino, 'The New Equal Protection' n 455 above, 748.

[457] See *Baehr v Lewin* 74 Haw 530, 555 (1993) (framing the issue as regarding the identification of a 'new' right). The issue concerning the recognition of a new right to same-sex marriage has been discussed above, p 127 ff.

Formal equality is also the starting point of same-sex marriage legal and political debate: same-sex marriage proponents assume that similarly situated couples should have equal access to marriage, whereas opponents generally deny that same-sex couples are placed in an equal position to different-sex couples.

Nonetheless, moving from these assumptions, much of the debate (and of the struggle) over same-sex marriage revolves around the *consequences* of formal equality. As Eskridge emphasises, 'although the case for same-sex marriage centrally focuses on the idea of formal equality, the debate appears to the casual observer to be overwhelmingly consequentialist'.[458]

Each consequence of marriage pertains to a different object of equality. Some consequences are attached to the recognition of the right to marriage as a fundamental right, others pertain to the right to personal choice regarding marriage, finally others flow from the recognition of an equal status of marriage.

In the legal (and sometimes in the scholarly) debate, the different claims of equality are often merged, due to the fact that is very difficult to draw clear lines of distinction among them and their consequences.[459] In the following pages I argue that the distinction is also made difficult by the fact the all the different claims of equality are strictly intertwined with arguments of liberty and dignity.

i. Equality and the 'Expressive' Value of Marriage

Proponents of equal marriage argue that same-sex couples should be allowed to marry (or to choose marriage as the form for their intimate relationship) on equal terms to different-sex couples because of the social and 'expressive'[460] value attached (by couples themselves and by their community) to marriage.

Marriage as a social institution has in fact 'an iconic and ideological status':[461] the spouses' mutual public statement of love and commitment in front of witnesses, relatives and friends has a value for the couple itself, because it validates and reinforces their mutual and (potentially) life-enduring bond, but also a *social* value, because it makes the union recognised and sanctioned in public.[462]

The public debate over same-sex marriage is almost entirely about marriage's expressive value. As early as in 1994, E Wolfson—'the godfather of same-sex

[458] WN Eskridge, 'The Ideological Structure of the Same-Sex Marriage Debate (and Some Postmodern Arguments for Same-Sex Marriage)', in R Wintemute and M Andenæs (eds), *Legal Recognition of Same-Sex Partnerships* (Oxford, Hart Publishing, 2001) 113, 114 (who stresses that a second feature of the debate is its abstract and ideological nature, because 'no one actually knows the consequences, especially the long-term consequences, of state recognition of same-sex marriage').

[459] See also J Halley, 'Recognition, Rights, Regulation, Normalisation' in R Wintemute and M Andenæs (eds), *Legal Recognition of Same-Sex Partnerships* (Oxford, Hart Publishing, 2001) 104.

[460] M Nussbaum, *From Disgust to Humanity. Sexual Orientation and Constitutional Law* (Oxford, Oxford University Press, 2010) 129.

[461] A Diduck and F Canagas, *Family Law, Gender and the State. Text, Cases and Materials*, 3rd edn (Oxford, Hart Publishing, 2012) 37.

[462] Nussbaum, *From Digust to Humanity*, n 460 above, 129. See *Obergefell v Hodges* 135 S Ct 2584 (2015), 2601 (arguing that 'just as a couple vows to support each other, so does society pledge to support the couple, offering symbolic recognition and material benefits to protect and nourish the union').

marriage movement' in the United States[463]—writing in support of the cause of same-sex marriage, argued that what couples see in marriage is 'the public affirmation of emotional and financial commitment and interdependence':[464]

> Today marriage is first and foremost about a loving union between two people who enter into a relationship of emotional and fiscal commitment and interdependence, two people who seek to make a public statement about their relationship, sanctioned by the state, the community at large, and, for some, their religious community.[465]

It has also been suggested that the marrying couple's statement has a normative significance because it involves an answering statement by society, which dignifies the conjugal bond.[466]

In Italy, where a heated debate led to the adoption of law no 76 of 2016[467] on civil unions, and marriage is still forbidden to same-sex couples, Gattuso effectively emphasises that 'the issue is not only about the "name" marriage, because the dispute is not merely terminological but involves the recognition of equality and full dignity for all citizens before the law'.[468]

Dignity, liberty and equality are therefore inextricably linked with the (social and expressive) significance of marriage. Gattuso states this in clear terms:

> If there is no difference between affective relationships of individuals regardless of their sexual orientation, there is no legal justification of two separate institutions, one reserved to opposite-sex couples (marriage between opposite-sex persons) and the other to same-sex couples (civil unions between same-sex persons).[469]

In common law countries, most courts[470] have recognised both the social and emotional importance of marriage in their cases on equal marriage. In *Halpern v Canada*,[471] for instance, seven same-sex couples contended before the Ontario Court of Appeal that marriage is 'a defining moment for people choosing to make

[463] On the importance of Evan Wolfson's contribution to marriage equality in the United States, K Yoshino, *Speak Now. Marriage Equality on Trial. The History of Hollingsworth v Perry* (New York, Broadway Books, 2015) 35 ff.

[464] E Wolfson, 'Crossing the Threshold: Equal Marriage Rights for Lesbians and Gay Men and the Intra-Community Critique' (1994) 21 *New York University Review of Law and Social Change* 567, 579.

[465] ibid.

[466] See Wolfson, 'Crossing the Threshold' n 464 above, 597. Nonetheless, after *Baehr v Lewin*, 74 Haw 530, 852 P 2d 44 (1993), the groundbreaking same-sex marriage case of the Supreme Court of Hawaii, LGBT movements did not develop the argument of marriage as 'a signal of approval' by the Government, because, as CR Feldblum, 'The Limitation of Liberal Neutrality Arguments' in R Wintemute and M Andenæs (eds), *Legal Recognition of Same-Sex Partnerships* (Oxford, Hart Publishing, 2001) 55, 56 ff, clarifies, such an argument would have implied a value choice by the Government. Instead, marriage proponents preferred to rest on liberal neutral equality grounds in order to justify marriage of same-sex couples. Against the 'stamp of approval argument', see also Eskridge, *The Case for Same-Sex Marriage* 51–52.

[467] Law no 76 of 20 May 2016.

[468] M Gattuso, 'La vittoria dei bambini arcobaleno' in Articolo29, *www.articolo29.it*, 22 June 2016 (transl mine).

[469] Gattuso, 'La vittoria dei bambini arcobaleno', n 468 above.

[470] In civil law countries, constitutional and supreme courts did not address similar issues concerning the expressive value of marriage, probably due to the more concise style of cases, but also to the tendency of the courts to develop arguments that find a textual support in statutory and constitutional texts, instead of 'social' arguments.

[471] *Halpern v Canada* (2003) 65 OR 3d 161 (Can Ont CA).

a life commitment to each other' and that, at the same time, it makes it possible to 'larger society to know and understand [the couple's] relationship for what it is, a loving committed relationship between two people'.[472]

The Ontario Court of Appeal accepted this argument, arguing that

> Marriage is, without dispute, one of the most significant forms of personal relationships. For centuries, marriage has been a basic element of social organization in societies around the world. Through the institution of marriage, individuals can publicly express their love and commitment to each other. Through this institution, society publicly recognizes expressions of love and commitment between individuals, granting them respect and legitimacy as a couple. This public recognition and sanction of marital relationships reflect society's approbation of the personal hopes, desires and aspirations that underlie loving, committed conjugal relationships. This can only enhance an individual's sense of self-worth and dignity.[473]

Similarly, many United States[474] and Canadian[475] federal and state court cases have emphasised that marriage is much more than a contract for opposite-sex as well as for same-sex couples: equal marriage implies dignity, respect and stature for the spouses.

For same-sex couples, 'normalisation' is also their 'exit from isolation' and the end of 'second-class treatment for same-sex couples'.[476] In the United States, *Loving v Virginia*,[477] the 1967 case that put an end to anti-miscegenation laws, is frequently cited as the first step in the struggle over marriage equality.[478]

[472] ibid, para 9.

[473] ibid, para 5.

[474] The list of cases cannot be exhaustive but see, *In re marriage cases* 43 Cal 4th 757 (2008), 830–31 (emphasising that 'One of the core elements of the fundamental right to marry is the right of same-sex couples to have their official family relationship accorded the same dignity, respect, and stature as that accorded to all other officially recognized family relationships'); *Goodridge v Department of Public Health*, 440 Mass 309, 329; *Lewis v Harris* 188 NJ 415 (2006), 458 (arguing that 'Plaintiffs seek not just legal standing, but also social acceptance, which in their view is the last step toward true equality'); *Perry v Brown*, 671 F 3d 1052 (9th Cir 2012) 1078 (emphasising that 'the word "marriage" has a unique meaning', and 'there is a significant symbolic disparity between domestic partnership and marriage. It is the designation of "marriage" itself that expresses validation, by the state and the community, and that serves as a symbol, like a wedding ceremony or a wedding ring, of something profoundly important'); *Varnum v Brien*, 763 NW 2d 862 (2009), 883 (concluding that 'the plaintiffs are similarly situated compared to heterosexual persons. Plaintiffs are in committed and loving relationships, many raising families, just like heterosexual couples. Moreover, official recognition of their status provides an institutional basis for defining their fundamental relational rights and responsibilities, just as it does for heterosexual couples').

[475] See *Halpern v Canada* n 471 above, para 9; *Hendricks c Québec (Procureur général)* [2002] RJQ 2506, para 131.

[476] See *Hendricks c Québec*, n 475 above, para 39 (explaining the value of marriage for the applicants with the following words: 'C'est leur entrée dans la normalisation et la sortie de l'isolement. L'inaccessibilité à cette institution les infantilise, les hommes gais et les lesbiennes ne peuvent pas choisir le type d'union qui leur convient. Ils demeurent des citoyens de second ordre'). For an opposite perspective on normalisation by progressive same-sex marriage proponents, see n 490 below and accompanying text.

[477] *Loving v Virginia* 388 US 1 (1967). On the *Loving* analogy, Y Merlin, *Equality for Same-Sex Couples. The Legal Recognition of Gay Partnerships in Europe and the United States* (Chicago, University of Chicago Press, 2002) 288 ff. For a different perspective on the importance of *Loving* in same-sex marriage debate in the United States, WN Eskridge, *The Case for Same-Sex Marriage. From Sexual Liberty to Civilized Commitment* (New York, The Free Press, 1996) 127 ff.

[478] In the aftermath of the Supreme Court's decision in *United States v Windsor* 133 SCt 2675 (2013), President Obama cited *Loving v Virginia*, n 477 above, as the first great achievement in the struggle for marriage equality. See 'Inaugural address' 2013 Daily Comp Pres Doc 32 (21 January 2013).

The most significant statements about the social and emotional value of marriage can be found in the United States Supreme Court's judgments in *United States v Windsor*[479] and in *Obergefell v Hodges*.[480]

In *Windsor*, writing for the Court, Justice Kennedy clarified what marriage means to same-sex couples:[481] he stressed that same-sex couples 'wish to define themselves by their commitment to each other'[482] and to affirm it 'before their children, their family, their friends, and their community'.[483] The right to marry, he argued, implies the couple's right '[to] live with pride in themselves and their union and in a status of equality with all other married persons'.[484]

In his majority opinion in *Obergefell* Justice Kennedy gave particular emphasis to the expressive and social value of marriage when mentioning its 'transcendent importance':

> The lifelong union of a man and a woman always has promised nobility and dignity to all persons, without regard to their station in life. Marriage is sacred to those who live by their religions and offers unique fulfilment to those who find meaning in the secular realm. Its dynamic allows two people to find a life that could not be found alone, for a marriage becomes greater than just the two persons. Rising from the most basic human needs, marriage is essential to our most profound hopes and aspirations.[485]

Although the immediate consequences of equal marriage might be tangible in term of rights and responsibilities,[486] these statements identify other more profound reasons in the exercise of individual freedom and dignity.

Eskridge puts it in clear terms when he writes that 'the second and more fundamental feature of the same-sex marriage debate is that it is abstract and ideological' because 'the consequentialist features of the debate are about theoretical and symbolic consequences than actual and tangible consequences'.[487] Thus, what makes the debate on same-sex marriage so intense, are the underlying institutional and theoretical commitments lying behind the different positions. Eskridge's analysis addresses the theoretical stances that inspire traditionalist opposition, the postmodern theories (stressing the oppressive cultural constraints of marriage) and, finally, the liberal arguments (emphasising the advancement of individual freedom of choice that marriage implies). Nonetheless, in my opinion it is possible to draw similar conclusions when the consequences of marriage in terms on dignity and social recognition of same-sex couples come into consideration.[488]

[479] *United States v Windsor* n 477 above.
[480] *Obergefell v Hodges* n 462 above.
[481] D NeJaime, '*Windsor*'s Right to Marry' (2013) 123 *Yale Law Journal Online* 219 (available at yalelawjournal.org/forum/windsors-right-to-marry, last visited 15 Sept 2016).
[482] *United States v Windsor* n 477 above, 133 S Ct, 2689.
[483] ibid.
[484] ibid.
[485] *Obergefell v Hodges* n 462 above, 135 S Ct, 2594.
[486] See below p 146 ff.
[487] Eskridge, 'The ideological structure', n 458 above, 115.
[488] On dignity discourse in same-sex marriage cases see below p 156 ff.

Justice Kennedy's opinion in *Obergefell* identified these implications of marriage in clear terms:

> The nature of marriage is that, through its enduring bond, two persons together can find other freedoms, such as expression, intimacy, and spirituality. There is dignity in the bond between two men or two women who seek to marry and in their autonomy to make such profound choices. It is the enduring importance of marriage that underlies the petitioners' contentions. This, they say, is their whole point. Far from seeking to devalue marriage, the petitioners seek it for themselves because of their respect—and need—for its privileges and responsibilities. And their immutable nature dictates that same-sex marriage is their only real path to this profound commitment.[489]

Although Justice Kennedy did not state it explicitly, his reasoning seemed to answer not only same-sex marriage opponents who thought that marriage would have been devalued if same-sex couples were allowed to marry, but also those within the LGBT community who contended that equal treatment would have normalised gay couples and contributed to the standardisation of same-sex relationship.[490]

The expressive value of marriage and the consequences of marriage equality with regard to dignity and freedom of same-sex couples have been also emphasised by the South Africa Constitutional Court since *Fourie*,[491] its 2005 ruling on same-sex marriage. Writing for the Court, Justice Sachs argued that the formalities for marriage 'make certain that it is known to the broader community precisely who gets married and when they get married'[492] because the words '"I do" bring the most intense private and voluntary commitment into the most public, law-governed and state-regulated domain'.[493]

Furthermore, it should be emphasised that for same-sex couples, marriage has a symbolic value also because it symbolises the ultimate achievement in the LGBT communities' long-term struggle for equality.

> The right to celebrate their union [Justice Sachs writes] ... signifies far more than a right to enter into a legal arrangement with many attendant and significant consequences, important though they may be. It represents a major symbolical milestone in their long walk to equality and dignity. The greater and more secure the institutional imprimatur for their union, the more solidly will it and other such unions be rescued from legal oblivion, and the more tranquil and enduring will such unions ultimately turn out to be.[494]

ii. Equality of Rights and Responsibilities Flowing from Marriage

Advocates of marriage equality also stress the many rights, protections and responsibilities flowing from marriage. Although, as mentioned above, it is difficult to draw

[489] *Obergefell v Hodges* n 462 above, 135 S Ct, 2594.

[490] See Eskridge, 'The Ideological Structure' n 458 above at 115 but see also Halley, 'Recognition, Rights, Regulation, Normalisation' n 459 above, 99 ff.

[491] *Minister of Home Affairs and Another v Fourie*, Case CCT 60/04 [2005] ZACC 19 paras 1 and 63–64.

[492] ibid, para 1.

[493] ibid, paras 63–64.

[494] ibid, para 137.

clear lines among the different implications of marriage equality, what comes into consideration here is actually the *legal status* of marriage: same-sex marriage proponents complain in fact about the unfairness of denying the same rights and mutual obligations to similarly situated couples.

Denial of some of the rights (for instance, parental rights)[495] and of the mutual obligations incumbent instead on those who are married (for instance, the symbolic duty of faithfulness)[496] has been one of the main features of first regulations of civil unions in many countries. For this reason, equal access to marriage, with all the rights and responsibilities thereto pertaining, symbolises at the same time the end of a discriminatory 'double-track system', which accorded a second-tier status to same-sex couples, reserving instead full rights to married opposite-sex couples only. In most constitutional cases, arguments of equality are again inextricably linked with dignity and liberty.

In *Lewis v Harris*,[497] for instance, the Supreme Court of New Jersey emphasised that even after the enactment of the New Jersey Domestic Partnership Act,[498] many of the rights and benefits accorded to married couples were denied to committed same-sex couples. As the state legislature had recognised that these rights and benefits were 'directly related to any reasonable conception of basic human dignity and autonomy',[499] the Supreme Court noted:

> It is difficult to understand how withholding the remaining rights and benefits from committed same-sex couples is compatible with a reasonable conception of basic human dignity and autonomy. There is no rational basis for, on the one hand, giving gays and lesbians full civil rights in their status as individuals, and, on the other, giving them an incomplete set of rights when they follow the inclination of their sexual orientation and enter into committed same-sex relationships.[500]

The idea that denial of the status of marriage amounts at the same time to a significant violation of gays' and lesbians' dignity and autonomy, has also been expounded by the United States Supreme Court since *Windsor*,[501] the 2013 case holding that the restriction of the definitions of 'marriage' and 'spouse'—by section 3 of the

[495] See for instance the regulation of PaCS in France, excluding eg inheritance rights and parental rights, or the regulation of civil partnerships (*eingetragene Lebenspartnerschaft*) in Germany that in the beginning excluded second adoption of the adopted child and treated partners as singles with respect to inheritance and income tax law and to survivors' benefits. See, below, Ch 5, p 187 ff.

[496] See law no 76 of 2016 regulating same-sex unions in Italy. Although this duty has no legal implications as far as eg parental rights are concerned, its exclusion places a stamp of inferiority on same-sex couples whose mutual commitment is considered less deep and strong than that of a different-sex couple. It also points to heterosexuality as a determinant of marriage. I have addressed this issue also above at Chapter 3, p 79. See E Falletti, 'Obbligo di fedeltà. Profili storici e di diritto comparato di un istituto non previsto nell'unione civile' (2016) *GenIus, Rivista sull'orientamento sessuale e l'identità di genere*, forthcoming.

[497] *Lewis v Harris* 188 N.J. 415 (2006). Cf K Franke, *The Perils of Marriage Equality. How African Americans and Gays Mistakenly Thought the Right to Marry Would Set Them Free* (New York, New York University Press, 2015), 109; Y Merin, Equality for Same-Sex Couples, n 477 above, 288 ff.

[498] New Jersey Domestic Partnership Act, L 2003, c 246.

[499] *Lewis v Harris*, n 497 above, 188 NJ 452.

[500] ibid.

[501] *United States v Windsor* n 477 above.

Defence of Marriage Act (DOMA)[502]—to different-sex couples was an unconstitutional deprivation of liberty and equal protection under the Fifth Amendment of the Constitution.

In concluding that DOMA injured the very class that New York state laws on equal marriage sought to protect, Justice Kennedy emphasised that 'New York was responding to the initiative of those who [sought] a voice in shaping the destiny of their own times'.[503] He argued:

> The States' interest in defining and regulating the marital relation, subject to constitutional guarantees, stems from the understanding that marriage is more than a routine classification for purposes of certain statutory benefits. Private, consensual sexual intimacy between two adult persons of the same sex may not be punished by the State, and it can form 'but one element in a personal bond that is more enduring'. … By its recognition of the validity of same-sex marriages performed in other jurisdictions and then by authorising same-sex unions and same-sex marriages, New York sought to give further protection and dignity to that bond. For same-sex couples who wished to be married, the State acted to give their lawful conduct a lawful status. This status is a far-reaching legal acknowledgment of the intimate relationship between two people, a relationship deemed by the State worthy of dignity in the community equal with all other marriages. It reflects both the community's considered perspective on the historical roots of the institution of marriage and its evolving understanding of the meaning of equality.[504]

Justice Kennedy enumerated the many negative effects of the definition of DOMA, concluding that the federal statute violated the principle of equality not only because it 'contrive[d] to deprive some couples married under the laws of their State, but not other couples, of both rights and responsibilities'[505] but also because it undermined the social and private value of marriage.[506]

In 2015, in *Obergefell v Hodges*,[507] the Supreme Court reiterated that denial of the status of marriage to same-sex couples amounted to a violation of their human dignity and autonomy and declared unconstitutional the operative section of DOMA (section 2) that allowed states to refuse to recognise same-sex marriages performed under the laws of other states.[508] After having clarified that throughout American history, states 'have made marriage the basis for an expanding list of governmental rights, benefits, and responsibilities' and 'have contributed to the fundamental

[502] Defense of Marriage Act (DOMA), 110 Stat 2419, sec 3, 1 US Code § 7—definition of 'marriage' and 'spouse' ('In determining the meaning of any Act of Congress, or of any ruling, regulation, or interpretation of the various administrative bureaus and agencies of the United States, the word "marriage" means only a legal union between one man and one woman as husband and wife, and the word "spouse" refers only to a person of the opposite sex who is a husband or a wife').

[503] *United States v Windsor* n 477 above, 133 S Ct, 2692.

[504] ibid, 133 S Ct, 2692–93.

[505] ibid, 133 S Ct, 2694

[506] ibid, 133 S Ct, 2694.

[507] *Obergefell v Hodges* n 462 above.

[508] Defense of Marriage Act, sec 2, 28 US Code § 1738C ('No State, territory, or possession of the United States, or Indian tribe, shall be required to give effect to any public act, record, or judicial proceeding of any other State, territory, possession, or tribe respecting a relationship between persons of the same sex that is treated as a marriage under the laws of such other State, territory, possession, or tribe, or a right or claim arising from such relationship').

character of the marriage right by placing that institution at the center of so many facets of the legal and social order',[509] Justice Kennedy reiterated:

> There is no difference between same- and opposite-sex couples with respect to this principle. Yet by virtue of their exclusion from that institution, same-sex couples are denied the constellation of benefits that the States have linked to marriage. This harm results in more than just material burdens. Same-sex couples are consigned to an instability many opposite-sex couples would deem intolerable in their own lives. As the State itself makes marriage all the more precious by the significance it attaches to it, exclusion from that status has the effect of teaching that gays and lesbians are unequal in important respects. It demeans gays and lesbians for the State to lock them out of a central institution of the Nation's society. Same-sex couples, too, may aspire to the transcendent purposes of marriage and seek fulfilment in its highest meaning.[510]

In recent years, other constitutional courts have similarly emphasised the implications of the recognition of equal rights and duties of marriage in terms of dignity of same-sex couples. Significant statements can be found in *Fourie*, when, writing for the South Africa Constitutional Court, Justice Sachs emphasised that 'the intangible damage to same-sex couples is as severe as the material deprivation'.[511] Analogously, the Canadian courts have repeatedly clarified how 'exclusion [from marriage] perpetuates the view that same-sex relationships are less worthy of recognition than opposite-sex relationships' and 'in doing so, it offends the dignity of persons in same-sex relationships'.[512]

Even European constitutional courts that, as mentioned earlier, have usually abstained themselves from addressing the intangible and symbolic meaning of marriage, have discussed the importance of the rights and duties of marriage in relation with the dignity and liberty of same-sex couples. In case no 198 of 2012 on the constitutionality of ley no 13 of 2015 which opened marriage to same-sex couples, Justice Perez Tremps for the Spanish Constitutional Tribunal argued that the recognition of equal access to marriage, regardless of sexual orientation, also safeguarded the personal dignity and the right to a free development of personality under article 10 of the Spanish constitution.[513] Similarly, the Portuguese constitutional court in its 2010 judgment on same-sex marriage stated that access to marriage stemmed from equality as well as from 'other constitutional values like dignity'[514] under Article 1 of the Portuguese Constitution.

C. Dignity as Synthesis of Liberty and Equality

Constitutional and supreme court cases reveal that courts direct much of their analysis on the consequences of marriage equality in terms of dignity and liberty of same-sex couples.

[509] *Obergefell v Hodges* n 462 above, 135 S Ct, 2601.
[510] *Obergefell v Hodges* n 462 above,135 S Ct, 2601–02.
[511] *Fourie*, n 491 above, paras 71–72.
[512] *Halpern v Canada* n 471 above, para 107.
[513] Case no198/2012, 6 November 2012, SCT, para 9.
[514] Case no 121 of 2010, 8 April 2010, para 19.

In the United States, there are no special provisions regarding human dignity in the federal Constitution; references to dignity were first made in the 1940s in dissenting opinions arguing for a more robust conception of individual liberties.[515] Nonetheless, in recent years the Supreme Court has relied increasingly on the idea of human dignity in its cases, attracting a significant amount of scholarly attention.[516] It has refused to adopt the view that dignity is a constitutional right derived from expressed rights of the Constitution,[517] and has treated dignity in relationship with liberty, under the Fifth and the Fourteenth Amendments. Furthermore, as clarified in Chapter 2, since *Lawrence v Texas*[518] the Supreme Court has been expounding the idea that liberty and equality are intertwined claims ('the double helix', in Tribe's words)[519] and that '[e]ach concept ... leads to a stronger understanding of the other'.[520]

The idea that liberty and equality are profoundly interlocked has been thoroughly explored by constitutional law scholarship in continental Europe and it is therefore probably no coincidence that Justice Kennedy is familiar with European constitutional law. After the Second World War, newly adopted European constitutions departed from the traditional negative conception of fundamental rights in order to guarantee the 'effectiveness' of rights and to answer to the demands of freedom from those factors of discriminations limiting the free development of human personality. Contemporary bills of rights mirror such a change of perspective, assuming that it is a duty of the State to enlarge the chances of realisation of multiple identities and guarantee an effective and equal enjoyment of rights.[521]

[515] N Rao, 'On the Use and Abuse of Dignity in Constitutional Law' (2008) 14 *Columbia Journal of European Law* 201, 202 ff.

[516] See A Barak, *Human Dignity. The Constitutional Value and the Constitutional Right* (Cambridge, Cambridge University Press, 2015); E Daly, *Dignity Rights: Courts, Constitutions, and the Worth of the Human Person* (University of Pennsylvania Press, Philadelphia, 2012); RC Glensy, 'The Right to Dignity' (2011) 43 *Columbia Human Rights Law Review* 65; MD Goodman, 'Human Dignity in Supreme Court Constitutional Jurisprudence' (2006) 84 *Nebraska Law Review* 740; VC Jackson, 'Constitutional Dialogue and Human Dignity: States and Transnational Constitutional Discourse' (2004) 65 *Montana Law Review* 15; J Paust, 'Human Dignity as a Constitutional Right: A Jurisprudentially Based Inquiry into Criteria and Content' (1984) 27 *Howard Law Journal* 145; N Rao, 'Three Concepts of Dignity in Constitutional Law' (2011) 86 *Notre Dame Law Review* 183 and 'On the Use and Abuse of Dignity' n 515 above; RB Siegel, 'Dignity and Sexuality: Claims of Dignity in Transnational Debates over Abortion and Same-sex Marriages' (2012) 10 *International Journal of Constitutional Law (ICon)* 355.

[517] See Barak, *Human Dignity* n 516 above, 186 ff.

[518] *Lawrence v Texas* 539 US 558 (2003), holding the Texas sodomy law unconstitutional. The case has been thoroughly analysed in Ch 2.

[519] On the relationship between equality and liberty in *Lawrence v Texas* n 518 above (the 'double helix') see LH Tribe, '*Lawrence v Texas*: the "Fundamental Right" That Dare not Speak its Name' (2004) 117 *Harvard Law Review* 1893, 1898 (arguing that 'It is a narrative in which due process and equal protection, far from having separate missions and entailing different inquiries, are profoundly interlocked in a legal double helix. It is a single, unfolding tale of equal liberty and increasingly universal dignity').

[520] *Obergefell v Hodges* n 480 above, 135 S Ct, 2603–04. On the history of complementarity between equality and liberty in constitutional jurisprudence in the United States, see KL Karst, 'The Liberties of Equal Citizens: Groups and the Due Process Clause' (2007) 55 *UCLA Law Review* 99, 103–04 and JS Schacter, '*Lawrence v Texas* and the Fourteenth Amendment's Democratic Aspirations' (2004) 13 *Temple Political & Civil Rights Law Review* 733, 749.

[521] P Ridola, 'Libertà e diritti nello sviluppo storico del costituzionalismo' in R Nania and P Ridola (eds) *I diritti costituzionali* (Torino, Giappichelli, 2006) 3, 131.

Therefore, instead of liberty in terms of equality or equality in terms of liberty, contemporary constitutions adopted the idea that liberty and equality mutually reinforce each other. This is exemplified for instance by Article 3, paragraph 2, of the Italian Constitution, stating that 'It is the duty of the Republic to remove those obstacles of an economic and social nature that, by in fact limiting the freedom and equality of citizens, impede the full development of the human person and the effective participation of all workers in the political, economic and social organisation of the country'.[522]

At the same time, European constitutional tradition has largely expounded the idea that liberty and equality, in their mutual relationship, find their ideal synthesis in the principle of human dignity. Although this book does not attempt to address thoroughly the theoretical stances that inspire the idea of human dignity, it is worth remembering that its roots trace back to classical Roman thought[523] and were subsequently expounded by the humanist writings of Pico della Mirandola in the mid-fifteenth century[524] and mostly by Kant's *Metaphysics of Morals*, who formulated the well-known principle that 'human beings are never to be treated merely as means but always to be valued as ends in themselves'.[525]

In Germany, human dignity (*Menschenwürde*) informs the substance and spirit of the constitutional order.[526] Article 1 of the Basic Law (*Grundgesetz*) states that 'human dignity shall be inviolable' (paragraph 1) and then emphasises the narrow relationship between human dignity and fundamental rights, declaring that 'the German people acknowledge inviolable and inalienable human rights as the basis of every community, of peace and justice in the world' (paragraph 2). Human dignity is almost always interpreted by the Constitutional Tribunal in conjunction with Article 2, which secures the general liberty interests of the individual in the right to life, physical integrity and personal development, and Article 3, which declares the principle of equality of all persons before the law.[527] Individual liberty is frequently limited by dignity, whereas equality informs and is informed by both dignity

[522] On liberty and equality in Art 3 of the Italian Constitution, see G Silvestri, *Dal potere ai principi. Libertà ed eguaglianza nel costituzionalismo contemporaneo* (Bari, Laterza, 2009) 73.

[523] In particular the Western roots of the principle of human dignity lie in the notion of *dignitas* embodying the idea of honour, the privileges and the deference due to rank and office. See MT Cicero, '*Rhetoricorum libri duo qui sunt de inventione retorica*' (De inv) II, 166. On the roots of the idea of dignity, see M Lewis, 'A Brief History of Human Dignity' in J Malpas and N Lickiss (eds), '*Perspectives on Human Dignity. A Conversation*' (Dordrecht, Springer, 2007) 93 and J Waldron, 'Dignity and Rank' (2007) 48 *European Journal of Sociology* 201.

[524] G Pico della Mirandola, *On the Dignity of Man* (1486) transl F Borghesi, M Sapio, and M Riva (Cambridge, Cambridge University Press, 2012) 107 ff, tracing the roots of Man's dignity in his ability in self-determination ('It is given to him to have that which he chooses and to be that which he wills').

[525] I Kant, *Groundwork of the metaphysics of morals*, transl M Gregor, introduction by CM Korsgaard (Cambridge, Cambridge University Press, 1997) 42.

[526] 45 BVerfGE 187 (1977). See G Dürig, 'Art 1' in Maunz, Dürig (eds), *Grundgesetz. Kommentar* (Beck, München, 1958); J Eckert, 'Legal Roots of Human Dignity in German Law' in D Kretzmer and E Klein (eds), *The Concept of Human Dignity in Human Rights Discourse* (The Hague, Kluwer, 2002) 41 ff; C Enders, *Die Menschenwürde in der Verfassungsordnung: Zur Dogmatik des Art 1 GG* (Tubingen, Mohr Siebeck, 1997); P Häberle, 'Menschenwürde und Verfassung, am Beispiel von Art 2 Abs 1 Verf Griechenland 1975' (1980) *Rechtstheorie*, 389 ff.

[527] See 27 BVerfGE1 (1962) (*Microcensus* case); 45 BVerfGE 187 (1977) (*Life Imprisonment* case) at para II.1.

and liberty. Therefore, the relationship among dignity, liberty and equality has been defined as 'symbiotic', because their meanings nourish and mutually reinforce each other.[528]

In Italy, Article 3 of the Constitution begins by declaring that 'all the citizens enjoy equal social dignity' (paragraph 1) and secures their formal equality before the law, whereas Article 2 'recognises and guarantees the inviolable rights of the person, both as an individual and in the social groups where human personality is expressed'. The principle of 'equal social dignity' in the Italian Constitution is not as broad as the German *Menschenwürde* because it aims at securing the dignity of individuals in their real living conditions and can consequently be interpreted as a premise of substantial equality. Nonetheless, the Italian constitutional scholarship has frequently interpreted the principle of 'equal social dignity' as a link of connection between the inviolable rights of liberties of the individuals (and social groups) and the principle of equality enshrined, respectively, in Articles 2 and 3 of the Constitution.[529] Furthermore, the Italian Constitutional Court identified a more general principle of human dignity as laying at the foundation of the protection of the inviolable rights of the person enshrined in Article 2.[530]

In the 1970s, with the fall of the dictatorships in Greece, Spain and Portugal, dignity was incorporated into the new constitutions.[531] The Spanish Constitution of 1978, influenced by the German interpretation of dignity as informing the whole constitutional order, states at Article 10, paragraph 1 that 'the dignity of the person, the inviolable rights which are inherent, the free development of the personality, the respect for the law and for the rights of others are the foundation of political order and social peace'.

The Spanish Constitutional Tribunal has repeatedly described dignity as 'a fundamental legal value',[532] emphasising that it pertains to the guarantee of the essential core (*contenido absoluto*) of fundamental human rights:

> In relation to individual rights, the principle expressed in Article 10(1) of the Constitution implies that as 'a spiritual and moral value inherent to the human person', dignity must remain inalterable in any circumstance, because it represents an invulnerable minimum that all the public powers must guarantee.[533]

[528] See, DP Kommers and RA Miller, *The Constitutional Jurisprudence of the Federal Republic of Germany* (Durham, Duke University Press, 2012). See also, E Klein 'Human Dignity in German Law' in D Kretzmer and E Klein (eds), *The Concept of Human Dignity in Human Rights Discourse* (The Hague, Kluwer, 2002) 145.

[529] See G Bognetti, 'The Concept of Human Dignity in European and US Constitutionalism' in G Nolte (ed), *European and US Constitutionalism* (Cambridge, Cambridge University Press, 2005) 85 at 95 ff; A Celotto, 'Art 3, 1 comma, Cost' in R Bifulco, A Celotto, M Olivetti, (eds) *Commentario alla Costituzione* (Torino, Utet, 2006) I, 72.

[530] See Italian Constitutional Court, case no 561 of 10 December 1987 and case no 161 of 23 May 1985 (reading dignity of man as a 'fundamental value' under Art 2 of the Constitution).

[531] See, C McCrudden, 'Human Dignity And Judicial Interpretation Of Human Rights' (2008) 19 *European Journal of International Law* 673.

[532] See Spanish Constitutional Tribunal, judgments no 53/1985 of 11 April 1985 and no 120/1990 of 27 June 1990. On the value of dignity in the Spanish Constitution, see J Gonzaléz Pérez, *La dignidad humana de la persona* (Madrid, Civitas, 1983); I Gutiérrez Gutiérrez, *Dignidad de la persona y derechos fundamentales* (Madrid, Marcial Pons, 2005); G Peces Barba, *La dignidad de la persona desde la Filosofía del Derecho* (Madrid, Dykinson, 2002).

[533] See case no 120/1990 n 532 above, F 4.

As belonging to the individual as 'a human person'[534] and informing the basic content of fundamental rights, dignity draws both on liberty and equality: following Kant's theory, the Spanish Constitutional Tribunal has interpreted dignity as a trait of the individual both 'as a free and responsible member of the legal community' and 'the object of the exercise of public powers'.[535]

In Ireland, Article 40 of the Constitution states that 'All citizens shall, as human persons, be held equal before the law'. The Supreme Court expounded this article, arguing that it enshrines 'a guarantee of equality as human persons' and

> a guarantee related to their dignity as human beings and a guarantee against any inequalities grounded upon an assumption, or indeed a belief, that some individual or individuals or classes of individuals, by reason of their human attributes or their ethnic or racial, social or religious background, are to be treated as the inferior or superior of other individuals in the community.[536]

In the 1990s, the German Constitution also inspired the new constitutions in Eastern Europe, explaining the choice to incorporate dignity in the new constitutional texts.[537] In 1989 Hungary enacted the first post-communist Constitution by way of a constitutional amendment. The new Article 54 opened the Bill of Rights with a reference to man's 'inherent right to dignity'.[538] The Hungarian Constitutional Court, following the German constitutional jurisprudence, expounded the meaning of dignity and its narrow relationship with the free development of human personality.[539]

The German influence is also apparent in the South Africa Constitution of 1996, where dignity is a value of supreme and foundational importance, enshrined alongside equality and freedom.[540] The South Africa Constitutional Court has explained the meanings of dignity in many judgments on human rights and discrimination.[541]

Against this background, it comes as no surprise that the nexus between liberty and equality and principle of human dignity, in its variety of meanings, have largely

[534] See case no 292/1994, 20 July 1994.

[535] Case no 11/1981, 8 April 1981 and case no 101/1991, 13 May 1991.

[536] *Quinn's Supermarkets Ltd v Attorney General* [1972] IR 1, 13–14. See C O'Mahony, 'There is no such right to dignity' (2012) 10 *International Journal of Constitutional Law (ICon)* 551, 554 ff.

[537] See Art 2(1) stating that 'Human dignity shall be inviolable'.

[538] Art 54 of the Constitution of Hungary of 1949, as amended in 1989, stated that 'In the Republic of Hungary everyone has the inherent right to life and human dignity'. The Constitution of Hungary of 2011, Art 2, following the German Basic Law, states that 'Human dignity shall be inviolable'.

[539] See Decision 48/1998 (IX 23) AB, § 3(b). See C Dupré, *Importing the Law in Post-Communist Transitions: The Hungarian Constitutional Court and the Right to Human Dignity* (Oxford, Hart Publishing, 2003) 73.

[540] Constitution of the Republic of South Africa of 1996, Art 1 (listing the values on which the new democratic order is founded, including 'Human dignity, the achievement of equality and the advancement of human rights and freedoms'); Art 7(1) (stating that 'This Bill of Rights is a cornerstone of democracy in South Africa. It enshrines the rights of all the people in our country and affirms the democratic values of human dignity, equality and freedom'); Art 10 ('Everyone has inherent dignity and the right to have their dignity respected and protected'); Art 36(1) (on the limitation of rights, stating that 'The rights in the Bill of Rights may be limited only in terms of law of general application to the extent that the limitation is reasonable and justifiable in an open and democratic society based on human dignity, equality and freedom') and Art 39(1) (including dignity among the values that courts must promote in the interpretation of the Bill of Rights).

[541] On dignity in South Africa Constitutional law, see Barak, *Human Dignity* n 516 above at 243 ff; McCrudden, 'Human Dignity And Judicial Interpretation', n 531 above, 655.

informed the debate over the rights of gays and lesbians in continental Europe and in countries, like South Africa, whose constitutional notion of dignity is inspired by the German tradition. In particular, the idea that dignity, liberty and equality are deeply intertwined and that the recognition of gay rights, in general terms, advances equality as well as dignity and liberty of same-sex couples can be considered a *leitmotiv* in constitutional and supreme courts' jurisprudence on same-sex marriage.

D. The Different Meanings of Dignity in Same-Sex Marriage Cases

It has been frequently pointed out that the concept of dignity is complex and multifaceted[542] and that it is difficult to identify, beyond a basic common core, a universalistic understanding of dignity across different jurisdictions.[543]

An analysis of the different meanings of dignity and of its widespread success in human rights legal discourse is beyond the scope of this book. Nonetheless, in order to analyse arguments of dignity and its intersections with liberty and equality in constitutional and supreme court cases on equal marriage, it is necessary to remember that the abundance of meanings of dignity is basically a consequence of the long history of this concept but also of the different legal functions dignity performs in constitutional interpretation.

Scholarly attempts to identify a common core of dignity[544] emphasise that, in its narrowest meaning, dignity pertains to the inherent worth of each individual.[545] According to this interpretation, dignity is not the result of an achievement, but an inherent quality of man, existing by virtue of human nature. Inherent dignity stresses the human potential, not its actual exercise.[546] It is related to formal equality but basically encompasses the liberal notion of negative freedom and the idea that the state should not restrain individual autonomy. The individual is free to exercise his autonomy consistent with the rights and freedoms of others.[547]

Based on a pluralist and neutral conception of human life, this interpretation of dignity can be traced back to Kantian moral philosophy. In Germany, in more recent times, it has been expounded by Dürig who argues that 'to reduce man to a mere object'

[542] See Case C-36/02 *Omega Spielhallen und Automatenaufstellungs-GmbH v Oberbürgermeisterin der Bundeststadt Bonn* [2004] ECR I-09609 ('there is hardly any legal principle more difficult to fathom in law than that of human dignity').

[543] McCrudden, 'Human Dignity And Judicial Interpretation' n 531 above, 655 and C McCrudden (ed), *Understanding Human Dignity* (Oxford, Oxford University Press, 2013). See also, M Finck, 'The Role of Human Dignity in Gay Rights Adjudication and Legislation: A Comparative Perspective' (2016) 14 *International Journal of Constitutional Law (ICon)* 26, 28.

[544] On the common core of dignity, see McCrudden, 'Human Dignity and Judicial Interpretation' n 531 above, and PG Carozza, 'Human Dignity and Judicial Interpretation of Human Rights. A Reply' (2008) 19 *International Journal of Constitutional Law (ICon)* 931.

[545] See J Waldron, 'Dignity and Rank' n 523 above and *Dignity, Rank and Rights* (ed Meir Dan-Cohen) (Oxford, Oxford University Press, 2012).

[546] See Rao, 'Three concepts of dignity' n 516 above, 187.

[547] See 75 BVerfGE 369, 380 (1987) ('The political satire case') (Arguing that the portrayal of sexual behaviour—which belongs to the protected core of intimate sphere—cannot violate an individual's human dignity. Accordingly, it cannot be considered constitutional in a legal order that recognises human dignity as its highest value.).

is forbidden by Article 1 of the German Basic Law. He qualifies dignity as an insuppressibly, inalienable and indefeasible quality of human being, not to be balanced with constitutional rights.[548]

Another interpretation of dignity emphasises that dignity is not an innate gift but the result of a process of development of human identity and personality.[549] According to this interpretation, dignity is strictly related to autonomy and self-determination and it is the product of a successful identity formation.[550] This meaning of dignity embodies a particular view of what constitutes the good life for man, what makes human life flourish for the individual as well as the community,[551] and assumes that the constitution guarantees the premises of this development. However, as has been emphasised, this interpretation may entail a paternalistic view of the State, 'prevent[ing] individuals from choosing a vocation or a way of life that might be "undignified" in the view of the social and political community'.[552]

Lastly, dignity is conceived as an aspect of the sociality of man. In German scholarship, Hofmann[553] argues that dignity is based on the promise of mutual recognition and reciprocal interaction. Therefore, stemming from the assumption of the equal worth of all individuals, dignity entails interpersonal respect, public recognition and mutual concern. According to this interpretation, dignity is strictly related to equality and to the idea that the State must guarantee protection in order to preserve individual self-image and standing in the community.[554]

It is clear that these different readings of the common core of dignity are strictly intertwined with the different theories on the function of dignity in constitutional interpretation. Although most interpretations consider dignity as the foundation of human rights, there are different variations of this approach: dignity is sometimes treated as a right or an obligation (and therefore, it is read in conjunction with equality and balanced with other constitutional rights),[555] but it is also conceived as a principle or a constitutional value, serving as a 'counter limit' to legislative action (*Schrankenschranke*) on fundamental rights[556] or as an interpretative

[548] See G Dürig, 'Der Grundrechtssatz von der Menschenwürde' (1956) 81 *Archiv des Öffentlichen Rechts* 117, 127, but see also Dürig, 'Art 1' n 526 above, interpreting dignity as 'an objective value' that cannot be balanced with other constitutional rights.

[549] A Podlech, 'Art 1 Abs I' in *Alternativkommentar zum Grundgesetz*, I (Newwied, Kriftel, 1989).

[550] N Luhmann, *Grundrechte als Institution* (Berlin, Duncker & Humblot, 1965) 57 ff.

[551] See Rao, 'Three concepts of dignity' n 516 above, 189 (emphasising that according to this interpretation, dignity is not intrinsic or inherent in the individual, because 'it can be gained or lost and depends on whether a person measures up to a socially defined standard of dignity').

[552] Rao, 'Three concepts of dignity' n 516 above, 189.

[553] H Hofmann, 'Die versprochene Menschenwürde' (1993) 118 *Archiv des öffentlichen Rechts* 353 ff.

[554] Rao, 'Three concepts of dignity' n 516 above, 188.

[555] The German Constitutional Tribunal has followed this approach when interpreting human dignity (Art 1(1) GG) in connection with the right to life and physical integrity (Art 2, para 2 GG) and the right to free development of human personality (Art 2, para 1 GG). This connection led the Tribunal to develop a general 'right to personality'. See J Luther, 'Ragionevolezza e dignità umana' in A Cerri and O Pfersmann (eds), *La ragionevolezza nella ricerca scientifica ed il suo ruolo specifico nel sapere giuridico* (Rome, Aracne, 2007) 185.

[556] See A Barak, 'The Constitutional Value and the Constitutional Right', in C McCrudden (ed), *Understanding Human Dignity* (Oxford, Oxford University Press, 2013) 12 ff. For a general overview about the different functions of dignity in constitutional interpretation, see also McCrudden, 'Human Dignity and Judicial Interpretation' n 531 above, 681; Daly, *Dignity Rights*, n 516 above and the many contributions in McCrudden (ed), *Understanding Human Dignity*, n 556 above, especially 361 ff.

tool.[557] The Constitutional Tribunal of Germany has mediated in many judgments between the idea of dignity as an absolute value and the interpretation that aims at relativising it.[558]

It is trite that dignity, in its different meanings, has become increasingly popular in judicial discourse on human rights. Appeals to dignity are so widespread in recent human rights discourse—even in countries like the United States whose constitutions do not contain explicit references to dignity[559]—that it has been argued that 'dignity' is frequently used as a 'rhetorical tool'.[560]

Limiting our investigation to same-sex marriage cases, dignity comes into consideration in all the three basic meanings I illustrated above. I will address them separately.

i. Dignity as a 'Claim of Recognition' and Equality

In constitutional cases on sexual orientation equality rights, dignity comes into consideration in the first place in relation to the sociality of same-sex couples and to their aspiration to social recognition and respect.

The Canadian courts have frequently emphasised this dimension of dignity and its relationship with equality of minorities and social groups.

> Human dignity—the Supreme Court of Canada clarified—means that an individual or group feels self-respect and self-worth. ... Human dignity is harmed when individuals and groups are marginalized, ignored, or devalued, and is enhanced when laws recognize the full place of all individuals and groups within Canadian society. Human dignity within the meaning of the equality guarantee does not relate to the status or position of an individual in society per se, but rather concerns the manner in which a person legitimately feels when confronted with a particular law.[561]

In same-sex marriage cases, in particular, dignity as recognition emerges in relation to the expressive value of marriage analysed in the first part of this section.[562]

As Taylor emphasises, the importance of recognition emerges both at the intimate level—'in which relationships are seen as key loci of self-discovery and self-affirmation' and 'we understand the formation of identity and the self as taking place in a continuing dialogue and struggle with significant others', and on the

557 See, C Enders, *Die Menschenwürde in der Verfassungsordnung: zur Dogmatik des Art 1 GG* (Tübingen, Mohr Siebeck, 1997) 501ff.

558 See P Häberle, 'Die Menschenwürde als Grundlage der staatlichen Gemeinschaft' in J Isensee, P Kirchhof (eds), *Handbuch des Deutschen Staats- und Verfassungsrechts*, 3rd edn, vol 1 (Heidelberg, Muller Verlag, 2004) 317 ff. For the theory of human dignity as an 'objective guarantee', see Dürig, 'Art 1' n 526 above.

559 Jackson, 'Constitutional Dialogue and Human Dignity' n 516 above, 15. See also Rao, 'Three Concepts of Dignity' n 516 above, 190 (arguing that in American constitutional law 'dignity presents a relatively new legal term; it has no firm footing and no established range of legal meanings').

560 C O'Mahoney, 'There Is No Such Thing as a Right to Dignity' (2012) 10 *International Journal of Constitutional Law (Icon)* 551, 552.

561 *Law v Canada* [1999] 1 SCR 497, 170 DLR (4th) 1, § 53.

562 See above p 142 ff.

social plane—where 'the understanding of identities are formed in open dialogue'.[563] Both levels emerge in same-sex marriage cases where, as Finck has recently pointed out, 'dignity captures what Nussbaum described as the transition from "disgust" to "humanity"'.[564] In this respect, 'dignity functions as the vocabulary that translates such socio-cultural change into legal change'.[565]

When the Ontario Court of Appeal emphasised in *Halpern*[566] the importance of marriage for the expression of love and mutual commitment of same-sex couples, it was interpreting dignity in relation to the self-fulfilment of the individual in the intimate sphere as well as a 'claim of recognition' on the public plane because marriage conveys a message of approbation by society.

In the United States, as illustrated earlier, Justice Kennedy relied on dignity and its relationship with equality in many relevant passages of *Windsor* and *Obergefell*.[567] When he emphasised what marriage meant to same-sex couples, arguing that it offered them 'recognition, stability, and predictability', Justice Kennedy was not only discussing the importance of marriage in the personal sphere of spouses, but also the freedom of couples and their families from the stigma attached to homosexuality.

As Taylor argues,

> equal recognition is not just the appropriate mode for a healthy democratic society. Its refusal can inflict damage on those who are denied it ... The projection of an inferior or demeaning image on another can actually distort and oppress, to the extent that the image is internalized.[568]

Furthermore, the right to marry, in Justice Kennedy's words, is fundamental because

> it safeguards children and families and thus draws meaning from related rights of childrearing, procreation, and education. Without the recognition, stability, and predictability marriage offers, children suffer the stigma of knowing their families are somehow lesser. They also suffer the significant material costs of being raised by unmarried parents, relegated to a more difficult and uncertain family life. The marriage laws at issue thus harm and humiliate the children of same-sex couples.[569]

The idea of a 'situated self'[570] and the interpretation of dignity as public recognition and respect for same-sex couples have been also expounded in South African constitutional cases on the rights of gays and lesbians. In *Fourie*,[571] on same-sex

[563] C Taylor, 'The Politics of Recognition' in A Gutmann (ed), *Multiculturalism and 'The Politics of Recognition'* (Chicago, Chicago University Press, 1992) 25, 36–37. According to Taylor, a 'politics of recognition' implies not only the recognition of 'an identical basket of rights and immunities for all' based on blindness to the differences and grounds of discrimination, but also the recognition of rights and entitlements for groups who have been demeaned or whose culture is at risk.

[564] See Finck, 'The Role of Human Dignity' n 543 above, 28 (citing Nussbaum, *From Disgust to Humanity*, n 460 above) and arguing that 'homosexuals are increasingly considered as "full humans" disposing of equal rights' and that dignity 'functions as the vocabulary that translates such socio-cultural change into legal change').

[565] ibid.

[566] See above p 144.

[567] See above p 145–6.

[568] Taylor, 'The Politics of Recognition' n 563 above, 36.

[569] *Obergefell v Hodges* n 462 above, 135 S Ct, 2590.

[570] JT Ismael, *The Situated Self* (Oxford, Oxford University Press, 2007).

[571] *Fourie*, n 491 above, 474.

marriage, the Constitutional Court thoroughly examined the different ramifications of recognising equality and dignity. When expounding the meaning of section 9(1) and (3)—including sexual orientation within the list of prohibited grounds of discrimination—Justice Sachs emphasised that the Constitution protected

> the right to be acknowledged as equals and to be embraced with dignity by the law. [Same-sex couples'] love that was once forced to be clandestine, may now dare openly to speak its name. The world in which they live and in which the Constitution functions, has evolved from repudiating expressions of their desire to accepting the reality of their presence, and the integrity, in its own terms, of their intimate life. Accordingly, taking account of the decisions of this Court, and bearing in mind the symbolic and practical impact that exclusion from marriage has on same-sex couples, there can only be one answer to the question as to whether or not such couples are denied equal protection and subjected to unfair discrimination.[572]

ii. From Exclusion to Inclusion: Dignity as Equal Value

The passages and the many citations in the previous pages regarding the expressive value of marriage also make it clear how courts, in Finck's words, frequently approach same-sex marriage issues in terms of 'the transition of homosexuals from exclusions to inclusion into full citizenship'.[573] In this perspective, recognition of the right for same-sex couples to marry assumes an idea of dignity as equal worth of all human beings and implies social acceptance. At the same time, denying a second-class status of same-sex couples, this implies the unconstitutionality of the 'separate but equal' regime.

The argument of passage from exclusion to inclusion of gays and lesbians can be considered a main theme in constitutional and supreme court cases on same-sex marriage. Even those courts that did not expound the relationship between equality and dignity or the different meanings of dignity, emphasised in clear terms that marriage is the final achievement in the long-term battle for 'freeing' an oppressed and discriminated minority. Finck reads this common thread as referencing to a 'unified concept of dignity' and suggests that it could convey the transnational meaning of dignity, explaining its widespread diffusion in same-sex marriage constitutional cases across different jurisdictions, including those that in the past had been less familiar with dignity discourse in constitutional law.[574]

I will take a position on this conclusion in the following pages,[575] but it is important to premise here that although it is not possible to make clear-cut distinctions in judicial discourses on dignity and equality, the passage 'from exclusion to inclusion' is clearly expounded by the courts when they illustrate the implications of equality in terms of recognition to married same-sex couples of the same rights and responsibilities already recognised to opposite-sex married couples.[576]

572 ibid, para 78.
573 Finck, 'The Role of Human Dignity' n 543 above, 37.
574 ibid, especially 36–37.
575 See below 166 ff.
576 See above 146 ff.

In the United States this implication of dignity—interpreted as equal value of all individuals and social acceptance and recognition—has been discussed by Justice Kennedy in personal statements[577] and in *Windsor* when addressing, as clarified above, the negative effects of DOMA. This law, he wrote, 'contrive[d] to deprive some couples married under the laws of their State, but not other couples, of both rights and responsibilities'[578] and undermined the social and private value of marriage.

In *Obergefell*, Justice Kennedy further developed dignity and inclusion of same-sex couples into full citizenship when stressing that same-sex marriage state bans

> are in essence unequal: same-sex couples are denied all the benefits afforded to opposite-sex couples and are barred from exercising a fundamental right. Especially against a long history of disapproval of their relationships, this denial to same-sex couples of the right to marry works a grave and continuing harm. The imposition of this disability on gays and lesbians serves to disrespect and subordinate them. And the Equal Protection Clause, like the Due Process Clause, prohibits this unjustified infringement of the fundamental right to marry.[579]

Against this constitutional background, he concluded that same-sex couples' 'hope is not to be condemned to live in loneliness, excluded from one of civilization's oldest institutions. They ask for equal dignity in the eyes of the law. The Constitution grants them that right'.[580]

State courts in the United States invoked human dignity, emphasising the second-class citizen status of gays and lesbians who have been denied the protection, benefits and obligations conferred to heterosexuals, including marriage, for a long time. As early as in *Goodridge v Department of Public Health*, for instance, the Supreme Judicial Court of Massachusetts noted that 'the Massachusetts Constitution affirms the dignity and equality of all individuals' and 'it forbids the creation of second-class citizens'.[581]

Accordingly, it pointed out that

> barred access to the protections, benefits, and obligations of civil marriage, a person who enters into an intimate, exclusive union with another of the same sex is arbitrarily deprived of membership in one of the community's most rewarding and cherished institutions. That exclusion is incompatible with the constitutional principles of respect for individual autonomy and equality under law.[582]

It is interesting to observe that according to the Supreme Court of California in *In Re Marriage Cases*, even 'the failure to designate the official relationships of

[577] Finck, 'The Role of Human Dignity' n 543 above, cites a passage from an interview Justice Kennedy gave to *The New Yorker*, in which he explained what the Supreme Court 'is trying to tell to the rest of world'.

[578] *United States v Windsor* n 477 above, 133 S Ct 2694.

[579] *Obergefell v Hodges* n 462 above, 135 S Ct, 2605–06.

[580] ibid, 135 S Ct, 2608.

[581] *Goodridge v Department of Public Health* 440 Mass 309 (2003), 312.

[582] ibid.

same-sex couples as marriage' constitutes a violation of dignity and equality of same-sex couples.[583] Observing that

> under the current statutes, the state ha[d] not revised the name of the official family relationship for all couples, but rather ha[d] drawn a distinction between the name for the official family relationship of opposite-sex couples (marriage) and that for same-sex couples (domestic partnership),[584]

the California Supreme Court held that

> one of the core elements of the right to establish an officially recognized family that is embodied in the California constitutional right to marry is a couple's right to have their family relationship accorded dignity and respect equal to that accorded other officially recognized families.[585]

Therefore, it concluded that the challenged legislation,

> assigning a different designation for the family relationship of same-sex couples while reserving the historic designation of 'marriage' exclusively for opposite-sex couples poses at least a serious risk of denying the family relationship of same-sex couples such equal dignity and respect. Although the provisions of the current domestic partnership legislation afford same-sex couples most of the substantive elements embodied in the constitutional right to marry, the current California statutes nonetheless must be viewed as potentially impinging upon a same-sex couple's constitutional right to marry under the California Constitution.[586]

In Canada, the Supreme Court analogously suggested that dignity—as social acceptance and equal worth of all individuals—implied the unconstitutionality of reserving a second-class citizen status to gays and lesbians. As the Supreme Court wrote in *Egan v Canada*, 'equality means that … society cannot tolerate legislative distinctions that treat certain people as second-class citizens, that demean them, that treat them as less capable for no good reason, or that otherwise offend fundamental human dignity'.[587]

The Constitutional Court of South Africa moved from a similar assumption when arguing in its same-sex marriage case, *Fourie*, that

> the sting of past and continuing discrimination against both gays and lesbians was the clear message that it conveyed, namely, that they, whether viewed as individuals or in their same-sex relationships, did not have the inherent dignity and were not worthy of the human respect possessed by and accorded to heterosexuals and their relationships. This discrimination occurred at a deeply intimate level of human existence and relationality.

[583] *In Re Marriage cases* 43 Cal 4th 757 (2008), 770–80 ('The legal issue we must resolve is not whether it would be constitutionally permissible under the California Constitution for the state to limit marriage only to opposite-sex couples while denying same-sex couples any opportunity to enter into an official relationship with all or virtually all of the same substantive attributes, but rather whether our state Constitution prohibits the state from establishing a statutory scheme in which both opposite-sex and same-sex couples are granted the right to enter into an officially recognized family relationship that affords all of the significant legal rights and obligations traditionally associated under state law with the institution of marriage, but under which the union of an opposite-sex couple is officially designated a "marriage" whereas the union of a same-sex couple is officially designated a "domestic partnership". The question we must address is whether, under these circumstances, the failure to designate the official relationship of same-sex couples as marriage violates the California Constitution').

[584] ibid, 43 Cal. 4th, 782.

[585] *In Re Marriage cases* n 583 above, 43 Cal 4th, 783.

[586] ibid.

[587] *Egan v Canada*, [1995] 2 SCR513 § 104–05.

> It denied to gays and lesbians ... the concepts of equality and dignity, which at that point were closely intertwined, namely that all persons have the same inherent worth and dignity as human beings, whatever their other differences may be.[588]

Starting from these remarks, the Constitutional Court concluded that

> the exclusion of same-sex couples from the benefits and responsibilities of marriage ... is not a small and tangential inconvenience resulting from a few surviving relics of societal prejudice destined to evaporate like the morning dew. It represents a harsh if oblique statement by the law that same-sex couples are outsiders, and that their need for affirmation and protection of their intimate relations as human beings is somehow less than that of heterosexual couples. It reinforces the wounding notion that they are to be treated as biological oddities, as failed or lapsed human beings who do not fit into normal society, and, as such, do not qualify for the full moral concern and respect that our Constitution seeks to secure for everyone. It signifies that their capacity for love, commitment and accepting responsibility is by definition less worthy of regard than that of heterosexual couples.[589]

In Europe, the idea that the inherent worth of all individuals imposes to grant same-sex couples the same rights as opposite-sex couples has also been expounded in terms of connections between democracy and dignity. In the House of Lords judgment in *Ghaidan v Godin-Mendoza*,[590] dealing with the recognition of tenancy rights to a surviving gay partner, Baroness Hale emphasised that 'the guarantee of equal treatment is also essential to democracy' and that 'democracy is founded on the principle that each individual has equal value'.[591]

> Treating some as automatically having less value than others not only causes pain and distress to that person but also violates his or her dignity as a human being. The essence of the Convention, as has often been said, is respect for human dignity and human freedom ... Second, such treatment is damaging to society as a whole. Wrongly to assume that some people have talent and others do not is a huge waste of human resources. It also damages social cohesion, creating not only an under-class, but an under-class with a rational grievance. Third, it is the reverse of the rational behaviour we now expect of government and the state. Power must not be exercised arbitrarily. If distinctions are to be drawn, particularly upon a group basis, it is an important discipline to look for a rational basis for those distinctions. Finally, it is a purpose of all human rights instruments to secure the protection of the essential rights of members of minority groups, even when they are unpopular with the majority. Democracy values everyone equally even if the majority does not.

iii. Dignity as Liberty and Self-Determination

Dignity finally comes into consideration in same-sex marriage cases in its third meaning, as autonomy and self-determination of human beings concerning the most intimate and personal life choices.

[588] *Fourie* n 491 above, para 50.

[589] ibid, para 71.

[590] *Ghaidan v Godin-Mendoza* [2004] UKHL 30. On this case, see above Ch 3 p 71 ff. For dignity arguments in *Ghaidan*, see Finck, 'The Role of Human Dignity', n 543 above, 43 and C Dupré, *The Age of Dignity: Human Rights and Constitutionalism in Europe* (Oxford, Hart Publishing, 2015).

[591] *Ghaidan v Godin-Mendoza*, n 590 above, 132 (Baroness Hale). On the connection between human dignity and democracy see Dupré, *The Age of Dignity*, n 590 above, ch 7.

In the United States, the Supreme Court refused to adopt the view that dignity is a constitutional right derived from the expressed rights of the Constitution,[592] but from as early as the 1960s it emphasised that dignity is a constitutional value lying 'at the root of any decent system of ordered liberty'[593] and to be taken into consideration in the interpretation of other rights enshrined in the Bill of Rights.[594]

In recent times, 'the idea that all individuals are deserving in equal measure of personal autonomy and freedom to "define [their] own concept of existence" instead of having their identity and social role defined by the state'[595] has been developed by Justice Kennedy's most memorable decisions on human rights.

As Tribe argues, he 'unified the two other operative clauses of the Amendment, Equal Protection and Due Process, in the name of "dignity," to generate a concept of great analytic strength and political power'.[596] In particular in *Lawrence*, as illustrated in Chapter 2, dignity came into consideration in relation to the adults' right 'to choose to enter upon a [same-sex] relationship in the confines of their homes and their own private lives'.[597] In *Obergefell*, Justice Kennedy endorsed at the same time other interpretations of the meaning of dignity, but also put dignity in relation with autonomy and liberty, stating that

> the fundamental liberties protected by [the Due Process Clause of the Fourteenth Amendment] include most of the rights enumerated in the Bill of Rights. ... In addition these liberties extend to certain personal choices central to individual dignity and autonomy, including intimate choices that define personal identity and beliefs.[598]

Tribe argues that, relying on broader postulates of the American constitutional order, Justice Kennedy's purpose was also to reply to the dissenters' main argument that a commitment to democracy renders the Court's intervention on marriage issues fundamentally illegitimate.[599] In other words, in Tribe's opinion, Justice Kennedy's conclusion that 'the idea of the Constitution is "to withdraw certain subjects from the vicissitudes of political controversy, to place them beyond the reach of majorities and officials and to establish them as legal principles to be applied by the courts"'[600]

592 See above p 157.
593 *Rosenblatt v Baer* 383 US 75, 92 (1966).
594 See *Cohen v California* 403 US 15, 24 (1971).
595 LH Tribe, 'Equal Dignity: Speaking Its Name' (2015) 129 *Harvard Law Review Forum* 16.
596 ibid.
597 *Lawrence v Texas* n 518 above ('Liberty gives substantial protection to adult persons in deciding how to conduct their private lives in matters pertaining to law').
598 *Obergefell v Hodges* n 462 above, 135 S Ct, 2597 but see also *Planned Parenthood of Southeastern Pennsylvania v Casey* 505 US 833 (1992) at 685 ('Our law affords constitutional protection to personal decisions relating to marriage, procreation, contraception, family relationships, child rearing, and education ... These matters, involving the most intimate and personal choices a person may make in a lifetime, choices central to personal dignity and autonomy, are central to the liberty protected by the Fourteenth Amendment. At the heart of liberty is the right to define one's own concept of existence, of meaning, of the universe, and of the mystery of human life. Beliefs about these matters could not define the attributes of personhood were they formed under compulsion of the State').
599 Tribe, 'Equal Dignity', n 595 above, refers in particular to *Obergefell v Hodges* n 462 above, 135 S Ct, 2611–12 (Roberts, dissenting), 2626–29 (Scalia, dissenting), 2631–32 (Thomas, dissenting) and 2640–41 (Alito, dissenting).
600 *Obergefell v Hodges* n 462 above, 135 S Ct, 2605 (quoting *West Virginia State Board of Education v Barnette* 319 US 624, 638 (1943)).

rests on broad and unwritten constitutional principles, including 'dignity and autonomy of the individual standing against the forces of coerced conformity'.[601] Such a vision of fundamental rights and underlying constitutional values assumes not only 'an educative and pedagogical vision of the Constitution' but also the view that the Court's cases serve to spur debate and educate both the public and the lower courts,[602] a thesis that I also advanced in this book when discussing the role of constitutional courts in promoting constitutional change.[603]

A similar vision of dignity, and its relationship with liberty and equality can also be found in other same-sex marriage cases at state level: in *Goodridge v Department of Public Health*, for instance, the Supreme Judicial Court of Massachusetts argued that

> The core concept of common human dignity protected by U.S. Const. amend. XIV precludes government intrusion into the deeply personal realms of consensual adult expressions of intimacy and one's choice of an intimate partner. The central role that decisions whether to marry or have children bear in shaping one's identity has been reaffirmed. The Massachusetts Constitution is, if anything, more protective of individual liberty and equality than the United States Constitution; it may demand broader protection for fundamental rights; and it is less tolerant of government intrusion into the protected spheres of private life.[604]

Furthermore, the state supreme courts analogously recognised that marriage involved 'the most intimate and personal choices a person may make in lifetime, choices central to personal dignity and autonomy'.[605]

In Europe, constitutional courts have analogously expounded the relationship between dignity and personal self-determination in their judgments on same-sex marriage. The Constitutional Tribunal of Spain, for instance, when concluding that equal marriage does not affect the institutional guarantee of marriage under Article 32 of the Constitution, emphasised that the recognition of the right to marry for same-sex couples also implied 'respect for their own sexual orientation' and defined this achievement as 'a step forward towards the guarantee of personal dignity and the free development of one's personality under article 10(1) of the Spanish Constitution of 1978 that lie at the foundation of the Spanish constitutional order'.[606]

[601] Tribe, 'Equal Dignity' n 595 above ('Thus the line of cases Justice Kennedy invokes conspicuously protects rights resting not on any particular clause, like the Freedom of Speech Clause or the Free Exercise of Religion Clause, but instead on the dignity and autonomy of the individual standing against the forces of coerced conformity—on principles underlying the written Constitution but nowhere expressly articulated in its text'.)

[602] Tribe, 'Equal Dignity' n 595 above ('The view that the Court's own opinions serve to spur debate and educate both lower courts and the public at large, even more noteworthy is his insistence that the greatest teacher in these matters is not any opinion drafted by the Justices but the Constitution itself.')

[603] See above, section I, p 102 ff.

[604] *Goodridge v Department of Public Health* n 581 above.

[605] See *Bostic v Rainey* 970 F Supp 2d 456, 22 (ED Va 2014) but see also *Kitchen v Herbert* 961 F Supp 2d 1181 (D Utah 2013) 21 (Individual choices pertaining to marriage were found to be protected because they are 'integral to a person's dignity and autonomy').

[606] See case no 198/2012, n 288 above, para 11. The Constitutional Tribunal also emphasises that dignity and the free development of one's personality under Art 10 of the Spanish Constitution 'should be directed to the full effectiveness of fundamental rights, apart from being one of the pillars of political order and social peace'.

In Italy, law no 76 of 2016[607] has introduced same-sex civil unions, while marriage is still precluded to same-sex couples. In 2010 the Constitutional Court held that gays and lesbians enjoy a constitutional and fundamental right 'to live freely their life as a couple'[608] under Article 2 (which recognises and guarantees the fundamental rights of individuals and social groups) and under Article 3 of the Constitution (which enshrines the principle of equality and social dignity of all citizens).

Finally, since its first case on same-sex marriage,[609] the Constitutional Tribunal of Portugal has developed the idea that marriage should be granted to all individuals in a state bound by the rule of law and whose bill of rights is based on the primacy of freedom and human dignity.

E. The Different Purposes of Dignity in Same-Sex Marriage Cases

Although none of the constitutional courts cited in the previous pages relies exclusively on dignity in order to conclude that marriage equality is mandated by (or complies with) the domestic constitutions, it is undeniable that same-sex marriage cases mirror the widespread diffusion of dignity discourse that dominates the present human rights adjudication.

Recent scholarship has analysed this development in a wider perspective, taking into account the different meanings of dignity and its relationship with equality and liberty in a wide variety of contexts. Identification of the various reasons behind the great expansion of dignity discourse in present human rights adjudication falls outside the subject area of this book, but the conclusions reached by recent scholarly works may cast some light both on the usage and the circulation of dignity discourse even in same-sex marriage cases.

McCrudden in particular has identified several reasons to explain the increasing popularity of the concept of dignity among judges and advocates: he argues in the first place that when courts have to decide how to resolve conflicts of rights (or conflicts between rights and values), dignity provides 'a language in which courts can indicate the weighting given to particular rights and other values in this context'.[610] This implies that once dignity enters the balancing, it determines the outcome of the case.

In my opinion, this role of dignity as the 'ultimate scale or principle against which to compare conflicting values'[611] is apparent in same-sex marriage cases as well as in legal debates on same-sex marriage. As in the past both 'pro-life' and 'pro-choice' movements invoked dignity respectively in relation to the inherent value of human life and to the right of self-determination of women, today dignity is invoked both in support and against same-sex marriage.[612] As clarified earlier, same-sex marriage

607 Law no 76 of 20 May 2016.

608 Case no 138 of 15 April 2010, para 8.

609 *Acórdão* no 359/2009 (9 July 2009).

610 McCrudden, 'Human Dignity And Judicial Interpretation' n 531 above, 716 ff.

611 ibid, 714.

612 See R Dworkin, *Life's Domininion: An Argument About Abortion, Euthanasia and Individual Freedom* (New York, Vintage Books, 1994) 238.

proponents emphasise the inherent value of all human beings, their need for social recognition and their right to self-determination with respect to fundamental life choices in order to support equal marriage. Conversely, traditionalists and religious authorities frequently emphasise the 'dignity of marriage'[613] in order to promote an opposite vision of the nature, the origin, the ends and importance of marriage. In their perspective, sex complementarity is required to preserve the dignity of marriage and to defend traditional sexual roles.[614] By contrast, same-sex marriage proponents object that the validity and dignity of opposite-sex marriage is not diminished by equal marriage because extending marriage to same-sex couples reinforces the importance of marriage to individuals and communities.[615]

In same-sex marriage cases, once the inherent value of all human beings regardless of their sexual orientation is assumed, dignity arguments tilt the balance in favour of equal marriage. Dignity triggers constitutional protection and it is interesting to note that even the Italian Constitutional Court—which in 2010 adopted an originalist interpretation of marriage and concluded that equal marriage is not mandated by the Constitution[616]—analogously appealed to dignity and used this argument to support the recognition of the constitutional and fundamental right of gays and lesbians 'to live freely their life as a couple'.

Nonetheless, in my opinion, dignity discourse is not a rhetorical tool: the idea of dignity, with all its ramifications in terms of equality and liberty of same-sex couples, has its roots—as clarified earlier—in an extensive and thorough scholarship. As Dupré argues in her recent book on dignity, although the judicial construction of human dignity 'may not always indicate a clear substantive meaning', when considered in the framework of European constitutionalism (and I would also add, American constitutionalism)[617] 'a much clearer picture of human dignity meanings and use begins to appear'.[618]

At the same time, I am not arguing that dignity is 'a broad abstraction':[619] when Justice Kennedy in *Windsor* noted that 'until recent years, many citizens had not even considered the possibility that two persons of the same sex might aspire to occupy the same status and dignity as that of a man and woman in lawful marriage',[620] or when the Spanish Constitutional Tribunal in 2012 argued that marriage between

[613] See C Tollefsen, 'The Dignity of Marriage' in C McCrudden (ed), *Understanding Human Dignity* (Oxford, Oxford University Press, 2013) 482 ff (citing Pope John Paul II , *Familiaris Consortio* (Vatican City, Libreria Editrice Vaticana, 1981) who spoke of the need 'to preserve and realise' the 'entire truth and the full dignity of marriage and the family' and the Pastoral Constitution of the Vatican Council II, *Gaudium and Spes* (Vatican City, Libreria Editrice Vaticana, 1965)).

[614] See, Siegel, 'Dignity and Sexuality' n 516 above, 374 ff.

[615] *Zappone and Gilligan v Revenue Commissioners* [2006] IEHC 404.

[616] See above, section II p 115 ff.

[617] See eg Tribe 'Equal Dignity' n 595 above (arguing that in American constitutional law, 'the conception of equal dignity in fact has a considerable doctrinal pedigree, one stretching across some of the most high-profile cases decided by the Court in the past half-century. The notion that *Obergefell* had no foundation is simply wrong').

[618] Dupré, *The Age of Dignity*, n 590 above, 82.

[619] Against J Rosen, 'The Dangers of a Constitutional Right to Dignity', *The Atlantic*, 29 April 2015 (www.theatlantic.com/politics/archive/2015/04/the-dangerous-doctrine-of-dignity/391796).

[620] *United States v Windsor* n 477 above, 133 S Ct, 2689.

two persons of the same-sex is integrated in Spanish society and legal culture[621] concluding that the legislator made 'a step forward … towards guaranteed personal dignity and the free development of one's personality', they were acknowledging 'a process of transition [of gays and lesbians] from exclusion to inclusion'.[622]

In other words, courts' argument is not merely descriptive. As I have already attempted to demonstrate in this book, courts' statements have a role which is detachable from the immediate purpose they serve: they help forging constitutional arguments and reinforcing constitutional values of liberty, equality and dignity enshrined in constitutional texts.[623] Dignity, with its flexible meaning, not only 'translates socio-cultural change in legal change':[624] it also strengthens that change, paving the way to further recognition of rights for gays and lesbians.

For this reason, remarks concerning the aspiration of same-sex couples to no longer be deprived of the opportunity to enjoy their fundamental rights and the rights stemming from marriage have at the same time a normative value. As Glensy emphasises, 'all the representations of the right to dignity … do not merely resolve a case, or set forth a legislative, constitutional, or international imperative, but instead provide something more—a statement of collective aspirations to be sought by all participating members of society'.[625]

McCrudden also suggests another reason for the widespread circulation of dignity discourse, in connection with 'the need to decide how far the rights which are to be interpreted should be seen as instantiating international standards, as opposed to how far they should be seen as protecting more national or local concerns where there is a conflict'.[626] He suggests that dignity 'gives us a conceptual tool to mediate the polarity of pluralism and the common good in a globalized world'.[627] He writes:

> Its role, in practice, is to enable local context to be incorporated under the appearance of using a universal principle. Dignity, in the judicial context, not only permits the incorporation of local contingencies in the interpretation of human rights norms; it requires it. Dignity allows each jurisdiction to develop its own practice of human rights.[628]

Addressing dignity discourse in transnational process with specific regard to debates over the regulation of sexuality, Siegel suggests instead that claims of dignity are popular as well as professional and that they are also asserted outside courts, due in particular to the role played by social movements and religious organisations.[629]

[621] See case no 198/2012 n 513 above, para 9.
[622] See Finck, 'The Role of Human Dignity' n 543 above, 29.
[623] See above, section I p 102 ff.
[624] Finck, 'The Role of Human Dignity', n 543 above, 45.
[625] Glensy, 'The Right to Dignity' n 516 above, 135–36.
[626] McCrudden, 'Human Dignity And Judicial Interpretation' n 531 above, 714.
[627] ibid, 719 (quoting Carrozza, 'Subsidiarity as a Structural Principle of International Human Rights Law' (2003) 97 *American Journal of International Law* 1, who argues that there 'is an inherent tension in international human rights law between upholding a universal understanding of human rights and respecting the diversity and freedom of human cultures'. Carozza identifies in the principle of subsidiarity a tool for instantiating international and local standards.)
[628] ibid.
[629] Siegel, 'Dignity and Sexuality' n 516 above, 536.

In my opinion, both the approaches capture some of the different aspects of dignity discourse in same-sex marriages cases at constitutional and supreme court level. Claims of dignity are shaped through debates at political and social movement level and advanced before lower courts[630] before being expounded at constitutional and supreme court level. But at the same time, especially newly established constitutional courts (such as, for instance, the South Africa Constitutional Court or East European constitutional courts) resort to dignity discourse in order to emphasise the rupture of their domestic legal systems with previous constitutional orders. Hungary's Constitutional Court, for instance, since its first case (no 8 of 1990),[631] developed a new concept of rights and used the argument of human dignity in order to set aside the provisions inherited from its past legal order and to reinterpret them in a liberal way.[632] The Constitutional Court of South Africa has similarly emphasised the country's need 'to locate [itself] in the mainstream of international democratic practice'.[633]

But dignity discourse also provides a conceptual tool to mediate among different instances coming from new (or newly recognised) groups and between the opposite aspirations to particularity and pluralism in present human rights adjudication. The idea of human dignity, as based on the inherent value of all human beings, satisfies an aspiration to the universal, but at the same time, when balanced with other constitutional rights or interpreted in the light of the general principles that inspire national constitutions, makes it possible to accommodate the social, moral, political specificities of each legal system.[634]

In the United States—where in recent times the Supreme Court has frequently emphasised the connection between liberty, equality and human dignity—Yoshino explains this change on the basis of the 'pluralism anxiety', as the United States, he writes, 'confront "new" kinds of people (introduced to the country through immigration) or newly visible people (introduced to the country by social movements)'. Yoshino argues that the 'apprehension of and about demographic diversity'[635] is transforming the Supreme Court's traditional civil rights jurisprudence and forging the traditional model of equal protection, pressing the Court away from traditional group-based identity politics.[636]

In his opinion, one of the main effects of this transformation lies in the limitation of the number of formally protected classifications, because 'pluralism anxiety has operated, and will continue to operate, as a serious obstacle to the recognition

[630] ibid, 378–79.

[631] Case no 8/1990 of 23 April 1990.

[632] C Dupré, *Importing the Law in Post-Communist Transitions. The Hungarian Constitutional Court and the Right to Human Dignity* (Oxford, Hart Publishing, 2003) 135.

[633] *Coetzee v Government of the Republic of South Africa, Matiso v Commanding Officer Port Elizabeth Prison* (CCT19/94, CCT22/94) [1995] ZACC 7 (22 September 1995), para 51.

[634] On the perennial challenge of mediating between the universal and the particular in human rights law, see PG Carozza, 'Uses and Misuses of Comparative Law in International Human Rights: Some Reflections on the Jurisprudence of the European Court of Human Rights' (1998) 73 *Notre Dame Law Review* 1217.

[635] Yoshino, 'The New Equal Protection', n 455 above, 747.

[636] ibid, 755 ff.

of classification-specific judicial protections'[637] by the Supreme Court. At the same time, Yoshino argues that pluralism anxiety is transforming constitutional civil rights jurisprudence, because 'it offers a way for the Court to "do" equality in an era of increasing pluralism anxiety'.[638] 'The Supreme Court has used liberty-based dignity analysis to mitigate its curtailment of group-based equality analysis. At the same time, 'the liberty-based dignity claim has been the Court's way of splitting the difference between a direct extension of equality analysis and its absolute foreclosure'.[639]

Opening its doors to liberty-based dignity arguments, the Supreme Court struck down the sodomy statutes in *Lawrence v Texas* instead of relying on equality arguments. By adopting this approach, Yoshino argues that the Supreme Court

> quieted pluralism anxiety. The Court evaded the charge that it was picking and choosing among groups by highlighting that the right in question belonged to all persons within the United States. *Lawrence* was ultimately not a group-based equality case about gays, but rather a universal liberty case about the right of all consenting adults to engage in sexual intimacy in the privacy of their homes.[640]

The United States Supreme Court's recent judgment in *Obergefell v Hodges*[641] confirms Yoshino's theory: the Supreme Court reiterated its intent not to rely exclusively on equality grounds. By placing a stronger emphasis on the intertwined nature of liberty and equality,[642] instead of relying on a standard equal protection argument, the Supreme Court asserted 'that due process ruling protects the true equality interests of gays and lesbians more than an equal protection decision ever could'.[643] Yoshino names this core component of *Obergefell* the 'antisubordination principle'.[644]

Other American scholars share the idea that the Supreme Court's decision not to rely (since *Lawrence*[645] to *Windsor*[646] and *Obergefell*)[647] on standard equal protection arguments or on the due process three-prong test[648] in favour of a new foundational principle should be considered 'a major shift in constitutional doctrine, one that will have ramifications in many cases to come'.[649]

[637] ibid, 763.
[638] ibid, 750.
[639] ibid, 776.
[640] ibid, 778. See above, Ch 1 p 85 ff.
[641] *Obergefell v Hodges*, n 462 above.
[642] K Yoshino, 'A New Birth of Freedom?' (2016) 129 *Harvard Law Review* 147, 148.
[643] Yoshino emphasises that there are some differences between *Lawrence* (n 518 above) and *Obergefell* (n 462 above) 'in that [the second] invokes both values—due process and equal protection—rather than relying solely on due process' he suggests that the similarities are 'more important than the differences' (see Yoshino, 'A New Birth of Freedom', n 642 above, 174).
[644] Yoshino, 'A New Birth of Freedom' n 642 above, 174 ('What emerges from *Lawrence* and *Obergefell* is a vision of liberty that I will call "antisubordination liberty".')
[645] *Lawrence v Texas*, n 518 above.
[646] *United States v Windsor*, n 477 above.
[647] *Obergefell v Hodges*, n 462 above.
[648] The three-prong test, based on tradition, specificity and negativity, has been formulated by the Supreme Court in *Washington v Glucksberg* 521 US 702 (1997) in order to provide guidance for the identification of new fundamental rights under the Due Process Clause of the 14th Amendment. See above 122 ff.
[649] Yoshino, 'A New Birth of Freedom?' n 642 above, 179.

Tribe, for instance, writes that 'the important doctrinal work done by Justice Kennedy's decision, ... represents the culmination of a decades-long project that has revolutionized the Court's fundamental rights jurisprudence'. Nonetheless he characterises *Obergefell*'s core argument in more expansive terms than Yoshino, arguing that its

> chief jurisprudential achievement is to have tightly wound the double helix of Due Process and Equal Protection into a doctrine of equal dignity—and to have located that doctrine in a tradition of constitutional interpretation as an exercise in public education. ... Equal dignity, a concept with a robust doctrinal pedigree, does not simply look back to purposeful past subordination, but rather lays the groundwork for an ongoing constitutional dialogue about fundamental rights and the meaning of equality.[650]

In my opinion, it is possible to identify an analogous relationship between the increasing reliance on liberty-based and equality-based dignity arguments and pluralism anxiety even in the judgments of other constitutional and supreme courts. Excluding more recent constitutions that explicitly prohibit different treatments based on sexual orientation,[651] with few exceptions[652] constitutional and supreme courts have been refraining from defining sexual orientation as an unconstitutional ground of discrimination or from qualifying gays and lesbians as a discriminated minority.

For instance, instead of applying 'traditional' formal equality patterns of adjudication and considering whether denial of marriage amounts to an unconstitutional discrimination under Article 14 of the Spanish Constitution, the Spanish Constitutional Tribunal stresses the violation of Article 10(1) concerning the guarantee of personal dignity and the free development of human personality,[653] although in its earlier judgments it had qualified 'sexual orientation' as an unconstitutional ground of discrimination.[654]

The principle of formal equality was dismissed as not relevant by the Italian Constitutional Court in case no 138 of 2010, mentioning instead, inter alia, human dignity and the right of same-sex couples 'to live freely their life as a couple'.

[650] LH Tribe, 'Equal Dignity: Speaking Its Name', n 595 above.

[651] See eg the Constitution of Mexico of 1917 (as amended in 2015), Art 1; New Zealand Human Rights Act 1993, Arts 27(2), 45 and 59; Constitution of Portugal of 1976 (as amended in 2005), Art 13(2); Constitution of South Africa of 1996, Art 9(3); Constitution of Sweden of 1974, as amended in 2012, Art 1(2). See also Northern Ireland Act 1998, art 75(1); Scotland Act 1998, Sch 5, Pt II, subheading 2, head L, L2 (interpretation).

[652] Against *Haig v Canada* (1992), 16 CHRR D/226 (Ont CA), *Egan v Canada* (1995) 2 SCR 513. See also on the interpretation of Art 14 of the European Convention on Human Rights and the principle that any difference in treatment based on sexual orientation requires 'very weighty' and 'particularly serious reasons' to justify it, *Karner v Austria* ECHR 2003-IX, § 37. The European Court of Human Rights has also clarified that a difference in treatment based solely on grounds of sexual orientation amounts to a discrimination under the ECHR in *Kozak v Poland* [2010] ECHR 280 § 91 and *Salgueiro da Silva Mouta v Portugal* ECHR 1999-IX. The violation of equality under Art 3(1) of the German Constitution (*Grundgesetz*) has been also emphasised by the First Senate of the German Constitutional Tribunal in the order of 7 July 2009 (1 BvR 1164/07) on the pension scheme for civil service employees, arguing that 'the mere reference [in the law] to the requirement of protecting marriage did not justify a differentiation' between marriage and civil partnerships.

[653] See above p 163.

[654] STC 41/2006 of 13 February 2006. Issues of equality have not been addressed even in the concurring and dissenting opinions (*votos particulares*).

The French Conseil constitutionnel in its 2013 reference case on same-sex marriage simply emphasised that 'the difference between couples comprised of a man and a woman and same-sex couples no longer justified the fact that the latter could no longer obtain the status and legal protection associated with marriage'.[655]

Yoshino's fascinating remarks on pluralism anxiety and its implications on traditional equality-based standards of review are applicable even to other constitutional experiences. In my opinion the widespread use of dignity discourse instead of formal equality arguments is also due to the fact that dignity, with its flexible meaning, makes it possible for constitutional courts to accommodate different conception of human rights and to answer new claims of recognition without adopting more rigid standards of adjudication as those resulting from pure formal equality arguments.

At the same time, it is worth noting that constitutional and supreme courts, compared to lower courts, are concerned not only with pluralism anxiety but also with the future implications of their judgments: in this respect, arguments of dignity provide a convenient language to recognise gay and lesbian rights and at the same time make it possible to accommodate equality arguments on more contingent grounds.

[655] Décision no 2013-669 DC, 17 May 2013, considérant no 22.

5

Addressing the Reality of Family Life: Parental Rights

I. THE DEBATE OVER PARENTAL RIGHTS AND THE PRINCIPLE OF THE BEST INTERESTS OF THE CHILD

WHEREAS THE EARLIER chapters of this book dealt with the protection of fundamental rights of single individuals or couples, issues concerning parental rights address also the rights of a third party, usually a minor.

In general terms, it is possible to identify some common lines in the debate over parental rights. The main arguments of advocates of parental rights for gays, lesbians and same-sex couples rest on formal equality: they argue that, as sexual orientation is an unconstitutional ground of discrimination, gays and lesbians and same-sex couples should be allowed to be parents on equal terms to heterosexuals and opposite-sex couples. As far as the position of children is concerned, they also contend that all children are entitled to the same rights, stability and protection, and that they cannot be discriminated against on the basis of their parents' sexual orientation.

Traditionalists oppose these arguments on different grounds: their main objection, at constitutional level, is that there is no fundamental 'right to have a child'. This apparently 'neutral' argument (claiming to be sexual-orientation blind) is often supported by assumptions concerning 'nature' and procreation: assuming that only the opposite-sex couple is 'natural'—because it is the only one that can 'naturally procreate'—opponents define the same-sex couple as unfit for parenting by nature. However, these arguments are frequently infused with prejudice against the morality of gays and lesbians: questioning the aptitude of gays and lesbians to child-rearing, traditionalists argue that children must be brought up within a 'traditional' family, composed of a mother and father anchored by the bond of marriage.

This short summary of the arguments at stake makes it clear why the debate over gay and lesbian parental rights frequently shifts away from formal equality discourse towards more factual arguments. On an abstract plane, advocates of parental rights support their claims with extensive evidence that sexual orientation does not affect the ability of gays and lesbians to raise a child, and that there is no harm for children to be brought up by a gay or lesbian parent or by a same-sex couple. On practical grounds, as I will clarify, prospective same-sex parents undergo more extensive checks and interviews than opposite-sex couples, in order to verify whether they are fit for child-rearing and so that the best interests of the child are actually served. As in same-sex marriage legal discourse, arguments of 'nature' and 'tradition' are axiomatic and play an evidentiary role.

Nonetheless, when a born child is also involved, an element breaks the similarity: the evaluation of best interests of the child. This principle—enshrined in the 1959 United Nations Declaration of the Rights of the Child,[1] in Article 3 of the 1989 Convention on the Rights of the Child[2] and, more recently, in Article 24(1) and (2) of the Charter of Fundamental Rights of the European Union[3] as well as in many legislative provisions at domestic level—is considered by the courts to be paramount and prevails over the other interests and arguments at issue.

In this chapter I will not discuss the meaning and interpretation of the principle of the best interests of the child in detail, addressing only incidentally the issues concerning the rights and interests of the minors involved, when necessary to the analysis of the constitutional rights of parents. Nonetheless, it is worth noting that, like dignity in same-sex marriage cases, once the principle of the best interests of the child is taken into account, it triggers constitutional protection.

There are several reasons that in my opinion explain the greater weight of the best interests of the child in constitutional balancing: in the tradition of continental family law, this principle rests on the same idea of human dignity as inherent value of all the individuals and, accordingly, on the assumption that the child is a right-holder.[4] At the same time, like dignity, the principle was left largely undefined in international documents, and therefore courts may adapt it to the needs of the instant case without providing adequate justifications of their conclusions.[5] The leading French scholar of private law, Jean Carbonnier, qualified the principle of the best interests of the child as a 'magical notion' and cautioned against the possible abuse of this formula and the risk of arbitrary judicial decisions.[6]

[1] United Nations Declaration of the Rights of the Child, 20 November 1959, UN res no 1386, principle 2 (declaring that the best interests of the child 'shall be a *paramount* consideration' (emphasis added) in the enactment of laws to ensure that the child is protected and given opportunities to develop in a healthy manner) and principle 7 (defining the best interests of the child as the 'guiding principle' to 'those responsible for his education and guidance').

[2] Convention on the Rights of the Child, 20 November 1989, 15 UNTS 3 (effective 2 September 1990). The principle of the best interests of the child is taken as a basic premise of the Convention. It is mentioned in the articles dealing with the relationships of parents and children, children and the state, foster care and juvenile delinquency and punishment. In particular Art 3 states that the child's best interests must be 'a *primary* consideration' (emphasis added) in all state actions concerning children. The principle also applies to adoption (Art 21).

[3] Charter of Fundamental Rights of the European Union, Art 24 (Rights of the child) states: '1. Children shall have the right to such protection and care as is necessary for their well-being. They may express their views freely. Such views shall be taken into consideration on matters which concern them in accordance with their age and maturity. 2. In all actions relating to children, whether taken by public authorities or private institutions, the child's best interests must be a primary consideration'.

[4] On the opposing visions underlying the interpretation of the principle of the best interests of the child in continental Europe and in the Anglo-Saxon tradition, see E Lamarque, *Prima i bambini. Il principio dei best interest of the child nella prospettiva costituzionale* (Milano, Franco Angeli, 2016).

[5] See M Freeman, 'Article 3. The Best Interests of the Child' in A Alen, J Vande Lanotte, E Verhellen, F Ang, E Berghmans and M Verheyde (eds), *A Commentary on the United Nations Convention on the Rights of the Child* (Leiden, Nijhoff Publishers, 2007) 27.

[6] See J Carbonnier, 'Note on Paris Court of Appeal, 10 April, 1959' (1960) *Dalloz* 673: 'Although the interest of the child might seem to convey a particular thought, it really is a meaningless ("magical") notion. Though it may be "the law", the issue that really is at issue is "abuse". Ultimately, the "interest of the child" will end up rendering superfluous all of the institutions of family law. There is nothing more fleeting, or more likely to lead to arbitrary judicial decision' (transl by J Rubellin-Devichi, 'The Best Interests Principle in French Law and Practise' 8 (1994) *International Journal of Law, Policy and the Family* 259).

International case law illustrates the flexibility of the principle of the best interests of the child and its frequent use for strengthening courts' conclusions. The European Court of Human Rights (ECtHR), for instance, has been interpreting the principle in order either to limit the right of family life of adults (under Article 8 ECHR) or to support specific rights of the child and tilting the balancing in his (or her) favour.[7]

The ambiguity and flexibility of the principle are easily apparent in *X and Others v Austria*,[8] a 2013 landmark case concerning second-parent adoption for same-sex couples.[9] In *X and Others*, the ECtHR held that the Austrian Government had violated the right to family life (under Article 14 in conjunction with Article 8 ECHR) by substantially denying to same-sex couples the right of adoption of one partner's biological child by the other partner, whereas this opportunity was granted to unmarried opposite-sex couples.[10] In this case, the best interests of the child had been invoked to support opposite conclusions. In its reasoning, the Court almost overlooked the principle of the best interests of the child, mentioning it only incidentally. After concluding that several reasons cast considerable doubt on the proportionality of an absolute prohibition on second-parent adoption for same-sex couples (for instance, no evidence suggested that it is detrimental to the child to be brought up by two mothers or two fathers), the Court emphasised that an evaluation of the best interests of the child in the instant case also supported the majority's conclusions.[11] An opposite perspective was adopted by dissenting judges who argued instead that the child 'had a mother and a father', and that the majority should have made more efforts to ascertain 'what best interests would have been served had his father been replaced by his mother's partner'.[12]

The Italian case law on equal marriage and parental rights of gays and lesbians is also illustrative of the argumentative potential of the principle of the best interests of the child. In the last few years, lower ordinary courts have relied extensively on the principle in order to dismiss narrow interpretations of constitutional clauses on marriage and family.[13] Despite in 2010 the Constitutional Court adopted an originalist interpretation of 'marriage' (Article 29 of the Italian Constitution), mentioning incidentally 'the (potential) creative purpose of marriage which distinguishes

[7] See *Mennesson and Others v France* and *Labassee v France* ECHR 2014-III; *D and Others v Belgium* App no 29176/13 (ECtHR, 8 July 2014); *Paradiso and Campanelli v Italy* [2015] ECHR 76 (concerning legal recognition for children born as a result of surrogacy arrangements).

[8] *X and Others v Austria [GC]* [2013] ECHR 425.

[9] The case will be analysed also below, p 189 ff.

[10] Art 182 § 2 of the Austrian Civil Code (*Allgemeines Bürgerliches Gesetzbuch*) that governed the effects of adoption by one adoptive parent severed the relationship with the child's biological parent. In particular, it stated that 'if the child is adopted by just an adoptive father (an adoptive mother), the relationship shall cease only in respect of the biological father (the biological mother) and his (her) relatives; in so far as the legal relationship with the other parent remains intact after the adoption, the court shall declare it to have been severed, subject to the consent of the parent concerned'. Therefore, while heterosexual couples (including unmarried ones) could establish an additional parent–child relationship between the child and its parent's partner, this was impossible for same-sex couples, as the same-sex partner would have replaced the biological parent.

[11] *X and Others v Austria* n 8 above, para 146.

[12] *X and Others v Austria* n 8 above, para 8 (joint partly dissenting opinion of Judges Casadevall, Ziemele, Kovler, Jočienė, Šikuta, De Gaetano and Sicilianos).

[13] See above Ch 4 p 115 ff.

it from homosexual unions',[14] lower courts and the Corte di Cassazione—Italy's highest (civil and criminal) court—have extended to gays and lesbians the right to adopt the child of their partner (stepchild or second-parent adoption), arguing that such a legal solution satisfied the best interests of children in the instant cases.[15] This achievement of the Italian LGBT community is even more remarkable if we take into consideration that Italian law on adoption[16] does not permit single-parent adoption (except 'in special cases'[17]), that the Constitutional Court has also abstained from qualifying same-sex couples as 'a family'[18] and until June 2016—when law no 76 of 2016[19] on same-sex civil unions came into force—there was no legal recognition of same-sex unions.[20]

The principle of the best interests of the child was extensively discussed by the German Constitutional Tribunal in its 2013 decision permitting the successive adoption of the adopted child within a same-sex civil partnership (*Sukzessivadoption*).[21] The German Civil Partnership Act (*Lebenspartnerschaftsgesetz*, LPartG) of 2002[22] granted the partner some parental rights of practical importance in everyday life[23] but introduced some relevant differences with marriage as far as parental rights were concerned: it still prohibits joint adoption by same-sex couples in a civil union, and before the Constitutional Tribunal's intervention, also forbade the secondary adoption when the child had been adopted and was not the biological child of the civil partner.[24] By contrast, spouses were free to adopt the adopted child of their

[14] Case no 138 of 2010 of 14 April 2010, para 9.

[15] See the recent judgment of Court of Cassation, no 12962 of 26 May 2016. On the importance of this ruling, see M Gattuso, 'La vittoria dei bambini arcobaleno' available in www.articolo29.it (last visited 15 September 2016) and A Schillaci, 'La sentenza perfetta. Paternità omosessuale e diritti del bambino' available in www.articolo29.it (last visited 15 September 2016) (qualifying the case as 'a perfect judgment').

[16] Law no 184 of 4 May 1983.

[17] The adoption by a single parent 'in special cases' is a particular kind of adoption, which art 44 of law no 184 of 1983 distinguishes from the 'full adoption' (*adozione legittimante*) (ie the joint adoption by a married opposite-sex couple) because it does not cancel the legal ties of the adopted child with the original family and it is always revocable by the juvenile court. It is permitted for instance when joint adoption is made difficult by particular circumstances (eg unsatisfactory conditions, health problems, child not available for adoption); for relatives who have an affective bond with a parentless child and in the case of adoption of the spouse's biological or adoptive child within a married opposite-sex couple (stepchild adoption). The last option has been extended to same-sex couples in the cases mentioned in n 15 above. Furthermore, juvenile courts have also granted this specific kind of adoption to gays and lesbians asking for the ratification of a single parent adoption obtained in a foreign country (see Court of Cassation, case no 3572 of 14 February 2011). Furthermore, a decree by the Tribunal of Bologna (Juvenile Court) granted a full adoption to a lesbian who had adopted a child in the United States (see Tribunale dei minorenni di Bologna, decree no 1948 of 17 April 2013).

[18] See above Ch 3, p 77 ff.

[19] Law no 76 of 20 May 2016 (which came into force on 5 June 2016).

[20] On the narrow interpretation of 'family' in the Italian legal system before law no 76 of 2016 (and the ECtHR judgment in *Oliari v Italy* [2015] ECHR 752) see above, Ch 3, p 76 ff.

[21] 1 BvL 1/11, 1 BvR 3247/09 of 19 February 2013 (First Senate).

[22] Act on the Termination of the Discrimination of Same-Sex Couples: Civil Partnerships (*Gesetz zur Beendigung der Diskriminierung gleichgeschlechtlicher Gemeinschaften: Lebenspartnerschaften*) of 16 February 2001 (Federal Law Gazette, *Bundesgesetzblatt*, BGBl I, p. 266). See above Ch 4, section I p 99 ff.

[23] Sec 9(1) and (2) LPartG.

[24] See AEH Sanders, 'When, if not Now? An Update on Civil Partnership in Germany' (2016) 17 *German Law Journal* 487, 499. The German regulation of same-sex relationships has been analysed in Ch 4, section I p 99 ff.

wife or husband (*Stiefkindadoption*).[25] The Constitutional Tribunal dismissed the arguments concerning the violation of same-sex parents' right of parenthood[26] and the fundamental right to family life[27] and did not address the discrimination against same-sex partners compared to married couples: it held instead that the law violated the right to equal treatment of the *children*.[28] In particular, it emphasised that

> The law disadvantages the adopted child of a registered civil partner in a manner that is unconstitutional, both compared to the adopted children of a spouse ... as well as compared to the biological children of a registered civil partner who may be adopted by the other civil partner pursuant to § 9 sec 7 LPartG.[29]

Arguing that the 'adopted children of a registered civil partner are ... denied the opportunities attached to successive adoption to develop and conduct their lives that are given to the adopted child of a married parent and the biological child of a civil partner',[30] the Tribunal also emphasised that

> the exclusion of step-parent adoption, which only applies to families in which one civil partner has an adopted child, can give the child the impression that its family relationship is less valuable than the family relationships of other step-children families where the parents are married or the child is the biological child of a registered civil partner.[31]

The Constitutional Tribunal also clarified that civil union and marriage are equal as far as stability and assumption of responsibility towards children come into consideration:

> there is no difference between adoption by a spouse and adoption by a registered partner. Through successive adoption by a registered civil partner, a child would become the joint child of the partners in the same way as it would through successive adoption by a spouse. ... Registered civil partnerships are intended to be just as enduring and to require just as much binding assumption of responsibility as marriages.[32]

In reaching its conclusions, the Tribunal dismissed the idea that the exclusion of successive adoption was justified by the interest of the child. Instead, it held, the opposite to be true:

> The best interests of the child does not speak against the adopted child of one civil partner being adopted by the other civil partner. On the contrary, they speak in favour of allowing this.[33]

Interpreting the best interests of the child not as a limit to adults' rights but as an argument supporting the constitutional rights of the child, in this case the principle

[25] See sec 1742 BGB.
[26] Art 6 (2) GG.
[27] Art 6 (1) GG.
[28] Art 3 (1) GG.
[29] 1 BvL 1/11, 1 BvR 3247/09, n 21 above, para 71.
[30] ibid, para 73.
[31] ibid, para 73.
[32] ibid, para 77. The Constitutional Tribunal also clarified that although the purpose of the denial of successive adoption was to prevent a child from being passed from family to family, 'there would be just as little risk in this case as in the case of spouses that the child would in such a way be passed from family to family'.
[33] ibid, para 78.

of the best interests of the child tilted the balance in favour of recognition of successive adoption. As the Tribunal emphasised: 'Successive adoption [does not] per se interfere with a child's best interest but tends to be beneficial in the constellations that are at issue'.[34]

II. THE CONSTITUTIONAL COURTS AND THE 'PROCREATIVE NATURE' OF MARRIAGE

In arguments regarding 'nature' and the legal traditional sex difference in marriage, the procreative purpose of marriage is axiomatic because traditionalists assume it as pertaining to the core definition of the institution. As Chief Justice Marshall incisively noted in *Goodridge v Department of Public Health*[35]—the 2003 judgment of the Supreme Judicial Court of Massachusetts on same-sex marriage—'the procreation argument focuses on the single unbridgeable difference between same-sex and opposite-sex couples and transforms that difference into the essence of civil marriage'.[36]

In the early United States cases on marriage, the Supreme Court held that marriage forms 'the foundation of the family and of society, without which there would be neither civilization nor progress'.[37] The Supreme Court has reiterated the connection between marriage and procreation until more recent times: in *Skinner v Oklahoma,*[38] for instance, when striking down a statute that allowed the state to sterilise 'habitual criminals' without their consent, the Supreme Court emphasised that the case was 'dealing with legislation which involve[d] one of the basic civil rights of man', adding that 'marriage and procreation are fundamental to the very existence and survival of the race'.[39] In *Loving v Virginia*[40]—the well-known 1967 case, which put an end to anti-miscegenation laws—marriage was still described as 'fundamental to our very existence and survival', an understanding that, as Justice Roberts emphasised in *Obergefell v Hodges*, 'necessarily implies a procreative component'.[41]

But the most detailed discussion of the fundamental right to marry in connection with 'procreation, childbirth, abortion, and child rearing' and the 'assumption that the one is simply the logical predicate of the others'[42] was expounded by the Supreme Court in *Zablocki,*[43] a 1978 decision concerning a Wisconsin statute that prohibited any resident of the state under obligation to support a minor child from obtaining a marriage licence without demonstrating to a court that he was in compliance with his child support obligations. The Supreme Court argued that

[34] ibid, para 82.
[35] *Goodridge v Department of Public Health* 440 Mass 309 (2003).
[36] ibid, 440 Mass, 333.
[37] *Maynard v Hill* 125 US 190, 211 (1885).
[38] *Skinner v Oklahoma ex rel Williamson* 316 US 535 (1942).
[39] ibid, 316 US, 541.
[40] *Loving v Virginia* 388 US 1, 12 (1967).
[41] *Obergefell v Hodges* 135 S Ct 2584, 2614 (2015).
[42] *Baehr v Lewin* 74 Haw 530, 553 (1993).
[43] *Zablocki v Redhail* 434 US 374 (1978).

'if appellee's right to procreate means anything at all, it must imply some right to enter the only relationship in which the State of Wisconsin allows sexual relations legally to take place'.[44]

Nonetheless, in its more recent cases the Supreme Court has rejected the idea that marriage is inextricably linked to procreation. In *Obergefell v Hodges,* writing for the Court, Justice Kennedy for instance focused on the reality of the 'hundreds of thousands of children presently raised by same-sex couples',[45] mentioning the many state laws that recognise parental rights to gays, lesbians and same-sex couples as providing 'powerful confirmation from the law itself that gays and lesbians can create loving, supportive families'. Nonetheless, he clarified that

> that is not to say the right to marry is less meaningful for those who do not or cannot have children. An ability, desire, or promise to procreate is not and has not been a prerequisite for a valid marriage in any State. In light of precedent protecting the right of a married couple not to procreate, it cannot be said the Court or the States have conditioned the right to marry on the capacity or commitment to procreate. The constitutional marriage right has many aspects, of which childbearing is only one.[46]

Justice Kennedy's interpretation was instead rebuked by dissenting Justices who endorsed the traditional definition of marriage as the union of 'a man' and 'a woman' ordered to procreation and childbearing. Assuming procreation and gender difference as determinants of marriage, Justice Roberts noted that the many changes that affected marriage in recent decades 'did not work any transformation of the core structure of marriage'.[47] Justice Alito admitted instead that the 'traditional understanding of the purpose of marriage does not ring true to all ears today ... because the tie between marriage and procreation has frayed'.[48] Nonetheless, he noted that many states 'have not yet given up on the traditional understanding'[49] and concluded that the Supreme Court lacked the power to declare this interpretation of marriage unconstitutional.[50]

In continental Europe the constitutional cases endorsing a narrow interpretation of marriage reveal a similar ambiguity in accommodating tradition and procreation with the reality of the many couples who choose not to have children (or who cannot procreate) and whose marriage is equally entitled to constitutional protection.

The Irish High Court, for instance, although admitting its uneasiness in rejecting the traditional definition of marriage in *Zappone,*[51] did not address the argument of

[44] ibid, 434 US, 386.

[45] *Obergefell v Hodges* n 41 above, 135 S Ct, 2600.

[46] ibid.

[47] ibid, 135 S Ct, 2614.

[48] ibid, 135 S Ct, 2641.

[49] ibid, 135 S Ct, 2641–42.

[50] ibid, 135 S Ct, 2642, Alito dissenting ('It is far beyond the outer reaches of this Court's authority to say that a State may not adhere to the understanding of marriage that has long prevailed, not just in this country and others with similar cultural roots, but also in a great variety of countries and cultures all around the globe.').

[51] *Zappone and Gilligan v Revenue Commissioners* [2006] IEHC 404. See above p. 116 ff.

procreation. Furthermore, as has been pointed out, in its earlier cases the Court also suggested that the institution of marriage should be separated from the concept of conceiving and rearing children.[52]

Analogously, the Italian Constitutional Court in case no 138 of 2010 on same-sex marriage did not state that marriage is inextricably linked to procreation. Nonetheless, as clarified earlier,[53] it incidentally suggested that procreation is the 'potential' difference between marriage and same-sex unions, a remark which probably aimed at setting the ground for a future differentiation as far as same-sex couples' parental rights are concerned.[54]

But in same-sex marriage cases the procreation argument is also advanced for the normative value that traditionalists attach to it. Traditionalists argue that if family and marriage are inherently 'heterosexual', the government should formalise and promote marriage also in order to encourage procreative conduct. Therefore, procreation comes into consideration in the legal debate over same-sex marriage not only as a determinant of the institution of marriage, but also as a relevant governmental interest justifying a different treatment between marriage and same-sex unions. It is no coincidence that—as Justice LaForme of the Ontario Superior Court of Justice emphasised in *Halpern*[55]—the emphasis on procreation as a justification for marriage arose once same-sex couples began asserting their claims for equal recognition of their relationships.

In California this argument was the primary rationale for Proposition 8, the voter ballot initiative that opponents of same-sex marriage created in order to amend the California Constitution to formally define marriage as an opposite-sex union.[56] The United States Court of Appeals for the Ninth Circuit in *Perry v Brown*[57] rejected the argument as flawed. It argued that there is no link between the governmental purpose 'to reward couples who procreate responsibly or to encourage couples who wish to procreate to marry first' and withdrawing access to marriage from same-sex couples who cannot procreate.[58] Although the Court of Appeals recognised that the governmental interest of promoting procreation could be legitimate under other circumstances,[59] it concluded that the nexus between promoting procreation and

[52] See J Ennis, 'Marriage: Redefined and Realigned with *Bunreacht na hÉireann*' (2010) 1 *Irish Journal of Legal Studies* 29, 42 (citing *Murray v Ireland* [1985] IR 532, 537 concerning a married couple without children defined as a 'family'; *McGee v Attorney General* [1974] IR 284, 302 holding that spouses have 'a correlative right to agree to have no children').

[53] See above p 14–15 and 78.

[54] See A Sperti, *Omosessualità e diritti. I percorsi giurisprudenziali ed il dialogo globale delle Corti costituzionali* (Pisa, Pisa University Press, 2013) 158.

[55] *Halpern v Canada (Attorney General)* 95 CRR (2d) 1 (Ontario Superior Court, 12 July 2002).

[56] Proposition 8 was created prior to the May 2008 final California Supreme Court decision in *In Re Marriage Cases* 43 Cal 4th 757 (2008), which struck down Proposition 22, a former ballot initiative which changed the California Family Code (adding sec 308.5) to define marriage as the union between a man and a woman. Same-sex marriage opponents' reasoning was that, by amending the state constitution, Proposition 8 would have given additional protection to traditional marriage, contrary to Proposition 22, which was only a statute and therefore subject to judicial review of legislation.

[57] *Perry v Brown* 671 F3d 1052 (9th Cir, 2012).

[58] ibid, 671 F3d, 1088.

[59] ibid, 671 F3d, 1086.

excluding same-sex couples from marriage 'cannot be credited as rational … given the realities of California law and of human nature'.[60]

At the same time, the argument is unsound because it implies that only 'natural' procreation is positive. The Court of Appeals did not address the issue in *Perry*, writing that it did not need to decide whether there is any sense 'in preferring biological parents over other couples'.[61] The objection was raised instead by the Constitutional Court of South Africa in its decisions on same-sex marriage[62] and by the Supreme Court of Canada in *Mossop*:[63] both Courts mentioned the reality of adoptive families and of those couples who are incapable of procreating or simply choose not to have children, emphasising that such 'a decision rests entirely within their protected sphere of freedom and privacy'.[64] The Supreme Court of Canada also stated that 'placing the ability to procreate as the inalterable basis of family could result in an impoverished rather than enriched vision'.[65]

In my opinion the same objection can also be raised when issues concerning medically assisted procreation or surrogacy are taken into consideration. I am referring for instance to the Italian debate on the recent law on same-sex unions in which traditionalists focused their fierce opposition against surrogacy, arguing that civil unions will implicitly promote it.[66]

In England and Wales, objections against the procreation argument were not successful. Before the adoption of the Marriage (Same-Sex) Couples Act 2013, two women who were legally married in Canada applied to have their marriage recognised in the UK as a marriage rather than as a civil partnership according to the Civil Partnership Act 2004. In 2006, the High Court (Family Division) relied on a narrow interpretation of marriage 'as a means not only of encouraging monogamy but also the procreation of children' and dismissed the petition finding no violation of Articles 14 in conjunction with Article 8 ECHR.[67]

Potter P also added:

> The belief that this form of relationship is the one which best encourages stability in a well regulated society is not a disreputable or outmoded notion based upon ideas of exclusivity, marginalisation, disapproval or discrimination against homosexuals or any other persons

[60] ibid, 671 F3d, 1087.

[61] ibid, 671 F3d, 1088.

[62] See *National Coalition for Gay and Lesbian Equality and Others v Minister of Home Affairs and Others* 2000 (2) SA 1 (CC); 2000 (1) BCLR 39 (CC); *Minister of Home Affairs and Another v Fourie*, Case CCT 60/04 [2005] ZACC 19.

[63] *Canada v Mossop* [1993] SCJ No 20. I discussed this case in Ch 3 p 56 ff.

[64] *Fourie* n 63 above, para 86.

[65] *Canada v Mossop* n 64 above, para 126.

[66] This objection was raised by Vatican authorities and found the support especially of right-wing political forces. During the parliamentary debates that led to the adoption of law no 76 of 2016, n 19 above, on same-sex civil unions, an amendment concerning a ban on surrogacy (which was already prohibited in Italy, under law no 40 of 2004) was introduced in the Senate by a member of the majority political party (*Partito Democratico*) (see on the issue, L Morrassutto, 'Vagiti e manette. L'emendamento Dalla Zuanna: una proposta tecnicamente irricevibile', available at www.articolo29.it. On 4 May 2016 the *Camera dei Deputati* voted four motions (see *Seduta* no 619 of 4 May 2016, www.camera.it) on the banning of all kinds of surrogacy. Some of the motions also gained the support of the Left.

[67] *Wilkinson v Kitzinger* [2006] EWHC 2022 (Fam), para 118.

who by reason of their sexual orientation or for other reasons prefer to form a same-sex union.

If marriage is, by longstanding definition and acceptance, a formal relationship between a man and a woman, primarily (though not exclusively) with the aim of producing and rearing children as I have described it, and if that is the institution contemplated and safeguarded by Article 12, then to accord a same-sex relationship the title and status of marriage would be to fly in the face of the Convention as well as to fail to recognise physical reality.[68]

In order to sidestep the many logical fallacies of the procreation argument, traditionalists also emphasise that permitting same-sex couples to marry would diminish the procreative potential for marriage because if same-sex couples were permitted to marry, significant numbers of opposite-sex couples would no longer do so. In other words, traditionalists argue that *equal marriage indirectly affects procreation* because it undermines the value that opposite-sex couples attach to marriage. I suggest that it is possible to read this argument as a completion of the 'regulatory costs argument', using Eskridge's formula: 'Legitimating an alternative "life-style", same-sex marriage would undermine different-sex marriage'[69] and, traditionalists would also add, indirectly procreation.

Nonetheless, in Canada courts have considered the logical nexus between same-sex marriage and 'the significant threat' to marriage and procreation weak.[70]

In continental Europe these issues have been instead addressed in connection with the different promotional duties about marriage and family that domestic constitutions impose on legislators.

Although the relevant structural differences among European countries on the issue should not be neglected, constitutional courts like the Spanish Constitutional Tribunal, the German Constitutional Tribunal and the Portuguese Constitutional Tribunal have dismissed the idea that equal marriage or same-sex civil union could undermine the 'institutional guarantee' of marriage, ie affect the duty of the State to promote the institution of marriage.[71]

The Spanish Constitutional Tribunal in particular concluded that equal marriage does not impair the exercise of the individual right to marry and that the legislator had not contravened its negative obligation not to harm the scope of freedom contained in the right to marry.[72] Writing for the majority, Justice Perez Tremps wrote:

What the legislator is doing further to the freedom of configuration granted to it by the Constitution is to change the way in which a constitutional right to marry is exercised. The changes [introduced by law 13/2005] have not affected [the] content [of marriage] or harmed the right to marry held by heterosexuals, given that the challenged law does not make any

[68] ibid, paras 119–20.

[69] WN Eskridge, 'The Ideological Structure of the Same-Sex Marriage Debate (and Some Postmodern Arguments for Same-Sex Marriage)' in R Wintemute and M Andenæs (eds), *Legal Recognition of Same-Sex Partnerships* (Oxford, Hart Publishing, 2001) 113, 115.

[70] See eg, *Egan v Canada* (1995) 2 SCR 513, para 211 and *EGALE Canada, Inc v Canada* (2003) 13 BCLR 4th 1 (Can BC CA) 127.

[71] Spanish Constitutional Tribunal, Case no 198/2012, 6 November 2012, SCT, paras 8 and 9; Portuguese Constitutional Tribunal case no 121 of 2010 (especially paras 18 ff); 105 BVerfGE 313 (2002). The 'institutional guarantee of marriage' has been analysed also above, Ch 4, section II p 138.

[72] Case no 198 of 2012, n 72 above, esp para 11.

> material amendment in the legal provisions governing the requirements and effects of civil marriage between opposite-sex couples. However, the option applied does not mean that an individual is denied or hindered in his/her constitutional right to marry or not to marry.[73]

In Germany the protection of marriage and the family under Article 6(1) of the Basic Law also requires a distinction to be maintained between civil unions and marriage (*Abstandsgebot*) which is derived in particular from the guarantee of the institution of marriage in Article 6(1) of the Basic Law and from the protection of marriage and the family as a fundamental principle.[74] In order to respect this separation, the Civil Partnership Act of 2001 introduced some differences between marriage and civil union, including—as mentioned in the foregoing pages—limitations with respect to parental rights.[75] Nonetheless, in 2002, applicants emphasised before the Constitutional Tribunal that 'the very name of the statute ma[de] it clear that it [was] intended to give the civil partnership equality of treatment with marriage'.[76] In particular they suggested that

> the Civil Partnerships Act introduces a family-law institution for same-sex couples largely furnished with the effects of marriage, and in doing so it infringes Article 6.1 of the Basic Law, which prevents the legislature from substantially restructuring the relationships in marriage and the family from the point of view of the law of persons, and which prohibits basing family law in equal measure on marriage and a same-sex civil partnership.[77]

The Tribunal dismissed this argument, saying that marriage should not be discriminated against, but also argued that the Constitution does not require other relationships to be treated less favourably than marriage.[78]

In the United States the Supreme Court addressed the same issue (that equal marriage could undermine the institution of marriage by leading to fewer opposite-sex marriages) from the perspective of same-sex couples, putting emphasis on the importance that they attach to marriage.[79]

In particular, in *Obergefell,* the respondents contended that equal marriage harmed the institution of marriage because 'it sever[ed] the connection between natural procreation and marriage'.[80] Justice Kennedy dismissed this assertion arguing that it 'rest[ed] on a counterintuitive view of opposite-sex couple's decision-making processes regarding marriage and parenthood'.[81] He wrote:

> Decisions about whether to marry and raise children are based on many personal, romantic, and practical considerations; and it is unrealistic to conclude that an opposite-sex couple would choose not to marry simply because same-sex couples may do so.[82]

[73] ibid.

[74] See Ch 4, section I p 99.

[75] See AEH Sanders, 'Marriage, Same-Sex Relationship, and the German Constitution' (2012) 13 *German Law Journal* 911, 926. The issue has been analysed earlier in this book (see Ch 4 p 99 ff).

[76] 105 BVerfGE 313 (2002).

[77] ibid, para 20.

[78] ibid, para 31.

[79] The structural issue is therefore inextricably linked to the human rights issue, due to the features of judicial review of legislation in the United States. See A Sperti, *Corti Supreme e conflitti tra poteri. Spunti per un confronto Italia-USA sugli strumenti e le tecniche del giudizio* (Torino, Giappichelli, 2005).

[80] *Obergefell* n 41 above, 135 S Ct, 2607.

[81] ibid.

[82] ibid.

He concluded that 'respondents have not shown a foundation for the conclusion that allowing same-sex marriage will cause the harmful outcomes they describe', adding that the issue involved only the rights of two consenting adults whose marriages would pose no risk of harm either to themselves or to third parties.[83]

III. THE OPTIMAL PARENTING ARGUMENT AND THE CHILD'S RIGHT TO A 'NORMAL' FAMILY LIFE

A. The Early Cases on Child Custody and Single-Parent Adoption

The procreation argument has been more fully developed also in order to justify another governmental interest that dominates equal marriage legal discourse: the optimal parenting rationale.

This rationale seems actually to involve two different arguments: the first assumes that it is beneficial for children to be raised by opposite-sex parents because of the complementarity of the two sexes or, as an alternative, by a single heterosexual adult who can provide a more appropriate role model. The second argument is that the state may better pursue its interest in optimal childrearing by allowing only heterosexuals to adopt children (and by prohibiting same-sex marriage). The 'politics of disgust' portrayed gays and lesbians as moral degenerates and, as a result, gay parenting was often perceived as a contradiction in terms.

It should be premised that the reality of gay and lesbian parenting first surfaced in courts within custody disputes following divorce. As Ball emphasises, by the end of the 1960s, the question of child custody (and visitation) was the first legal issue involving the rights of gays and lesbians in the United States. It began appearing repeatedly in court dockets, and family law judges were the first jurists to address claims concerning sexual orientation discrimination,[84] well before the debate over equal marriage arose.

In 1985, in the United States, the Supreme Court of Virginia addressed the question of 'whether [a] child's best interests [were] promoted by an award of custody to a parent who carrie[d] on an active homosexual relationship in the same residence as the child'.[85] The Court concluded that 'the father's continuous exposure of the child to his immoral and illicit relationship render[ed] him an unfit and improper custodian as a matter of law'.[86] At the same time, as sexual intercourse between persons of the same sex was illegal in Virginia at that time,[87] the state Supreme Court also emphasised that

> the conditions under which this child must live daily are not only unlawful but also impose an intolerable burden upon her by reason of the social condemnation attached to them,

[83] ibid.

[84] See CA Ball, *The Right to Be Parents: LGBT Families and the Transformation of Parenthood* (New York, New York University Press, 2012) 23.

[85] *Roe v Roe* 324 SE 2d 691 (1985).

[86] ibid, 324 SE 2d, 692.

[87] Sexual acts between persons of the same sex were decriminalised in Virginia in 2003, as a consequence of the United States Supreme Court's judgment in *Lawrence v Texas* 539 US 558 (2003).

which will inevitably afflict her relationships with her peers and with the community at large.[88]

The same year, the Superior Court of Pennsylvania, in a similar case,[89] addressed the case of a mother who was living in a fully acknowledged lesbian relationship after her divorce, and requested for custody of her child. The Court reasoned that

> there are sufficient social, moral and legal distinctions between the traditional heterosexual family relationship and illicit homosexual relationship to raise the presumption of regularity in favor of the licit, when established, shifting to the illicit, the burden of disproving detriment to the children.[90]

The Court concluded that the woman had failed to prove that the 'total exposure to her lifestyle' met her children's best interests, and accordingly granted her only monthly weekend partial custody.

Until about the mid-1990s English courts also perceived homosexuality as potentially affecting children's well-being. Although sexual orientation did not formally constitute a bar on adoption, courts feared the consequences of children's exposure to same-sex relationships. In *Re D* for instance, Lord Wilberforce warned that

> new attitudes at the time should not entitle the courts to relax the vigilance and severity with which they should regard the risk of children, at critical ages being exposed or introduced to ways of life which as this case illustrates, may lead to severance from normal society, to psychological stress and unhappiness ... which may scar him for life.[91]

Until 1997, when Singer J challenged the cruelty to gay and lesbian parents in the case of *Re W*, arguing that nothing in the Adoption Act 1976 precluded a person from seeking or obtaining an adoption order even if that person is cohabiting in a same-sex relationship,[92] gay and lesbian parents were frequently faced with the argument that children might suffer embarrassment and be stigmatised as a result of their parents' sexual orientation. This argument was also frequently coupled with the assertion that heterosexual parents could offer a 'normal family life'.[93]

The European Court of Human Rights addressed the issue in 1999[94] when the applicant—a gay man living with his partner—was prevented by his ex-wife from visiting their daughter, in breach of an agreement they had concluded after divorce. The Lisbon Court of Appeal admitted that 'no doubt is being cast on the father's love for his daughter or on his ability to look after her', but concluded that the child's interest were better served by awarding parental responsibility to her mother. The Court also emphasised that

> The child should live in a family environment, a traditional Portuguese family, which is certainly not the set-up her father has decided to enter into, since he is living with another man

[88] *Roe v Roe* n 86 above, 324 SE 2d, 694.

[89] *Constant V v Paul CA* 344 Pa Sup Ct 49, 496 A.2d 1 (1985).

[90] ibid, 344 Pa Sup Ct, 66.

[91] *Re D (An Infant) (Adoption: Parent's Consent)* [1977] AC 602, 629.

[92] *Re W (Adoption: Homosexual Adopter)* [1997] 2 FLR 406.

[93] See *C v C (A Minor) (Custody: Appeal)* [1991] 1 FLR 223. For further analysis, see A Diduck and F Canagas, *Family Law, Gender and the State. Text, Cases and Materials*, 3rd edn (Oxford, Hart Publishing, 2012) 438 ff.

[94] *Salgueiro da Silva Mouta v Portugal* ECHR 1999-IX.

> as if they were man and wife. It is not our task here to determine whether homosexuality is or is not an illness or whether it is a sexual orientation towards persons of the same sex. In both cases it is an abnormality and children should not grow up in the shadow of abnormal situations; such are the dictates of human nature.[95]

Before the ECtHR, the father alleged that the Lisbon Court of Appeal had based its decision only on the ground of his sexual orientation and that, as a result, he had suffered an unjustifiable interference with his right to family life under Article 14 in conjunction with Article 8 ECHR. The ECtHR concluded in his favour, arguing that the applicant's homosexuality had 'swayed the final decision [of the Lisbon Court of Appeal] in a decisive manner and for the first time suggested that sexual orientation is an illegitimate ground of discrimination covered by Article 14 ECHR'.[96] The Court accordingly concluded that the difference in treatment was 'not acceptable under the Convention'.[97]

These cases illustrate how prejudices and stereotypes have deeply affected the family lives and parental relationships of gays and lesbians.

In reaching their conclusions, the American courts as well as the Lisbon Court of Appeal mainly focused on the principle of the best interest of the child; but their blatantly homophobic approaches to the issue tilted the balancing against same-sex parents, imposing on them an additional evidentiary burden.[98]

A similar approach also influenced courts' decisions concerning single parent adoption. The ECtHR, despite its conclusions in *Salgueiro*, for instance, was less supportive in *Fretté v France*,[99] a 2002 case concerning a French gay man who was denied a single parent adoption[100] despite his 'undoubted personal and intellectual qualities and aptitude for bringing up children' because 'the type of home that he was likely to offer a child could pose substantial risks to the child's development'.

The ECtHR admitted that the applicant's avowed homosexuality was the decisive factor in the French court's conclusions[101] but denied that the refusal of adoption amounted to a violation of the applicant's right to private life. The Court mentioned in particular, 'the total lack of consensus as to the advisability of allowing a single

[95] Lisbon Court of Appeal (Tribunal da Relação), judgment of 9 January 1996 para 30.

[96] *Salgueiro da Silva Mouta v Portugal* n 95 above, para 28. See R Wintemute, 'Lesbian and Gay Inequality 2000: The Potential of the Human Rights Act 1998 and the Need for an Equality Act' (2000) 6 *European Human Rights Law Review* 603, 620 (emphasising that 'this case makes absolutely clear that the sexual orientation of one of the parties ... can no longer be cited as a negative factor'). See also P Johnson, *Homosexuality and the European Court of Human Rights* (Abingdon, Routledge, 2013) (emphasising that 'the explicitness of the homophobic language used by the domestic authorities was decisive in persuading the court to regard the difference in treatment as discriminatory under Article 14').

[97] *Salgueiro da Silva Mouta v Portugal* n 95 above, para 36. The ECtHR could not also find 'a reasonable relationship of proportionality existed between the means employed and the aim pursued' (para 37).

[98] On the gay and lesbian parent's burden of disproving detriment to the child see also *Doe v Doe*, 16 Mass App Ct 499, 452 NE 2d 293 (1983); *Gottlieb v Gottlieb*, 108 AD 2d 120, 488 NYS 2d 180 (1st Dep't 1985). Custody disputes concerning parents' sexual orientation raised similar issues in Argentina (see *LSF y ACP*, Family Tribunal of the 4th Court District of the City of Cordoba, Argentina RU 2003-5, 5, DJ 2003-3, 236, 6 August 2003).

[99] *Fretté v France* ECHR 2002-I, (2004) 38 EHRR 21.

[100] Art 343-1 of the French Civil Code.

[101] *Fretté v France* n 100 above, para 33.

homosexual to adopt a child'[102] and the division in the scientific community over the 'consequences on a child's psychological development and, more generally, his or her future life'[103] of the deprival of a dual maternal and paternal role model. As no child had been identified for adoption yet, the Court's reasoning took the best interests of the child into account only in the abstract, confirming an instrumental usage of the principle.

At the same time it should be emphasised that the ECtHR relied also on an apparently neutral constitutional argument: it noted that the Convention does not recognise 'a right to adopt as such' and moreover, that 'the right to respect for family life presupposes the existence of a family and does not safeguard the mere desire to found a family'.[104] As a result, the ECtHR argued that

> in the instant case, the decision to dismiss the applicant's application for authorisation could not be considered to infringe his right to the free expression and development of his personality or the manner in which he led his life, in particular his sexual life.[105]

The ECtHR tacitly overturned *Fretté* in *EB v France,*[106] a 2008 decision concerning a French woman in a stable same-sex relationship who was denied authorisation for a single-parent adoption because of her sexual orientation. The situation was therefore different from that addressed in *Fretté,* because the applicant was cohabiting with a long-term female partner who—according to psychologists and welfare reports—'show[ed] a clear lack of interest in Ms B's plan to adopt'.[107] Despite the applicant's 'undoubted personal qualities and aptitude for bringing up children', the French judicial authorities justified their refusal of authorisation on the basis of the 'absence of identificational markers due to the lack of a paternal role model or referent' and 'the ambivalence of the commitment of each member of the household to the adoptive child'.[108]

The ECtHR defined as 'inescapable'[109] the conclusion that the applicant's sexual orientation 'was consistently at the centre of deliberations in her regard and omnipresent at every stage of the administrative and judicial proceedings',[110] and concluded that Ms EB had suffered a 'difference in treatment', in violation of Article 14 (prohibition of discrimination) in conjunction with Article 8 (right to respect for private and family life).

EB v France is a remarkable decision because it clearly formulates the principle that 'a person seeking to adopt cannot be prevented from doing so merely on the ground of his or her homosexuality'.[111] This implies that when a State has gone beyond its minimum obligation by consenting to adoption outside 'traditional' marriage,

[102] ibid, para 36.
[103] ibid, para 36.
[104] ibid, para 32.
[105] ibid, para 32. The idea that there is no constitutional right to have a child was advanced also by the French Conseil constitutionnel in its 2013 decision on equal marriage. See below p 193 ff.
[106] *EB v France* IHRL 3284 (ECtHR, 2008).
[107] ibid, para 15 but see also para 76.
[108] Conseil d'Etat, 1/2 SSR, no 230533, 5 June 2002.
[109] *EB v France* n 107 above, para 88.
[110] ibid.
[111] See ibid, dissenting opinion of Judge Costa, joined by Judges Türmen, Ugrekhelidze and Jočienė.

it cannot discriminate on the basis of sexual orientation. It has been suggested[112] that the radical shift from *Fretté* was probably justified by the Court's intention of setting a significant precedent, because a revised version of the European Convention on the Adoption of Children was in preparation when the case was released.[113]

Nonetheless, the complex issues addressed in *EB v France* were very divisive:[114] the Court's assertion that the facts of the case 'undoubtedly fall within the ambit of Article 8' was for instance rejected by Judge Mularoni who argued that, as there is no right to adoption under the Convention, it is 'illogical' to infer that the 'right to seek authorisation "undoubtedly" falls under Articles 8 and that Article 14 taken together with Article 8 is applicable'.[115] Judge Zupančič stated instead that 'adoption is a privilege rather than a right', and that it is inconsistent to find a violation of Article 14,[116] whereas Judge Loucaides advanced a more blatantly homophobic argument, stressing that gays and lesbians 'must, like any other persons with some peculiarity, accept that they may not qualify for certain activities which, by their nature and under certain circumstances, are incompatible with their lifestyle or peculiarity'.[117]

It should also be noted that the judges devoted great attention to the best interests of the child and to the necessity of providing a referent of the other sex 'capable of fostering the well-adjusted development of an adopted child', and discussed the place Ms EB's partner would have occupied in the child's life.[118] All these issues were analysed on an abstract plane (because, obviously, no child had yet been selected for adoption) and, as in *Fretté,* the burden of proving the existence of any scientific reasons to deny that gay and lesbians parents are as fit as heterosexual parents was on the French Government. In this respect, the Court admitted that if France 'had failed to prove in *Fretté* and in the instant case that there was a consensus in the scientific community, this was because there was no known study on the subject'.[119]

Despite its final conclusions, the background issues reveal that the ideal of 'order of family life'[120] the Court had in mind still referred to the heterosexual parenthood and to complementarity of sexes; but it is also important to emphasise that since *EB,* the Court has been taking for granted the reality of gay and lesbian parenting and childrearing.

[112] L Hart, 'Individual Adoption by Non-Heterosexuals and the Order of Family Life in the European Court of Human Rights' (2009) 36 *Journal of Law and Society* 536, 552.

[113] European Convention on the Adoption of Children (Revised), 27 November 2008.

[114] The judges unanimously declared the application admissible, but they held by 10 votes to 7 that there was a violation of Article 14 taken in conjunction with Article 8, and by 11 votes to 6 on the award of pecuniary damages to Ms EB. On the complexity of the case, see Johnson, *Homosexuality and the European Court of Human Right*; E Falletti, 'Homosexual Single Individuals' Right to Adopt Before the European Court of Human Rights and in the French Legal Context' (2011) 18 *Human Rights Brief* 26, 28.

[115] *EB v France,* n 107 above, dissenting opinion of Judge Mularoni.

[116] ibid, dissenting opinion of Judge Zupančič.

[117] ibid, dissenting opinion of Judge Loucaides.

[118] ibid, para 22.

[119] ibid, paras 66 and 70.

[120] On the sociological issues concerning the order of family life and the 'symbolic order of kinship as a cultural ideal' in ECtHR cases, see Hart, 'Individual Adoption', n 113 above, 552 ff.

B. Second-parent Adoption

The United States state courts were also the first to address, in the early 1990s, the claims of discrimination brought by gays and lesbians who wanted to adopt their partner's biological child.

As early as in 1992, for instance, a New York Superior Court held that the interests of the child were best served by granting to the lesbian partner of a biological mother the right to adopt the biological mother's child.[121]

In the following year, the Vermont Supreme Court[122] concluded that it was surely in the best interests of the children and the State to facilitate second-parent adoptions, so that the rights and responsibilities of the adults could be determined and legal disputes could be resolved within the framework of domestic relations laws. The Vermont Supreme Court emphasised that it was not called upon to approve or disapprove the relationship between the mother and her partner, but to address the reality of their family life: the partner had acted as a parent to the children since their birth, and to deny legal protection to their relationship as a matter of law was inconsistent with the children's best interests.[123] For these reasons the Supreme Court of Vermont also concluded that the lesbian partner of a biological mother could adopt the children without termination of the biological mother's parental rights according to state statutes.

Nonetheless, at that time, these cases did not reflect a general trend. Just before the United States Supreme Court decision in *Obergefell*, which in 2015 made same-sex marriage legal throughout the country, some states within the United States—where same-sex marriage was not legal—still prohibited second-parent adoption to same-sex couples even if they were married in another state,[124] and others had laws that limited or prohibited adoption rights to unmarried same-sex couples.[125] The last

[121] *Matter of Adoption of Evan* 583 NYS 2d 997 (Sur Ct 1992). ('[T]his is not a matter which arises in a vacuum. Social fragmentation and the myriad configurations of modern families have presented us with new problems and complexities that cannot be solved by idealizing the past. Today a child who receives proper nutrition, adequate schooling and supportive sustaining shelter is among the fortunate, whatever the source. A child who also receives the love and nurture of even a single parent can be counted among the blessed. Here this Court finds a child who has all the above benefits an two adults dedicated to his welfare, secure in their loving partnership, and determined to raise him to the very best of their considerable abilities. There is no reason in law, logic or social philosophy to obstruct such a favourable situation'; ibid at 1002). See also *Petition of LS for Adoption of Minor (T)*, 1991 WL 219598 (DC Super Ct 1991) (unreported opinion).

[122] *In re Adoption of BLVB* 160 Vt 368, 628 A 2d 1271 (1993).

[123] *In re Adoption of BLVB* 160 Vt, 377 ('There is not a scintilla of evidence in the record to suggest that the adoptions are not in the best interests of these children.').

[124] The state of Mississippi had the most restrictive adoption ban in the United States, prohibiting same-sex couples from jointly adopting, or a person from adopting his same-sex partner's child. A federal district court recently held the ban unconstitutional in *Campaign for Southern Equality v Mississippi Department of Human Services* 2016 US Dist LEXIS 43897 (2016) making gay adoption legal in all 50 states.

The Supreme Court recently held in *VL v EL* 136 S Ct 1017 (2016) that the Alabama Supreme Court erred in refusing to grant full faith and credit to a Georgia court's judgment of adoption making the petitioner a legal parent of the children that she and the respondent had raised together.

[125] Eg, in Kansas the Kansas Court of Appeals ruled in *Adoption of IM* 48 Kan App 2d 343 (2012) that Kansas could not permit second-parent or co-parent adoption by unmarried couples. A similar decision was released by the Kentucky Court of Appeals (*SJLS v TLS* 265 SW 3d 804 (Ct App Ky 2008)), in Nebraska

(and most restrictive) adoption ban in force in the State of Mississippi was declared unconstitutional only in 2016, making both second-parent adoption and joint adoption legal across all the nation. It is surprising that this ban survived the Supreme Court decision in *Obergefell v Hodges,* the only constitutional court judgment so far to overturn the argument of procreation maintaining that the right to marry 'safeguards children and families and thus draws meaning from related rights of childrearing, procreation, and education'.[126]

In France, before 2013, same-sex couples who entered a *pacte civil de solidarieté* (PACS) under law no 944 of 1999[127] were denied parental rights because Article 365 of the Code Civil reserved the opportunity to adopt the partner's biological child (*adoption simple*) only to married (opposite-sex) couples. Same-sex couples submitted the issue to ordinary courts and to the Cour de Cassation that in 2007[128] reiterated that Article 365 CC was applicable only to married couples, and rejected the request for authorisation to a second-parent adoption to a lesbian couple, arguing that the best interests of the child were not served because second-parent adoption would have severed the legal ties with the biological parent.

In 2010 the issue was submitted also to the Conseil constitutionnel, under its recently introduced power of judicial review of legislation.[129] Relying on the Cour of Cassation's conclusions, the Conseil constitutionnel held that Article 365 cc did not impair the right of a same-sex couple 'to enjoy a normal family life'.[130] Nonetheless, it excluded that 'the right to a normal family life' implied the 'right to establish a legal bond of adoptive filiation'[131] and did not even address the issue of discrimination between children of married couples and children of unmarried couples.[132] Therefore, the Conseil dismissed the issue, concluding that it fell within the legislator's discretionary powers to introduce a difference between married and unmarried couples regarding parental rights, and to assess that such a difference best served the interests of the children.[133]

Against this background the issue was submitted to the ECtHR that in *Gas and Dubois v France*[134] addressed the case of a French lesbian couple and their daughter who had been conceived through anonymous donor insemination. The two women

(*In re Adoption of Luke* 640 NW 2d 374 (Neb 2002)). In 2014, the Idaho Supreme Court (*In the Matter of the Adoption of John Doe & John Doe I* 156 Idaho 532; 328 P 3d 512 (2014)) reversed a magistrates' court decision that had refused to allow a woman to adopt her lesbian partner's children.

126 *Obergefell v Hodges*, n 41 above, 135 S Ct, 2600.

127 Loi no 99-944 of 15 November 1999 (*relative au pacte civil de solidarité*).

128 Cour de Cassation, Arrêt nos 221 and 224, 20 February 2007.

129 The *question prioritaire de constitutionnalité* (QPC) was introduced by a constitutional reform (*loi constitutionnelle no 2008-724 of 23 July 2008 de modernisation des institutions de la Ve République*), art 29. The QPC concerning Art 365 Code Civil was submitted to the Conseil constitutionnel by the Cour of Cassation. On the case, see C Severino, *La doctrine du droit vivant* (Paris, Economica-PUAM, 2003).

130 Conseil constitutionnel, Décision no 2010-39 QPC, 6 October 2010, considérant no 3.

131 ibid, considérant no 8. The Conseil constitutionnel in particular emphasised that the law is unconstitutional for denying legal status only when the denial also impairs the right to enjoy a normal family life.

132 Conseil constitutionnel, case no 2010-39, n 131 above, considérant no 3.

133 ibid, considérant no 9 (arguing also the issue did not involve a discriminatory treatment and was not subjected to a strict scrutiny and a proportionality test).

134 *Gas and Dubois v France* ECHR 2012-II.

had raised the child together, but for legal purposes she had only one parent, namely the second applicant, because the French authorities had rejected their application for an *adoption simple*. The applicants alleged that the refusal infringed their right to respect for their private and family life in a discriminatory manner (under Article 14 in conjunction with Article 8).

The ECtHR unanimously dismissed the applicants' argument, finding no violation of Convention rights. It held that the situation of the couples could not be considered equal to that of married couples, because marriage confers a special status on those who are married. The ECtHR also emphasised that under Article 12 of the European Convention (as interpreted in *Schalk and Kopf v Austria*)[135] the State had no duty to open marriage to same-sex couples.[136] Furthermore, the Court found that the legal regulation of *adoption simple* in France did not discriminate on the ground of sexual orientation of partners because even opposite-sex couple in a comparable legal situation would likewise have had its application rejected.[137] Nonetheless, as illustrated in Chapter 4, the issue is now settled by law no 404 of 2013,[138] which opened marriage to same-sex couples, extending to them also full parental rights.[139]

Gas and Dubois should be now read also in the light of the more recent ECtHR landmark decision in *X and Others v Austria*[140] concerning second-parent adoption. As illustrated in the first pages of this chapter,[141] in *X and Others* the ECtHR found that Austria had violated Article 14 of the ECHR in conjunction with Article 8 for substantially denying to same-sex couples the opportunity to adopt the biological child of their partner in comparison with unmarried different-sex couples that instead enjoyed this right.[142] At the same time, the ECtHR found that the difference was inseparably linked to the fact that the first and third applicants formed a same-sex couple, and was thus based on their sexual orientation.[143]

Nonetheless, the Court found no discrimination when the applicants' situation was compared with that of a married couple in which one spouse wished to adopt the other spouse's child.[144] Confirming its conclusions in *Gas and Dubois*, the Court emphasised that 'Article 12 of the Convention does not impose an obligation on the Contracting States to grant same-sex couples access to marriage … nor can a right to same-sex marriage be derived from Article 14 taken in conjunction with Article 8'.[145]

[135] *Schalk and Kopf v Austria* ECHR 2010-I, (2010) ECHR 1996. The European Court has reiterated its findings also in *Hämäläinen v Finland* App no 37359/09 (ECtHR [GC], 16 July 2014); *Oliari v Italy* [2015] ECHR 752 and, recently in *Chapin and Charpentier v France* App no 40183/07 (ECtHR, 9 June 2016). See also *Vallianatos and others v Greece [GC]* [2013] ECHR 1110.

[136] See *Gas and Dubois v France* n 135 above, paras 66–68.

[137] *Gas and Dubois v France* n 135 above, para 69.

[138] Loi no 2013-404, 17 May 2013 (*ouvrant le mariage aux couples de personnes de même sexe*).

[139] On the issues concerning parental rights in case no 404 of 2003, see below, p 193 ff.

[140] *X and Others*, n 8 above.

[141] See above p 173.

[142] This followed from Art 182 § 2 of the Austrian Civil Code stating that any person who adopts replaces the biological parent of the same sex. Although neutral at first glance, Art 182 § 2 of the Civil Code excluded second-parent adoption in a same-sex couple because adoption could not serve to create a parent–child relationship in addition to the relationship with the biological parent.

[143] *X and Others* n 8 above, para 130.

[144] ibid, para 105.

[145] ibid, para 106.

Therefore, when a state chooses to limit marriage to different-sex couples and to provide 'same-sex couples with an alternative means of legal recognition, it enjoys a certain margin of appreciation as regards the exact status conferred'.[146] Furthermore, the Court stated that following its reasoning in *Gas and Dubois,* 'there is no obligation under Article 8 of the Convention to extend the right to second-parent adoption to unmarried couples'.[147]

Although the ECtHR clarifies that it was 'not called upon to rule on the issue of second-parent adoption by same-sex couples as such, let alone on the question of adoption by same-sex couples in general' but only on 'a narrowly defined issue of alleged discrimination between unmarried different-sex couples and same-sex couples in respect of second-parent adoption'[148] in Austrian legislation, the decision implied that when a state has chosen to provide an alternative legal status that places same-sex couples and different-sex couple in 'a relevantly similar situation',[149] it could not then differentiate between them in regard, for instance, to parental rights.[150] In this respect, it is worth noting that, in a final passage, the Court stresses 'the importance of granting legal recognition to de facto family life'[151] and emphasises also that

> in contrast to individual adoption or joint adoption, which are usually aimed at creating a relationship with a child previously unrelated to the adopter, second-parent adoption serves to confer rights *vis-à-vis* the child on the partner of one of the child's parents.[152]

With regard to the 'optimal parenting rationale', the European Court argued that the provisions at issue were justified by the Austrian Government on the basis of protection of the 'traditional family', 'based on the tacit assumption that only a family with parents of different sex could adequately provide for a child's needs'.[153]

The Court accepted that 'protection of the family in the traditional sense might be, in principle, a weighty and legitimate reason apt to justify a difference in treatment',[154] but it also emphasised that the principle of proportionality must be assessed in the circumstances of the case and that, as the Convention is 'a living instrument',[155] the interpretation of Article 8 'must necessarily take into account

[146] ibid.
[147] ibid, para 136.
[148] *X and Others*, n 8 above, para 134.
[149] Compare esp *X and Others*, n 8 above, para 112.
[150] See R Wintemute, 'Marriage, adoption, and donor insemination for same-sex couples: does European case law impose any obligations on Italy?' (2014) 2 *GenIUS* 35, 39 (available at www.articolo29.it), arguing that 'the net effect of *Schalk & Kopf* ... and *Gas & Dubois* ... is to establish a "Marriage Wall" in Europe. Governments that wish to do so may stay behind the "legal safety" of the "Marriage Wall", knowing that the EConHR permits them to restrict marriage to different-sex couples, and joint and second-parent adoption of children to married different-sex couples. If they venture outside the "Marriage Wall", by voluntarily granting rights to unmarried different-sex couples, the ECtHR's *Karner* principle will require them to grant the same rights to unmarried same-sex couples'.
[151] *X and Others*, n 8 above, para 145.
[152] ibid, para 145.
[153] ibid, para 137.
[154] ibid, para 138 (see also *Karner v Austria* ECHR 2003-IX, 38 EHRR 24, para 40 and *Kozak v Poland* [2010] ECHR 280, para 98).
[155] ibid, para 139.

developments in society and changes in the perception of social, civil-status and relational issues, including the fact that there is not just one way or one choice when it comes to leading one's family or private life'.[156] With regard to the specific circumstances of the case, the Court noted that many considerations cast considerable doubt on the proportionality of the absolute prohibition on second-parent adoption by the Austrian Government in the instant case. It emphasised in particular that the Austrian Government

> did not adduce any specific argument, any scientific studies or any other item of evidence to show that a family with two parents of the same sex could in no circumstances adequately provide for a child's needs. On the contrary, they conceded that, in personal terms, same-sex couples could be as suitable or unsuitable as different-sex couples when it came to adopting children.[157]

Therefore, the ECtHR concluded that 'unless any other 'particularly convincing and weighty reasons'[158] might justify an absolute prohibition, its consideration militate in favour of allowing the courts to carry out an examination through a case-by-case approach, in order to better assess the best interests of the child in each individual case.[159] Therefore, although the European Court of Human Rights did not give special prominence to the best interest of the child in the reasoning, its final remarks[160] suggest the conclusion that the principle was functional to the purpose the Court wanted to achieve.

Other constitutional and supreme court cases on second-parent adoption and the German Constitutional Tribunal decision[161] suggest a similar conclusion. This can also be explained by the fact that, in comparison to the past (for instance in *Fretté*),[162] courts have now acknowledged the lack of any scientific evidence that gay and lesbian families do not provide the optimal environment for child-rearing.[163] As it is now evident that this objection is not supported by any scientific study or

[156] ibid, para 139.

[157] ibid, para 142.

[158] ibid, para 146.

[159] ibid. It should be also emphasised that the European Court also rejected the Austrian Government's argument concerning the lack of a 'European consensus' on the matter, arguing that in the instant case what came into consideration was the difference in treatment between unmarried couples, and not the access of same-sex couples to second-parent adoption (*X and Others* n 8 above, para 149).

[160] See above p 173, but also the European Court's remarks at *X and Others*, n 7 above, para 152 ('The Court emphasises once more that the present case does not concern the question whether the applicants' adoption request should have been granted in the circumstances of the case. It concerns the question whether the applicants were discriminated against on account of the fact that the courts had no opportunity to examine in any meaningful manner whether the requested adoption was in the second applicant's interests, given that it was in any case legally impossible.').

[161] See above at n 174 and accompanying text.

[162] See *X and Others*, n 8 above, para 102.

[163] ibid, para 142; German Constitutional Tribunal, 133BVerfGE 59, para 80; Cassazione Civile, sez I, case no 601 of 11 January 2013; Spanish Constitutional Tribunal, case no 198 of 2012, n 72 above, para 12; Supreme Court of Israel, *Yaros-Hakak v Attorney General*, CA 10280/01, 10 January 2005 (mentioning several scientific studies denying harm to children from being raised by homosexual couples) and in particular Justice Barak's dissenting opinion (para 34). See also M Strasser, 'Adoption and the Best Interests of the Child: on the Use and Abuse of Studies' (2004) 38 *New England Law Review* 629, 633 (arguing that 'one regrettable aspect of the debate regarding adoption by lesbians and gay men is that irrelevant statistics are cited to justify policies which would harm both adults and children').

any other item of evidence, courts require a *specific* evidence of actual and potential harm to the child before taking into account the parent's sexual orientation. This implies that, in recent cases—as Ball argues—if the courts make a correct use of the 'nexus test',[164] the gay and lesbian parent is almost always able to persuade the court that authorising second-parent adoption meets the child's best interests.

The counterargument relies in fact on a precautionary principle, in particular on the idea that given the inconclusive findings of scientific research it is justified in the interests of the child to reserve adoption to opposite-sex couples.[165] But this abstract argument is frequently proven less powerful when opposed to the existence of de facto family life and to the practical evaluation of the best interests of the child in the instant case.

C. Joint Adoption

Joint adoption is a more controversial kind of adoption at political and social level because, unlike custody and second-parent adoption issues, the rights and best interests of no identified child come into consideration. This puts the question on a more abstract plane, giving strength to the 'neutral' argument that there is neither a right to adopt, nor a general right to have a child. The more abstract nature of the issue also implies that the question is conceived as falling within the exercise of legislative discretionary powers because, traditionalists argue, only political and democratically legitimated powers are able to assess whether the interests of the child are best served by a total equivalence of rights between same-sex and opposite-sex couples or by the application of the precautionary principle.[166]

In Europe, issues concerning the right of same-sex couples to jointly adopt a child mostly arose at constitutional level within disputes concerning equal marriage and the consequent recognition to same-sex couples of all the rights and duties stemming from marriage. Therefore, whereas recognition of the right to adopt the partner's

[164] Ball, *The Right to Be Parents*, n 85 above, 8.

[165] See the argument of Alliance Defending Freedom in *X and Others*, n 8 above, summarised at para 91.

[166] At the time of writing, joint adoption by same-sex couples is legal in countries which opened marriage to same-sex couples whereas, within the Council of Europe, it was forbidden in countries which do not admit same-sex marriage and in particular in countries like Germany, Switzerland and Italy, which adopt a separate and parallel framework of recognition for same-sex couples, reserving joint adoption only to married (opposite-sex) couples. The introduction of same-sex marriage in many countries has softened the conflict over the denial of joint adoption to unmarried couples. In England the Adoption and Children Act 2002 (s 144(4)) states that a couple means a married or civil-registered couple or 'two people (whether of different sex or the same-sex) living as partners in an enduring family relationship'. The provision therefore opened adoption to same-sex couple under the same conditions established for different-sex couples, although, before the adoption of the Marriage (Same-Sex Couples) Act 2013 some practical difficulties remained. Outside Europe, joint adoption is admitted in all 50 states of the United States (see above p 187 f) that hold unconstitutional the Mississippi adoption ban. Nonetheless, some states still limit joint adoption to married same-sex couples. Joint adoption is also legal all the provinces of Canada, in South Africa and in some South American countries like Argentina, Brazil, Colombia, Mexico, Puerto Rico and Uruguay.

biological child has been also achieved through constitutional litigation, the right to jointly adopt a child has been mostly the result of legislative intervention, and constitutional courts have frequently addressed the issue on a second step, within the exercise of their judicial review powers.

In France the issue of joint adoption has dominated the political debate on equal marriage (*mariage pour tous*). Before the adoption of law no 404 of 2013,[167] which opened marriage to same-sex couples and extended to them the right to jointly adopt a child (as well as second parent adoption), this right was recognised only to married (opposite-sex) couples.

In case no 669 of 2013,[168] when addressing the constitutionality of law no 404, the Conseil constitutionnel focused extensively on the issue of parental rights and on the legislative choice to recognise the right of adoption to married same-sex couples 'under the same conditions established for married heterosexual couples'.[169] The applicants argued, inter alia, that

> the possibility given to two individuals of the same sex to adopt a child, violate[d] the "principle of constitutional standing of bilinear filiation based on sexual alterity" proclaimed by the laws of the Republic, as well as the constitutional right of all children to establish their filiation from their father and their mother.[170]

Applicants also emphasised 'the right of the child to lead a normal family life as well as the protection of the superior interest of the child'.[171]

The Conseil constitutionnel dismissed these arguments, reiterating that the issue was a '*question de société*', falling within the legislative discretionary powers.[172] Nonetheless it decisively rejected the optimal parenting argument ('*filiation bilinéaire fondée sur l'altérité sexuelle*'),[173] arguing that the freedom proclaimed under Article 2 of the 1789 Declaration of the Rights of Man and the Citizen 'implied the duty to respect private life' and that 'no requirement of constitutional law stipulates … that the parental bonds established through adoptive filiation must reproduce those of biological filiation'.[174]

At the same time, the Conseil constitutionnel emphasised that there is no 'right to a child': same-sex couples must always show evidence that they are suitable for adoption and child-rearing, and they will not be exempted 'from the rules, conditions

167 Loi no 2013-404.

168 Conseil constitutionnel, décision no 2013-669 DC, 17 May 2013.

169 Art 13 of law no 404 of 2013 introduced the new Art no 6–1 of the Civil Code (stating that 'Le mariage et la filiation adoptive emportent les mêmes effets, droits et obligations reconnus par les lois, à l'exclusion de ceux prévus au titre VII du livre Ier du présent code, que les époux ou les parents soient de sexe différent ou de même sexe').

170 Case no 669 of 2013, n 169 above, considérant no 46.

171 ibid.

172 ibid ('Considering that it is not for the Constitutional Council to substitute its appraisal for that of the legislator regarding the consideration, for the purpose of establishing a bond of adoptive filiation, of the difference between same-sex couples and couples comprised of a man and a woman'). See against, B Mathieu, 'Decision du Conseil constitutionnel sur le mariage homosexuel' (30 May 2013) available in www.bertrandmathieu.fr.

173 ibid, considérant no 56.

174 ibid, considérant no 51.

and controls established in relation to adoptive filiation'.[175] Therefore, the Conseil concluded, the child is afforded equal protection either when parents of the same sex or parents of the opposite sex adopt them.[176]

One year before the Conseil constitutionnel released its ruling on equal marriage, the Spanish Constitutional Tribunal expounded quite similar arguments in case no 198 of 2012, concerning the legitimacy of law no 13 of 2015, which opened marriage also to same-sex couples redrafting Article 175, section 4, of the Civil Code in order to eliminate any referral to the sexual orientation of the adopting parents. The petitioners argued that the revised Civil Code provision was 'contrary to the mandate to provide integral protection to children' under the Spanish Constitution,[177] 'mak[ing] the legitimation or standardisation of homosexual relations prevail over a minor's interest'.[178]

Both the French Conseil constitutionnel and the Spanish Constitutional Tribunal argued that the Civil Code provision requiring 'an examination conducted on the potential adopting parents, irrespective of their sexual orientation' safeguarded the best interests of the child. Accordingly the Tribunal excluded that the legislator, in the exercise of its discretionary powers, had infringed the obligation to protect the family[179] and in particular the children.[180] The Spanish Constitutional Tribunal also emphasised that Spanish legal system 'does not acknowledge a fundamental human right to adopt'.[181]

As both the French and the Spanish constitutional cases address the legitimacy of recently introduced legislative reforms, their judgments devoted great attention to the structural issues concerning the legitimate exercise of legislative powers in the light of the principle of the protection of the best interests of the child.

Conversely, in countries where joint adoption issues were instead raised before the introduction of same-sex marriage, the courts showed greater deference to national legislator, and future legislative choices and also focused extensively on equality and dignity of same-sex couples.

The difference is best illustrated by the South Africa Constitutional Court's decision in *Du Toit*,[182] concerning the complaint brought by two women in a longstanding relationship who were forbidden to jointly adopt two children because legislative provisions restricted adoption to married couples only[183] (and, at that time, same-sex marriage had not been introduced in South Africa). As the partners could only have access to individual adoption and were therefore denied the opportunity to

[175] Case no 669 of 2013, n 169 above, considérant no 52 ('Same-sex couples who wish to adopt a child shall be subject, in the same manner as those comprised of a man and a woman, to a procedure aimed at establishing their capacity to provide a home to a child in order to adopt it').

[176] ibid, considérant no 53.

[177] Spanish Constitution, Art 39, § 2.

[178] Case no 198 of 2012 n 72 above, para 12.

[179] Spanish Constitution, Art 39, § 1.

[180] Case no 198 of 2012, n 72 above, para 12.

[181] ibid.

[182] *Du Toit v Minister for Welfare and Population Development* Case CCT 40/01 of 10 September 2002.

[183] Child Care Act s 17(1) and (2).

establish a joint legally recognised bond with their children, they were concerned about the instability of their children's legal situation in the event of death or separation of one of them. They also alleged that the law unfairly discriminated against gays and lesbians in violation of the principle of equality (Article 9(3) of the Constitution) and that the absolute prohibition of joint adoption by same-sex parents was against the best interests of the children placed in the families of adoptive parents involved in same-sex life partnerships.[184]

The Constitutional Court held the regulation of adoption to be unconstitutional and justified its conclusion by stating that it protected not only the rights of applicants in respect of their children, but 'all permanent same-sex life partners' who want[ed] to adopt jointly or undertake joint guardianship'.[185] The Court also found that the adoption legislation introduced an illegitimate discrimination based on sexual orientation[186] and violated the right of human dignity of gays and lesbians.[187] The Court recognised that the interest at stake could be 'best cured by the passing of legislation of Parliament',[188] and suggested that in the meantime the interests of the prospective adoptive children could be 'adequately addressed by the high courts as the upper guardians of all minor children'.[189]

[184] South Africa Constitution of 1996, art 28(1)(b) (guaranteeing the child's right to a family or parental care).

[185] *Du Toit* n 183 above, para 42.

[186] ibid, para 23.

[187] ibid, para 27.

[188] ibid, para 41.

[189] ibid.

6

Concluding Remarks

IN THIS BOOK I have analysed constitutional cases on sexual orientation equality following a path where the recognition of the rights of gays, lesbians and same-sex couples went together with their increasing visibility and inclusion as individuals, couples and families.

However, the recognition of equal marriage and of parental rights does not mark the end of the long battle for full equality by gays and lesbians. Just as, in 1954, *Brown v Board of Education* did not bring an end to claims of recognition of coloured people in the United States and, in the early 1970s, *Roe v Wade* and other constitutional court cases on abortion did not definitively close the issue of abortion and reproductive rights in many jurisdictions, so the landmark constitutional cases on equal marriage will not make gays and lesbians 'full citizens', enjoying equal rights. Other claims are now finding their way into the courts and among them, in my opinion, the most interesting are those involving the demands of gays and lesbians not to have their rights modelled on opposite-sex relationships or on established gender-based social roles and, on a different plane, the issues where freedom of religion and conscientious objection seem to be invoked in order to sidestep any issue of discrimination.

My main purpose in this book has been to analyse how courts have expounded arguments of dignity, liberty and equality in their rulings on gay rights. However, I would like to emphasise in conclusion that by recognising the fundamental rights of gays and lesbians, courts—especially constitutional and supreme courts—have also advanced the cause of equality of *all* individuals. Therefore, the legacy of the cases analysed in this book lies not only in their contribution to the transition 'from exclusion to inclusion' of gays and lesbians, but also in a new reading of fundamental rights, which will influence the debate on human rights for many years to come.

Bibliography

Ackerman, B, 'The Rise of World Constitutionalism' (1997) 83 *Vanderbilt Law Review* 771

Bala, N and Jaremko Bromwich, R, 'Context and Inclusivity in Canada's Evolving Definition of the Family' (2000) 16 *International Journal of Law, Policy and the Family* 145

Balkin, JM, 'Tradition, Betrayal, and the Politics of Deconstruction' (1990) 11 *Cardozo Law Review* 1613

Balkin, JM, 'Obergefell and Tradition' in *Balkinization*, 28 June 2015 (balkin.blogspot.com)

Ball, CA, *The Right to Be Parents: LGBT Families and the Transformation of Parenthood* (New York, New York University Press, 2012)

Bamforth, N, *Sexuality, Morals and Justice. A Theory of Lesbian and Gay Rights Law* (London, Cassell, 1997)

Bamforth, N, 'Introduction' in N Bamforth (ed), *Sex Rights. The Oxford Amnesty Lectures 2002* (Oxford, Oxford University Press, 2005), 1

Bamforth, N, 'Families but not (yet) marriages? Same-sex partners and the developing European Convention "margin of appreciation"' (2011) 23 *Children & Family Law Quarterly* 128

Barak, A, 'The Constitutional Value and the Constitutional Right' in C McCrudden (ed), *Understanding Human Dignity* (Oxford, Oxford University Press, 2013) 12

Barak, A, *Human Dignity. The Constitutional Value and the Constitutional Right* (Cambridge, Cambridge University Press, 2015)

Barsotti V, Carozza PG, Cartabia M and Simoncini, A, *Italian Constitutional Justice in Global Context* (Oxford, Oxford University Press, 2015)

Bartlett, KT, 'Tradition as Past and Present in Substantive Due Process Analysis' (2012) 62 *Duke Law Journal* 535

Behnabib, S, *The Claims of Culture: Equality and Diversity in the Global Era* (Princeton, Princeton University Press, 2002)

Bifulco, R, Celotto, A, and Olivetti, M (eds), *Commentario alla Costituzione* (Torino, Utet, 2006)

Blumberg, G, 'Legal Recognition of Same-sex Conjugal Relationships: The 2003 California Domestic Partner Rights and Responsibilities Act in Comparative Civil Rights and Family Law Perspective' (2004) 51 *UCLA Law Review* 1555

Boele-Woelki, K and Fuchs, A (eds), *Legal Recognition of Same-Sex Couples in Europe* (Cambridge, Intersentia, 2003)

Boele-Woelki, K and Fuchs, A (eds), *Legal Recognition of Same-Sex Relationships in Europe. National, Cross-Border and European Perspectives*, 2nd edn (Cambridge, Intersentia, 2012)

Bognetti, G, 'The Concept of Human Dignity in European and US Constitutionalism' in G Nolte (ed), *European and US Constitutionalism* (Cambridge, Cambridge University Press, 2005) 85

Bonini Baraldi, M, 'Family vs solidarity. Recent epiphanies of the Italian reductionist anomaly in the debate, on de facto couples' (2008) 4 *Utrecht Law Review* 175

Bonini Baraldi, M, *La famiglia de-genere* (Sesto San Giovanni, Mimesis, 2010)

Borrillo, D, 'The "Pacte Civil de Solidarité" in France: Midway Between Marriage and Cohabitation' in R Wintemute and M Andenæs (eds), *Legal Recognition of Same-Sex Partnerships* (Oxford, Hart Publishing, 2001) 475

Brandao AM and Machado TC, 'How Equal Is Equality? Discussions About Same-Sex Marriage in Portugal' (2012) 15 *Sexualities* 662

Brown, RL, 'Tradition and Insight' (1993) *Yale Law Journal* 177

Bruni, F, 'One Country's Big Gay Leap', *International New York Times*, 9 October 2011, p SR3

Butler, J, *Undoing Gender* (New York, Routledge, 2004)

Caggia, F and Zoppini, A, 'Articolo 29' in R Bifulco, A Celotto and M Olivetti (eds), *Commentario alla Costituzione*, vol 1 (Torino, Utet, 2006) 601 ff.

Campbell Black, H, *Black's Law Dictionary*, 6th edn (St Paul, West Publishing, 1990)

Cappelletti, M, *Judicial Review in the Contemporary World* (New York, Bobbs-Merrill, 1971)

Carozza, PG, 'Uses and Misuses of Comparative Law in International Human Rights: Some Reflections on the Jurisprudence of the European Court of Human Rights' (1998) 73 *Notre Dame Law Review* 1217

Carozza, PG, 'Subsidiarity as a Structural Principle of International Human Rights Law' (2003) 97 *American Journal of International Law* 1

Carozza, PG, 'Human Dignity and Judicial Interpretation of Human Rights. A Reply' (2008) 19 *International Journal of Constitutional Law (ICon)* 931

Celotto, A, 'Art 3, 1 comma, Cost' in R Bifulco, A Celotto, M Olivetti (eds), *Commentario alla Costituzione* (Torino, Utet, 2006), I, 72

Charbonneau, G and Pansier, FJ, 'Et in Terra Pacs. Commentaire du Pacte civil de solidarité créé par la loi du 14 novembre 1999 et à la lumière de la décision du Conseil constitutionnel' (1999) 323–24 *Gazette du Palais* 2

Choudhry, S, 'Globalization in Search of Justification: Toward a Theory of Comparative Constitutional Interpretation' (1999) 74 *Indiana Law Journal* 819 (1999)

Choudhry, S (ed), *The Migration of Constitutional Ideas* (Cambridge, Cambridge University Press, 2006)

Cicero, MT, *Rhetoricorum libri duo qui sunt de inventione retorica (De inv.)*, II, 166

Curry-Summer, I, 'A Patchwork of Partnership: Comparative Overview of Registration Schemes in Europe' in K Boele-Woelki and A Fuchs (eds), *Legal Recognition of Same-Sex Couples in Europe* (Cambridge, Intersentia, 2003) 71

Daly, E, *Dignity Rights. Courts, Constitutions and Worth of the Human Person* (Philadelphia, University of Pennsylvania Press, 2012)

Danisi, C, *Tutela dei diritti umani, non discriminazione e orientamento sessuale* (Napoli, Editoriale Scientifica, 2016)

de Vergottini, G, *Oltre il dialogo tra le Corti. Giudici, diritto straniero, comparazione* (Bologna, Il Mulino, 2010)

de Visser, M, *Constitutional Review in Europe. A Comparative Analysis* (Oxford, Hart Publishing, 2014)

Devlin, P, *The Enforcement of Morals* (Oxford, Oxford University Press, 1965)

Diduck, A and Canagas, F, *Family Law, Gender and the State. Text, Cases and Materials*, 3rd edn (Oxford, Hart Publishing, 2012)

Dorsen, N, Rosenfeld, R, Sajó, A and Baer, S, *Comparative Constitutionalism. Cases and Materials* (St Paul MN, West Publishing Company, 2003)

Dupré, C, *Importing the Law in Post-Communist Transitions: The Hungarian Constitutional Court and the Right to Human Dignity* (Oxford, Hart Publishing, 2003)

Dupré, C, *The Age of Dignity: Human Rights and Constitutionalism in Europe* (Oxford, Hart Publishing, 2015)

Dürig, G, 'Der Grundrechtssatz von der Menschenwürde' (1956) 81 *Archiv des öffentlichen Rechts* 117

Dürig, G, 'Article 1' in T Maunz and G Dürig (eds), *Grundgesetz. Kommentar* (München, Beck, 1958)

Dworkin, R, *Life's Dominion: An Argument About Abortion, Euthanasia and Individual Freedom* (New York, Vintage Books, 1994)

Dworkin, R, *Is Democracy Possible Here?* (Princeton, Princeton University Press, 2006)

Eberle, EJ, *Dignity and liberty: constitutional visions in Germany and in the United States* (Westport CT, Praeger, 2001)

Eckert, J, 'Legal Roots of Human Dignity in German Law' in D Kretzmer and E Klein (eds), *The Concept of Human Dignity in Human Rights Discourse* (The Hague, Kluwer, 2002) 41

Edmiston, WF and Duménil, A, *La France contemporaine* (Boston, Heile Cencage, 2009)

Enders, C, *Die Menschenwürde in der Verfassungsordnung: Zur Dogmatik des Art 1 GG* (Tubingen, Mohr Siebeck, 1997)

Ennis, J, 'Marriage: Redefined and Realigned with *Bunreacht na hÉireann*' (2010) 1 *Irish Journal of Legal Studies* 29

Epstein, S, 'Gay Politics, Ethnic Identity: the Limits of Social Constructionism' in E Stein (ed), *Forms of Desire: Sexual Orientation and the Social Constructionist Controversy* (New York, Garland, 1990)

Eskridge, WN, *The Case for Same-Sex Marriage. From Sexual Liberty to Civilized Commitment* (New York, The Free Press, 1996)

Eskridge Jr, WN, *Gaylaw: Challenging the Apartheid of the Closet* (Cambridge MA, Harvard University Press, 1999)

Eskridge Jr, WN, 'The Ideological Structure of the Same-Sex Marriage Debate (and Some Postmodern Arguments for Same-Sex Marriage) in R Wintemute and M Andenæs (eds), *Legal Recognition of Same-Sex Partnerships* (Oxford, Hart Publishing, 2001) 113

Eskridge Jr, WN, *Equality Practice. Civil Unions and the Future of Gay Rights* (New York, Routledge, 2002)

Eskridge Jr, WN, 'Backlash Politics: How Constitutional Litigation Has Advanced Marriage Equality in the United States' (2003) 93 *Boston University Law Review* 275

Eskridge Jr, WN and Hunter, ND, *Sexuality, Gender and the Law* (New York, Foundation Press, 2004), 97

Falletti, E, 'Homosexual Single Individuals' Right to Adopt Before the European Court of Human Rights and in the French Legal Context' (2011) 18 *Human Rights Brief* 26

Falletti, E, 'Obbligo di fedeltà. Profili storici e di diritto comparato di un istituto non previsto nell'unione civile' (2016) 2 *GenIus, Rivista sull'orientamento sessuale e l'identità di genere*

Favoreau, L, 'Constitutional review in Europe' in L Henkin and AJ Rosenthal (eds), *Constitutionalism and Rights: The Influence of the United States Constitution Abroad* (New York, Columbia University Press, 1989)

Feldblum, CR, 'The Limitation of Liberal Neutrality Arguments' in R Wintemute and M Andenæs (eds), *Legal Recognition of Same-Sex Partnerships* (Oxford, Hart Publishing, 2001) 55

Ferejohn, J and Pasquino, P, 'Constitutional Adjudication: Lessons from Europe' (2003–04) 82 *Texas Law Review* 1671

Ferrarese, MR, *Il diritto al presente* (Bologna, Il Mulino, 2002)

Ferrari, GF, and Gambaro, A (eds), *Corti nazionali e comparazione giuridica* (Napoli, ESI, 2006)

Ferreres Comella, V, 'The European Model of Constitutional Review of Legislation: Toward Decentralization'? in (2004) 3 *International Journal of Constitutional Law* 461

Fidalgo de Freitas, T and Tega, D, 'Judicial Restraint and Political Responsibility: A Review of the Jurisprudence of the Italian, Spanish and Portuguese High Courts on Same-Sex Couples' in D Gallo and L Paladini and P Pustorino (eds), *Same-Sex Couples before National, Supranational and International Jurisdictions* (Heidelberg, Springer, 2015) 287

Finck, M, 'The Role of Human Dignity in Gay Rights Adjudication and Legislation: A Comparative Perspective' (2016) 14 *International Journal of Constitutional Law (ICon)* 26

Fontana, D and Braman, D, 'Judicial Backlash or Just Backlash? Evidence From a National Experience' (2012) 112 *Columbia Law Review* 731

Forde-Marzui, K, 'Tradition as Justification: The Case of Opposite-Sex Marriage' (2011) 78 *University of Chicago Law Review* 28

Franke, K, *The Perils of Marriage Equality. How African Americans and Gays Mistakenly Thought the Right to Marry Would Set Them Free* (New York, New York University Press, 2015)

Freeman, M, 'Article 3. The Best Interests of the Child' in A Alen, J Vande Lanotte, E Verhellen, F Ang, E Berghmans and M Verheyde (eds), *A Commentary on the United Nations Convention on the Rights of the Child* (Leiden, Nijhoff Publishers, 2007)

Fried, C, 'Privacy' (1968) 77 *Yale Law Journal* 475

Gallo, D and Paladini, L and Pustorino, P (eds), *Same-Sex Couples before National, Supranational and International Jurisdictions* (Heidelberg, Springer, 2015)

Gattuso, M, 'Cosa c'è nella legge sulle unioni civili: una prima guida' in *Articolo29*, www.Articolo29.it

Gattuso, M, 'La vittoria dei bambini arcobaleno' in *Articolo29*, www.Articolo29.it

Gentili, G, 'Canada' in T Groppi and MC Ponthoreau (eds), *The Use of Foreign Precedents by Constitutional Judges* (Oxford, Hart, 2013) 44

Gilissen, J, 'Le Probleme des Lacunes du Droit dans l'Evolution du Droit Medieval et Modeme' in C Perelman (ed), *Le Probleme des Lacunes en Droit* (Bruxelles, Bruylant, 1968) 197

Ginsburg, T, 'The Global Spread of Constitutional Review' in GA Caldeira, DR Keleman and KE Whittington (eds), *Oxford Handbook of Law and Politics*, Oxford Handbooks on Political Science (Oxford, Oxford University Press, 2008) 81

Gittins, D, *The Family in Question. Changing Households and Familiar Ideologies*, 2nd edn (Houndmills, Macmillan Press, 1993)

Glendon, MA, 'Power and Authority in the Family: New Legal Patterns as Reflections of Changing Ideologies' (1975) 23 *American Journal of Comparative Law* 1

Glendon, MA, *The Transformation of Family Law. State, Law and the Family in the United States and Western Europe* (Chicago, Chicago University Press, 1989)

Glendon, MA, Gordon, MW and Osakwe, C, *Comparative Legal Traditions* (St Paul MN, West Publishing Co, 1994)

Glenn, P, *Legal Traditions of the World*, 5th edn (Oxford, Oxford University Press, 2014)

Glennon, L, '*Fitzpatrick v Sterling Housing Association Ltd:* An Endorsement of the Functional Family?' (2000) *International Journal of Law, Policy and the Family* 226

Glensy, RC, 'The Right to Dignity' (2011) 43 *Columbia Human Rights Law Review* 65

Gonzales Beilfuss, C, 'All or Nothing: the Dilemma of Southern Jurisdictions' in K Boele-Woelki and A Fuchs (eds), *Legal Recognition of Same-Sex Relationships in Europe. National, Cross-Border and European Perspectives*, 2nd edn (Cambridge, Intersentia, 2012) 46

Gonzaléz Pérez, J, *La dignidad humana de la persona* (Madrid, Civitas, 1983)

Goodman, MD, 'Human Dignity in Supreme Court Constitutional Jurisprudence' (2006) 84 *Nebraska Law Review* 740

Greenhouse, L and Siegel, R, 'Before (and After) Roe v. Wade' (2011) 120 *Yale Law Journal* 2028

Grigolo, M, 'Sexualities and the ECHR: Introducing the Universal Sexual Legal Subject' (2003) 14 *European Journal of International Law* 1023

Groppi, T, 'The Italian Constitutional Court: Towards a Multi-level System of Judicial Review? (2008) 3 *Journal of Comparative Law* 100

Groppi T and Ponthoreau MC (eds), *The Use of Foreign Precedents by Constitutional Judges* (Oxford, Hart Publishing, 2013)

Gröschner, R, 'Ehe und Familie, Elternrecht, Mutterschutz, uneheliche Kinder (Arktikel 6)' in H Dreier (ed), *Grundgesetz Kommentar*, 2nd edn, vol 1 (Tubingen, Mohr Siebeck, 2004) 750

Guastini, R, *Le fonti del diritto. Fondamenti teorici* (Milano, Giuffrè, 2010)

Gutiérrez Gutiérrez, I, *Dignidad de la persona y derechos fundamentales* (Madrid, Marcial Pons, 2005)

Häberle, P, 'Menschenwürde und Verfassung, am Beispiel von Art. 2 Abs. 1 Verf. Griechenland 1975' (1980) *Rechtstheorie*, 389 ff.

Häberle, P, *Rechtsvergleichnung im Kraftfeld des Verfassungsstates* (Berlin, Dunker & Humblot, 1992)

Häberle, P, 'Die Menschenwürde als Grundlage der staatlichen Gemeinschaft' in J Isensee, P Kirchhof (eds), *Handbuch des Deutschen Staats- und Verfassungsrechts*, 3rd edn (Heidelberg, Muller Verlag, 2004), vol 1, 317 ff

Halley, J, 'Recognition, Rights, Regulation, Normalisation' in R Wintemute and M Andenæs (eds), *Legal Recognition of Same-Sex Partnerships* (Oxford, Hart Publishing, 2001) 104

Hantrais, L and Letablier, MT, *Families and Family Policies in Europe* (London, Routledge, 2014)

Harris-Short, S and Miles, J, *Family Law: Text, Cases and Materials* (Oxford University Press, Oxford, 2011)

Hart, L, 'Individual Adoption by non-Heterosexual and the Order of Family Life in the European Court of Human Rights' (2009) 36 *Journal of Law and Society* 536

Helfer, LR, 'Will the UNHRC Require Recognition of Same-Sex Marriages?' in R Wintemute and M Andenæs, M (eds), *Legal Recognition of Same-Sex Partnerships* (Oxford, Hart Publishing, 2001) 732

Herdegen, M, 'Article 1' in T Maunz and G Dürig (eds), *Grundgesetz. Kommentar* (München, Beck, 2009)

Hildebrandt, A, 'Routes to decriminalization: A Comparative Analysis of the Legalization of Same-Sex Sexual Acts' (2014) 17 *Sexualities* 230

Hirschl, R, *Towards Juristocracy* (Cambridge MA, Harvard University Press, 2004)

Hirschl, R, 'The Question of Case Selection in Comparative Constitutional Law' (2005) 53 *American Journal of Comparative Law* 125

Hitchings E, '*Mendoza v Ghaidan*: Two Steps Forward, One Step Back' (2003) 15 *Family Law Quarterly* 313

Hoare, L, 'France's gays are assimilating. What comes next?', *Slate.com* (10 August 2015)

Hofmann, H, 'Die versprochene Menschenwürde' (1993) 118 *Archiv des öffentlichen Rechts* 353

Hooghe M and Meeusen C, 'Is Same-Sex Marriage Legislation Related to Attitudes Toward Homosexuality? Trends in Tolerance of Homosexuality in European Countries Between 2002 and 2010' (2013) 10 *Sexuality Research and Social Policy* 258

ILGA Europe, *Attitudes towards marriage equality in 51 countries*, Survey of May 2015, www.old.ilga.org

Jackson, VC, 'Constitutional Dialogue and Human Dignity: States and Transnational Constitutional Discourse' (2004) 65 *Montana Law Review* 15

Jackson, VC, 'Constitutional Comparison: Convergence, Resistance, Engagement' (2005) 119 *Harvard Law Review* 109

Jackson, VC, *Constitutional Engagement in a Transnational Era* (Oxford, Oxford University Press, 2009)

Jackson, VC and Tushnet, M, *Comparative Constitutional Law*, 2nd edn (New York, Foundation Press, 2006)

Jaurena i Salas, F, 'The Law of Stable Unions of Couples the Catalonia Autonomous Community of Spain' in R Wintemute and M Andenæs (eds), *Legal Recognition of Same-Sex Partnerships* (Oxford, Hart Publishing, 2001) 505

Jemolo, AC, *La famiglia e il diritto* (Naples, Annali del Seminario Giuridico dell'Università di Catania, 1949)

Johnson, P, '"An Essentially Private Manifestation of Human Personality": Constructions of Homosexuality in the European Court of Human Rights', (2010) 10 *Human Rights Law Review* 67

Johnson, P, *Homosexuality and the European Court of Human Rights* (Abingdon, Routledge, 2013)

Kant, I, *Groundwork of the metaphysics of morals*, transl M Gregor, introduction by CM Korsgaard (Cambridge, Cambridge University Press, 1997)

Karst, KL, 'The Liberties of Equal Citizens: Groups and the Due Process Clause' (2007) 55 *UCLA Law Review* 99

Keck, ME and Sikkink, K, *Activists Beyond Borders: Advocacy Networks in International Politics* (Ithaca, Cornell University Press, 1998)

Klarman, MJ, 'Brown and Lawrence (and Goodridge)' (2005) 104 *Michigan Law Review* 431

Klarman, MJ, '*Windsor* and *Brown:* Marriage Equality and Racial Equality' (2013) 127 *Harvard Law Review* 127

Klarman, MJ, *From the Closet to the Altar. Courts, Backlash and the Struggle for Same-Sex Marriage* (Oxford University Press, Oxford, 2013)

Klein, E, 'Human Dignity in German Law' in D Kretzmer and E Klein (eds), *The Concept of Human Dignity in Human Rights Discourse* (The Hague, Kluwer, 2002) 145

Koh, HH,'International Law as Part of Our Law' (2004) 98 *American Journal of International Law* 43

Kommers, DP and Miller, RA, *The Constitutional Jurisprudence of the Federal Republic of Germany* (Durham, Duke University Press, 2012)

L'Heureax-Dubé, C, 'From Many Different Stones: A House of Justice' (2003) 41 *Alberta Law Review* 659

Lamarque, E, 'Interpreting Statutes in Conformity with the Constitution: The Role of the Italian Constitutional Court and Ordinary Judges' (2010) 1 *Italian Journal of Public Law* 91

Lamarque, E, *Prima i bambini. Il principio dei best interest of the child nella prospettiva costituzionale* (Milano, Franco Angeli, 2016)

Lecis Cocco Ortu, AM, 'Le unioni di persone dello stesso sesso in Francia: dai PaCS alla sentenza sul *mariage homosexual*' (2011) 2 *Ianus* 213

Lewis, M, 'A Brief History of Human Dignity' in J Malpas and N Lickiss (eds), '*Perspectives on Human Dignity. A Conversation*' (Dordrecht, Springer, 2007), 93

Luhmann, N, *Grundrechte als Institution* (Berlin, Duncker & Humblot, 1965), 57 ff

Lund, N and McGinnis, JO, '*Lawrence v Texas* and the Judicial Hubris' (2004) 102 *Michigan Law Review* 1555, 1583

Luther, J, 'Ragionevolezza e dignità umana' in A Cerri and O Pfersmann (eds), *La ragionevolezza nella ricerca scientifica ed il suo ruolo specifico nel sapere giuridico* (Rome, Aracne, 2007) 185

Malfatti E, Panizza S, Romboli R, *Giustizia costituzionale*, 5th edn (Torino, Giappichelli, 2016)

Malpas, J and Lickiss, N (eds), '*Perspectives on Human Dignity. A Conversation*' (Dordrecht, Springer, 2007)

Markesinis, B, and Fedtke, J, *Judicial Recourse to Foreign Law. A New Source of Inspiration?* (London, Routledge, 2006)

Martín Casals, M, 'Same-Sex Partnerships in the Legislation of Spanish Autonomous Communities' in K Boele-Woelki and A Fuchs (eds), *Legal Recognition of Same-Sex Couples in Europe* (Cambridge, Intersentia, 2003) 58

Martiny, D, 'Private International Law Aspects of Same-Sex Couples under German Law' in K Boele-Woelki and A Fuchs (eds), *Legal Recognition of Same-Sex Relationships in Europe. National, Cross-Border and European Perspectives* (Cambridge, Intersentia, 2012) 189

Massa Pinto, I and Tripodina, C, 'Sul come per la Corte costituzionale le "unioni omosessuali non possono essere ritenute omogenee al matrimonio". Ovvero tecniche argomentative impiegate per motivare la sentenza 138/2010' (2010) *Diritto Pubblico*, n 1-2, 471

Mathieu, B, 'Decision du Conseil constitutionnel sur le mariage homosexuel' (30 May 2013), www.bertrandmathieu.fr

McCrudden, C, 'Human Dignity and Judicial Interpretation of Human Rights' (2008) 19 *European Journal of International Law* 656

McCrudden, C (ed), *Understanding Human Dignity* (Oxford, Oxford University Press, 2013)

McFadden, P, 'Provincialism in United States Courts' (1995) 81 *Cornell Law Review* 4

Merlin, Y, *Equality for Same-Sex Couples. The Legal Recognition of Gay Partnerships in Europe and the United States* (Chicago, University of Chicago Press, 2002)

Meulders-Klein, MT, 'Individualisme et communautarisme: l'individu, la famille et l'État en Europe occidentale' (1993) 23–24 *Droit et société* 163

Michelman, FI, 'Reflection' (2004) 82 *Texas Law Review* 1737

Millbank, J, 'The Role of Functional Family in Same-Sex Family Recognition Trends' (2008) 20 *Child & Family Law Quarterly* 155

Morrassutto, L, 'Vagiti e manette. L'emendamento Dalla Zuanna: una proposta tecnicamente irricevibile' in *Articolo29*, www.Articolo29.it

NeJaime, D, 'Constitutional Change, Courts and Social Movements' (2013) 111 *Michigan Law Review* 877

NeJaime, D, '*Windsor*'s Right to Marry' (2013) 123 *Yale Law Journal Online* 219, www.yalelawjournal.org/forum/windsors-right-to-marry

Note: 'Looking for a Family Resemblance: the Limits of the Functional approach to the Legal Definition of Family' (1991) 4 *Harvard Law Review* 1640

Nussbaum, M, *From Disgust to Humanity. Sexual Orientation and Constitutional Law* (Oxford, Oxford University Press, 2009)

O'Donovan, K, *Sexual Divisions in Law* (London, Weinfeld & Nicholson, 1985)

O'Mahoney, C, 'There is no such thing as a right to dignity' (2012) 10 *International Journal of Constitutional Law (Icon)* 551

Paust, J, 'Human Dignity as a Constitutional Right: A Jurisprudentially Based Inquiry into Criteria and Content' (1984) 27 *Howard Law Journal* 145

Peces Barba, G, *La dignidad de la persona desde la Filosofía del Derecho* (Madrid, Dykinson, 2002)

Peces Barba, G, *Lecciones de derechos fundamentales* (Madrid, Dykinson, 2004)

Pico della Mirandola, G, Oration *On the Dignity of Man*, 1486, transl, F Borghesi, M Sapio, and M Riva (Cambridge, Cambridge University Press, 2012) 107 ff

Pierceson, J, *Same-Sex Marriage in the United States. The Road to the Supreme Court* (Lanham, Rowman & Littlefield Publishers, 2013)

Pizzorusso, A, *Delle fonti del diritto* (Bologna, Zanichelli, 1977)

Pizzorusso, A, 'Italian and American Models of the Judiciary and of Judicial Review of Legislation: A Comparison of Recent Tendencies' (1990) 38 *American Journal of Comparative Law* 373

Pizzorusso, A, *Sistemi giuridici comparati* (Milano, Giuffrè, 1998)

Pocar, V and Ronfani, P, *La famiglia e il diritto* (Bari, Laterza, 2003)

Podlech, A, 'Art. 1 Abs I' in *Alternativkommentar zum Grundgesetz*, I (Newwied, Kriftel, 1989)

Ponthoreau, MC, 'Le recours à l'argument de droit compare par le juge constitutionnel. Quelques problèmes théoriques et techniques', in F Mélin-Soucramanien (ed), *L'interprétation constitutionnelle* (Paris, Dalloz, 2005) 167

Portalis, JEM *Discours préliminaire du premier projet de Code civil* (1801)

Posner, RA, 'No Thanks, We Already Have Our Own Laws: The Court Should Never View a Foreign Legal Decision as a Precedent in Any Way' (2004) 7/8 *Legal Affairs*, legalaffairs.org/issues/July-August-2004/featureposnerjulaug04.msp

Posner, RA, 'The Supreme Court, 2004 Term: Foreword: A Political Court' (2005) 119 *Harvard Law Review* 31, 84–90

Post, R and Siegel, R, 'Originalism as Political Practice: The Right's Living Constitution' (2006) 75 *Fordham Law Review* 545

Rao, N, 'On the Use and Abuse of Dignity in Constitutional Law' (2008) 14 *Columbia Journal European Law* 201

Rao, N, 'Three concepts of dignity' (2011) 86 *Notre Dame Law Review* 183

Regan, MC, *Family Law and the Pursuit of Intimacy* (New York University Press, New York, 1993)

Repetto, G, 'At the Crossroads Between Privacy and Community: the Legal Status of Same-Sex Couples in German, Austrian and Swiss law' in D Gallo and L Paladini and P Pustorino (eds), *Same-Sex Couples before National, Supranational and International Jurisdictions* (Heidelberg, Springer, 2015) 263

Report of the Committee on Sexual Offences and Prostitution ('Wolfenden Report') (London, Her Majesty's Stationery Office, 1957)

Reyniers, P, 'Same-Sex Couples in France and Belgium: the Resilient Practise of Judicial Deference' in D Gallo and L Paladini and P Pustorino (eds), *Same-Sex Couples before National, Supranational and International Jurisdictions* (Heidelberg, Springer, 2015) 249

Ridola, P, 'Libertà e diritti nello sviluppo storico del costituzionalismo' in R Nania and P Ridola (eds) *I diritti costituzionali* (Torino, Giappichelli, 2006) 3

Rodriguéz Martinez, ME, *La legislación autonómica sobre uniones de hecho. Revisión desde la Constitución* (Valencia, Editorial Tirant lo blanch, 2003)

Rodríguez Ruiz, B, 'Matrimonio, género y familia en la Constitución Española: Transcendiendo la familia nuclear' (2011) 91 *Revista española de derecho constitucional* 69

Romboli, R, 'Il diritto "consentito" al matrimonio ed il diritto "garantito" alle coppie omosessuali in una pronuncia in cui la Corte dice "troppo" e "troppo poco" (2010) *Giurisprudenza costituzionale* 1629

Rose, N, 'Beyond the public/Private Division: Law, Power and the Family' (1987) 14 *Journal Law and Society* 61

Rosen, J, 'The Dangers of a Constitutional Right to Dignity', *The Atlantic*, 29 April 2015, www.theatlantic.com/politics/archive/2015/04/the-dangerous-doctrine-of-dignity/391796

Rosenberg, GN, 'Courting Disaster: Looking for Change in the Wrong Place' (2006) 54 *Drake Law Review* 795

Rosenberg, GN, *The Hollow Hope: Can Courts Bring About Social Change?*, 2nd edn (Chicago, Chicago University Press, 2008)

Rosenfeld, M, 'Constitutional Adjudication in Europe and the United States: Paradoxes and Contrasts' (2004) 2 *International Journal of Constitutional Law* 633

Rosenfeld, M, Sadurski, W and Toniatti, R, 'Central and Eastern European Constitutionalism a Quarter of a Century After the Fall of the Berlin Wall: Introduction to the Symposium' (2015) 13 *International Journal of Constitutional Law* 119

Rosenfeld, M and Sajó, A (eds), *The Oxford Handbook of Comparative Constitutional Law* (Oxford, Oxford University Press, 2012)

Rousseau, D, 'L'art italien au Conseil constitutionnel: les décisions de 6 et 14 octobre 2010' (2010) *Gazette du Palais* 12

Rubellin-Devichi, J, 'The Best Interests Principle in French Law and Pracise' 8 (1994) *International Journal of Law, Policy and the Family* 259

Sáez, M (ed), *Same Sex Couples—Comparative Insights on Marriage and Cohabition* (Heidelberg, Springer, 2015)

Salford, H, 'Concepts of Family Under the EU Law: Lessons From the ECHR' (2002) 16 *International Journal of Law, Policy and the Family* 410

Sánchez, MM, *Matrimonio homosexual y Constitución* (Valencia, Editorial Tirant lo Blanch, 2008)

Sanders, AEH, 'Marriage, Same-Sex Relationships, and the German Constitution' (2012) 13 *German Law Journal* 911

Sanders, AEH, 'When, if not Now? An Update on Civil Partnership in Germany' (2016) 17 *German Law Journal* 487

Saraceno, C and Naldini, M, *Sociologia della famiglia* (Bologna, Il Mulino, 2013)

Schabas, WA, *The European Convention on Human Rigths. A Commentary* (Oxford, Oxford University Press, 2015)

Schacter, JS, 'Lawrence v. Texas and the Fourteenth Amendment's Democratic Aspirations' (2004) 13 *Temple Political & Civil Rights Law Review* 733

Schacter, JS, 'Sexual Orientation, Social Change and the Courts' (2006) 54 *Drake Law Review* 861

Schacter, JS, 'Courts and the Politics of Backlash: Marriage Equality Litigation Then and Now' (2009) 82 *Southern California Law Review* 1153

Scheffler, S, *Equality and Tradition. Questions of Value in Moral and Political Theory* (Oxford, Oxford University Press, 2010)

Schillaci, A (ed), *Omosessualità, eguaglianza, diritti* (Roma, Carocci, 2014)

Schillaci, A, 'La sentenza perfetta. Paternità omosessuale e diritti de bambino', *www.articolo29.it*

Schimmel, R and Heun, S, 'The Legal Situation of Same-Sex Partnership in Germany: An Overview' in R Wintemute and M Andenæs (eds), *Legal Recongnition of Same-Sex Partnerships* (Oxford, Hart Publishing, 2001) 575

Sedwick, E, *Epistemology of the Closet* (Harmondsworth, Penguin, 1990)

Severino, C, *La doctrine du droit vivant* (Paris, Economica-PUAM, 2003)

Shapiro, M, Stone Sweet, A, 'The New Constitutional Politics of Europe' (1994) 26 *Comparative Political Studies* 397

Siegel, RB, 'Dignity and Sexuality: Claims of Dignity in Transnational Debates over Abortion and Same-sex Marriages' (2012) 10 *International Journal of Constitutional Law* 355

Siegel, RB, 'Foreword: Equality Divided' (2013) 127 *Harvard Law Review* 9

Silvestri, G, *Dal potere ai principi. Libertà ed eguaglianza nel costituzionalismo contemporaneo* (Bari, Laterza, 2009)

Slaughter, AM, 'A Global Community of Courts' (2003) 44 *Harvard International Law Journal* 191

Slaughter, AM, *A New World Order* (Princeton, Princeton University Press, 2004)

Songer, D, *The Transformation of the Supreme Court of Canada: An Empirical Examination* (Toronto, Toronto University Press, 2008)

Sperti, A, *Corti Supreme e conflitti tra poteri. Spunti per un confronto Italia-USA sugli strumenti e le tecniche di giudizio* (Torino, Giappichelli, 2005)

Sperti, A, 'Il dialogo tra le corti ed il ricorso alla comparazione nell'esperienza più recente' (2006) *Rivista di diritto costituzionale*, 125

Sperti, A, 'United States of America: First Cautious Attempts of Judicial Use of Foreign Precedents in the Supreme Court's Jurisprudence' in T Groppi and MC Ponthoreau (eds), *The Use of Foreign Precedents by Constitutional Judges* (Oxford, Hart Publishing, 2013) 393

Sperti, A, *Omosessualità e diritti. I percorsi giurisprudenziali ed il dialogo globale delle Corti costituzionali* (Pisa, Pisa University Press, 2013)

Stein, E, 'Uses, Misuses—and Nonuses of Comparative Law' (1977) 72 *Northwestern University Law Review* 198

Stone Sweet, A, 'The Politics of Constitutional Review in France and Europe', (2007) 5 *International Journal of Constitutional Law* 69

Stone Sweet, A and Shapiro, M, *On Courts, Politics and Judicialization* (Oxford, Oxford University Press, 2002)

Strasser, M, *On Same-Sex Marriage, Civil Unions and the Rule of Law. Constitutional Interpretation at the Crossroads*, (Westport, Praeger, 2002)

Strasser, M, 'Adoption and the Best Interests of the Child: on the Use and Abuse of Studies' (2004) 38 *New England Law Review* 629

Sunstein, CR, 'Due Process Traditionalism' (2008) 106 *Michigan Law Review* 1543

Taylor, C, 'The Politics of Recognition' in A Gutmann (ed), *Multiculturalism and 'The Politics of Recognition'* (Chicago, Chicago University Press, 1992) 25

Théry, I and Biet, C, *La famille, la loi, l'Etat. De la Revolution au code civil* (Paris, Iprimerie Nationale, Ed du Centre George Pompidou, 1989)

Thomlinson, E, 'Same-sex relationships: going with the grain or judicial vandalism?' (2004) 63 *Cambridge Law Journal* 577

Tollefsen, C, 'The Dignity of Marriage' in C McCrudden (ed), *Understanding Human Dignity* (Oxford, Oxford University Press, 2013)

Torres, G, 'Some Observations on the Role of Social Change on Courts' (2006) 54 *Drake Law Review* 895

Tribe LH, '*Lawrence v Texas*: the "Fundamental Right" That Dare not Speak its Name' (2004) 117 *Harvard Law Review* 1893

Tribe, LH, 'The Constitutional Inevitability' of Same-Sex Marriage (2012) 71 *Maryland Law Review* 471

Tribe, LH, 'Equal Dignity: Speaking Its Name' (2015) 129 *Harvard Law Review Forum* 16

Tribe, LH and Dorf, MC, 'Levels of Generality in the Definition of Rights', (1990) 57 *University of Chicago Law Review* 1057

Tushnet, M, 'The Possibilities of Comparative Constitutional Law' (1999) 108 *Yale Law Journal* 1225

Villaverde, JML, 'And the Story come to an End: the Constitutionality of Same-Sex Marriages in Spain' in M Sáez (ed), *Same Sex Couples—Comparative Insights on Marriage and Cohabition* (Heidelberg, Springer, 2015), 13

Waldron, J, 'Dignity and Rank' (2007) 48 *European Journal of Sociology* 201

Waldron, J, *Dignity, Rank and Rights*, ed Meir Dan-Cohen (Oxford, Oxford University Press, 2012)

Warren, S and Brandeis, L, 'The Right to Privacy' (1890) 193 *Harvard Law Review* 220

Weeks, J, *Sex Politics and Society. The Regulation of Sexuality Since 1800* (London, Longman, 1989)

Whitman, JQ, 'The Two Western Cultures of Privacy: Dignity Versus Liberty' (2004) 113 *Yale Law Journal* 1151

Wintemute, R, *Sexual Orientation and Human Rights: The United States Constitution, the European Convention, and the Canadian Charter* (Oxford, Clarendon Press, 1995)

Wintemute, R, 'Lesbian and Gay Inequality 2000: The Potential of the Human Rights Act 1998 and the Need for an Equality Act' (2000) 6 *European Human Rights Law Review* 603

Wintemute, R, 'Strasbourg to the Rescue? Same-Sex Partners and Parents Under the European Convention' in R Wintemute and M Andenæs, M (eds), *Legal Recognition of Same-Sex Partnerships* (Oxford, Hart Publishing, 2001) 713

Wintemute, R, 'Sexual Orientation and the Charter: The Achievement of Formal Legal Equality (1985–2005) and Its Limits' (2004) 49 *McGill Law Journal* 1143

Wintemute, R, 'From "Sex Rights" to "Love Rights": Partnership Rights as Human Rights', in N Bamforth (ed), *Sex Rights. The Oxford Amnesty Lectures 2002* (Oxford, Oxford University Press, 2005)

Wintemute, R, 'Marriage, adoption, and donor insemination for same-sex couples: does European case law impose any obligations on Italy?' (2014) 2 *GenIUS* 35

Wintemute, R and Andenæs, M (eds), *Legal Recognition of Same-Sex Partnerships* (Oxford, Hart Publishing, 2001)

Wolfson, E, 'Crossing the Threshold: Equal Marriage Rights for Lesbians and Gay Men and the Intra-Community Critique' (1994) 21 *New York University Review of Law and Social Change* 567

Yoshino, K, 'The New Equal Protection' (2011) 124 *Harvard Law Review* 747

Yoshino, K, *Speak Now. Marriage Equality on Trial. The History of Hollingsworth v Perry* (New York, Broadway Books, 2015)

Yoshino, K, 'A New Birth of Freedom?' (2016) 129 *Harvard Law Review* 147

Yoshino, K, and Kavey, M, 'Immodest claims and Modest Contributions: Sexual Orientation in Comparative Constitutional Law' in M Rosenfeld and A Sajó (eds), *The Oxford Handbook of Comparative Constitutional Law* (Oxford, Oxford University Press, 2012) 1079

Zagrebelsky, G, 'Corti costituzionali e diritti universali' (2006) *Rivista Trimestrale di Diritto Pubblico* 297

Zylan, Y, *States of Passion: Law, Identity, and Social Construction of Desire* (Oxford, Oxford University Press, 2011)

Index

Note: Alphabetical arrangement is word-by-word, where a group of letters followed by a space is filed before the same group of letters followed by a letter, eg 'ethnic origin' will appear before 'ethnicity'. In determining alphabetical arrangement, initial articles and prepositions are ignored.

abortion, 2, 33, 82, 176,196
adoption:
  couples incapable of procreation, 179
  Austria, *see* Austria
  Canada, *see* Canada
  France, *see* France
  Germany, *see* Germany
  Italy, *see* Italy
  joint, 18, 192–95 (*see also individual countries*)
  Portugal, *see* Portugal
  second-parent (or stepchild), 187–92 (*see individual countries*)
  single parent, 182–86 (*see also individual countries*)
  South Africa, *see* South Africa
  Spain, see *Spain*
  successive, 102, 174–76
  Switzerland, *see* Switzerland
  United Kingdom, *see* United Kingdom
  United States, *see* United States
affection, between partners or spouses, 63, 65–66, 70, 75, 132
age discrimination, 141
anti-miscegenation laws, 120, 144, 176
antisubordination principle, 168
assimilation,
  between family and the opposite-sex couple, 76
  and diversity, 140
Australia, Tasmania, 20, 47–8
Austria:
  second-parent (or stepchild) adoption in, 173–74
  families, 63, 65–7
autonomy,
  in relation to dignity, 147–48, 154–55, 161–64
  of civil partnership, 101
  of ordinary courts, 104
  of self, 31–32, 34–6, 42–43, 45, 52, 54, 56, 62, 146,155, 161–62
  see also self-determination

backlash, judicial, 80–5, 88–9, 91, 103, 109, 113
Balkin, J, 131
Ball, CA, 182, 192
Bamforth, N, 66
Belgium,
  constitutional court (*Cour d'arbitrage*) 3, 132
  definition of family in, 50
  introduction of same-sex marriage in, 86, 132n
belief:
  and autonomy, 31,34, 162
  discrimination, 36, 120,141, 153
best interests of children, *see* children
birth discrimination, 140
Bonini Baraldi, M, 77
'boomerang pattern of influence' of *Dudgeon* at international level, 45–8
British Columbia:
  same-sex marriage, 81, 136

California:
  Constitution, marriage, procreation argument, 178–79
  Proposition 8, 178
  Supreme Court, dignity and equality, 159–60
Canada:
  Charter of Rights, *see* Table of Legislation
  traditional definition of marriage, 111
  dignity, 81, 144, 156–57, 160
  equal marriage, lower courts' contribution to paths towards, 81–82, 107, 135–36
  equality, 143–44, 156, 160
  family:
    definition, 56, 86
    formalistic definition of, 58
    functional definition of, 59–61
    'unexamined consensus' in definition of 'family', 56–61, 67, 69, 80
  Human Rights Act 1985, 56–58
  same-sex marriage, 10, 80–2
    procreation argument, 179–80
    separation of powers, 135
    tradition in cases, 111, 114, 118, 132–35
  sexual orientation discrimination, 57, 80
  Supreme Court:
    citation by foreign courts, 10, 14, 137
    dignity, 160
    essential core of marriage, identification of, 118
    foreign precedents use, 10, 14, 139
    legal tradition, 114, 118, 134–35
    same-sex marriage, procreation argument, 179
  see also individual provinces
Carozza, PG, 141
Central and Eastern Europe:
  constitutional courts, 3, 167

Charter of Rights, Canada, *see* Table of Legislation
children:
  best interests, 171–76, 182–88, 191–92, 194–95
  custody on divorce, 83, 182–84
  definition of 'family', 58–59, 70, 73, 107
  gays' and lesbians' aptitude to bring up, 3, 102, 108, 186
  gays' and lesbians' right to bear or to raise, 33, 63–65, 75, 163, 171
  in French civil code, 52
  'normal family life', rights to, 18, 96, 182–95
  principle of protection of family and, 88, 93, 99
  protection through 'traditional' family, *see* 'optimal parenting argument'
  protection through same-sex marriage, 157, 188
  as right-holders, 172
  'right to have a child', 171, 192
Chirac, Jacques, 92
circular reasoning risk, 100, 121, 132–34
Civil Codes, *see* Table of Legislation
civil law legal systems:
  and centralised judicial review of legislation, 107, 109
  common law legal systems, convergence between, 4
  families, regulation, 52, 58
  sex-difference in marriage tradition, 111
civil partnerships, 55
  Germany, 99–102, 175, 181
  to same-sex marriage from, 80–5
  see also same-sex civil unions and individual countries
civil rights:
  equality and diversity in debate, 140–41
  United States, 167–68
civil solidarity pact (PaCS, *pacte civil de solidarieté*), France, *see* France
civil unions, same-sex, *see* same-sex civil unions
closed-ended formulaic approach, 124
Code Napoléon, *see* Table of Legislation
cohabitation:
  in the definition of family, 66, 71, 74–75
  France (*concubinage*), 92
  in German definition of marriage, 100
  unmarried, 77–8, 80, 183, 185
colour discrimination, 140
common law:
  civil law systems, convergence between, 4
  equal marriage cases, 143–44
  families, regulation, 16, 52–4, 67
  open-ended approach, 123–24
  sex-difference in marriage tradition, 111–13
common law spouses, 80–81, 99
common life
  (*vie commune*), France, 93–4
  in Italian regulation of same-sex civil unions, 79
comparative law
  idea of marriage in, 8–9, 137
  use of materials of, 9–11, 13, 42, 75, 138
comparative method, 6–8
concubinage (*cohabitation*), France, 92
Conseil constitutionnel, France, *see* France
Cour d'arbitrage, *see* Belgium
consensual same-sex sexual acts, 37–8
consequences of marriage
  legal, 99, 142
  in terms of dignity, 146, 149
constitutional change,
  in connection with the model of judicial review, 85
  and judicial backlash, 82–85
  constitutional courts' role in, 4, 6, 16–17, 40, 48, 80–85, 103
  ordinary courts role in, 105
constitutional courts, 1, 2, 7
  centralised, 3
  constitutional change, *see* constitutional change
  cooperation with legislators, 89, 108
  dialogue with foreign counterparts, 3, 21, 8–15, 137–40
  European, 106, 149, 167
  foreign legal developments, reliance on, 8–15,137–40
  global community of, 3
  judicial backlash, *see* judicial backlash
  legal tradition, 117
  newly established, 2, 10
  ordinary courts and, different roles:
    advancement of rights, 136
    promoting equal marriage, 102–109
  procreative nature of marriage and, 176–82
  see also individual countries
constitutional tribunals, *see* constitutional courts
constitutionalism, 2, 165
constitutions:
  construing legislation in conformity with, 104
  definition of families, 50, 54
  'effectiveness of rights', 150
  evolutionary interpretation of, 138–39
  European:
    dignity, 151–54, 167
    liberty and equality, 150–54
  grounds of discrimination in, 169
  liberal interpretations, 136
  sex difference in definitions of marriage, 109–15
  see also individual countries
constructionist theories of homosexuality, 23
contraception:
  United States privacy and self-determination jurisprudence, 64
Convention of the Rights of the Child, *see* Table of Legislation
Council of Europe, 7, 20, 21, 37, 42, 61, 66, 192n
Cour de Cassation, *see* France
criminalisation of same-sex sexual acts, 16, 27–8, 30, 36, 41–42, 49, 125–26
cultural tradition in same-sex marriage cases, 119–22

customs, 114
Cyprus, legalisation of sexual acts, 19, 46

de Montaigne, Michel, 114
Declaration of the Rights of Man and of the Citizen, *see* Table of Legislation
decriminalisation:
  sexual acts, 1, 19–48, *see* individual countries
  sodomy laws, 15 *see* individual countries
demographic diversity, 167
Diduck, A, 70–1, 118
dignity, 44
  as autonomy and self-determination, 35, 147–48, 151–52, 154–55, 161–64
  Canada, *see* Canada
  common core, 154–55
  different meaning of, same-sex marriage cases, 154–64
  England and Wales, *see* England and Wales
  as fundamental legal value, 152, 155
  Germany, *see* Germany
  Greece, *see* Greece
  human identity, result of process of development of, 155
  Hungary, *see* Hungary
  identity formation and, 155
  as inherent worth of the individual, 35, 41, 144, 154, 158–61
  Ireland, *see* Ireland
  Italy, *see* Italy
  Kantian notion of, 151, 154
  of marriage, 100, 143–144, 146, 148, 165
  as obligation, 155
  personality, result of process of development of, 155
  Portugal, *see* Portugal
  and 'pluralism anxiety', 167–70
  purposes, 164–70
  as recognition claim, 156–58
  in relation to equality, 35, 42, 73, 143, 149, 153, 156–58
  in relation to liberty, 35, 143, 147, 151, 153
  in relation to privacy, 36, 42
  as respect, 144–45
  as rhetorical tool, 156
  as right, 155
  of same-sex couples, 73, 76, 79, 146, 149, 165, 169
  same-sex marriage, *see* same-sex marriage
  sexual orientation equality, 156–58
  as social recognition, 145, 148, 156–58
  social and expressive value of marriage, 143
  sociality of man, as aspect of, 41, 44, 153, 155
  South Africa, *see* South Africa
  Spain, *see* Spain
  as synthesis of liberty and equality, 149–54
  unified concept of, 158
  United States, *see* United States
  widespread judicial use of, 35, 141, 166–67
discrimination:
  age, 141
  belief, 141
  birth, 140
  colour, 140
  disability, 141
  ethnic origin, 141
  genetic features, 141
  grounds:
    enumerated, 58
    European Convention on Human Rights, 140
    European Union Charter of Fundamental Rights, 141
  language 140
  national minority association discrimination, 140
  national origin discrimination, 140
  overt, 1
  political, 140
  property, 140
  race, 140
  religious, 140
  sex 140
  sexual orientation, *see* sexual orientation
  social origin, 140, 141
  status 140
  vicious cycle perpetuating, 119–22
diversity:
  assimilation and, 140
  demographic, 167
  equality and, in civil rights debate, 140–41
  within equality, 150
divorce:
  child custody, 182–84
  Germany, 101
  'imposed', Italy, 78
Dorf, MC, 127, 128–31
double track model, 97, 147*see also* 'separate but equal'
Due Process Clause, *see* United States
Dupré, C, 165
Dürig, G, 154–55

Eastern Europe, *see* Central and Eastern Europe
England and Wales:
  adoption, 192n
  child custody on divorce, 183
  decriminalisation of same-sex sexual acts, 29
  definition of 'families', 53–4, 67–74
  definition of 'spouse', 71–74
  dignity, 161
  marriage, 53
  procreation argument, 179–80
enumerated rights, 122–32
equal marriage, 1, 4, 5
  'constitutional inevitability' of, 1, 81
  as final achievement of LGBT movements, 15, 109n
  as label, 141
  promoting, different roles of constitutional and ordinary courts, 102–109
  see also individual countries, marriage; same-sex marriage

equality:
  adjudication in pluralism anxiety, 168–70
  between same-sex civil unions and marriage, 181
  between spouses, 51, 77, 118–19
  Canada, *see* Canada
  diversity and, in civil rights debate, 140–41
  diversity within, 150
  European constitutions, 150–54
  expressive value of marriage and, 142–46
  formal, 142, 152, 154, 169–71
  France, *see* France
  Germany, *see* Germany
  implications, 141–49
  Ireland, *see* Ireland
  Italy, *see* Italy
  liberty and, dignity as synthesis of, 149–54
  marriage, 4, 81–82, 107, 114, 164
  Portugal, *see* Portugal
  in relation dignity, 35, 42, 74, 143, 147, 149, 153–58, 166–67
  in relation to liberty, 31–32, 57, 143, 147, 150–54, 163–67
  in relation to privacy, 47–48
  of responsibilities flowing from marriage, 146–49
  of rights flowing from marriage, 146–49
  in same-sex marriage cases, 141–48
  same-sex marriage, *see* same-sex marriage
  sexual orientation equality, *see* sexual orientation
  South Africa, *see* South Africa
  Spain, *see* Spain
  substantial, 152
  Tasmania, 47–8
  United States, *see* United States
Eskridge Jr, WN, 81, 82–4, 103, 107, 142, 145, 180
essential core, marriage, 17, 115–19, 131, 136, 138, 152
essentialist theories of homosexuality, 23–4
ethnic origin discrimination, 141
ethnicity, 140
European Convention on Human Rights (ECHR), *see* Table of Legislation
European Convention on the Adoption of Children, *see* Table of Legislation
European Court of Human Rights (ECtHR), 1
  best interests of the child, 173, 184–86
  child custody on divorce, 183–84
  construction of homosexuality, 21–27
  family:
    definition, 50
    early cases, 61–65
    same-sex couple as, 65–67, 159, 166
    life, right to, 62–67, 106
  Dudgeon v United Kingdom as a global landmark case, 19–21, 30, 37, 46–47
  privacy, 21, 26–30, 39, 41, 61–5
  private life v family life, 61–5
  sexual orientation, ground of discrimination, 22, 41, 72, 183–84
  second-parent adoption, 187–92
  single parent adoption, 184–86
European model of constitutionalism, 2, 165
European Union Charter of Fundamental Rights, *see* Table of Legislation

families:
  affection, 65
  Austria,*see* Austria
  Canada *see* Canada
  definition:
    'common sense' in, 67–71
    formalistic, 58
    functional, 56–61, 67–71, 72, 76
    heteronormative, 61–62
    as natural institution founded on marriage, 50–51, 54, 77
    as social institution, 51, 55
    traditional, 36, 63, 67, 178, 190
    'unexamined consensus' in, 56–61
  England, *see* England
  European Court of Human Rights, *see* European Court of Human Rights
  Finland, *see* Finland
  France, *see* France
  Germany, *see* Germany
  Greece, *see* Greece
  heterosexuality and, 67, 73–4, 76–7, 87
  Ireland, *see* Ireland
  Israel, *see* Israel
  Italy, *see* Italy
  life, *see* family life
  long-term commitment, 65
  Luxembourg, *see* Luxemburg
  narrow interpretation, 76–9
  from 'perception of the ordinary man' to functional definition of, 67–71
  Poland, *see* Poland
  Portugal, *see* Portugal
  private life v family life, 61–5
  public–private dichotomy, 49–56
  in relation to marriage, 50, 77, 89, 97–100, 105, 110, 115, 129, 181
  regulation models, 49–56
  respect, 65
  same-sex couples:
    recognition as 'family', 55–61, 65–71, 94, 108, 174
    as spouses, 71–4
  South Africa, *see* South Africa
  Spain, *see* Spain
  status, 56–61, 67
  tenancy successions, 67–74
  United States, *see* United States
family life:
  collective right, 64
  de facto, 67, 77, 190, 192
  'normal', children's rights to, 182–95
  private life and, distinguishing, 61–5
  in relation to marriage, 138

same-sex relationships, 29–30
see also families; parental rights
Federal Constitutional Tribunal, Germany, *see* Germany
Fedtke, J, 12
Finck, M, 157, 158
Finland:
families, constitutional definition, 50
Forde-Marzui, K, 120
foreign precedents, 8–15
see also comparative law; judicial cross-fertilisation; individual countries
formulaic approach, closed-ended, 124
forward-looking dimension of tradition, 131
France:
adoption,:
joint, 93, 95, 193–94
single parent, 184–86
second-parent, 93
Civil Code, families and, *see* Table of Legislation
child, right to have a, 193
civil solidarity pact (PaCS, *pacte civil de solidarieté*), 92–4, 96, 107, 147n, 188
common life (*vie commune*), 93–4
concubinage (cohabitation), 92
Conseil constitutionnel, 3, 93–96, 106, 108, 170
judicial review of legislation (*question prioritaire de constitutionnalité*, QPC), 3, 188
role of, constitutional change, 107
style of cases, 8n
Cour de Cassation, 94–5
adoption, 188
equal marriage, 94–5, 97, 107, 193
families:
Civil Code and, 52, 54, 97
constitutional definition, 50
institutional theory of, 52
'pacsée couple' as, 93
homosexuality, 92
joint life, 93–4
life as couple, 94
marriage, 93, 95
institutional theory of, 52
equality, 97
pacsée couples, 92–6
principle of bilinear filiation, 193
same-sex couples' rights, 92
same-sex marriage (*mariage pour tous*), 92–7, 193
vie commune (common life), 93–4
vie de couple (life as couple), 94
frozen concepts theory, 77, 90, 117, 134, 137
functional, definition of families, 67–71, 72, 76
functionalists, 59–61

Gattuso, M, 143
gay marriage, *see* same-sex marriage
gender, 15n, 140
-based social roles, 196
diversity in marriage, 17, 72–3, 88–9, 96, 105, 110–11, 117
diversity in definition of 'spouse', 76, 141, 177
ground of discrimination, 132, 140
neutral sodomy laws, 47
reassignment surgery, 64, 78
genetic features discrimination, 141
Georgia, sodomy law, 124, 125
Germany:
adoption, 101
successive, 102, 174
civil partnerships (*eingetragene Lebenspartnerschaft*), 98–102, 139, 174, 181
constitutional tradition, influence of German, 41–2, 44, 89, 153–54
Constitution:
dignity, 151–56
liberty, 151–2
Constitutional Tribunal, *see* Federal Constitutional Tribunal *below*
dignity, 44, 100, 151–56
divorce, 101
double track model, 97, 108
equality, 51,151, 153, 155
families:
constitutional definition, 50–1
constitutional protection, 97
in relation to marriage, 97, 100, 110, 181
Federal Constitutional Tribunal, 44, 97, 98–102, 104, 108
adoption, 191
best interests of the child, 174–76
civil unions, 181
definition of marriage, 98, 100–01
dignity, 151–52
foreign legal developments, reliance on, 139
marriage, 181
role of, constitutional change, 107–8
judicial review of legislation, 104
marriage:
constitutional protection, 97–8
distinction from civil union (*Abstandsgebot*), 181
'institutional guarantee' (*Institutgarantie*), 98, 180
'objective value', 98
in relation to family, 110
right to, 98
State protection, 51
same-sex marriage, debate on, 99, 102
separate but equal model, *see* double-track
Gittins, D, 55
Glensy, RC, 166
global community of courts, 3
global mass communications, judicial cross-fertilisation, 4
Greece:
dignity, 152
families, constitutional definition, 50–1

Hawaii:
  same-sex marriage, 1, 82, 113, 139
Hoffmann, H, 155
homosexuality:
  construction, 15, 22, 108, 113, 157, 183
  decriminalisation, 12, 21, 24, 90
  private dimension of:
    courts and decriminalisation of sexual acts, 19–48
  as private manifestation of human personality, *Dudgeon* recognition as, 21–6
  protection in social life, 29–30, 55
  as 'social harm'. 30
  social perception, *see* construction
  Wolfenden Report, *see* Wolfenden Report
human dignity, *see* dignity
human identity:
  dignity as result of process of development of, 155
human personality:
  homosexuality as private manifestation of, *Dudgeon* recognition as, 21–6
human rights, 167
  Canada, 3, 56–7
  dignity as foundation of, 155
  legislation, Portugal, 91
  universalism, 4
humanness:
  sexual orientation as aspect of, 24
Hungary,
  dignity, 153, 167
  constitutional court, 153

ICCPR, *see* International Covenant on Civil and Political Rights, *see* Table of Legislation
identity formation, dignity and, 155
India, sodomy statute, 12
individuality, 44
institutional guarantee:
  Germany, 98, 180
  Portugal, 180
  Spain, 119, 132, 138, 163, 180
institutional theory of family and marriage, France, 52
International Covenant on Civil and Political Rights (ICCPR), *see* Table of Legislation
intimate association, right, 65
Iowa, same-sex marriage, 133
Ireland:
  Constitution:
    as 'living instrument'. 117
    equality, 153
    legal tradition, 116
  dignity, 153
  families, constitutional definition, 50–1, 129
  High Court:
    legal tradition, 116–17, 133
    procreative nature of marriage, 177–78
    use of foreign cases, 10, 13, 139–40
  legalisation of sexual acts, 46
  marriage:
    essential core, 117
    originalist interpretation, 116–17, 132
    tradition, 133,139, 177
  same-sex marriage, 10, 13
    tradition in cases, 116–17, 131–32
isolation, exit from, 144
Israel:
  families, definition, 75
  same-sex partners, 14
Italy:
  Civil Code, *see* Table of Legislation
  Constitution, 105–106
    best interests of the child, 173–74
    equality between spouses, 51, 77
    family, 50–1, 129
    formal equality, 152, 169
    interpretation, in conformity with, 104
    legal tradition, 116
    liberty, 151
    marriage, 77–8, 105, 105, 115–16, 129
    social dignity, 152
    social solidarity, 77
    substantial equality, 152
  Constitutional Court:
  dignity, 152, 164, 165, 169
    equality between same-sex and opposite-sex couples, 134
    essential core of marriage identification of, 136
    family, 77–8, 110
    gender reassignment, 78
    legal tradition, 115–16, 117–18, 134
    marriage, 78, 105, 110, 115–7, 173
    parental rights, 173
    procreative nature of marriage, 178
    role of, constitutional change, 107–8
    same-sex couples, legalisation of, 9, 106–8
    same-sex marriage, 131, 173
    tradition, 115–6, 134
  Court of Cassation, 115
  dignity:
    of same-sex couples, 79, 143, 169
    social, 152, 164
  families:
    in civil unions law, 76–9
    constitutional definition, 50–1, 76–9, 105, 110, 115, 129, 174
    as 'natural institutions', 50–51, 54
    model of regulation, 52
    in relation to marriage, 115
  foreign precedents use, 9–10
  gender reassignment, regulation, 78
  judicial review of legislation, 85
  judicial cross-fertilisation in, 4
  living law doctrine (*dottrina del diritto vivente*), 95
  parental rights, 173–4
  rights of gays and lesbians:
    lower courts' contribution to paths towards, 107

same-sex civil unions, 97, 105–9, 134, 143–64, 179
same-sex marriage, 131–32
second-parent adoption, 51
sexual orientation equality:
constitutional and ordinary courts, approaches by, 104–105
surrogacy, 179

Johnson, P, 22, 24, 27, 29, 61–2
joint adoption, 192–95
joint life, France, 93–4
Jospin, Lionel, 93
judicial backlash, 6, 80–5, 88–9, 91, 103, 109, 113
judicial cross-fertilisation, 4, 8, 11
use of, interpretation of marriage, 137–40
see also comparative law; foreign precedents
judicial reviews of legislation, 2–3, 6, 17, 85, 90n, 95, 103–6, 109,138, 188,193
see also individual countries

Kaganas, F, 70–1, 118
Kant, I, 44, 151, 153
Keck, ME, 46

Lamarque, E, 104
language, as ground of discrimination,140
legal status of marriage, *see* status
legislation, judicial reviews, *see* judicial reviews of legislation
liberty:
dignity as synthesis of equality and, 149–54
European constitutions, 150–54
Italy, *see* Italy
marriage significance links with, 143
personal relationships, 30–3
in relation to dignity, 32, 35–6, 140–43, 147–154, 161–70
in relation to equality, 32, 35–6, 57, 140–43, 147–54, 162–70
in relation to privacy, 33–4, 43–4, 65, 179
as self-determination and autonomy, 26, 30–7, 44, 96
South Africa, *see* South Africa
Spain, *see* Spain
'spatial and more transcendent dimension' of, 35
United States, Constitution, XIV Amendment, 26, 32–6, 124–8, 148, 150, 162, 167
see also United States
life as couple, France, 94
'living law doctrine' (*dottrina del diritto vivente*), Italy, 95
'living tree', Constitution, Canada, 57–8, 134
'logic of the closet', 26–30, 34, 43, 49, 64
long-term commitment, same-sex couples, 64–5, 70, 185
Luxembourg:
families, constitutional definition, 50

Mamère, Noël, 94
Markensinis, B, 12
marriage:
bond, 35, 98, 119, 132, 138, 142, 146, 148
formal, 71, 74, 109
definition, 2, 5, 17, 75
at constitutional level, 50–52
in civil codes, 52
in the common law, 53
as contract, 109
as an institution, 109
as a legal relationship, 109
as social institution, 142
denial of status of, 147–9
determinants:
affection, 132
procreation, 5, 176–82
sex difference in, 5, 72–4, 78–9, 109–15, 137, 176
dignity of, 165
emotional value, 145
equal, *see* equal marriage, same-sex marriage and individual countries
essential core identification, 17, 115–19, 131, 136, 138, 152
expressive value, equality and, 142–46
family and, relationship between, 50–52, 76
institutional guarantee, *see* Germany, Portugal, Spain
institutional theory family and, 52
judicial cross-fertilization in marriage cases, 8–15
legal status, 148
new image, 132, 137–40
procreative nature, 113
constitutional courts and, 176–82
progressive interpretations of constitutional clauses on, 134–37
purposes, 77
responsibilities flowing from, equality and, 146–49
right to, 81, 85
rights and responsibilities flowing from, 146–49
same-sex, *see* same-sex marriage
same-sex relationship, distinction from, 78
sexual privacy within, protection, 62
social value, 142, 145
tradition, 115–22
cultural, 119–122
legal, 115–18
see also individual countries
marriage-like relationships, 73
Martín Casals, M, 86–8
Massachusetts, same-sex marriage, 83, 120, 159, 163
McCrudden, C, 164, 166
Mexico, same-sex marriage, 9, 139n
Millbank, J, 59
Minnesota, same-sex marriage, 120
Mississippi, adoption, 188
Montaigne, Michel de, 114

morality, 25, 30
  enforcement as state purpose, 30, 36–7, 40, 42–3
  tradition and, 119
morals, protection of, 24–5
Mossop, 56–61, 67, 69, 80, 179
Moulders-Klein, MT, 52
multi-faceted notion of privacy in *Lawrence*, 33–6

national origin discrimination, 140
nationality, ground of discrimination, 140
natural institution founded on marriage, families as, 50–51, 54, 77
nature:
  arguments of, same-sex marriage cases, 96, 112–4, 146, 171
  procreative, marriage 176–82
New Jersey:
  same-sex marriage, 121, 133, 147
  sex-difference in marriage tradition, 112
New Zealand:
  tradition in same-sex marriage cases, 112–13
non liquet, prohibition of, 103
normalisation, 144
normative value of tradition in same-sex marriage cases, 122–34, 178
Northern Ireland:
  decriminalisation of sexual acts, 19–24, 45
Nussbaum, M 28–9, 30, 34–5, 65, 108–109, 157

Ontario:
  Court of Appeal, dignity, 157
  same-sex marriage, 133, 136, 143–44
  Superior Court, procreation argument, 178
optimal parenting argument, 182–95
ordinary courts:
  constitutional courts and, different roles:
    advancement of rights, 136
    promoting equal marriage, 102–109
  see also Canada, Italy

PaCS (*pacte civil de solidarieté*, civil solidarity pact), France, 92–4, 96, 107, 147n, 188
parental rights, 1, 5
  best interests of the child principle, 171–76
  child custody early cases, 182–84
  constitutional courts and 'procreative nature' of marriage, 176–82
  debate over, 171–76
  joint adoption, 192–95
  'normal family life', children's rights to, 182–95
  optimal parenting argument, 182–95
  second parent adoption, 187–92
  single parent adoption, 184–86
parliaments, 6
particularity, 167
Pennsylvania:
  child custody on divorce, 183
  same-sex marriage, 120
Perry v Brown, 178–79
personal relationships:
  liberty of all individuals in, *Lawrence* and, 30–3
personality:
  dignity as result of process of development of, 155
Pico della Mirandola, G, 151
pluralism, 166, 167–68, 169,170
Poland, families, 63–4
political discrimination, 140
Portalis, J-E-M, 52
Portugal:
  child custody on divorce, 183–84
  Civil Code, *see* Table of Legislation
  Constitution, 89–91
    dignity, 152, 164
  Constitutional Tribunal, 90–2, 106, 108
    cooperation with parliament, same-sex marriage, 89–92, 106–9
    dignity, 149, 152
    foreign legal developments, reliance on, 138–39
    equality, 149
    legal tradition, 117, 119, 134, 136–37
    role of, constitutional change, 107–8
  families, constitutional definition, 50–1
  homosexuality decriminalisation, 90
  judicial review of legislation, 85
  marriage, 90–1
    as a right, 164
    institutional guarantee, 180
  same-sex de facto unions *(união de facto)*, legalisation, 90
  same-sex marriage, 89–92, 108
    tradition in cases, 117, 119
  sexual orientation
    discrimination, 89
    as ground of discrimination, 183–4
powers, separation of, 134–37
privacy:
  decisional aspect, 34
  in European Court of Human Rights cases, 21, 26–30, 39, 61–5
  'logic of the closet', 26–30, 34, 43, 49, 64
  multi-faceted notion of, 33–6
  private-public dimension, 45
  South Africa, *see* South Africa
  spatial dimension of, 26, 30–1, 33–7, 49, 168
  Tasmania, *see* Tasmania
  United States, *see* United States
private dimension of homosexuality:
  courts and decriminalisation of sexual acts, 19–48
private life:
  family life and, distinguishing, 61–5
private, sexual acts in, 27–8
procreative nature of marriage, 113, 137, 173, 177–80, 188
  constitutional courts and, 176–82
progressive interpretations of constitutional clauses on marriage, 134–39

property
in the definition of 'family', 54, 59
in the definition of marriage, 111n
public, sexual acts in, 28
public–private dichotomy, families, 49–56

Quebec, same-sex marriage, 136

race, ground of discrimination, 140
regulation models, families, 49–56
'regulatory costs argument', 180
religion, 140
discrimination, 140
tradition in same-sex marriage cases, 119–22
reproductive rights of women, 2, 195
Republic of Ireland, *see* Ireland
responsibilities flowing from marriage, equality, 146–49
rights:
advancement:
constitutional courts and ordinary courts, different roles, 136
children, right to 'normal family life', 182–95
dignity as right, 155
enumerated, 122–32
families, 1
flowing from marriage, equality of, 146–49
parental, *see* parental rights
reproductive rights of women, 2, 195
unenumerated, 122–32
United Nations Declaration of the Rights of the Child, *see* Table of Legislation
Rosenberg, GN, 84

same-sex civil unions, *see* individual countries
same-sex couples
dignity, 73, 76, 79, 146, 149, 165, 169
exit from isolation, 144
normalisation, 144
recognition:
as 'family', 56–61, 65–71, 94, 108, 174
as 'spouses', 71–4, 80
role of courts in promoting marriage for, 102–09
second-class, status, 158
see individual countries
same-sex de facto unions *(união de facto)*, Portugal, 90
same-sex marriage
Canada, *see* Canada
from civil partnerships to, 80–5
courts and constitutional change, 80–5
dignity in cases:
as claim of recognition and equality, 156–58
different meanings, 154–64
different purposes, 164–70
as equal value, 158–61
from exclusion to inclusion, 158–61
as liberty and self-determination, 161–64
social and expressive value of marriage, 143
as synthesis of liberty and equality, 149–54
effect on opposite-sex marriage, 181
equality in cases:
expressive value of marriage and, 142–46
implications, 141–49
of rights and responsibilities flowing from marriage, 146–49
foreign precedents use, 9–10
judicial backlash, 80–5, 103
'new image', 137–140
procreation argument, 178
right to, 124–30, 189
role of courts in promoting, 102–09
tradition:
argument in constitutional cases, 109–15
backward-lookind and forward-looking dimension of, 130–34
circular reasoning risk, 132–34
cultural, 119–22
definition of tradition in constitutional cases on, 109–22
indeterminacy, 119–22
legal, 115–19
normative value of, 122–34
progressive interpretations of constitutional clauses on marriage, 134–37
religious, 119–22
separation of powers concerns, 134–37
unenumerated rights, 122–32
vicious cycle perpetuating discrimination, 119–22
see also equal marriage; marriage; individual countries
same-sex sexual acts, *see* sexual acts
Sanders, AEH, 101
Scheffler, S, 115, 130–1
second-parent adoption, 173–74, 187–92
see also adoption, parental rights
self-determination:
dignity and, 155, 161–64
liberty as 26, 30–7, 44, 96
United States, *see* United States
separate but equal model, 29n, 97, 109n, 158
see also double-track model
separation of powers concerns, same-sex marriage cases, 134–37
sex and contraception:
United States privacy and self-determination jurisprudence, 64
sex difference in marriage, 5, 72–4, 78–9, 109–15, 137, 176
sex, ground of discrimination, 48n, 63, 140
sexual acts:
decriminalisation, 1, 19–48
different-sex, 125
in private, 20, 23, 25–8, 30, 36–7, 41, 44, 47
in public, 28
same-sex:
consensual, 26, 35–8, 41–3, 47, 125, 148
criminalisation, 27–8, 42, 45, 126
legalisation, 45–8
see also sexual conduct

'sexual closet', *see* 'logic of the closet'
sexual conduct:
  regulation 24–5, 36
  separation from public sphere, 27
  see also same-sex sexual acts
sexual orientation:
  as affecting the ability to raise a child, 171, 183–5, 191–2
  as aspect of humanness, 24
  as ground of discrimination, 32–3, 41, 47–8, 57, 60, 63, 65, 72–3, 80, 83, 89, 141, 158, 169, 184
  equality, *see* civil unions; equality; marriage; same-sex marriage
  essentialist approach to, 23–4
  judicial cross-fertilization, cases on, 8–15
  in relation to liberty and self-determination, 31, 48 (*see also* liberty)
  in relation to privacy, 28
  see also homosexuality
sexual practices:
  sexual orientation separation from, 22–3
Siegel, RB, 166
Sikkink, K, 46
Silva, Cavaco, 91
single parent adoption, 184–86
situated self, 157–58
social acceptance, 13, 109n, 135, 138,158–9
  see also stigma
social dignity, *see* Italy
social formations, 77–8
social institution:
  families as, 51, 55
  marriage as, 142
social movements, 2
social origin discrimination, 140, 141
social solidarity, Italy, 77
sociality, 44
  of man, dignity as aspect of, 155
sodomy laws, 12, 46, 124, 125
  decriminalisation, 15, 46
  South Africa, 41, 42
  United States, 15, 20, 30–2, 34, 36, 40, 125–6
  United Kingdom, 25
  see also sexual acts
South Africa:
  adoption, 192n, 194–5
  Constitution, 14,
    dignity, 20, 153–4
    marriage, 121–22
    privacy, 20
  Constitutional Court, 3, 167
    adoption, 194–95
    dignity, 42, 146, 153, 167
    family, definition, 121
    foreign legal developments, reliance on, 9–10, 14, 20, 42, 139
    marriage, definition, 75, 121–2, 139
    privacy, 41–45
    same-sex marriage, 122, 139, 146, 149, 160–1, 179
  decriminalisation of sexual-acts, 41–5
  equality, 41–2, 145, 149, 195
  family, same-sex couples as, 74–76, 122
  liberty, 44
  marriage:
    definition, 112, 121
    expressive value, 149
    procreation as determinant of, 179
    rights and responsibilities flowing from, 149
    tradition, 121–22, 139
    'spouses', definition, 74–76
  privacy, 42, 43–5
  same-sex marriage, 14, 146, 149, 160–61, 179
    procreation argument, 179
    tradition in cases, 112, 121–22, 139
  sexual orientation discrimination, 41
  sodomy laws, 41–43
Southern Europe, constitutional courts, 3
Spain:
  backlash, 88–9
  Civil Code, adoption, 194
  children:
    best interest, 194
    protection in same-sex marriage, 194
    right to adopt, 194
  Constitution, 88
    dignity, 149, 152–53, 163, 169
    family, definition, 50–51
    free development of personality, 149
    marriage, definition, 50–51, 110, 134–7, 163
  Constitutional Tribunal:
    adoption, 194
    dignity, 149, 152–53, 163, 165–66, 169
    essential core of marriage identification of (*contenido absoludo*), 118, 138, 152
    foreign legal developments, reliance on, 8, 13, 15, 137–38
    liberty, 149
    progressive interpretation of constitutional clauses, 88, 118–9, 134–7
    role of, constitutional change, 107–8
    same-sex marriage, 65–66, 86–9, 104, 108, 118–19, 132, 134–38, 163, 180–1
  equality between spouses, 118–19
  families:
    constitutional definition, 51, 81
    in relation to marriage, 89, 138
  foreign precedents use, 8, 13, 15
  judicial review of legislation, 104
  liberty, 149–154
  marriage:
    definition, 50–1, 88, 110–1, 129, 135–6
    essential core of, 118–9
    'institutional guarantee', 119, 132, 138, 163, 180
    model of regulation, 52
    'new image', 137–8
    right to, 180
    'social institution', 51

same-sex marriage (*matrimonio igualitario*), 13, 15, 86–9
tradition in cases, 118–19, 132, 134–35
sexual orientation discrimination, 88
sodomy laws decriminalisation, 15
spatial aspect of privacy, 26, 30–1, 33–37, 49, 168
spouses, 68–9
common law, 80
definition, 2
same-sex couples as, 71–4, 80
stability, 157
status:
citizen, 159–60
denial of status of marriage, 147–49
discrimination, 140
families, 56–61, 67
legal, of marriage, 66, 93, 96n, 112, 119, 122, 142, 144n, 145–49, 170, 180, 189–90
second-class, same-sex couples, 158
stepchild adoption, *see* second-parent adoption; adoption; parental rights
stigma,
due to denial of marriage, 35, 157
due to denial of 'duty of faithfullness', Italy, 79
due to sodomy laws, 31, 38, 42
gays and lesbians and their families, 157, 173
Stone Sweet, A, 104
successions in tenancies, 67–74
successive adoption, 102, 174–76
surrogacy, 7, 179

Tasmania, 20–21, 47–8
Taylor, C, 156–7
tenancy successions, 67–74
tradition, 40, 44
backward-looking interpretation, 130–32, 134, 136
cultural, 119–22
forward-looking dimension of, 130–1
legal, 115–19
procreation argument, 180
religious, 119–22
in same-sex marriage cases, *see* same-sex marriage
surrogacy opposition, 179

transjudicial dialogue, *see* judicial cross-fertilisation; individual countries
Tribe, LH, 32, 81, 127, 128–31, 162, 169

UK, *see* England and Wales; Northern Ireland; United Kingdom
unenumerated rights, 122–32
right to same-sex marriage as, 129–31
United Kingdom:
see also England and Wales; Northern Ireland
United Nations Declaration of the Rights of the Child, *see* Table of Legislation
United States:
adoption, 187–88
animus towards gays and lesbians, 38
anti-miscegenation laws, 120, 144, 176
autonomy, 35–6
children, early cases on custody, 182–3
citizenship, 159
civil rights, 167–68
Constitution:
Due Process Clause, 17, 33, 36, 123–24, 128, 159, 162
equality (Equal Protection Clause), 31–2, 36, 39–40, 133, 150, 159, 162–3, 167
Fourteenth Amendment, 26, 30–1, 38, 123, 127, 129, 150, 162
Fifth Amendment, 148, 150
liberty, 26, 31–2, 37, 41, 163
dignity, 31–2, 35–6, 38–9, 41, 143–150, 156–57, 159–60, 162–63, 165–69
different purposes, same-sex marriage cases, 167–69
as equal value, 159–60
as liberty and self-determination, 161–3
in relation to equality, 157, 167–8
as synthesis of liberty and equality, 167–69
family:
functional approach to, 60
traditional, 36, 82–3
same-sex couples as, 65–67, 159, 166
enforcement of morality, legitimate State interest, 37
judicial review, 106n
liberty, 33–7, 65, 124–130, 147–50, 161–63, 167–69
marriage:
definitions, 110, 112
denial of status of, 147–49
equality, 82, 84, 107, 114, 144–50, 157, 159, 163, 168–70, 181–82
emotional and expressive value of, 142–46
interracial, 120, 144, 176
procreative nature, 176–8
rights and responsibilities, 147–9
politics of disgust, 107, 113–4
recognition politics, 82–3
same-sex marriage, 15, 82–5, 127–32, 145–49, 157, 159–63, 165, 168–9, 187–8
judicial backlash, 82–85
as unemerated right, 127–32
sexual acts, decriminalisation, 19–21, 30–40, 126–7, 150
see also sodomy laws (United States)
sexual orientation:
discrimination, 32–3, 41, 182–84
sodomy laws, 15, 20, 30–2, 36, 40–1, 125–6
Supreme Court:
abortion, 33, 82, 196
equality adjudication in 'pluralism anxiety', 168–70
privacy, 30–1, 33–36, 39, 41, 64–5
same-sex marriage jurisprudence, *see* same-sex marriage above
sex and contraception, privacy and self-determination jurisprudence, 64–5
unenumerated rights identification, 123–32

tradition in same-sex marriage cases, 112, 113, 120–21, 122–34
see also individual states
Universal Declaration of Human Rights, *see* Table of Legislation
unmarried cohabitation, 77–8
USA, *see* United States

Vermont:
same-sex civil unions, 83
Supreme Court, second-parent adoption, 187
vicious cycle perpetuating discrimination, 119–22
vie commune (common life), France, 93–4
vie de couple (life as couple), France, 94
Virginia:
child custody on divorce, 182
same-sex marriage, 120
virtuous cycle, 1–2

Wintemute, R, 64
Wisconsin, procreative nature of marriage, 176–77
Wolfenden Report, 20, 23–25, 27–8, 37
Wolfson, E, 142–3
women's reproductive rights, 2
workplace benefits, same-sex couples, 1, 30

Yoshino, K, 31, 123–24, 126, 141, 167–69, 170

www.ingramcontent.com/pod-product-compliance
Lightning Source LLC
LaVergne TN
LVHW052309200926
848481LV00002B/513